Employee Relations

About the author

David Farnham is Professor of Employment Relations at the University of Portsmouth. His other publications include: *Personnel in Context*; *The Corporate Environment*; *Understanding Industrial Relations* (with J. Pimlott); *Managing the New Public Services* (with S. Horton); and *Public Administration in the United Kingdom* (with M. McVicar). Marjorie Corbridge is Senior Lecturer in Human Resources Management, Sylvia Horton is Principal Lecturer in Public Sector Studies and Stephen Pilbeam is Senior Lecturer in Human Resources Management at the University of Portsmouth.

Management Studies 2 Series

The IPM examination system provides a unique route into professional personnel practice. After the Professional Management Foundation Programme, the IPM Stage II syllabus covers the core subject areas of Employee Resourcing, Development and Relations. This Management Studies 2 series forms the essential reading for all students at this level.

Other titles in the series:

Case Studies in Personnel Management
Diana Winstanley and Jean Woodall

Employee Development
Rosemary Harrison

Employee Resourcing
Derek Torrington, Laura Hall, Isabel Haylor and Judith Myers

MANAGEMENT STUDIES 2

Employee Relations

David Farnham

Institute of Personnel Management

First published in 1993
Reprinted 1994

© David Farnham 1993

Phototypeset by The Comp-Room, Aylesbury
and printed in Great Britain
by Short Run Press, Exeter

British Library Cataloguing in Publication Data

Farnham, David
Employee Relations. – (Management
Studies, Stage 2))
I. Title   II. Series
658.315

ISBN 0-85292-474-7

INSTITUTE OF PERSONNEL MANAGEMENT
IPM House, Camp Road, Wimbledon, London SW19 4UX
Tel: 081-946-9100   Fax: 081-947-2570
Registered office as above. Registered Charity No. 215797
A company limited by guarantee. Registered in England No. 198002

Contents

List of figures

List of tables

List of exhibits

List of abbreviations

ACAS	Advisory Conciliation and Arbitration Service
ADT	approved deferred trust scheme
AEU	Amalgamated Engineering Union
AEEU	Amalgamated Engineering and Electrical Union
AMMA	Assistant Masters and Mistresses Association
APEX	Association of Professional Executive Clerical and Computer Staff
ASB	Amalgamated Society of Boilermakers
BIFU	Banking Insurance and Finance Union
C and P	custom and practice
CAC	Central Arbitration Committee
CBI	Confederation of British Industry
CEuC	Commission of the European Community
CIR	Commission on Industrial Relations
CO	Certification Officer
COHSE	Confederation of Health Service Employees
CoM	Council of Ministers
CPSA	Civil and Public Services Association
CRTUM	Commissioner for the Rights of Trade Union Members
CSC	*Confédération des Syndicats Chrétiens*
DGB	*Deutscher Gewerkschaftsbund*
EA 1980	Employment Act 1980
EA 1982	Employment Act 1982
EA 1988	Employment Act 1988
EA 1989	Employment Act 1989
EA 1990	Employment Appeal Tribunal
EC	European Community
EETPU	Electrical Electronic Telecommunications and Plumbing Union

ELM	external labour market
EMU	European monetary union
EPA 1975	Employment Protection Act 1975
EPCA 1978	Employment Protection (Consolidation) Act 1978
EqPA 1970	Equal Pay Act 1970
EqPAR 1983	Equal Pay Amendment Regulations 1983
ESO	employee share ownership
ETUC	European Trade Union Confederation
EuP	European Parliament
EWC	European works council
FBP	fall back position
FGTB	*Fédération Général du Travail de Belgique*
GMBU	General Municipal and Boilermakers Union
HASAWA 1974	Health and Safety at Work etc. Act 1974
HRM	human resource management
ICFTU	International Confederation of Free Trade Unions
ILM	internal labour market
ILO	International Labour Organisation
IPM	Institute of Personnel Management
IRA 1971	Industrial Relations Act 1971
ISP	ideal settlement point
ISTC	Iron and Steel Trades Confederation
IT	information technolotgy
ITs	industrial tribunals
JCC	joint consultative committee
LO	*Landesorganationen i Sverige*
LLM	local labour market
MBL 1977	Employee Participation in Decision Making Act 1977
MSF	Manufacturing Science and Finance Union
NALGO	National and Local Government Officers Association

NAS/UWT	National Association of Schoolmasters/Union of Women Teachers
NCU	National Communications Union
NFC	National Freight Corporation
NGA	National Graphical Association
NHS	National Health Service
NSA	new-style agreements
NUCPS	National Union of Civil and Public Servants
NUM	National Union of Mineworkers
NUPE	National Union of Public Employees
NURMTW	National Union of Railway Marine and Transport Workers
NUT	National Union of Teachers
PF	Police Federation
PRB	pay review body
PRP	performance-related pay
PSBR	public sector borrowing requirement
QWA	quality work assured
RCN	Royal College of Nursing of the United Kingdom
RRA 1976	Race Relations Act 1976
RSP	realistic settlement point
SAYE	save as you earn
SC	Social Charter
SCE	Standing Committee of Employment
SCPC	Standing Commission on Pay Comparability
SDA 1975	Sex Discrimination Act 1975
SERPS	State Earnings Related Pension Scheme
SOGAT	Society of Graphical and Allied Trades
TCO	*Tjänstemannens Centralorganisation*
TGWU	Transport and General Workers Union
TQC	total quality control
TQM	total quality management
TUA 1984	Trade Union Act 1984
TUC	Trades Union Congress
TULRA 1974	Trade Union and Labour Relations Act 1974

TULRCA 1992	Trade Unions and Labour Relations (Consolidation) Act 1992
TUPER 1981	Transfer of Undertakings (Protection of Employment) Regulations 1981
UCATT	Union of Construction Allied Trades and Technicians
UCW	Union of Communication Workers
UMA	union membership agreement
UN	United Nations
UNICE	Union of Industrial and Employers' Confederations of Europe
USA	United States of America
USDAW	Union of Shop Distributive and Allied Workers
WA 1986	Wages Act 1986
WIRS 1980	Workplace Industrial Relations Survey 1980
WIRS 1984	Workplace Industrial Relations Survey 1984
WIRS 1990	Workplace Industrial Relations Survey 1992

Preface

> Employee Relations is that part of personnel management that enables competent managers, through the development of institutions, procedures and policies, to reconcile within acceptable limits to the organisation the interests of employers as the buyers of labour services and those of employees as the suppliers of labour services.
>
> IPM, *Professional Education Scheme Syllabus*, 1993–94

This introductory book covers the syllabus requirements of Employee Relations 1 and Employee Relations 2 in the Professional Education Scheme of the Institute of Personnel Management (IPM). Like its companion volumes in this series, by Derek Torrington and his colleagues (Torrington *et al.* 1992) and Rosemary Harrison (1992), this book is a study guide for personnel management students, rather than a conventional textbook. It differs from related books in the field (Farnham and Pimlott 1994; Kessler and Bayliss 1992; Salamon 1992; Towers 1992) in three main respects. First, it focuses on 'employee relations' rather than 'industrial relations'. In this sense, the book is written from a *managerial perspective* and seeks to provide a framework within which students of personnel management will be able to identify and understand the role of management in employee relations, operationally, strategically and contextually. Compared with other texts, this one also gives far more emphasis to the individual facets of the employment relationship, to non-union variants of employee relations and to other aspects of employee relations management.

This does not mean that this book is written from a narrow, prescriptive point of view. It seeks to be analytical, academic and rigorous in its approach but emphasises the contingent nature of employee relations management. Contingency means that there are not only choices and alternative approaches for managements in taking employee relations decisions but also constraints and limitations on management discretion.

Second, in line with its managerial thrust, compared with other texts, this book provides far more opportunities for *developing competency* in personnel management students by enabling them to apply employee relations knowledge and skills to practical situations. This practical approach to employee relations is underlined not only by the conceptual, theoretical and empirical content of the chapters but also by the assignments at the end of them. These assignments require students to do wider reading, to undertake activities and to problem-solve issues. Assignments may be done individually or in groups and they may be presented orally, in writing or both. Where an assignment refers to 'your organisation', and the student is not in current employment, this may be interpreted by the reader as meaning 'any organisation with which you are familiar'.

Although this book focuses largely on British experience and practice in employee relations, its third feature is that it incorporates some *international comparisons*. This is to enable personnel management students to understand external trends and alternative approaches in employee relations in countries and national cultures other than their own.

Part 1 focuses on The Components of Employee Relations. This part of the book provides an overview of employee relations concepts, actors, processes, contexts and skills. Chapter 1 explores the elements of employee relations in terms of the interests of the buyers and sellers of labour services, the agreements and rules made by them, the conflict-resolving processes they use and the major external influences on employee relations behaviour. In Chapter 2, the major parties to employee relations – management, management organisations, employee organisations and state agencies – are identified and their roles discussed. Chapter 3 analyses the main processes and outcomes of employee relations. These include: management-led approaches; joint approaches; third-party intervention; industrial sanctions; legal enactment; and worker participation in Europe.

Chapter 4 examines the economic and legal contexts of employee relations management. The topics discussed range from Keynesianism and supply-side economics to the statutory floor of employment protection rights, the law and trade disputes and the 'Social Charter' of the European Community. In Chapter 5, the basic employee relations skills required of managers are reviewed and examined, such as negotiating, handling grievances, dealing with discipline and managing redundancy.

Part 2 of the book focuses on Managing Employee Relations. Chapter 6 analyses the changing economic, technological, social and political environments within which employee relations management takes place and the implications for management strategy. In Chapter 7, the role of the state in employee relations is considered. It discusses the traditional role of the state, the 'Employee Relations Consensus' between 1945 and 1979 and the changing policies of the state in the 1980s and 1990s. Chapter 8 focuses on management and trade unions. This includes: developments in union policy, structure and practice; union responses to the changing employee relations environment; the law and union membership; and trade union recognition.

Chapter 9 focuses on collective bargaining. It examines some of the theoretical issues relating to collective bargaining, the emerging patterns of collective bargaining and the knowledge and skills underpinning negotiating practice. In Chapter 10, alternative patterns of employee relations management, other than that of collective bargaining, are considered. These include: employee involvement practices; employee communication; joint consultation; and worker participation. Finally, in Chapter 11, attention is switched to industrial action. The topics addressed here include the forms industrial action takes, the influences on it and the law and industrial action.

In getting this book to press, I would particularly like to acknowledge the efforts of Matthew Reisz, Siobhan Bremner and Finn Jensen at IPM House. I would also like to thank my colleagues Marjorie Corbridge and Stephen Pilbeam for writing Chapter 5 and Sylvia Horton for writing Chapter 6. Thanks also go to Jim Basker for kindly producing the author and subject indexes. The result is, we believe, a text which is up to date, will be of practical use to students and teachers of employee relations and will make students aware of the complex influences on employee relations management.

David Farnham

References

BAYLISS, F. and KESSLER, S. 1992. *Contemporary Industrial Relations.* Basingstoke: Macmillan.

FARNHAM, D. and PIMLOTT, J. 1994 (forthcoming). *Understanding Industrial Relations.* London: Cassell.

HARRISON, R. 1992. *Employee Development.* London: IPM.

SALAMON, M. 1992. *Industrial Relations: Theory and Practice.* London: Prentice Hall.

TORRINGTON, D., HALL, L., HAYLOR, I. and MYERS, J. 1992. *Employee Resourcing.* London: IPM.

TOWERS, B. (ed.) 1992. *A Handbook of Industrial Relations Practice.* London: Kogan Page.

Part One
The Components of Employee Relations

Chapter 1

The elements of employee relations: an overview

Employee relations in market economies take place wherever work is exchanged for payment. Therefore, the essence of employee relations is paid employment or the pay–work bargain between employers and employees. An employee is someone who works under a contract of employment, sometimes called 'a contract of service', for an employer. A contract of employment contrasts with 'a contract for services'. These are made between independent contractors and those buying their specialist services, such as fee-paid, self-employed management consultants selling their consultancy skills to companies. To determine whether or not a worker has the legal status of an employee or that of an independent contractor, the courts apply a number of tests. These include the type of work, the nature of the orders given, the method and frequency of payment, the power to dismiss and the understanding between the parties. But the crucial test is that of 'control'. In other words, who has the ultimate right to tell the worker what to do? If one person can tell another what job to do, how it is to be done and when, where and with whom, then that party is the employer in law and the other is an employee.

The pay–work bargain between employer and employee is influenced by a series of factors, including:

- the institutional arrangements by which employment decisions are made;
- external factors such as the economic, political and legal contexts of the exchange relationship;
- the ideas and values underpinning employment activity.

Organisations, whatever their ownership, size or outputs, employ people to work for them, hiring them for the knowledge, skills and capabilities which individual workers possess, and reward them accordingly. People, in turn, seek paid employment to earn incomes so that they can spend the money they earn, as consumers in the market place. There are also other more complex reasons why people work but the economic imperative is the fundamental one.

Employee relations, therefore, are concerned with the interactions amongst the primary parties who pay for work and those who provide it in the labour market (employers and employees), those acting as secondary parties on their behalf (management or management organisations and trade unions) and those providing a third-party role in employment matters (state agencies and European Community (EC) institutions). Employee relations practices in any organisation are a product of a number of factors. The principal ones are:

- the *interests* of the buyers and sellers of labour services (or human resource skills);
- the *agreements and rules* made by them and their agents;
- the *conflict-resolving processes* that are used;
- the *external influences* affecting the parties making employment decisions.

Interests in employee relations

The economic imperatives

Today's employers are normally organisations. As employers, organisations vary widely in their patterns of ownership, size of employment units, numbers of employment units and types of workers employed. Business organisations in the private sector are characterised by being driven by the profit motive and market factors and are found in the primary economic sector (agriculture, mining and fishing), the secondary sector (manufacturing and construction) and the tertiary sector (services). Larger enterprises often operate on several sites, employing a wide variety of human resource skills including managerial, professional, technical, administrative and what are traditionally called 'manual' groups of workers. Some private enterprises are heavily unionised, whilst others are non-unionised. Larger firms tend to have well-organised, professional personnel departments, the smaller ones do not.

Public sector organisations, other than a few commercial public corporations, are generally driven by welfare or political goals, having been set up by the state to provide a series of services to the general public (Farnham and Horton 1993). These are normally financed by some form of taxation on individuals or corporations but their services are 'free' at the point of consumption by those using them. The public sector is usually classified as consisting of the public corporations, central government, including the National Health Service, and the local authorities (Fleming 1989; Central Statistical Office 1991). Public sector organisations tend to be large, complex enterprises, employing a wide variety of occupational groups and skills, with relatively high levels of union membership and bureaucratically driven personnel policies and departments.

Since business organisations are driven by the profit motive and market values, one of the main aims of those directing them and those responsible for their economic effectiveness is to obtain a financial surplus of revenues over costs at the end of each accounting cycle. Unless they achieve this financial target, businesses cannot, in the medium term at least, survive as viable economic units. At the extremes, firms may be either labour intensive, as in parts of the service sector, or capital intensive, as in hi-tech production industries. In either case, the cost-effective utilisation and managing of human resources is essential to organisational success. Private employers can only stay profitable where:

- total pay and employment costs are kept within planned human resource budgets;
- worker productivity per head is increased;
- or, where human resource budgets are exceeded, pay is cut or the numbers employed in the enterprise at current pay levels are reduced.

Whilst public sector organisations are not driven by market factors, in that they are 'not for profit' enterprises (Starks 1991), they have to operate as efficiently as possible and provide 'value for money' to their political stewards, in Parliament or local government, and to those who pay for them as taxpayers. Like their private sector counterparts, they also have to utilise and manage their human resources cost-effectively, especially since they tend to be labour intensive organisations where some 75 per cent of their costs are labour costs. If labour costs increase in public sector organisations, a number of governmental and employer responses are possible. These include:

- raising taxes;
- increasing public borrowing;

- introducing 'charges' for services;
- increasing labour productivity;
- cutting back public services;
- reducing their staffing establishments.

Individual men or women in employment, or those seeking work, in contrast, have their own economic interests in doing so. These might be wanting:

- the best pay available to them;
- good promotion prospects;
- the best fringe benefits such as pensions, medical insurance and job training;
- the best working conditions such as short hours of work, holidays with pay and sick pay;
- a safe and healthy working environment;
- security of employment.

All these elements of the employment package involve economic costs to employers.

Labour market and managerial relations

With employers buying labour skills and work effort and workers selling these in the labour market, there are potential conflicts of interest in the determination of the pay–work bargain or in the *market relations* between them. Put crudely, the economic interests of employers are such that they want the lowest possible employment costs commensurate with obtaining and retaining the skills and commitment of their workforce. The economic interests of the workforce, in contrast, are that they want the best possible terms and conditions of employment commensurate with their job security and employment prospects. The more that is paid out in pay or non-pay benefits to employees, the less there is available to corporate shareholders or for investment purposes and vice versa. Even in the public sector, the higher the employment costs for hiring and retaining staff, the higher the taxes that are needed or the higher the level of public borrowing required to pay for them. These, then, are the underlying conflicts between employers and employees in the labour market under capitalism.

There are other potential conflicts of interest between employers and employees, once labour has been hired in the workplace. These derive from the *managerial relations* between the parties arising out of the pay–work bargain (Flanders 1968). Employers generally want employees who will be compliant with or committed to employer rules and management decisions. If organisations are to achieve their economic targets of profitability, efficiency, productivity and growth – or, at a minimum, survival – managers, who are responsible for organisational success and effectiveness, want employees who respond willingly and flexibly to managerial decisions and initiatives. Managers want to be free to take and implement decisions in the interests of enterprise efficiency and workplace order, without being constrained by individual or collective employee resistance.

Employees, on the other hand, normally want a say in how their work is organised, how the decisions affecting their working lives are taken and how any complaints and grievances relating to their rewards, working arrangements and job content may be resolved. It is potential conflicts over job control which are at the root of managerial relations between managers and employees in the workplace.

Where conflict between employers and employees remains unresolved, in either their market or managerial relations, industrial conflict can result. Employers may take sanctions against their employees, or the employees and their unions may take sanctions against their employers. The situation then becomes a power struggle, with the stronger side trying to force the weaker side to concede to its demands. The outcome of such conflicts depends on the balance of power between the two sides and on other factors such as the availability of third-party intervention, the law and public opinion.

'Good' employee relations

Since there are heavy economic costs to all parties to the employment relationship if they fail to reach agreements and understandings amongst themselves, employers and employees – the latter through their unions where these are recognised – normally emphasise their common interests in the pay–work bargain, rather than their differences. Employers seek predictable labour costs, a stable workforce and cooperative employees. Employees, and recognised unions, in turn, seek reasonable terms and conditions of employment, continuous employment and fair management decisions. It is to the benefit of both employers and employees to focus on their common interests and the mutuality of the employment relationship – their pay–work bargain and other arrangements between them – by resolving their potential conflicts either constitutionally, to avoid damaging and expensive industrial conflict, or by interpersonal negotiation.

For employers, industrial conflict results in lost revenues and loss of reputation for fair dealings with their employees. For employees, industrial conflict means lost pay and possible job losses if the employer's business prospects are damaged. 'Good' employee relations, from both the employers' and employees' points of view, mean establishing institutional arrangements to reconcile their conflicts of interest, build on their common interests and avoid costly confrontations between them.

The state also has an interest in 'good' employee relations. This is expressed through government policies, the law, the state's employee relations agencies and its role as an employer in its own right. One concern of government, as the ultimate source of power in society, is to ensure that any unresolved conflicts between employers and employees, over either their market or managerial relations, do not degenerate into what it considers to be unacceptable or unlawful behaviour, which might damage the economy or threaten social order. This is a difficult role to fulfil, since if government is seen to intervene in a way which is perceived as being too much in favour of one of the parties, at the expense of the other, then the legitimacy of its actions may be disputed. Second, government seeks to provide a framework of law, including state enforcement agencies, within which the parties to employee relations are expected to conduct themselves. It provides the parties with rights and responsibilities, and the means for adjudicating them (Wedderburn 1986). Third, as an employer, government seeks to provide its own 'good' employment practices, so as to facilitate the effective recruitment and retention of appropriately qualified public servants (Farnham 1993; see also Chapter 7 below).

Agreements and rules

Formal, written agreements and rules in employee relations are the principal means for containing any potential conflicts arising from the pay–work bargain, although unwritten 'understandings' (custom and practice) also provide guidelines to behaviour between the buyers and sellers of labour services in the labour market and the workplace (Brown 1972; Terry 1977).

Employment rules may be made unilaterally, bilaterally or trilaterally. Unilateral rules are made by:

- employers and managers (company rules);
- management organisations (policy statements);
- workers (customs and practices);
- trade unions (union rules);
- the state (statute and common law);
- the EC (directives and regulations).

Agreements are made bilaterally between:

- employers and employees (contracts of employment);
- employers or employers' associations and trade unions (collective agreements).

Wages councils, organised on a tripartite basis amongst employers, unions and independent persons, determined, until recently, minimum wages for certain low-paid groups of workers (wages regulation orders).

Substantive agreements or substantive rules cover the pay and conditions of employment associated with particular jobs. They include rates of pay, additional payments, overtime pay, hours of work, holiday arrangements, holiday pay, sick pay, maternity pay and so on. By specifying the economic rights and obligations attached to particular jobs, substantive agreements or substantive rules regulate the market relations between the buyers and sellers of labour services. Procedural agreements or procedural rules, such as grievance and disciplinary procedures, adjust any differences between the parties to the pay–work bargain, whether in interpreting existing agreements or rules (conflicts of right) or in making new agreements or rules (conflicts of interest).

Substantive and procedural agreements and rules may be regulated internally or externally. Company rules, for example, are internally regulated, as are customs and practices, since changing them does not require the consent of external authorities, such as trade unions, management organisations or the state. All other types of substantive and procedural arrangements – whether policy statements by management organisations, union rules, statute and common law, EC directives and regulations, contracts of employment, collective agreements – are externally regulated. In practice, each of these methods of determining employment rules shades into the others but differentiating them conceptually is important for analytical purposes.

The employee relations agreements and rules, outlined above, are made at different decision-making levels. Directives and regulations derive from decisions made in EC institutions, whilst statute and common law stem from Parliament and the courts. Industry-wide collective agreements, the policy statements of management organisations and wages regulation orders are determined at multi-employer level. Apart from departmental customs and practices, and externally generated union rules, all other agreements and employee relations rules are made at employer or site level: company rules, contracts of employment, company collective agreements and workplace collective agreements.

Conflict-resolving processes

Unilateral employer regulation – company rules or 'the right to manage' – is only one of several types of employment rules. Given the potentially conflictual nature of the employment relationship, there are a number of institutional arrangements by which conflicts of interest between the primary parties to the pay–work bargain (employers and employees) and the secondary parties (management or management organisations and trade unions) may be resolved. Some are collective processes, others are individual ones. Collective processes are those where employees are represented indirectly in employment decision-making with employers and managers, by either trade unions or similar bodies. Individual processes are those where there are direct, face-to-face contacts between employers or managers and their subordinates.

Both collective and individual processes, in turn, can be subdivided into voluntary or legal methods of conducting employee relations. Voluntary methods are those determined independently and autonomously by the parties to employee relations, such as 'free' or 'voluntary' bargaining between employers and trade unions. Legal methods are those supported by the law, whether derived from common law, statutory or European sources. They provide the parties with legal rights and obligations and are ultimately enforceable by the courts, such as in employment protection, health and safety matters or the regulation of industrial conflict.

Figure 1: *Conflict resolution and employee relations*

```
┌─────────────────────────────────────────────────────────────┐
│                          Methods                              │
│   P                       voluntary                           │
│   r                          │                                │
│   o              joint       │      employer                  │
│   c            regulation    │     regulation                 │
│   e                          │                                │
│   s   collective ────────────┼──────────────── individual     │
│   s                          │                                │
│   e            regulated     │       state                    │
│   s           collectivism   │     regulation                 │
│                              │                                │
│                           legal                               │
└─────────────────────────────────────────────────────────────┘
```

Combining collective and individual processes with voluntary and legal methods, as shown in Figure 1, we observe that there are four major institutional approaches to resolving conflict in employee relations. These are:

• joint regulation;
• employer regulation;
• state regulation;
• regulated collectivism.

At any one time, the ways in which the pay–work bargain is determined, interpreted and implemented – within any organisational or national setting – involve, to varying degrees, a combination of these approaches to resolving potential employee relations conflict. But one of them may be the dominant approach.

Joint regulation

This involves a combination of collective processes and voluntary methods and includes:

• collective bargaining;
• joint consultation.

Collective bargaining takes place between employer and union representatives and is based on the assumption that both the market and managerial relations between the primary parties to employee relations are power based, with the balance of power weighted in favour of employers and individual managers. This is because any individual employee has a far greater need for a particular job, and the pay–work bargain attached to it, than an employer has for any particular worker (Webb and Webb 1913). Without collective bargaining, individual workers are disadvantaged in the labour market since, where labour supply is plentiful, each worker is competing with others for jobs, enabling pay and conditions to be cut to the lowest possible standards by market-driven employers. Equally, in their managerial relations, without collective bargaining, workers are subject to internal, unilateral employment decisions about their work, over which they have no control.

With collective bargaining, in contrast, there is assumed to be a fairer balance of power between the buyers and sellers of labour, with employers and unions jointly responsible for implementing the substantive and procedural collective agreements determined between them. These terms, conditions and procedures then become incorporated into the individual contracts of employment of the employees covered by the bargaining arrangements. In this way, collective bargaining is a process for identifying, institutionalising and resolving any conflicts of interest or of rights in employee relations (see Chapter 9).

Joint consultation is the process whereby employer and employee representatives, who may or may not be union representatives, come together, normally at workplace and/or employer levels, to discuss matters of common interest. There are a number of different approaches to joint consultation (Marchington 1989) but the basic distinction between joint consultation and collective bargaining is that it is a collaborative rather than an adversarial process. Joint consultation tends to exclude matters which are subject to negotiation and to focus on matters of a non-controversial nature. It discusses issues prior to management taking a decision, or prior to negotiation, but it does not itself generally involve the taking of decisions. In this sense, the joint consultative process retains the power of management as a group to take and implement decisions, after consultations have been completed (see Chapter 10).

Employer regulation

This involves a combination of individual processes and voluntary methods which are employer and management driven. These include:

- the right to manage;
- employee involvement;
- profit-sharing;
- pay review bodies.

The right to manage is basically concerned with all those decisions, over employment and related issues, which management claim the exclusive right to determine unilaterally. Where trade unions are absent, the employer's freedom to make decisions unilaterally is restricted only by what the law prescribes. Where unions are recognised by the employer, however, management's right to determine and apply employment rules is further restricted. But there are always areas of organisational decision-making, normally incorporated into company or 'works' rules, which remain exclusive to management alone.

There are a number of types of employee involvement. One is team briefing. This is a system of direct communication between line managers and their work teams, based on the principle of cascading information downwards, on a regular and formal basis, from management to employees. It aims to inform employees and work groups what is happening in their organisation, and why. It also reinforces the role of line managers as leaders of their work teams. Another type of employee involvement is quality circles. These comprise small groups of employees meeting regularly and voluntarily to discuss and solve quality and work-based problems. Quality circles are normally led by first line managers who have been provided with training to improve the effectiveness of quality circles. Quality circles are sometimes monitored by steering committees higher up the organisation (see Chapter 10).

Profit-sharing is also an employer-driven process. It is primarily aimed at emphasising the common, rather than the divergent, interests of employers and employees and at reinforcing this financially. Profit-sharing is where cash bonuses are paid voluntarily by employers to employees out of corporate profits. In practice, these cash bonuses are provided in one of the following ways:

- on a discretionary basis;
- as a fixed proportion of profits;
- as a proportion above a stated profit threshold;
- in relation to dividends paid on share capital.

Profit-sharing does not provide employees with a share in the ownership of an enterprise but simply with an additional monetary claim, over and above their pay and non-pay rewards, based on corporate success (see Chapter 10).

Pay review bodies (PRBs) are appointed by the prime minister for certain groups of public servants. It is a politically driven approach to employee relations. The role of PRBs is to make recommendations to the prime minister about the pay for particular public servants, although the government is not automatically bound by the decisions made. PRBs are established where it is felt that collective forms of pay determination for particular groups – such as top civil servants, doctors and dentists, and the armed services – are inappropriate, although in some cases union evidence is given to the review body, such as for schoolteachers, and this is taken into account in making its recommendations.

State regulation

This combines individual processes with legal methods and includes:

- contracts of employment;
- employment protection rights;
- individual conciliation by the Advisory Conciliation and Arbitration Service (ACAS);
- union membership rights;
- employee share ownership.

Contracts of employment are, in many respects, the focal point of relations between the primary parties to employment – employers and employees, or individual managers and their staff. In essence, a contract of employment is a legal agreement between an employer and an individual employee, whereby the employee undertakes to obey the lawful and reasonable orders of the employer, or its managerial agents, and to take reasonable care in carrying out his or her employment duties, in exchange for remuneration. There is also a duty of fidelity to the employer. The employer, in turn, is bound in duty to pay wages, take reasonable care for the employee's safety and exercise due consideration in dealing with the employee. In practice, many features of the contract of employment are undefined, since they are settled by the courts through the legal device of 'implied terms'. The other main legal sources of the contract of employment include (Lewis 1990):

- statutory statements;
- collective agreements;
- works rules;
- customs and practices.

Employment protection rights are incorporated in legislation which provides a floor of minimum statutory employment rights for individual employees, below which no one may fall. These rights include (see also Chapters 3 and 4):

- not to be 'unfairly' dismissed;
- minimum periods of notice;
- itemised pay statements;
- not to be discriminated against on the grounds of gender, nationality or ethnic origin;
- not to be made redundant without a minimum payment;
- maternity pay and leave.

ACAS is empowered by the Trade Union and Labour Relations (Consolidation) Act (TULRCA) 1992 to provide individual conciliation where employees think that their employment protection rights, such as not to be 'unfairly' dismissed or to statutory maternity pay and leave, have been infringed by an employer. Cases unresolved by ACAS may go to industrial tribunals.

Union membership rights, for individual trade unionists, include: not to be unreasonably excluded or expelled from a trade union; to elect union office holders by secret ballot; to endorse official trade union industrial action by secret ballot; to determine union political funds by secret ballot; and not to be unjustifiably disciplined by the individual's union (see Chapters 4 and 8).

Employee share ownership (ESO), introduced by the Finance Acts 1978 and 1980, provides employees with not only a stake in the ownership of the firm in which they work but also a right to participate in the distribution of its profits. Technically ESO is a legal regulation of an optional, voluntary employee relations practice. It is government- and employer-driven and is aimed at increasing the identification of employees with their employers, making them more conscious of the market pressures on their firms and ensuring they gain financially from corporate profitability. There are certain types of ESO which attract tax advantages such as Approved All Employee Profit Sharing Schemes and Save As You Earn Schemes. Under approved schemes, employees are not liable for income tax on gains in exercising share options.

Regulated collectivism

This involves collective processes, underpinned by the law, and includes:

- wages councils;
- conciliation, arbitration and mediation;
- trade union rights;
- pension fund trustees;
- unilateral industrial sanctions;
- in the European context, co-determination.

Third-party intervention and trade union rights

Wages councils were established in law to settle the minimum hourly rates of pay and overtime pay in particular industries, where there was no collective bargaining machinery. First set up in 1909, they were abolished in 1993. They consisted of employer, union and independent representation, including an independent chair. Wages councils determined the pay rates of workers covered by their terms of reference, at regular intervals, and issued wages regulation orders setting out their decisions. These were legally enforceable on all employers in the industries covered by them.

Voluntary conciliation, arbitration and mediation in Britain is provided by ACAS, through the TULRCA 1992, where either a trade dispute is threatened, or negotiations between an employer and a union have broken down. Collective conciliation is the process whereby, with negotiations having broken down, and normally when the agreed procedures to avoid disputes are exhausted, ACAS officers provide assistance to both sides to get them talking again. Their intervention often provides a basis for resolving such conflicts. Arbitration is the process whereby a third party, normally a single arbitrator or a panel of arbitrators, hears the cases of each side, deliberates on their evidence and determines a settlement. Each side agrees in advance to be bound by the decision of the arbitrator and to accept the award. Mediation is the process whereby a third party, normally an individual nominated by ACAS, with the approval of both sides, makes recommendations to the parties which may provide a basis for settling their differences.

Certain legal rights are provided for 'independent' unions having a certificate of independence from the Certification Officer (CO), where they are recognised by employers for collective bargaining purposes. These legal rights include (see also Chapters 3 and 7):

- the appointment of safety representatives and the establishment of safety committees;
- consultation on collective redundancies;
- information and consultation on business transfers;
- secret ballots on employers' premises;
- public funds to finance secret postal ballots for specific issues.

Pension fund trustees, whether employee or union representatives, have the right to be consulted where an employer:

- wishes to contract out of the State Earnings Related Pension Scheme (SERPS);
- introduces pension benefits without contracting out of SERPS;
- replaces one contracted-out scheme with a new one;
- wishes to amend a contracted-out scheme.

Industrial sanctions

Industrial sanctions are normally taken, within a framework established by the law, where there are no alternative conflict resolving processes left. They may be used unilaterally either by employers, management organisations and managers against employees and their unions or by employees and their unions against employers. They are a method of last resort and are used by one party to force the other to concede a demand, often of principle, which cannot be resolved by persuasion, negotiation, compromise or third-party intervention. Industrial sanctions involve the blunt use of employer, union or worker power against the other party. To remain 'constitutional', in other words within the accepted rules of employee relations, they should be taken only after any agreed procedures for avoiding conflict have been used and a 'failure to agree' has been recorded.

Employers use a range of industrial sanctions. These include, in order of severity:

- tight supervision;

- harsh discipline;
- demotions;
- withdrawing overtime;
- changing working practices unilaterally;
- lockouts;
- closing sites or workplaces;
- reinvesting in plant and machinery elsewhere.

Formal sanctions by employees and unions against employers and management, in turn, include (see also Chapter 11):

- lax time-keeping;
- working inefficiently;
- working to rule;
- overtime bans;
- stoppages of work.

Co-determination

Co-determination, as yet unestablished in Britain, is the process embodied in law whereby employees are enabled to participate in certain areas of managerial decision-making within the business organisations employing them. In Germany, for example, the law provides for the establishment of works councils at plant or site level (Berghan and Karsten 1989). Works councils are elected by the workforce in all plants or sites where there are five or more employees. They exist to protect the interests of workers in the plant and to ensure that effect is given to legislation, safety regulations and collective agreements affecting employees. They also have the right to participate in certain management decisions relating to the operation of the plant, the conduct of employees and the distribution of working hours. The employer also has to seek the consent of the works council on certain other issues.

   Other forms of co-determination by employee reprsentatives in management are provided for by federal law in Germany. These operate at company level. In the mining, iron and steel industries, for example, there is numerical parity of 'capital' and 'labour' representatives on the (upper-tier) supervisory boards of these enterprises. These appoint and dismiss members of the (lower-tier) management board and supervise them. Additionally, the labour director, who is a member of the management board, cannot be appointed against the wishes of the majority of the employee representatives. In limited companies employing more than 2,000 persons, 50 per cent of the supervisory board are shareholder representatives, with the employees' side divided between those employed by the company and those who are external trade union representatives (see Chapters 3 and 10).

External influences

Employee relations in the labour market and the workplace do not take place in a vacuum. The resolution of potential employment conflict between the buyers and sellers of labour services are affected by a variety of economic and political factors.

The micro-economic level

A major determinant of pay rates and the numbers of workers employed by an organisation is the demand for labour relative to its supply. Other things being equal, where labour demand exceeds labour supply, pay rates rise. Where labour supply exceeds labour demand, pay rates fall. There is also the union 'mark-up' differential between union and non-union labour. This is the extent by which unions are able to raise pay rates for their members over and above the market rates for equivalent non-union labour. The union mark-up varies widely across occupations and over time. Stewart (1983), for example, indicates a union mark-up of about 8 per cent in British manufacturing as a whole, with shipbuilding and paper and printing, at that time, having mark-ups of around 18 per cent and 11 per cent respectively. Clearly, the union mark-up varies over time but these figures give some idea of the 'gap' between union and non-union pay.

The determinants of an employer's demand for labour are complex. It depends partly on the structure of the external labour market, its internal labour market and its local labour market, but more particularly on the buoyancy, or not, of its product markets (Brown 1973) or, in the public services, on the ceiling placed on public spending by government (Beaumont 1992). The total supply of labour available to the economy is determined by the size of the population of working age, with the amount supplied being a function of the labour force participation rate, the number of hours that people are willing to work and the amount of effort provided by people at work. From an employer's point of view, the available labour supply is affected by its quality, its relative mobility and its potential productivity.

A firm's external labour market (ELM) is the numbers of workers that are either available for work or potentially available for new jobs. Within the ELM, pricing and allocating decisions are controlled largely by economic variables, but employer decisions are crucial (Rubery 1989). In practice, because of differences in the quality of labour, in terms of aptitudes, skills and training, the ELM is highly segmented by occupation, industry, geography, gender, race and age (Dex 1989; Jenkins 1989; and Ashton 1989). One theory, the dual labour market hypothesis, is that the ELM is dichotomised into primary and secondary sectors. The primary sector is characterised by 'good' jobs and the secondary sector by 'bad' ones. Good jobs have high pay, high status, excellent promotion prospects, attractive fringe benefits and security of employment. Bad jobs, with the opposite characteristics, are allocated to those excluded from the primary sector, because they lack investment in 'human capital' or are discriminated against. In the secondary sector, where unions are weak or unrecognised, pay rates are established largely by competition, since with full employment there are sufficient jobs available for all those seeking work at current pay rates, or, in conditions of unemployment, labour supply exceeds labour demand and pay rates fall. Work in the secondary sector is generally low paid, unattractive and unstable.

Internal labour markets (ILMs) are the arrangements by which labour is supplied and demanded within a firm without direct access to the ELM. Employment policies are directed towards those employed in the firm, with most jobs being filled by the promotion or transfer of workers who are already working in the company (Robinson 1970). ILMs, therefore, consist of sets of employment relationships, embodying formal and informal rules, which govern each job and the relationships amongst them. The reasons for ILMs include:

- union pressure for internal promotion, based on seniority;
- on-the-job training which makes the jobs unique;
- low-cost recruitment;
- good employment practice;
- more reliable selection;
- scarcity of skills in the ELM.

Local labour markets (LLMs) are largely the consequence of the financial and psychological costs and disadvantages, to workers, of extensive time spent travelling to work. These costs further segment a labour force which is already stratified by the characterisitics outlined above. They tend to restrict a firm's labour market to that which is accessible from a limited geographical area, for less skilled occupational groups at least. This definition of LLMs assumes that their key characteristic is that the bulk of an area's working population continually seeks employment there and that local employers recruit most of the labour from the area.

The macro-economy

Government economic policy also affects the buyers and sellers of labour. One approach is Keynesian demand management which dominated British macro-economic policy during the 1940s, 1950s and 1960s (Worswick and Ady 1952; Dow 1964; Worswick and Trevithick 1984). Its focus is on the level of aggregate demand in the economy. This is the total sum spent on goods and services, consisting of consumption, investment, government expenditure and expenditure on exports less imports. With the economy expanding and aggregate demand rising, demand for goods, services and labour increases, unemployment falls and union bargaining power is strengthened. When the economy slows down, because of falls in consumption or investment, demand for goods, services and labour decreases, unemployment rises and union bargaining power is weakened.

Governments using Keynesian demand management techniques seek to influence the level of aggregate demand by counter-cyclical fiscal and monetary policies. These are aimed at trying to slow down the economy when it is booming, because 'full employment' contributes to pay and price inflation, and at trying to boost the economy during recession, because unemployment is rising. Governments cut their spending and raise taxes when the economy is overheating and increase their spending, by public borrowing, and cut taxes when the economy is in recession (see Chapter 4).

The ways in which employers and unions in the private and public sectors react to these policy instruments is crucial in determining whether or not governmental policy succeeds. If pay bargainers fail to respond to the labour market signals given by government, and pay increases rise faster than national productivity, then the 'pay–price' and 'pay–tax/public borrowing' spirals are fuelled, resulting in inflation, low growth and balance of payments problems. If, on the other hand, employers resist 'felt-fair' union pay claims, then increases in trade disputes are likely. For these reasons, Keynesian demand management policies are normally linked with 'prices and incomes' policies, necessitating employer and union cooperation with government, aimed at restraining price and pay rises in line with rises in productivity and efficiency in the corporate sector (Jones 1987; see also Chapter 7 below).

Another approach is where governments focus on 'supply-side' measures, as they have done in Britain since the mid-1970s. Supply-side economics emphasises that the principal determinant of the rate of growth of an economy, in both the short and long run, is the allocation and efficient use of labour and capital. It is a restatement of neo-classical macro-economic principles. These are based on the notion of 'rational expectations' and a 'natural rate of unemployment' that emerges as a result of efficient market clearing. By this view, the natural rate of unemployment cannot be reduced by raising aggregate demand and attempts to disturb this equilibrium are self-defeating. This is because they will be anticipated and neutralised by economic agents in the market place (Brittan 1988; Green 1989; Levacic 1988).

Supply-side economic policies focus on removing impediments to the supply of and efficient use of the factors of production. They are concerned with the determinants of the natural rate of unemployment, rather than with the level of effective demand in the short run as in Keynesian macro-economics. Amongst these impediments are claimed to be disincentives to work and invest, because of tax structures and tax levels, and institutional barriers, such as trade unions, to the efficient allocation of resources. The policy prescriptions flowing from this analysis are (see also Chapters 4 and 7):

- deregulating labour and product markets, thus making them more competitive and efficient;
- privatisation;
- cutting public borrowing;
- cutting taxes.

The employee relations implications of these supply-side policies are that they result in the strengthening of employer bargaining power in the labour market and managerial rights in the workplace. In the private sector, in order to remain competitive in tight product markets, companies seek increased workforce productivity and efficiency. These are only made possible by reducing unit labour costs and increasing labour flexibility. This results in rising unemployment – unless pay rates fall, new product markets are found or growth rates are high. This weakens union wage bargaining power. In the public sector, there are similar employer pressures to raise efficiency, keep public spending under control and resist union pay claims which are 'not affordable' or not responsive to 'market forces'. The right to manage, in turn, is reinforced at the workplace, because of fear of unemployment and job losses, and union resistance to changes in working practices, new technology and managerial assertiveness is weakened.

Politics, the state and the law

Politics, the state and the law are never neutral in employee relations. The roles of the state – as legislator, economic manager, employer or third-party conciliator – its governmental agents, and the courts are crucial in determining the contexts within which employee relations decisions are taken (see Chapter 7).

During the nineteenth century, in the age of classical *laissez-faire*, or the doctrine that economic decisions are best guided by the autonomous decisions of free individuals in the market place, the state's role in employee relations was a minimalist and restrictive one. This reflected the dominant power structures in a society based on landed wealth, a growing entrepreneurial class of manufacturers and merchants and an undemocratic, elitist Parliament and political system (Fox 1985). Wide differentials in wealth, class, status and power separated 'master' from 'servant', capitalist from worker, entrepreneur from wage earner and even craftsman from labourer. And common law, described by Kahn-Freund (1983: page 18) as 'a command under the guise of an agreement', dominated the employment contract between the primary parties to the pay–work bargain.

By the early twentieth century, with the slow emergence of trade unionism amongst working people and the gradual democratisation of the parliamentary system, there were three main political and legal legacies of classical *laissez-faire* for employee relations. One was the emergence of a unified 'Labour Movement', linking the now legally emancipated unions with the newly created Labour Party (see Chapter 7). This political alliance was in reaction to the dominance in

Employee Relations

Parliament of the business and commercial classes and meant that employee relations were now inevitably politicised and dichotomised between those representing the interests of the capitalist and labouring classes respectively (Farnham 1976). Second, there was a mistrust of the law by working people, especially of the courts, in the ways it affected trade unions, collective bargaining and the regulation of industrial conflict. Their preference was for autonomy in collective bargaining with employers and for non-intervention by the courts and the judges in employee relations. The third legacy was the central importance of the common law in regulating the individual contract of employment.

With the steady growth in the size, power and scope of the state in the twentieth century (White and Chapman 1987), and the continued democratisation of society (Middlemas 1979), it was inevitable that the roles of government and the law would increase in employee relations. Crouch (1979) provides four models of state or public policy on employee relations under advanced capitalism. These are summarised in Figure 2. He describes them as:

- voluntary collective bargaining;
- neo-*laissez-faire*;
- corporatism;
- bargained corporatism.

The model which predominates depends on whether the state is organised on 'corporatist' or 'liberal' principles and whether the position of trade unions within it is 'weak' or 'strong'. A corporatist state is where the economy is largely privately owned but the interests of capitalists, workers and government are integrated and mediated, through centralised institutional mechanisms, to ensure political and economic stability. A liberal state, in contrast, is one based on private enterprise but where the political and economic spheres are disassociated. Economic decisions are decentralised, with businesses, individuals and workers exercising freedom of choice in the market place. A crucial development in economic liberalism is the acceptance of trade unionism, or collectivism. Combination takes place to offset the inequalities between workers as sellers of labour services and capitalists as buyers in the market place, resulting in 'collective' liberalism or collective *laissez-faire*.

Figure 2: *State policies on employee relations*

```
                        Trade Unions
    T                       strong
    h                   voluntary        |
    e                   collective       |   bargained
                        bargaining       |   corporatism
    S
    t       liberal  ────────────────────┼──────────────── corporatist
    a
    t                   neo-laissez      |   corporatism
    e                     faire          |
                                         |
                             weak
```

Source: Crouch (1979)

Governments, with their economic and legal policy preferences, determine whether employee relations operate in corporatist or liberal contexts and whether trade unions are weak or strong. The centralised, corporate state, with weak trade unions – as in postwar Japan – provides *corporatism* as the employee relations model. This often comprises a combination of supply-side economic policies, union pay constraint and legal limitations on trade unions. Where unions are strong in a corporate state, the model is described as *bargained corporatism*. This is a situation, as in Britain during the second world war and in the late 1970s, where union leaders accepted politically imposed restraints on 'free collective bargaining' in return for other gains for their members, such as concessions on social policy, laws favourable to union organisation and a share in economic and political decision-making.

In the liberal, market-centred state, *voluntary collective bargaining* provides the model for employee relations where unions are strong. This was the dominant model for much of the post-war period, especially in the 30 years after 1945, apart from 1970–71. It was characterised largely by bi-partisan Conservative or Labour governments, with demand management economic policies and legal abstention in employee relations. Where unions are weak in the liberal state, the model is described as *neo-laissez-faire*. This was the case in the interwar period and since the early 1980s. During this period, Conservative governments supported supply-side economic policy and legal intervention in employee relations. These proscribed union activities and industrial action (Moran 1977; Gamble 1988; Farnham 1990; see also Chapter 7 below).

Assignments

(a) Why do people work? What do they get from working? And what are the main implications of employee needs at work for employers and their employee relations policies? Give examples from your own organisation.

(b) Provide examples of employment costs to your organisation for employing various categories of staff, breaking them down into costing classifications. What factors have to be taken into account by the employer in 'costing' the likely effects of a stoppage of work by a key group of employees in the organisation?

(c) Read Brown (1972) and Terry (1977) and analyse what is meant by the term 'custom and practice'. Why do workers use it and why do employers accept it? Looking at your own organisation, identify some current 'customs and practices', indicating management's reaction to them and why they are tolerated. Provide other examples of 'C and P' which management have recently claimed back, how this was done and why.

(d) Interview some managers, including someone in personnel, at least one trade union representative and some employees and ask them to define what they consider to be 'good employee relations'. Comment on and compare their answers and approaches. Rank in order of relative importance the conflict resolving processes in your organisation used to maintain 'good employee relations', commenting on them as appropriate.

(e) Identify and evaluate the types of labour market from which your employer recruits its employees. How are these labour markets segmented and what are the implications for employee relations?

(f) Read Lewis (1990) and identify the main common law duties of employers and employees under the contract of employment.

(g) Summarise Flanders' analysis of the trade unions' role in politics (1970: pages 24–37). Examine the relevance of his arguments today. Alternatively, discuss his analysis of job regulation and its part in rule making in employee relations (pages 86–94).

(h) Evaluate Kahn-Freund's 'reflections on law and power' in employee relations (1977: pages 1–17). Outline how the role of the law in employee relations has evolved since then and its relevance for management.

References

ASHTON, D. 1989. 'Educational institutions, youth and the labour market'. In GALLIE, D. (ed.) 1989. *Employment in Britain*. Oxford: Blackwell.

BERGHAN, V. and CARSTEN, D. 1989. *Industrial Relations in West Germany*. Oxford: Berg.

BEAUMONT, P. 1992. *Public Sector Industrial Relations*. London: Routledge.

BRITTAN, S. 1988. *A Restatement of Economic Liberalism*. London: Macmillan.

BROWN, W. 1972. 'A consideration of custom and practice'. *British Journal of Industrial Relations*. X(1), March.

BROWN, W. 1973. *Piecework Bargaining*. London: Heinemann.

CENTRAL STATISTICAL OFFICE 1991. 'Employment in the public and private sectors'. *Economic Trends*. 458, December.

CROUCH, C. 1979. *The Politics of Industrial Relations*. Glasgow: Fontana.

DEX, S. 1989. 'Gender and the labour market'. In GALLIE, D. (ed.) 1989. *Employment in Britain*. Oxford: Blackwell.

DOW, J. 1964. *The Management of the British Economy, 1945 to 1960*. Cambridge: Cambridge University Press.

FARNHAM, D. 1976. 'The Labour Alliance: reality or myth?' *Parliamentary Affairs*. XXIX(1), Winter.

FARNHAM, D. 1990. 'Trade union policy 1979–89: restriction or reform?' In SAVAGE, S. and ROBINS, L. (eds). *Public Policy under Thatcher*. Basingstoke: Macmillan.

FARNHAM, D, 1993. 'Human resources management and employee relations'. In FARNHAM, D. and HORTON, S. (eds) 1993. *Managing the New Public Services*. Basingstoke: Macmillan.

FARNHAM, D. and HORTON, S. (eds) 1993. *Managing the New Public Services*. Basingstoke: Macmillan.

FLANDERS, A. 1968. 'Collective bargaining: a theoretical analysis'. In FLANDERS, A. 1970. *Management and Unions*. London: Faber and Faber.

FLEMING, A. 1989. 'Employment in the public and private sectors'. *Economic Trends*. 434, December.

GAMBLE, A. 1988. *The Free Economy and the Strong State*. London: Macmillan.

GREEN, F. 1989. *The Restructuring of the British Economy*. London: Harvester.

JONES, R. 1987. *Wages and Employment Policy, 1936–85*. London: Allen and Unwin.

JENKINS, R. 1989. 'Discrimination and equal opportunity in employment: ethnicity and race in the United Kingdom'. In GALLIE, D. (ed.) 1989. *Employment in Britain*. Oxford: Blackwell.

KAHN-FREUND, O. 1977. *Labour and the Law*. London: Stevens.

KAHN-FREUND, O. 1983. *Labour and the Law*. (3rd ed.) London: Stevens.

LEVACIC, R. 1988. *Supply Side Economics*. Oxford: Heinemann.

LEWIS, D. 1990. *Essentials of Employment Law*. London: IPM.

MARCHINGTON, M. 1989. 'Joint consultation in practice'. In SISSON, K. (ed.) 1989. *Personnel Management in Britain*. Oxford: Blackwell.

MIDDLEMAS, K.. 1979. *Politics in Industrial Society.* London: Deutsch.

MORAN, M. 1977. *The Politics of Industrial Relations.* London: Macmillan.

RUBERY, J. 1989. 'Employers and the labour market'. In GALLIE, D. (ed.) 1989. *Employment in Britain.* Oxford: Blackwell.

ROBINSON, D. (ed.) 1970. *Local Labour Markets and Wage Structure.* Farnborough: Gower.

STARKS, M. 1991. *Not for Profit Not for Sale.* Bristol: Policy Journals.

STEWART, M. 1983. 'Relative earnings and individual union membership in the UK'. *Economica.*

TERRY, M. 1977. 'The inevitable growth of informality'. *British Journal of Industrial Relations.* 15(1).

WEBB, S. and WEBB, B. 1913. *Industrial Democracy.* NY: Longmans.

WEDDERBURN, Lord 1986. *The Worker and the Law.* Harmondsworth: Penguin.

WHITE, G. and CHAPMAN, H. 1987. 'Long-term trends in public expenditure'. *Economic Trends.* 408, October.

WORSWICK, D. and ADY, P. 1952. *The British Economy 1945–50.* Oxford: Oxford University Press.

WORSWICK, D. and TREVITHICK, 1984. *Keynes and the Modern World.* Cambridge University Press.

Chapter 2

The Parties in Employee Relations

In advanced market economies, employee relations are largely institutionalised. This means that the primary parties to the employment relationship (employers and employees) are bound together by a network of formally agreed rules, agreements and procedures, such as contracts of employment, employment handbooks, grievance, disciplinary and promotion procedures, and by informal customs and practices. These provide both parties with a series of interdependent, *individual* rights and obligations, emphasising the mutuality of their relationship, which are aimed at reconciling any potential conflicts between them authoritatively and fairly. These rights and obligations between employers and employees are economic, legal and constitutional in character but they are underpinned by a set of normative and moral values associated with fairness, equity and trust in the employment relationship (Hyman and Brough 1975; Fox 1974; Fox 1985).

Another institutional feature of employee relations is the secondary nature of many employment relationships. The secondary parties (management or management organisations and unions) are also bound together by a network of formally agreed rules, agreements and procedures.These include union rules, collective agreements and negotiating and consultative procedures (see Chapters 1, 9 and 10). These link the parties together in a web of mutually independent, *collective* rights and obligations aimed at reconciling any potential conflicts between them legitimately and peacefully. They are economic and constitutional in character, with their own procedural and substantive, normative order (Flanders and Fox 1969).

The last institutional feature of employee relations is the existence of third parties, normally agents of the state. These bodies are created to influence the decisions of the primary and secondary parties and to ensure either 'fair play' or changes in the balance of power amongst them. The values associated with third-party institutions have varied between those of evenhandedness, balance and legitimacy, on the one side, and of bias, controversy and coercion on the other (see Chapter 7).

Management

The term 'management' is used in two main senses. First, management is the set of activities carried out by those individuals with decision-taking and executive responsibilities in organisations. It focuses on the jobs, tasks and activities which managers do. This definition of management incorporates three aspects of managing: what managers do; how they do it; and how they are grouped in organisations, vertically and horizontally. It recognises that managers are themselves employees who are employed for the knowledge, skills and expertise which they bring into organisations as part of the internal and occupational divisions of labour. Management in this sense focuses on four areas of managing: the nature of managerial work (Mintzberg 1975; Stewart 1982); managerial processes (Fayol 1949; Likert 1961; Peters and Waterman 1982); management levels (Chandler and Daems 1980); and the functional areas of management such as operations, finance, marketing and personnel (Farnham 1990).

The second way in which the term management is used is to describe the group of people in organisations who are collectively responsible for the efficient and effective running of the enterprises they manage. By this view, management is the authority system or the power group which has the responsibility for ensuring the financial viability, organisational success and ultimate accountability of an enterprise to its primary beneficiaries, whether these are shareholders, government ministers or local politicians. Management in this sense focuses on the *agency* roles of managers in terms of their responsibilities for enterprise effectiveness, corporate efficiency and employee relations. It is this meaning of the term 'management' that is primarily used in this book.

One objective of management collectively is to ensure the profitability and/or efficiency of the organisations in which they work. They have to ensure the most efficient use of enterprise resources and the achievement of enterprise goals. In practice, however, managements also have to take account of the broader social and economic consequences of their decisions, not just the short-term economic ones. In this respect, Brown (1965) amongst others argues that managements have to reconcile a number of conflicting aims and objectives. These include making their enterprises economically viable, whilst at the same time seeking to be responsive to shareholder, customer, supplier and employee interests. Managements, in short, are concerned not only with profits and efficiency, or with 'value for money' in the public sector, but also with being socially responsible to the wider communities with which they interact. They also want good working relations with their employees.

This means that employees are only one of the many executive concerns of management. Customers, banks, suppliers and government inspectorates all make demands on management. Employee relations are an important part of the management function but they are only one of management's many organisational roles and corporate responsibilities. This makes the managing of employee relations problematic in any organisation. At one extreme, managements can develop sophisticated employee relations strategies, policies and procedures, which take account of the other, often conflicting, demands made on management. Here the employers' objective is to promote the best employment practices associated with 'model' employing organisations. At the other extreme, managements may act in ways meeting only the minimum employment standards required by the law and local labour market pressures.

Employee relations management

For these and related reasons, medium and larger organisations in both the private and public sectors use employee relations specialists. They are variously described as personnel officers, industrial relations advisers, employee relations managers or, most recently, as human resource managers. It is these members of management who represent the human resource function within the management structure and in its dealings with employee or union respresentatives. In 1992, the IPM estimated that there were some 150,000 people working in the personnel function in Britain, with employee relations accounting for 35 per cent of all personnel activity (Institute of Personnel Management 1992).

The traditional management role in employee relations has been an uninterested, reactive and fire-fighting one. Top management literally did not want to know about employee relations (Winkler 1974). According to Miller (1987), this pattern of reactive, 'non-strategic' employee relations management implies an employee relations function which is characterised by being:

- separate from an organisation's corporate strategy;
- short term;

- of no interest to the board of directors.

It is also identified with a definition of employee relations focusing principally on unionised, lower-status groups of workers.

Managing collective bargaining

The steady growth of trade unions throughout the twentieth century, together with employer recognition of trade unions and public policy support for collective bargaining, meant that the joint determination of terms and conditions of employment became the centrepiece of British employee relations by the 1960s (Ministry of Labour 1965). Indeed, the conclusion of the Donovan Commission (1968: page 50) was that 'collective bargaining is the best method of conducting industrial relations'. It added, however, that multi-employer, industry-wide bargaining was no longer capable of imposing its decisions on the participants. The Commision therefore recommended that management should take the initiative and responsibility for reforming collective bargaining at company and plant levels. The means was to be the development of proactive personnel policies, management-led authoritative, collective bargaining machinery, comprehensive procedural agreements and joint arrangements for discussing health and safety at work, within companies or plants. Multi-employer, industry-wide bargaining would deal with those issues, such as overtime premia, length of working week or holiday periods, which it could most effectively regulate (see Chapter 7).

From the late 1960s, Donovan's recommendations were gradually extended and acted upon in much of the corporate sector, with parallel developments in the public sector. The changes must not be exaggerated, however, as recent research by Storey (1992: page 259) shows that whilst old-style industrial relations 'fire-fighting' is increasingly being disavowed by managements, there is hardly 'an instance where anything approaching a ''strategic'' stance towards unions and industrial relations could readily be discerned as having taken its place.' Nevertheless, the outcome has been the steady expansion in numbers of personnel and employee relations specialists to help deal with the workplace issues arising from decentralised collective bargaining, the increasing scope of employment legislation and trade union organisation locally (Millward and Stevens 1986; Millward *et al.* 1992).

In this role, employee relations specialists are a resource upon which senior line management can draw for advice, expertise and technical know-how. The sorts of tasks in which they are involved include:

- participating in negotiating and joint consultation;
- assisting in the drafting of collective agreements;
- advising on employment legislation;
- advising in grievance and disciplinary cases;
- handling redundancies;
- providing inputs to personnel policy-making and decision-taking.

It is essentially an advisory rather than an executive role which typifies this approach to employee relations management.

Human resource management (HRM) and the new industrial relations

Another development, largely since the 1980s, has been the emergence of more strategic approaches to managing employee relations. This has taken place in some larger organisations, especially in the corporate sector, in response to increased product market competition, changes in market structures and technological change. Some of these developments are identified in the debate about HRM (Storey 1989; Storey 1992; Sissons 1989). This debate distinguishes between 'hard' HRM, focusing on human resource strategy and employee utilisation, and 'soft' HRM, with its greater emphasis on the 'human' aspects of management and concern with people in organisations. Whatever the exact nature of HRM, survey evidence reveals a positive picture of strategic HRM by the early 1990s, with 63 per cent of UK organisations surveyed claiming to have personnel or human resource directors, 83 per cent claiming a corporate strategy and 73 per cent claiming a personnel or HRM strategy (Price Waterhouse Cranfield 1990).

Other developments have given rise to a related debate focused on the relationship between the claimed rise of HRM and the apparent decline of trade union power. Bassett (1986) and Wickens (1987), on the basis of limited case study material, proclaim the arrival of a 'new industrial relations' based on single-union, 'no-strike' deals or even no unions at all. Dunn (1990) notes that the rhetoric of industrial relations has changed. From being based on the metaphor of 'trench warfare', it is now based on that of the 'new frontier', which is more consistent with HRM and the notion of a new industrial relations than it is with traditional personnel management.

Models of employee relations management

From this outline analysis, it is clear that the roles and status of employee relations specialists in organisations are now secure but are quite different from what they were when Donovan reported. Employee relations management clearly operates in a variety of modes and at different organisational levels. Some are operating in roles akin to what Tyson (1987) describes as the 'contracts manager' model of the personnel function. This is where employee relations specialists are particularly valued for their capacity to make quick decisions and informal agreements with trade union representatives, and their other activities are largely advisory. Others are operating as what Tyson describes as HRM 'architects'. This is a creative view of personnel and employee relations which aims at contributing to corporate success through explicit human resources policies and integrated systems of labour control between personnel and line managers. The architect model is particularly associated with the management of change, proactive personnel planning and systems of employee involvement (see Chapter 10).

Managerial approaches to employee relations

In its role as agent of the employer, management has a variety of employment activities to carry out. These include: attracting, recruiting, rewarding, motivating, retaining, directing, disciplining, exiting, negotiating and consulting with employees at work. In undertaking these activities, managements can choose, explicitly or implicitly, from a multiplicity of approaches to employee relations. A critical influence is management style. Management style, according to Purcell (1987: page 535), implies:

> a distinctive set of guiding principles, written or otherwise, which set parameters to and signposts for management action in the way employees are treated and particular events handled. Management style is therefore akin to business policy and its strategic derivatives.

It is management style, in short, which circumscribes the boundaries and direction of acceptable management action in its dealing with employees.

Frames of reference

Some writers suggest that it is management's 'frame of reference' which determines their predominant style of employee relations management. Fox (1966) identifies two major frames of reference, the unitary and the pluralist. The main elements of the unitary view are:

- organisations consist of teams of people, working together for common aims, where there are no conflicts of interest between managers and subordinates;
- strong leadership is required from management to achieve common organisational purpose;
- trade unions are illegitimate intrusions into the right to manage.

Pluralism, in contrast, emphasises:

- organisations are coalitions of competing interests, where management's role is to mediate amongst different interest groups;
- trade unions are legitimate representatives of employee interests;
- stability in employee relations results from concessions and compromises between managers and unions in the collective bargaining process.

Fox (1974) develops his analysis further in identifying four 'ideal' typologies of employee relations management. He describes managements as being:

- *traditionalists*, with unitary, anti-union policies;
- *sophisticated paternalists*, with unitary, enlightened, employee-centred human resource policies;
- *sophisticated moderns*, with pluralist, joint management–union decision-making in defined areas;
- *standard moderns*, where unions are recognised but employee relations fire-fighting predominates.

Purcell and Sisson (1983) divide the standard modern management style into 'constitutionalists' and 'consultors'. Constitutionalists codify the limits of collective bargaining, whilst consultors place greater emphasis on joint consultation and joint problem-solving.

Individualism and collectivism

Purcell (1987: pages 535–6) claims that the unitary and pluralist frames of reference are limited in defining management styles. He identifies two main dimensions of management style: *individualism* and *collectivism*. Individualism focuses on 'the feelings and sentiments of each employee' and encourages the capacities of individual employees and their roles at work. He distinguishes between 'high' and 'low' degrees of individualism. High individualism emphasises the resource status of employees, with employers wanting to develop and nurture their employees' talents and abilities. Related employment policies include careful selection, internal labour markets, staff appraisal, merit pay and extensive communication systems, all of which are associated with a 'neo-unitary' approach to employee relations (Farnham and Pimlott 1990). Low individualism emphasises the commodity status of employees, with employers concentrating on the control of both labour costs and the labour process. Profits are the priority and employment policies include recruiting in secondary labour markets, tight workplace discipline and little security of employment. Intermediate between high and low individualism is 'paternalism'. This synthesises caring, welfare employment policies with the subordinate position of lower-level employees in the organisational hierarchy.

Collectivism is the 'extent to which the organisation recognises the right of employees to have a say in those aspects of management decision-making which concern them' (Purcell 1987: page 538). Collectivism is operated through trade union organisation or other forms of employee representative system, thus giving employees a collective voice in organisational decision-making. There are two aspects of collectivism: the levels of employee participation – whether these are 'high' or 'low' – and the degree of legitimacy given to collective organisation by management. High-level employee participation such as co-determination, pension fund trustees and employer-wide collective bargaining, takes place at the corporate level. Low-level employee participation, in contrast, takes place at workgroup, departmental or workplace levels. Management tolerance of collectivism ranges from willing cooperation, at one extreme, to grudging acceptance at the other.

The important point which Purcell makes is that the links between individualism and collectivism in employee relations are complex. Whilst some employers have more individualist management styles, such as IBM, and some have more collectivist ones, such as the Ford Motor Company, elements of both individualism and collectivism are not incompatible with each other, as in some Japanese-owned companies.

> Management styles operate along the two dimensions and . . . action in one area, toward individualism, for example, is not necessarily associated with changes in the collectivism scale (page 541).

In practice, individualist styles of employee relations management tend towards non-unionism, whilst collectivist ones lead to union recognition. Thus whether an employer recognises trade unions for representational, consultative, negotiating or co-determination purposes is a critical and visible expression of management style and approach to employee relations. This does not mean, however, that internal training, promotion ladders and welfare provisions for individual employees are precluded. On the other hand, where trade unions are recognised and employees given a collective voice in employee relations, and the unions are subsequently derecognised, this is clearly an expression of a shift towards a more individualist style of employee relations management (Claydon 1989).

Employee relations policies

It is difficult to define the concept of an 'employee relations policy' with precision. In essence, it represents an employer's intentions and objectives about employment-related and human resource matters and the ways in which these are communicated to managers, employees, the wider community and, where they are recognised, to trade unions and their representatives. In practice, employee relations policies are an amalgam of explicit written statements and implicit unwritten assumptions about how employees are to be treated and managed as individuals and as members of trade unions. They are dynamic, organisationally specific and contingent on the external and internal environments within which organisations operate. Management style is an important determinant of an organisation's employee relations policies but the internal and external contingencies are crucial.

The contingencies acting on management in determining an organisation's employee relations policies include:

- legislation;
- other employers' policies;
- organisational size, ownership and location;
- union power;
- prevailing 'good practice';
- most importantly, the links between the organisation's business strategy and its employment and human resource strategy.

Policy choices

One way of analysing management's policy choices in employee relations is outlined in Figure 3. This identifies four potential policy choices for management. First, management can pursue a policy of *worker subordination*. This is based on low degrees of individualism and collectivism, with high levels of management discretion. Policy is operated through firm management control. Second, the policy of *union incorporation* is where there is a relatively high degree of collectivism, a low degree of individualism and policy is operated, in key employment areas, through joint management–union regulation. The third policy choice is *employee commitment* which incorporates a high degree of individualism and a low degree of collectivism, with policy being operated through management-driven programmes of HRM and employee involvement. Fourth, the policy of *worker participation* involves high degrees of both individualism and collectivism, with policy being operated through management–employee co-determination linked, possibly, with employee involvement measures. Indeed worker participation policies are entirely compatible with union incorporation and/or employee commitment policies. In practice, of course, managements can adopt different employee relations policies for different groups of workers or different policies for the same group of workers at different times.

Figure 3: *Management policies on employee relations*

		Individualism	
		low	high
Collectivism	low	worker subordination	employee commitment
	high	union incorporation	worker participation

Business strategy and managing personnel

A more sophisticated analysis is that of Thomason (1991). He examines the links between business strategy and management approaches to acquiring and utilising human resources and identifies three historical shifts in business strategy. They are not watertight compartments but are indicative of the main emphases of business strategy in different historical periods, different enterprises over time and some enterprises at any one time. The three approaches are:

- a *product differentiation strategy*, associated with the early industrial revolution;
- a *low-cost leadership strategy*, associated with industrial rationalisation which began about 100 years ago;
- a *customer/client satisfaction strategy*, associated with the 'new wave' rationalisations, in response to global competition and technical change, since the 1960s.

The differentiation strategy depends upon a core skilled workforce, supplemented by peripheral workers recruited for less-skilled work, organised in factories and workshops. The low-cost strategy depends upon the external labour market, where jobs are broken down into small tasks and repetitive activities, in line with the principles of scientific management. In contrast, in organisations seeking special relationships with their customers or clients, emphasis is placed on quality, reliability and product or service delivery and intra-organisational teamwork. This business strategy depends on, first, the development of internal labour markets and job training for existing employees. Second, job tasks and activities are reorganised, with the focus being on flexibility, versatility, multi-skilling and commitment. Third, managements try to create and transmit new corporate cultures to their employees (Anthony 1990), emphasising the primacy of client relationships, quality and teamwork.

Thomason's analysis leads to four possible labour control processes for management. The first stresses the need for quality output and, where recruitment takes place in the external labour market, uses an *employee selection strategy*. The second, which emphasises low-cost production and recruitment in the external labour market, uses an *employee supervision strategy*. This provides a framework of agreed or imposed employment rules and procedures. The third, based on price competition and demand for high-quality products, relies on a *human resources development strategy*, aimed at staff flexibility. The fourth, stressing customer satisfaction and recruitment from the internal labour market, focuses on a *human resources partnership strategy*. This aims at integrating employees into the organisation and at employee commitment.

Management organisations

There are a range of organisations acting on behalf of management interests in employee relations. Some, such as the IPM and the Institute of Directors, are based on individual or personal membership. This section focuses on management organisations that are based on collective or corporate membership and have specific roles in employee relations and related areas.

Employers' associations

An employers' association is defined in law as any organisation of employers, individual proprietors or constituent organisations of employers whose principal purpose includes the regulation of relations between employers and workers or between employers and trade unions. Employers' associations recruit member firms vertically, on an industry-wide basis.

Objectives, functions and ideology

The idea of employers within an industry combining together for employee relations purposes is not a new one. The first such bodies were formed in the nineteenth century in response to trade union organisation. Their central objective was to protect employer interests collectively in dealings with the unions (Clegg 1979). However, unlike in the USA (where, despite anti-trust laws, there have been powerful producer cartels), there has always been a much stronger ideological reluctance by British companies to combine amongst themselves for business purposes. Companies have generally jealously guarded their 'trade secrets' and corporate independence in commercial matters, with the result that membership of employers' associations has often been resisted by some British companies.

One of the main traditional roles of employers' associations has been to bargain collectively for their members, with the trade unions, on a multi-employer or industry-wide basis. The theory underlying this is that multi-employer collective agreements on pay and conditions take labour costs out of competition for all employers in the industry, thus allowing companies to compete in product markets other than by undercutting their competitors' employment costs. A corollary to this is that combination amongst employers also protects individual employers against being 'picked off', one by one, by the union(s) during a trade dispute.

In early 1992, the Certification Officer, who is required by law to maintain a list of employers' associations under Section 2 of the Trade Union and Labour Relations (Consolidation) Act 1992, listed 131 such organisations, with another 146 bodies that were unlisted. This compares with 148 listed and 187 unlisted associations in 1986 and 196 listed and 280 unlisted associations in 1977 (Certification Office 1992; 1987; 1978). Despite the reduction in the numbers of employers' associations operating in Britain since the late 1970s, employers' associations continue to have a role in employee relations, especially in industries where labour costs are a high proportion of total costs, or where the industry is dominated by a large number of relatively small companies in competitive product markets, such as electrical contracting, building construction, and printing. Here two-tier bargaining is the norm, with multi-employer bargaining – through such organisations as the Electrical Contractors Association and British Printing Industries Federation – setting a floor of terms and conditions for the industry.

Current activities

In these and similar cases, employers' associations continue to provide a number of services to member firms. These include:

- employer representation in industry-wide bargaining;
- intelligence, information and data collection;
- assistance in operating procedures to avoid disputes;
- policy guidelines and advice on employee relations;
- consultancy and training for managements;
- representing employers at industrial tribunals;
- protection for employers taking part in trade disputes against the trade unions in their industry.

In acting as specialist centres of employee relations knowledge and expertise, employers' associations, like trade unions, are serviced by a cadre of full-time officers who work closely with elected representatives from member companies in determining policy, representing employer interests and fire-fighting on behalf of employers when necessary (Watson 1988).

A main reason why there has been a decline in the absolute numbers and the relative importance of employers' associations in the last decade is the declining importance of multi-employer pay bargaining arrangements in the private sector (Brown and Walsh 1991). Further, the traditional reluctance to combine by private employers has been reinforced by recent changes in business structure, especially decentralised cost centres (Marginson *et al.* 1988), increased product market competition and devolved employee relations policies. In these circumstances, companies, and sometimes plants within multi-site companies, are less inclined to join employers' associations for employee relations purposes. They prefer the autonomy of determining their own employment policies, reward structures and decentralised bargaining arrangements for dealing with trade unions. Indeed, some writers argue that decentralised bargaining provides distinct advantages to managements by keeping local union officials and full-time officers away from strategic decision-making (Kinnie 1987). In some cases, employers have even opted for union derecognition and no bargaining at all (Gregg and Yates 1991).

Another reason for the relative decline in importance of employers' associations is political. Since the late 1970s, governments have adopted market-centred economic policies rather than corporatist ones (see Chapters 1, 4 and 7). Apart from a few cases such as the National Farmers' Union, this has generally diminished the role of employers' associations as pressure groups representing the interests of employers nationally in discussions in Whitehall, and government departments. Moreover, with shifts towards greater EC integration and a single European market for labour, capital, goods and services, the role of industry-wide employers' associations is further weakened. The political role of employers' associations is now more effectively carried out by central organisations such as the Confederation of British Industry (CBI), which recruits horizontally and vertically, and supranational ones such as the Union of Industrial and Employers' Confederations of Europe (UNICE) (see below), than by industry-based ones.

The Confederation of British Industry (CBI)

Unlike some of its European counterparts, such as in Germany, Ireland and the Netherlands, the CBI – ever since its formation in 1965 – has been ambivalent about taking on a corporatist role in employee relations in collaboration with unions and government at the central level. In recent years, its activities have mainly focused on 'speaking up' for British business. Although the CBI has an Employment Affairs Directorate, Employment Policy Committee and Industrial Relations and Wages and Conditions Committee, it is, as a management organisation, only indirectly involved in employee relations and then only in so far as these affect corporate efficiency, productivity and competitiveness.

The CBI's objectives are:

- to provide the means for British industry to influence economic and related policy;
- to develop the contribution of British industry to the national economy;
- to encourage economic efficiency;
- to provide advice and services to its members.

In its role in 'speaking up' for British business, the CBI claims to provide five key benefits to its members. These are: strength in unity; greater competitive edge; a powerful and effective advocate for business interests; a vital resource offering expert advice; and a forum generating ideas and business contacts (Confederation of British Industry 1992).

Recent CBI policy has focused on the need to minimise the burdens on business – through promoting investment, curbing inflation and creating appropriate tax policies – and to tackle national competitive handicaps. This means shaping a 'Europe of free and fair trade', achieving a skills revolution and improving the UK's transport infrastructure. It is a set of policies based on market rather than corporatist values and on the virtues of free enterprise. Its policy prescriptions on employee relations are limited but direct. First, since the 1980s, the CBI has continually expressed its opposition to a tightly regulated labour market and has been strongly opposed to harmonised EC employment legislation and minimum standards of employment protection. Its arguments are that this would adversely affect EC competitiveness and restrict the necessary flexibility of the labour market. It continues to oppose the EC Social Action Programme, aimed at bringing the Social Charter to life. Second, recent CBI actions on employment affairs have concentrated on helping its members protect labour cost competitiveness and labour flexibility. The CBI has continually argued the case for linking employee pay to corporate performance and productivity growth. It has also taken part in the public debate about the merits of decentralised pay bargaining (Confederation of British Industry 1991).

The CBI claims to represent the interests of more than 250,000 member organisations embracing all sectors of industry and commerce. Many of its members are multinational businesses or parent companies with subsidiaries, but over half its members are firms with under 200 employees. This means that the CBI recruits both horizontally across industries and vertically within them. To fulfil its tasks, it has a President's Committee, 17 standing committees and 13 regions, each with an elected council. These bodies are serviced by six Directorates: Company Affairs; Education and Training; Employment Affairs; Economic Affairs; International Affairs; and a Regional and Smaller Firms Directorate. The CBI is also active in Europe though UNICE.

The Union of Industrial and Employers' Confederations of Europe (UNICE)

UNICE was created in 1958 and comprises over 30 central employers' federations from over 20 European countries. Its purposes include:

- promoting the common professional interests of the firms represented by its members;
- providing the framework through which member organisations can coordinate their European policies;
- ensuring that European decision makers take UNICE's policies and views into account.

UNICE's main activities are:

- maintaining effective contacts with all European institutions;
- organising members into working groups and committees to examine European policies and proposed legislation;
- promoting UNICE's policies and opinions at EC and national level.

UNICE's principal contacts are with the Commission of the European Communities (CEuC), the European Parliament (EuP), the Council of Ministers (CoM) and the Economic and Social Committee. It also works with other European-level governmental organisations and international non-governmental organisations such as the European Trade Union Confederation (ETUC).

The main priorities of UNICE are:

- creating a favourable climate for enterprise;
- promoting European technology, research and development;
- strengthening European economic and social cohesion;
- developing social diaologue between UNICE and the ETUC;
- liberalising world trade on the principles of reciprocity and fair competition.

It does this through its Council of Presidents, an Executive Committee, a permanent Secretariat in Brussels and a series of policy committees which assist in policy formulation, suggest actions to be taken and implement UNICE decisions (Union of Industrial and Employers' Confederations of Europe 1990).

Employee organisations

Trade unions

A trade union is any organisation of workers, or constituent or affiliated organisations, whose principal purposes include the regulation of relations between its members and their employers, managements or employers' associations. The CO listed 287 unions in Britain in early 1992, with a total of 9.8 million members, although over 80 per cent of this membership was concentrated in the 23 largest unions with over 100,000 members each. This compares with 375 listed unions and 10.8 million members in 1986 and 485 listed unions and 12.1 million members in 1977 (Certification Office 1992; 1987; 1978).

Objectives, functions and ideology

Trade unions organise by occupation or industry. Where they are occupationally based, unions recruit horizontally across industries and vertically within them. Where they are industrially based, they recruit vertically within an industry, as in Germany's 17 *Industriegewerkschaften* or industrial unions. Because of their deep historical roots, the complex structures of British industry and the variegated patterns of union mergers and amalgamations, British trade unions are rarely based on occupational or industrial lines alone. They tend to recruit both across and within industries, resulting in union membership competition and multi-union representation structures with employers (see Chapter 8 below; Coates and Topham 1988).

Like employers' associations, trade unions exist to protect the interests of their members. The essential rationale of trade unions therefore is to defend and extend their members' individual employment interests, in both their market relations and managerial relations with employers, through collective organisation and strength. Trade union organisation, in other words, is based on an ideology of collectivism, or worker solidarity, summed up in the slogan 'Unity is Strength'. The industrial objectives of trade unions include participating in:

- the determination of pay and conditions;
- the maintenance and improvement of health and safety standards within the workplace;
- how work and job tasks are organised;
- agreed employee relations procedures for resolving grievances, disciplinary and related issues;
- 'fair' dealings with management;
- improving security of employment in the workplace.

Many unions also have political objectives since, as organisations, they want to influence political decision-making when it affects the interests of their members as employees and citizens, and the interests of unions as employee interest groups. To these ends, the unions seek to influence, first, government economic policies, such as those covering the labour market, the training of human resources, union bargaining power, taxation and public spending. Second, unions are also interested in government legal policy and the ways that it affects individual employment rights and union collective rights to organise, to be recognised by employers and to take industrial action against employers. Third, they want to influence government social policies, in terms of pensions, state benefits and the 'social wage'. Unions also play an international role by seeking links with unions in other countries. They want to influence international labour policy and protest when brother and sister unionists overseas are persecuted or discriminated against by employers or the political authorities (see Chapter 8).

Current activities

Unions use a variety of methods to further their industrial objectives as the collective agents of employee participation in employee relations. These include unilateral regulation, collective bargaining, joint consultation and industrial action. In parts of Europe, such as in Sweden, Germany and Denmark, unions also participate with management in co-determination systems, which provide legal rights for employee representatives in enterprise decision-making (Incomes Data Services 1991).

In furthering their political objectives, unions in Britain use a number of methods. These include lobbying governments, seeking consultations with ministers and maintaining close links with the Labour Party (McIlroy 1988). The political role of the unions is made possible through the device of 'political funds' and the 'political levy'. Under the TULRCA 1992, unions can include the furtherance of political objects amongst their aims and adopt political fund rules. These provide for union expenditure on political objects but any payments made in furthering them must come out of a separate political fund. Union members not wishing to pay the political levy may 'contract out' of paying it. The main uses of union political funds include:

- to affiliate union members to the Labour Party, thereby enabling unions to influence Labour Party policy;
- to sponsor Labour Members in Parliament;
- to conduct political campaigns on behalf of their members.

In 1990, 54 unions had political funds, with 6.1 million members contributing to them (Certification Office 1992).

Trade unions are voluntaristic and democratic bodies, with all the strengths and weaknesses associated with these characteristics. With the closed shop unlawful, individuals generally join the trade union of their choice, according to their occupation, where they work and what unions are recognised. Once recruited, members are allocated to a union branch which is the basic unit of trade union organisation.

Branches are linked to regions or divisions which, in turn, are linked to national union headquarters (Farnham and Pimlott 1990).

Unions are democratic bodies in the sense that decisions at workplace, divisional and national levels are only taken after membership debate and by majority voting. Every member is entitled to stand for union office, in accordance with the union rule book and the law, and to participate on an equal basis in union decision-making procedures. In workplaces, shop stewards, workplace representatives and health and safety representatives are elected to speak on behalf of their members with management. Workplaces, branches and divisions, in turn, are serviced and supported by full-time, professional union officers.

Staff associations and professional bodies

The term 'staff associations' is difficult to define with precision but in essence they have three main characteristics:

- their membership is confined to employees of a single employer, where the employees are almost always in non-manual, white-collar work;
- they do not normally regard themselves as 'trade unions' in the accepted meaning of the term;
- they are generally found in the private sector rather than in public sector employment, especially in the financial services such as banks, insurance and building societies.

Staff associations are sometimes encouraged by employers and managements in order to keep unions out of their businesses. Such organisations, confined to a single employer, are rarely effective negotiating bodies. They lack adequate financial resources, find it difficult to bargain on equal terms with the employer and, though operating at low cost, are poorly protected against unexpected hostility from a previously paternalist or benevolent employer (Certification Office 1981). On the other hand, it is sometimes the employees themselves who, in seeking collective representation with the employer, are reluctant to join a union for ideological, political or social reasons. With their relatively low membership subscriptions and lack of militancy, staff associations sometimes provide an acceptable alternative to trade unions for certain types of white-collar employee.

Professional bodies are not primarily employee relations agencies.

They normally seek to:

- control the education and training of new members to the 'profession', acting as 'qualifying associations';
- maintain professional standards amongst members;
- advance the standing and status of the profession in the wider community.

(See Millerson 1964.)

Where professional bodies take on a dual function, in seeking to protect and improve their members' employment interests, such as in pay determination or collective bargaining, this is more likely to happen in the public sector rather than the private sector. In the education and the health services, for example, there are groups of professional employees who use their professional bodies in this dual capacity, such as amongst nurses, midwives and teachers.

The Trades Union Congress (TUC)

The TUC is 'the unions' union'. It is a long-established body, formed in 1868, and is the sole central coordinating body of the British trade union movement. In comparison with most other European countries, this is fairly unusual since in Europe there are often rival central trade union centres, representing different political, confessional and occupational interests. The TUC is an autonomous body composed of individually affiliated union organisations which pay an annual affiliation fee, based on their membership size. In 1991, the TUC had 74 affiliated unions, with a total membership of 8.2 million. This represented about 85 per cent of total union membership in Britain at that time. These compare with 89 affiliated unions, with 9.6 million members, in 1986 and 108 affiliated unions, with 11.6 million members, in 1981 (Trades Union Congress 1991; 1986; 1981).

The objectives of the TUC are:

- to promote the interests of all or any of its affiliated organisations;
- to improve the economic and social conditions of workers in all parts of the world;
- to affiliate to or assist any organisation having similar objectives to the TUC;
- to assist in the complete organisation of all workers eligible for union membership;

- to assist in settling disputes between members of affiliated organisations and their employers, between affiliated organisations and their members and between affiliated organisations themselves.

The TUC gives effect to these objectives in a number of ways. These include:

- developing policies on industrial, economic and social matters and campaigning actively for them;
- assisting unions in dispute;
- regulating relations between affiliated unions and promoting inter-union cooperation;
- providing services to affiliated unions;
- nominating representatives on statutory and consultative bodies;
- participating in international trade union organisations.

The TUC's policy-making congress meets annually in the first week of September and is attended by more than 1,000 delegates. The General Council, which governs the TUC between congresses, is elected by congress and has nine standing committees:

- Economic;
- Education and Training;
- Employment Policy and Organisation;
- Equal Rights;
- European Strategy;
- Finance and General Purposes;
- International;
- Social Insurance and Industrial Welfare;
- Trade Union Education.

There are two special committees: the Special Review Body, established in 1987 to improve union organisation and promote trade unionism; and the Environment Action Group. These committees are serviced by the TUC's headquarters staff in London but the TUC also has nine regional offices, linked to regional councils, in the provinces (Trades Union Congress 1990).

The European Trade Union Confederation (ETUC)

The ETUC, whose secretariat is in Brussels, is the umbrella organisation of the major national trade union confederations in Europe. It comprises 39 organisations in 21 Western European countries, representing over 45 million workers or some 40 per cent of their 110 million workforce (Trades Union Congress 1991). Formed in 1973, the ETUC has the following membership:

- unitary trade unions confederations, such as the TUC and *Deutscher Gewerkschaftbund* (DGB) in Germany;
- those which are predominantly blue-collar or white-collar union groups, such as the *Landesorganisationen i Sverige* (LO) and the *Tjänstemannens Centralorganisation* (TCO) in Sweden;
- union federations with particular ideological or political tendencies, such as the socialist *Fédération Generale du Travail de Belgique* (FGTB) and the Christian *Confédération des Syndicats Chrétiens* (CSC) in Belgium;
- 12 European industry committees, drawn from affiliated unions in particular sectors.

The major objectives of the ETUC are to represent and promote the social, economic and cultural interests of workers at the European level and to safeguard and strengthen democracy in Europe. To achieve its objectives, the ETUC negotiates within a number of European bodies where it is officially recognised. It also has statutory rights of consultation and *de facto* rights of consultation on specific matters, engages in policy discussions with heads of governments and ministers and takes direct action jointly with unions in different countries (European Trade Union Institute 1987). In the EC, the ETUC makes representations at various levels including the Commission of the European Community, the European Parliament, the Council of Ministers, the Standing Committee of Employment and the European Council. Additionally, the Ministerial Committee of the Council of Europe has a liaison committee which includes members of the General Secretariat of the Council of Europe, the ETUC and UNICE.

The International Confederation of Free Trade Unions (ICFTU)

The ICFTU was formed in 1949. It now has 141 affiliated organisations in some 97 countries on five continents, with a membership of about 86 million. It is a confederation of national trade union centres, with a secretariat in Brussels and permanent offices in Geneva and

New York. Its motto is 'Bread, Peace and Freedom' (International Confederation of Free Trade Unions 1988). The objectives of the ICFTU include:

- promoting the interests of working people throughout the world;
- working for rising living standards, full employment and social security;
- reducing the gap between the rich and poor;
- working for international understanding, disarmament and world peace;
- helping workers to organise themselves and secure the recognition of their organisations as free bargaining agents;
- fighting against oppression, dictatorship and discrimination of any kind;
- defending fundamental human and trade union rights.

The ICFTU helps to defend workers' rights, fight poverty, reduce international tensions and promote peace. It also has very close relations with the International Labour Organization (ILO), which is the only international body made up of government, employer and worker representatives. Because of ICFTU representation, the ILO has established many international standards to protect workers' rights and denounce violations of trade union rights by governments. The ICFTU insists that all countries should respect basic trade union rights such as freedom of association, free collective bargaining and the right to strike. The ICFTU represents the trade union movement at international conferences, in the United Nations (UN) and in various specialised UN agencies. Finally, the ICFTU maintains close relations with the International Trade Secretariats associated with it, such as the International Metal Workers' Federation and the International Transport Workers' Federation.

State agencies

Industrial tribunals (ITs) and the Employment Appeal Tribunal (EAT)

ITs are independent judicial bodies set up to hear matters of dispute in employee relations, quickly, informally and cheaply. ITs have a legally qualified chair, with two other members each of whom are drawn from panels appointed by the Secretary of State for Employment – one after consultation with employee organisations, the other after consultation with employers' organisations. Anyone can present cases at ITs, which deal with a variety of appeals, applications and complaints. ITs also determine questions of compensation delegated to them. About 50 ITs sit daily in England and Wales, with the number of hearings annually in the region of 12,500.

The jurisdiction of ITs derives from a series of employment laws and EC regulations, enacted on a piecemeal basis since the mid-1970s. The legal rights stemming from them are largely directed at individual workers and individual trade unionists. The principal legislative provisions include:

- Equal Pay Act 1970 and Equal Pay Amendment Regulations 1983;
- Health and Safety at Work etc. Act 1974;
- Sex Discrimination Act 1975;
- Race Relations Act 1976;
- Employment Protection (Consolidation) Act 1978;
- Transfer of Undertakings (Protection of Employment) Regulations 1981;
- Wages Act 1986;
- Trade Union and Labour Relations (Consolidation) Act 1992.
- Trade Union Reform and Employment Rights Act 1993.

Although the matters that may be considered by ITs are wide ranging (Department of Employment 1991; Dickens and Cockburn 1986), about 60 per cent relate to claims of unfair dismissal. The other main applications relate to the Wages Act 1986 (10 per cent), redundancy payments (8 per cent), employment protection provisions (7 per cent), contracts of employment (5 per cent), race discrimination (4 per cent), sex discrimination (3 per cent), with all other items under 1 per cent each (Central Office of Industrial Tribunals 1990).

The EAT was established by Sections 86 and 87 of the Employment Protection Act (EPA) 1975. It sits regularly in London and Edinburgh and consists of appointed judges and lay members, with special knowledge or experience of employee relations as employer or worker representatives. It hears appeals from the decisions of ITs on questions of law only. It is not the function of the EAT to re-hear the facts of the case as they were put to an IT. Nor does the EAT have power to interfere with the judgement reached by ITs on those facts. Any appeal to the EAT must show that in reaching its decision the tribunal made an error in its interpretation or application of the law. Like in tribunals, any person may appear before the EAT, including employer and union representatives. The EAT hears several hundred cases each year.

The Advisory Conciliation and Arbitration Service (ACAS)

ACAS was created by the Employment Protection Act (EPA) 1975. Its prime statutory duty, now incorporated in the Trade Union and Labour Relations (Consolidation) Act (TULRCA) 1992, is to promote 'the improvement of industrial relations' (Section 209). Until 1993, this duty had included the particular role 'of encouraging the extension of collective bargaining and the development and, where necessary, reform of collective bargaining machinery.' This is now no longer the case. Clearly, ACAS's role is now less circumscribed by legislation than it was in the past. ACAS is independent of government, employers and trade unions but its governing council is drawn from employers, employee organisations and independent experts in employee relations.

In carrying out its statutory duties, ACAS undertakes three main activities:

* resolving disputes;
* providing conciliation services for individuals;
* giving advice, assistance and information on industrial relations and employment issues.

In 1991 ACAS had 1,386 requests for collective conciliation, 157 for arbitration and mediation and 60,605 for individual conciliation. It also carried out 2,658 in-depth visits to organisations and 15,167 advisory visits (Advisory Conciliation and Arbitration Service 1992).

ACAS's role in resolving disputes is through collective conciliation, arbitration and mediation (see Chapter 3). Collective conciliation is the process whereby employers and trade unions are helped to reach mutually acceptable settlements of disputes through neutral, third-party intervention by an ACAS conciliation officer. It is voluntary, and agreements reached in conciliation are determined by the parties themselves, normally only after agreed procedures are exhausted or when both sides agree that there are overriding considerations requiring it. In

1991, ACAS's completed conciliations included pay and conditions of employment (41 per cent), followed by redundancy (19 per cent), union recognition (14 per cent), dismissal and discipline (12 per cent), other union matters (7 per cent) and changes in working practices (4 per cent).

Voluntary arbitration is provided where the parties in dispute invite one or more impartial persons to make a decision which both parties agree in advance to accept. It is normally regarded as a means of last resort for determining a peaceful settlement, where disputes cannot be resolved by other methods. In accordance with the TULRCA 1992, ACAS has to ensure that:

- the consent of both parties is obtained;
- conciliation is considered;
- any agreed procedures have been used and a failure to agree recorded.

Arbitration may proceed, however, where ACAS believes there to be special circumstances for using it. In 1991, the issues referred to ACAS arbitrators (and mediators) were discipline and dismissal (35 per cent), other pay and conditions of employment (22 per cent), grading (22 per cent) and annual pay (17 per cent).

Mediation is where a third party, appointed by ACAS, assists the parties to reach their own negotiated settlement, by making appropriate suggestions to both sides. These recommendations are similar to those of an arbitrator's award but the parties do not agree in advance to accept them. Mediation tends to constrain the parties more than conciliation does but is more flexible and decisive.

ACAS also has a statutory duty to promote settlements of complaints, by individuals, which have been or could be made to an IT. ACAS completes some 70 per cent of the cases it receives annually. Of these, about 40 per cent are settled by conciliation, some 30 per cent are withdrawn and about 30 per cent proceed to ITs. The largest part of ACAS's workload concerns unfair dismissal. This is followed by claims under the Wages Act 1986, sex discrimination, equal pay and racial discrimination.

The advisory and information services provided by ACAS complement its conciliation services. The key areas where ACAS currently focuses its advisory services are:

- orderly, dispute-free collective bargaining;
- the orderly and voluntary resolution of individual employment issues;
- effective and felt-fair payment and reward systems;
- improved communication, consultation and employee involvement practices;
- the effective use of human resources at work, including participative approaches to change.

The Central Arbitration Committee (CAC)

The CAC is a standing, independent arbitration body, working nationally in employee relations. It was set up as 'the Industrial Court' in 1919 and its current status and constitution are embodied in the TULRCA 1992. The CAC has three panels, one consisting of the independent chair and deputy chairs and two of members with experience as employers and employees. Cases are normally heard by a committee of three, with one member from each panel. The CAC deals with issues relating to national disputes, a single employer or a particular employee group. It provides voluntary arbitration in trade disputes at the request of one party, but with the agreement of the other. It also determines claims by trade unions for disclosure of information for collective bargaining purposes. Its workload tends to be light, with most claims referring to disclosure of information.

The Certification Officer (CO)

The CO, originally established under Section 3 of the EPA 1975, has six main functions, now stemming from the TULRCA 1992 (Certification Office 1992):

- ensuring that the statutory procedures governing union political funds are complied with and dealing with complaints about the conduct of political fund ballots;
- overseeing the statutory procedures for union amalgamations, mergers and transfers of engagement, including complaints about the conduct of merger ballots;
- maintaining lists of trade unions and employers' associations and seeing that their accounts are properly audited;
- determining the independence of trade unions;

- reimbursing certain expenditures incurred by independent unions in conducting secret postal ballots;
- dealing with complaints by members that a union has failed to comply with the provisions for certain union elections.

The Commissioner for the Rights of Trade Union Members (CRTUM)

The CRTUM was created under the Employment Act 1988 and her duties are now incoporated in the TULRCA 1992. She has two sets of powers. The first is to grant assistance to union members contemplating or taking legal action against a union arising out of an alleged or threatened breach of a member's statutory union membership rights. These include the rights:

- to restrain a union from organising industrial action without a proper ballot;
- to elect union leaders at regular intervals, by secret postal ballot;
- to prevent a union unlawfully spending money on party political matters;
- to complain if a union does not hold a political fund ballot;
- to prevent unlawful use of union funds or property;
- to ensure a union keeps a membership register.

Second, the CRTUM may also grant assistance when a union member complains that a union has failed to observe the requirements of its own rule book. Typical areas of complaint include:

- the appointment, election or removal of persons from union office;
- union disciplinary proceedings;
- authorising or endorsing industrial action;
- balloting members;
- imposing levies for industrial action;
- following the agreed proceedings of conferences or committees.

The means by which individual union members can enforce these rights are through the courts, ITs or the CO, depending on the unlawful act. In general, the Commissioner has wide discretion in deciding whether to grant assistance or not. Assistance includes paying for legal advice or legal representation, or making arrangements for such advice or representation to be provided.

Assignments

(a) Read Hyman and Brough (1975: especially pages 229–53) and comment on their analysis of the role of social values in employee relations, particularly the concept of 'fairness'. Alternatively read Flanders and Fox (1969: pages 241–76). What did they identify as the sources of 'normative disorder' in British industrial relations at that time and how did these manifest themselves? What relevance does their analysis have for employee relations today?

(b) Interview an employee relations manager and find out the sort of job tasks and activities which he or she does. To whom is this person accountable and what sort of performance targets are set by senior management for this individual?

(c) To what extent is the management style of your employer based on individualism and/or collectivism? Provide illustrations of its employment policies and practices to substantiate your diagnosis.

(d) Read Farnham and Pimlott (1990: pages 3–21) and compare and contrast the unitary (including 'neo-unitary') and pluralist concepts of employee relations.

(e) What are the pros and cons of an employer joining an employers' association:

1. in a labour intensive industry, where the firm is medium-sized, is one of many operating in a competitive product market, and where there are strong trade unions in the workplace and industry?

2. in a capital intensive industry, where the firm is a large one operating in a heterogeneous product market, and where the unions are weak in the workplace and industry?

3. in a capital intensive industry, where the firm is medium-sized and is operating in a homogeneous product market and the unions are strong in the workplace and industry?

(f) Using McIlroy (1988: Chapter 1), how do you account for the absolute and relative decline in trade union organisation during the 1980s?

(g) Interview some trade union members and find out: why they are union members, including the benefits of this; what they see as the purposes of trade unions; and what the main problems facing their union are.

(h) Read Chapter 1 of ACAS's current *Annual Report*. What were the major trends in employee relations for that year? How may these trends be explained? Also read the CRTUM's *Annual Report* and comment on the applications for assistance to the Commissioner during the previous year.

(i) Read Clegg (1976: pages 309–16). What is his defence of pluralism in employee relations?

References

ADVISORY CONCILIATION AND ARBRITRATION SERVICE 1992. *Annual Report 1992*. London: ACAS.

ANTHONY, P. 1990. 'The paradox of the management of culture or "he who leads is lost"'. *Personnel Review*. 19(4).

BASSETT, P. 1986. *Strike Free: New Industrial Relations in Britain*. London: Macmillan.

BROWN, W. 1960. *Explorations in Management*. London: Heinemann.

BROWN, W. and WALSH, J. 1991. 'Pay determination in Britain in the 1990s: the anatomy of decentralisation'. *Oxford Review of Economic Policy*. 7(1).

CENTRAL OFFICE OF INDUSTRIAL TRIBUNALS 1990. *Fact Sheet (for England and Wales)*. London: COIT.

CERTIFICATION OFFICE 1978. *Annual Report of the Certification Officer 1977*. London: CO.

CERTIFICATION OFFICE 1981. *Annual Report of the Certification Officer 1980*. London: CO.

CERTIFICATION OFFICE 1987. *Annual Report of the Certification Officer*. London: CO.

CERTIFICATION OFFICE 1992. *Annual Report of the Certification Officer 1991*. London: CO.

CHANDLER, A. and DAEMS, H. (eds) 1980. *Managerial Hierarchies*. London: Harvard University Press.

CLAYDON, T. 1989. 'Union derecognition in Britain in the 1980s'. *British Journal of Industrial Relations*. 28(2).

CLEGG, H. 1976. 'Pluralism in industrial relations'. *British Journal of Industrial Relations*. XII(2).

CLEGG, H. 1979. *The Changing System of Industrial Relations in Britain*. Oxford: Blackwell.

COATES,T. and TOPHAM, T. 1988. *Trade Unions in Britain*. London: Fontana.

CONFEDERATION OF BRITISH INDUSTRY 1991. *Annual Review and Report for 1990*. London: CBI.

CONFEDERATION OF BRITISH INDUSTRY 1992. *The Voice of British Business.* London: CBI.

DANIEL, W. and MILLWARD, N. 1983. *Workplace Industrial Relations in Britain.* London: Heinemann.

DEPARTMENT OF EMPLOYMENT 1991. *Trade Union Immunities.* London: HMSO.

DICKENS, L. and COCKBURN, D. 1986. 'Dispute settlement institutions and the courts'. In LEWIS, R. (ed.) 1986. *Labour Law in Britain.* Oxford: Blackwell.

DONOVAN, Lord 1968. *Royal Commission on Trade Unions and Employers' Associations 1965–1968: Report.* London: HMSO.

DUNN, S. 1990. 'Root metaphor in the old and new industrial relations'. *British Journal of Industrial Relations.* 28(1).

EUROPEAN TRADE UNION INSTITUTE 1987. *European Trade Union Confederation: Profile.* Brussels: ETUI.

FARNHAM, D. 1990. *Personnel in Context.* London: IPM.

FARNHAM, D. and PIMLOTT, J. 1990. *Understanding Industrial Relations.* London: Cassell.

FAYOL, H. 1949. *Industrial and General Administration.* (Translated by G. Storrs). London: Pitman.

FLANDERS, A. and FOX, A. 1969. 'Collective bargaining: from Donovan to Durkheim'. In FLANDERS, A. 1970. *Management and Unions.* London: Faber and Faber.

FOX, A. 1966. *Industrial Relations and Industrial Sociology: Royal Commission on Trade Unions and Employers' Associations Research Paper 3.* London: HMSO.

FOX, A. 1974. *Beyond Contract: Work, Power and Trust Relations.* London: Faber and Faber.

FOX, A. 1985. *History and Heritage.* London: Allen and Unwin.

GREGG, P. and YATES, A. 1991. 'Changes in wage-setting arrangements and trade union presence in the 1980s'. *British Journal of Industrial Relations.* 29(3).

HYMAN, R. and BROUGH, I. 1975. *Social Values and Industrial Relations.* Oxford: Blackwell.

INCOMES DATA SERVICES 1991. *Industrial Relations.* London: IPM.

INSTITUTE OF PERSONNEL MANAGEMENT 1992. *Occupational Mapping Report.* London: IPM.

INTERNATIONAL CONFEDERATION OF FREE TRADE UNIONS 1988. *Bread, Peace and Freedom.* Brussels: ICFTU.

KINNIE, N. 1987. 'Bargaining within the enterprise: centralised or decentralised?' *Journal of Management Studies.* 24(5), September.

LIKERT, R. 1961. *New Patterns of Management.* NY: McGraw-Hill.

MCILROY, J. 1988. *Trade Unions in Britain Today.* Manchester: Manchester University Press.

MARGINSON, P., EDWARDS, P., MARTIN, R., SISSON, K. and PURCELL, J. 1988. *Beyond the Workplace: Managing Industrial Relations in Multi-Establishments.* Oxford: Blackwell..

MILLER, P. 1987. 'Strategic industrial relations and human resource management – distinction, definition and recognition'. *Journal of Management Studies.* 24(2), July.

MILLERSON, G. 1964. *The Qualifying Associations.* London: Routledge.

MILLWARD, N. and STEVENS, M. 1986. *British Workplace Industrial Relations 1980–1984.* Aldershot: Gower.

MILLWARD, N., STEVENS, M., SMART, D. and HAWES, W. 1992. *Workplace Industrial Relations in Transition.* Aldershot: Dartmouth.

MINISTRY OF LABOUR 1965. *Royal Commission on Trade Unions and Employers' Associations: Written Evidence of the Ministry of Labour.* London: HMSO.

MINTZBERG, H. 1975. *The Nature of Managerial Work.* NY: Prentice Hall.

PETERS, T. and WATERMAN, R. 1982. *In Search of Excellence.* NY: Harper and Row.

PRICE WATERHOUSE CRANFIELD 1990. *Price Waterhouse Cranfield Survey 1990.* Cranfield.

PURCELL, J. 1987. 'Mapping management styles in employee relations'. *Journal of Management Studies.* 24(5), September.

PURCELL, J. and SISSON, K. 1983. 'Strategies and practice in the management of industrial relations'. In BAIN, G. (ed.) 1983. *Industrial Relations in Britain.* Oxford: Blackwell.

SISSONS, K. (ed.) 1989. *Personnel Management in Britain.* Oxford: Blackwell.

STEWART, R. 1982. *Choices for the Manager.* London: McGraw-Hill.

STOREY, J. (ed.) 1989. *New Perspectives on Human Resource Management.* London: Routledge.

STOREY, J. (ed.) 1992. *The Development of the Management of Human Resources.* Oxford: Blackwell.

THOMASON, G. 1991. 'The management of personnel'. *Personnel Review.* 20(2).

TRADES UNION CONGRESS 1981. *Annual Report.* London: TUC.

TRADES UNION CONGRESS 1986. *Annual Report.* London: TUC.

TRADES UNION CONGRESS 1990. *Annual Report.* London: TUC.

TRADES UNION CONGRESS 1991. *Annual Report.* London: TUC.

TYSON, S. 1987. 'The management of the personnel function'. *Journal of Management Studies.* 24(5).

UNION OF INDUSTRIAL AND EMPLOYERS' CONFEDERATIONS 1990. *The Voice of European Business and Industry.* Brussels: UNICE.

WATSON, D. 1988. *Managers of Discontent.* London: Routledge.

WICKENS, P. 1987. *The Road to Nissan.* Basingstoke: Macmillan.

WINKLER, J. 1974. 'The ghost at the bargaining table: directors and industrial relations'. *British Journal of Industrial Relations.* July.

Chapter 3

Employee relations processes

There are a number of conflict-resolving and decision-making processes in employee relations. Some of these are voluntary, others are legal and can involve either collective or individual methods of conducting employee relations. Employee relations decision-making, in turn, may be unilateral, bilateral or trilateral. This chapter explores these processes in more detail and examines their outcomes, as systems of employee relations rules.

Personal contracts

With the growth of individualist employee relations policies and patterns of employment since the 1980s (see Chapters 7 and 10), the use of personal contracts of employment, between employers and employees, has been extended within some organisations, especially for managerial and professional staff. A personal contract is the outcome of individual bargaining between an employer and an employee. It normally incorporates an individual salary for the post holder and other specific terms and conditions of employment, pertinent to that individual and the job being done. Personal contracts have always been more common amongst management staff than amongst non-management employees in large organisations, and for all employees in non-union small firms. However, the practice has spread in both the private and public sectors in recent years and has become more common now amongst other groups of employees, such as technical and professional workers, that have traditionally had their terms and conditions of employment determined collectively rather than individually. Personal contracts are typically linked to staff appraisal and performance review, staff development and performance-related pay.

Like all employees, those on personal contracts are entitled to receive written particulars from their employer setting out the main terms of their employment. This applies to all employees working

eight or more hours per week under contracts of one month or
The information must be provided within two months of commei
employment. Exhibit 1 illustrates the information typically include
such written statements.

Exhibit 1: *Written particulars of the main terms and conditions of employment*

This nomally includes:

- the identity of the parties
- commencement of employment
- continuous employment
- hours of work
- holidays
- sickness and injury arrangements
- pensions
- notice period
- job title
- expected length of temporary employment (where appropriate)
- place of work
- collective agreements affecting the contract
- terms relating to abroad
- how grievances and disciplinary matters are to be resolved

In one senior management contract, known to the author, most of the items in Exhibit 1 are included but it is stated, regarding hours of work (Portsmouth and South East Hampshire Health Authority 1991), that: 'managers are required to work such hours as are necessary for the full performance of their duties.' It goes on to add that continuation of the appointment is 'subject to satisfactory performance', with the duties of the post being reviewed in 'accordance with the Individual Performance Review arrangements for senior managers.'

> The primary objective of this will be to help . . . achieve the best possible level of performance, but unsatisfactory performance, as assessed under the Individual Performance Review arrangements, may be regarded as grounds for action under the Authority's disciplinary and dismissal procedures.

In this case, this could result from failure to meet agreed objectives after two successive reviews where unsatisfactory performance is identified. Clearly, compared with collectively determined terms and conditions, personal contracts give senior managers much tighter control over the job activities, work performance and pay rewards of the employees covered by such contracts. Personal contracts thus enhance management control of the work process.

Collective bargaining

Collective bargaining (or joint negotiation) is a voluntary process involving autonomous employers and independent trade unions and remains a common pattern of employee relations in Britain (see Chapters 8 and 9). Its purpose is to determine:

- the terms and conditions of employment, for particular groups of employees;
- the ways in which employment issues such as individual grievances, collective disputes and disciplinary matters are to be resolved at workplace and corporate levels.

Autonomous employers are normally self-governing organisations, operating in the market or public sectors. Independent trade unions are organisations of workers, which are not under the domination or control of an employer, whose activities are not liable to interference from an employer. Unions meeting the criteria for 'independence' set out in Section 5 of the TULRCA 1992 may apply for a certificate of independence from the CO.

Collective bargaining is a power relationship, based on a management policy of union incorporation in the enterprise, and is one of power-sharing, or joint regulation, with management. Its outcomes, resulting from negotiations between management and union representatives, are collective agreements. In Britain, collective agreements are voluntary and non-legally enforceable. In other countries, collective agreements are normally legally binding contracts between employers and unions, with any breaches of such agreements resulting in legal action being taken by the aggrieved party against the other. The relative advantage in collective bargaining is determined by the balance of bargaining power between the two parties in the negotiating process. Where the power balance favours the employer side, this is to the relative disadvantage of the union and its members. Where the power balance favours the union side, this is to the relative disadvantage of the employer and management. The essence of an effective collective bargaining relationship between employers and trade unions is the willingness of both parties to seek negotiated and agreed settlements, by concessions, exchanges and compromises between them, so that each side feels mutually bound, responsible and committed to their joint bargaining outcomes (Clegg 1976).

Any set of collective bargaining arrangements comprises a framework or structure within which the employer and union sides participate. Parker and his colleagues (1971) use the term 'bargaining structure' to describe the permanent features distinguishing the collective bargaining process in any particular industry or organisation. They identify four interrelated features within any collective bargaining structure. These are bargaining levels, bargaining units, bargaining scope and bargaining forms.

Bargaining levels

The bargaining level is where collective bargaining between employer and union representatives takes place. This may be at:

- multi-employer level (otherwise described as industry-wide or national level);
- single employer or company level;
- establishment or plant level.

Multi-employer bargaining was common amongst private sector employers in Britain in the 1930s, 1940s and 1950s. For multi-employer bargaining to operate, it is necessary for employers to organise themselves into employers' associations or federations (see Chapter 2), thus providing a collective voice for employer interests in the bargaining process. Unions, in turn, often collaborate at national level through multi-union confederations, consisting of a number of independent trade unions working together. Multi-employer bargaining has also been a common practice in the public services such as local government, the civil service and the National Health Service (NHS). This is changing rapidly, however, with the public services being broken up into a series of executive agencies, NHS trusts and directly managed units in schools, colleges and universities (Farnham and Horton 1993).

Multi-employer bargaining is also common in parts of Europe. In

Denmark, for example, industry-wide collective agreements in the private sector are concluded every other year between individual unions and industrial employers' associations. All such agreements, which are legally enforceable, must be ratified by union members in a ballot before they can be signed and implemented by the negotiating parties. In Italy, industry-wide bargaining has traditionally been important because it is the level at which minimum wage rates are set for each industry. These cover the private sector, publicly owned companies and the small business or craft sector. There are around 25 major industries in Italy and about 100 national industry agreements, which are binding on all employers, irrespective of whether they are members of signatory organisations (Incomes Data Services 1991).

Single employer or company bargaining takes place between one employer and the union (or unions) it recognises at corporate level. These arrangements are common either in medium to large, multi-site companies where the employer wants standardised terms, conditions and employment policies across the company, or in single-site companies, which are not involved in multi-employer bargaining arrangements. Company bargaining is becoming more common in Britain, as companies move away from multi-employer bargaining so as to provide themselves with more flexibility, better cost-effectiveness and greater control in the bargaining process. Most collective bargaining in the Republic of Ireland is carried out at company level (Gungicle and Flood 1990). In the Netherlands, where there used to be a highly centralised collective bargaining system, and where multi-employer bargaining still predominates, company bargaining has increased in importance in recent years, especially in the large corporate sector.

Enterprise or plant bargaining in large multi-site companies takes place between local managers and local union officials. This has been a growing trend in Britain, since the 1980s. Patterns vary but, in the private sector, some of the driving forces have been changes in business strategy, decentralised cost and profit centres and management wishes to keep union officials away from strategic decision-making levels. Marginson and his colleagues (1988) show, even where there is plant bargaining, that management freedom to bargain locally may be limited and that guidelines and controls are set at corporate centre. There have also been pressures from government to encourage more decentralised bargaining and pay flexibility in the public services, though not to the extent that has happened in the private sector.

In the USA and Japan, plant bargaining is the norm. In the USA, this

is because of its business structures, industrial and commercial region-
alisation, immense geographical size and preferred management strategies in employee relations (Kochan *et al.* 1986). In Japan, most
collective bargaining takes place at enterprise level. Employers favour
it because of their paternalist personnel and employment policies. And
the unions support it because of their cooperative working arrangements with the employers and their origins as factory and company-
based wartime production committees (Shirai 1983).

Bargaining units

A bargaining unit, which is closely related to the bargaining level in an
industry or organisation, is the group of employees covered by a particular set of substantive or procedural collective agreements. Separate
bargaining units, for example, may cover manual workers, clerical and
administrative workers and supervisory workers respectively. A bargaining unit may be narrow or wide in terms of the group of workers it
covers. A narrow bargaining unit, by definition, covers a limited group,
such as the skilled craftworkers in a manufacturing organisation. A
wide bargaining unit covers a much more comprehensive group, such
as all the manual workers within an industry, organisation or plant.

There has been a tendency in recent years for bargaining units, especially at company and workplace levels, to become wider. Bargaining
units are more likely than in the past to be of a 'single table' type. A
single bargaining table covers all the recognised groups of workers at
employer or enterprise level including:

- non-manual and manual groups;
- workers represented by TUC and non-TUC unions;
- skilled, semi-skilled and less skilled workers.

It is an employee relations approach which rationalises and simplifies
the bargaining process for employers, harmonises conditions of
employment within the employment unit and integrates and focuses
collective bargaining for the unions.

Bargaining units are interconnected with bargaining levels. The bargaining unit is particularly concerned with the representative function
of the trade unions recognised by the employer, whilst the bargaining
level concentrates on the management side of the negotiating table.
Within a bargaining unit, it is a joint panel of unions, or a single trade

union, that acts as the bargaining agent on behalf of the employees, with the unions normally determining the representative arrangements on behalf of their members. Bargaining levels, in contrast, are predominantly employer-determined and are influenced by a combination of product market, business structure and technological factors (Advisory Conciliation and Arbitration Service 1983; Palmer 1990).

Bargaining scope

Bargaining scope begins where the right to manage ends. It defines the range of subjects and matters covered within procedural and substantive agreements and may be extensive or limited in content. Again the tendency in Britain in recent years has been for bargaining scope to narrow, as employers and managers become more assertive and confident in the collective bargaining process. This has been helped by relatively high levels of unemployment, falling union membership and better trained management negotiators. Unless changes favourable to unions and their members are made to the balance of power in the labour market, the legal framework of employee relations and personnel policy, bargaining scope is unlikely to be extended in the future.

Bargaining forms

Bargaining forms are the ways in which collective agreements are recorded. They may be formal and written, on the one hand, or unwritten and informal on the other. The tendency in recent years has been towards greater formality in recording collective agreements. This is to avoid arguments about the content and application of collective agreements and to provide stability in collective bargaining arrangements when those who have negotiated procedural or substantive agreements change jobs or roles.

Collective agreements

Collective agreements are the outcome of collective bargaining and are jointly determined employment rules which may be procedural or substantive in nature. Procedural collective agreements set out:

- the responsiblities and duties of management and unions in employee relations;

- the steps or stages through which the parties determine employee relations decisions jointly;
- what happens when the parties to employee relations fail to agree.

Substantive collective agreements, in contrast, cover the terms and conditions of employment relating to specific categories of jobs and employment groups.

In Britain, unlike in other Western European and North American countries, collective agreements between managements and unions are not legally enforceable. This means that neither party can sue the other where agreements are broken, for example, when either management or unions fail to act in accordance with agreed procedures. Collective agreements become incorporated, however, into the individual contracts of employment of all the employees covered by the bargaining unit, whether they are trade union members or not.

Procedural agreements

There is no such thing as a 'model' procedural agreement. Each employer and the union(s) that they recognise determine their own set of procedural agreements according to a number of contingent factors. These include:

- the size and organisational structure of the company, public service or industry;
- the level(s) at which collective bargaining takes place;
- the history, location(s) and ownership of the organisation;
- the dominant style and philosophy of management;
- the union(s) with which the management deal;
- union power and organisation.

For the purposes of this analysis, the main types of procedural clauses found in 'traditional' collective agreements between management and unions in the private sector, at employer or enterprise level, are outlined in Exhibits 2–6 below. These clauses typically cover:

- general principles;
- union recognition, union representation and facilities;
- the rights and duties of the parties;

- grievances and the avoidance of disputes;
- discipline.

These traditional procedural agreements, which often include multi-union representation, contrast with a less common form of collective agreement, based on single-union representation, called 'new style' or 'single-union' deals. Their procedural clauses incorporate a different approach to the ones outlined below (see Chapter 3).

General principles clauses

These clauses set out the intentions of the various parties to collective bargaining and the general spirit with which their relationship is to be conducted. The subject matter of these clauses is illustrated in Exhibit 2.

Exhibit 2: *General principles clauses in procedural agreements*

These cover:

- the basis on which discussions and negotiations between the company and the unions take place;
- a general statement emphasising the need for good working relations between the company and the unions;
- a company statement recognising the right of the unions to represent and negotiate on behalf of their members;
- a company statement recognising the right of employees to join and belong to a union;
- a union statement recognising the company's responsibility to plan, organise and manage the company efficiently and cost-effectively;
- a joint statement reinforcing the common, shared objectives of the company and unions in contributing to its prosperity, increased productivity and operating efficiency;
- a joint statement committing the company and the unions to refrain from any form of industrial action, until agreed procedures have been exhausted.

Union recognition, workplace representation and facilities procedure

These clauses set out the unions having recognition rights and how union representatives are to be elected and treated within the procedural arrangements. The subject matter of these procedures is illustrated in Exhibit 3.

Exhibit 3: *Union recognition and facilities procedure*

This covers:

- company recognition of workplace representatives, elected in accordance with union rules;
- the appointment of workplace representatives, their numbers, constituencies and coordination into a joint panel of unions or joint union committee;
- the conditions permitting workplace representatives to undertake union duties and activities and the facilities for these including time off, pay, administrative support and union training.

The rights and duties of management and unions

These clauses define the roles and responsibilities of the parties in the collective bargaining relationship. The subject matter of these clauses is illustrated in Exhibit 4.

Exhibit 4: *Rights and responsibilities of the parties within procedure*

These cover:

- the importance of the effective use of procedures to all the parties and of mutual confidence and trust amongst them in the conduct of good employee relations;
- the right of workplace representatives to take up grievances, disciplinary and other matters on behalf of individuals and workgroups;
- the responsibility of workplace representatives to act on behalf of their members where this is justified;
- the responsibility of workplace representatives to act fairly, honestly and in a manner befitting their functions;
- the responsibilities of management to ensure procedures are used, that workplace representatives are treated fairly, honestly and with the respect due to their positions and that the cases presented to them are given a fair hearing;
- the rights of management to object to any breach of procedure through union channels and to expect unions to keep to the principles, spirit and stages of agreed procedures;

- the rights of unions to nominate elected workplace representatives to designated areas and to the joint panel of unions or joint union committee;
- the responsibility of the unions to see that their workplace representatives adhere to the principles, spirit and stages of agreed procedures.

Procedures for settling grievances and avoiding disputes

These clauses provide means for settling and resolving grievances and disputes between the parties and normally follow a series of stages, with both the employer and the unions undertaking to refrain from taking coercive industrial action against the other, including lockouts or stoppages of work (i.e. retaining existing arrangements – the *status quo*), whilst the procedures are being used. Grievance procedures normally cover individual issues (see Chapter 5) and collective 'disputes' procedures normally cover matters of concern to groups of employees. The subject matter of these clauses is illustrated in Exhibits 5 and 6.

Individual issues

Exhibit 5: *Procedure for individual grievances*

These clauses provide for meetings involving:

- Stage 1: the union member and immediate supervisor
  (if the issue is not resolved, it is referred to . . .)

- Stage 2: the union member, workplace representative and supervisor
  (if the issue is not resolved, it is referred to . . .)

- Stage 3: the union member, workplace representative and next level of management
  (if the issue is not resolved, it is referred to . . .)

- Stage 4: the joint panel of unions or joint union committee and appropriate managers, including the personnel manager
  (if the issue is not resolved, and at the request of either management or the union, it is referred to . . .)

- Stage 5: the personnel manager, union full-time official and other invited parties

(if the issue is not resolved, it is referred to . . .)

- Stage 6: the human resources director, union full-time official and other invited parties
(if the issue is not resolved, it *may* be referred to . . .)

- Stage 7: an external party agreed to by management and the union.

Collective issues

Exhibit 6: *Procedure to avoid collective disputes*

- For a group managed by the same supervisor, these clauses provide for meetings involving:
    - Stages 2–7 above

- For a group involving members of one union in more than one department, these clauses provide for meetings involving:
    - the joint panel of unions or the joint union committee and the personnel manager
      (if it is not resolved, it is referred to . . .)
    - Stages 5–7 above

- For a group with members of more than one union in more than one department, these clauses provide for meetings involving:
    - the joint panel of unions or joint union committee and appropriate management representatives, including the personnel manager
      (if it is not resolved, it is referred to . . .)
    - senior management representatives and appropriate union full-time officials.

Disciplinary procedure

The objective of this procedure is to help individuals whose conduct (or performance) gives cause for dissatisfaction, to improve their behaviour (see Chapter 5). Individuals being disciplined have the right to be accompanied by their union representative. The subject matter of these clauses is illustrated in Exhibit 7.

Exhibit 7: *Disciplinary procedure*

The stages typically incorporate interviews involving:

- Stage 1: the individual and the supervisor, which can result in a verbal warning;

- Stage 2: unless an improvement in employee conduct (or performance) results, the supervisor reviews the situation with the individual, which, following investigation, can result in a first written warning;

- Stage 3: where there is still no improvement in employee conduct (or performance), the supervisor consults his/her manager, which, following investigation, can result in a second written warning;

- Stage 4: where there continues to be no improvement in employee conduct (or performance), the manager consults with his/her manager who, if still dissatisfied with the conduct, following investigation, can dismiss the individual.

Where appropriate, Stages 2 or 3 above may be the first steps used in implementing the procedure. Cases of defined and established gross misconduct, for example, may result in instant dismissal, with an individual being suspended on full pay pending a hearing. Appeals systems are normally built into disciplinary procedures, thus allowing individuals to appeal against disciplinary sanctions determined by management.

Other procedures

These clauses include procedures covering:

- recruitment;
- induction;
- promotion;
- redeployment;
- training;
- redundancy;
- retirement.

New-style agreements

New-style collective agreements – sometimes mistakenly described as 'single-union deals' – are typically found in 'hi-tech', foreign-owned, 'greenfield site' companies (Rico 1987). Some new-style procedural clauses are of the same types as those found in traditional procedures, although they incorporate different provisions and emphases, but others are quite distinctive and different from those in normal procedural arrangements between employers and unions. Like traditional procedures, new-style procedures include clauses covering:

- general principles;
- union recognition and facilities;
- grievances and the avoidance of disputes;
- discipline.

Yet they commonly focus on (see also Chapters 1 and 9):

- single-union recognition, not multi-union recognition;
- the role of employee representatives in procedure, not union representatives;
- single machinery for dealing with negotiation, consultation and information, not multiple machinery;
- the need for two procedures for avoiding disputes, not a single procedure – with one for dealing with conflicts of rights (for interpreting *existing* agreements) and the other for dealing with conflicts of interest (in making *new* agreements).

Additional procedural clauses typically found in new-style agreements include:

- 'no-strike' arrangements;
- 'pendulum' arbitration for disputes of interest, where the arbitrator rules for the final position of one side or the other;
- 'labour flexibility' clauses.

The subject matter of typical procedural clauses incorporated in new-style agreements is illustrated in Exhibit 8 (see also Chapter 8).

Exhibit 8: *Procedural clauses in new-style collective agreements*

These cover:

- single-union recognition;

- employee representation within the company;
- single employment status for all employees;
- employee flexibility and multi-skilling, with security of employment and opportunities for training and retraining for employees;
- a company council, or forum, incorporating advisory, information, consultative and negotiating functions;
- no-strike or peace clauses;
- binding pendulum arbitration.

Substantive agreements

These cover how much the various groups of employees are paid for the jobs they do, in terms of either immediate or postponed payments (such as pensions), and the conditions of employment associated with these jobs. Substantive agreements define the market relations between the primary parties to the employment contract and they therefore involve financial costs to the employer and economic rewards for the employees. The main categories are summarised in Figure 4 but the lists are neither exclusive nor exhaustive.

Figure 4: *Main categories of substantive agreement*

Pay	Conditions
Hourly wage rates	Working hours
Annual salaries	Length of working week
Shift work payments	Shift working hours
Unsocial hours payments	Shift working systems
Pay structures	Clocking in arrangements
Payments for performance	Working time arrangements
Pay bonuses	Refreshments facilities
Overtime payments	Overtime arrangements
Holiday pay	Holiday arrangements
Sick pay	Sick pay schemes
Maternity pay	Maternity leave
Redundancy payments	Pensions schemes
'Call-in payments'	Sabbatical leave

Joint consultation

In Britain, voluntary collective bargaining and voluntary joint consultation have traditionally been seen as separate and complementary processes, with collective bargaining focusing on the divergent interests of employers and employees and consultation focusing on their common interests. In practice, where bargaining and consultation co-exist, the distinction between them is often institutionalised by having separate negotiating and consultative machinery and separate agendas for their activities. This has meant in many cases that collective bargaining has been concerned with pay determination and conditions of employment and joint consultation with welfare, health and safety, training and efficiency, even where the same representatives are involved in the separate processes in the same organisation.

Although Flanders (1964) argues that this distinction between bargaining and consultation is artificial, McCarthy (1966) accepts the distinction but claims that there is an inverse relationship between trade union power and joint consultation. When union power is strong, joint consultation is neutralised and, when it is weak, joint consultation is reinvigorated. The McCarthy thesis is fairly persuasive, up to a point, since as Millward and Stevens (1986) show there was a significant growth of joint consultative committees (JCCs) in Britain during the early 1980s which was a period of generally high unemployment, declining union membership and assertive styles of management. By the time of the third Workplace Industrial Relations Survey (WIRS) in 1990, however, the overall proportion of workplaces with JCCs had fallen 'between 1984 and 1990, from 34 per cent to 29 per cent' (Millward *et al.* 1992: page 153). This could be accounted for by the fact that by 1990, there were fewer larger workplaces with recognised unions, where JCCs had previously been common. In the 1960s and 1970s, in contrast, during a period of strong trade union power, successful joint consultation was not widely practised in either private or public industry. Union representatives preferred negotiation because it influenced employment decisions and consultation did not.

One of the problems of analysing joint consultation as an employee relations process is that it has a variety of objectives, subject matter, representative structures and managerial approaches to it. Marchington (1989) identifies four models of joint consultation, in terms of the links between collective bargaining and employee respresentation. The aims of each of the four models are, respectively:

- to prevent the establishment of independent trade unionism;
- to make JCCs a marginal activity within the enterprise;
- to upgrade joint consultation, as a substitute for collective bargaining;

- to make JCCs a valuable adjunct to collective bargaining.

Clearly, from Marchington's research, management's motives for setting up and participating in joint consultation, and its attitudes towards it, are crucial determinants of its effectiveness, efficacy and impact on employee relations behaviour.

The *non-union* model is established by management to prevent unions organising in the workplace. It is based on information-giving from management, either of a 'hard' business nature or on 'soft' welfare and social matters. Non-union consultative committees are normally chaired by a senior line or personnel manager, and the employee representatives, chosen from amongst the workforce, are encouraged to identify with management and not to challenge management prerogatives or management's decision-making authority. JCCs of this sort are usually at establishment level and are not linked to committees on other sites in multi-plant firms.

The *marginal* model of joint consultation is one in which the JCC has a symbolic role and the JCC's employee representatives are kept busy on non-controversial issues. Fairly trivial information is provided to employee representatives. These JCCs tend to be chaired by the personnel manager and the employees are represented by both union and non-union members. Like the non-union model, the marginal model of joint consultation is organised at plant or establishment level with no links to other parts of the organisation.

The *competitive* model aims to reduce union influence, by upgrading joint consultation so as to render collective bargaining less meaningful. Hard, high-level information is provided by management to shop stewards and other employee representatives. Meetings are chaired by senior line managers at establishment level, although in larger organisations there may be departmental JCCs, allowing ideas and information to be passed up and down the organisation to reinforce the line management chain of command. According to Marchington (1988), this sort of consultation may be linked with other types of employee involvement such as quality circles, team briefings and similar direct forms of management-employee communications (see Chapter 10).

The purpose of the *adjunct* model of joint consultation is to provide a problem-solving forum, for management and union representatives, at plant and company levels, in parallel with the collective bargaining machinery. With this approach, collective bargaining tends to deal with matters of conflict between management and unions, such as pay and conditions of employment, whilst joint consultation fills in the gaps left by negotiation. This type of joint consultation therefore deals with issues of common and shared interest between the parties but may also be seen as a process preceding the negotiation of matters of conflict. The adjunct consultative process tends to be based on high trust and mutual colloboration between management and union representatives, with hard, high-level information, covering trading prospects, business plans and customer relations, being provided by management. Adjunct JCCs are likely to be chaired by the most senior line manager in the plant or company and there are normally links between JCCs at workplace and corporate levels in multi-site companies. Managements are also likely to encourage workplace representatives to have their own discussions prior to JCC meetings, to reinforce good working relations amongst management, unions and staff.

Conciliation, arbitration and mediation

Where the secondary parties to employee relations (management/management organisations and unions) are unable to resolve their employee relations differences by agreed negotiating or consultative procedures, or where no procedures exist, then the only means by which they can avoid damaging industrial conflict is by voluntary conciliation, arbitration or mediation. Normally, these are provided through the agency of ACAS (see Chapters 1 and 2).

Conciliation

Where the parties in dispute request or agree to collective conciliation, it is ACAS which provides a conciliator. The task of the conciliator is to help employer and unions settle their differences by agreement. Conciliators work through confidential, informal meetings between the parties, sometimes separately, sometimes jointly. They also work with certain broad assumptions. These include:

- that the parties wish to reach agreement;
- that they wish to avoid or end disruptive industrial conflict;
- that they will be generally cooperative in the conciliation process.

To be effective, conciliators have to gain the confidence of all parties to the dispute and establish good working relations with them. This depends on the personal qualities, knowledge, experience and, most importantly, the neutrality and impartiality of the conciliator.

According to ACAS (Advisory Conciliation and Arbitration Service 1979: page. 8):

> The process of conciliation is a dynamic one, requiring a continuous assessment of developments as they occur, and the conciliator adapts his conduct of each case accordingly.

The initial stage in collective conciliation is the preliminary briefing meeting. The conciliator's prime objective at this stage is to obtain a clear understanding of the issues in dispute and the attitudes of the parties. This involves collecting information from a variety of sources including oral evidence, documents, press cuttings and informed observers. It is at this stage that the conciliator has to decide whether it is appropriate to proceed with conciliation or not.

Conciliation normally consists of a series of 'side' meetings, with each party separately, and joint meetings chaired by the conciliator. Each party is free to choose its own representatives, though the level of seniority and extent of representation is important. The length of meetings varies and, at an appropriate time, the conciliator tries to direct the discussions into an accommodation between the parties. If successful, this can result in a settlement. If not, the conciliation process fails.

Side meetings enable each set of participants to speak freely, to reduce tensions and to adopt a problem-solving approach. Proposals and counter-proposals are examined, with a view to inducing movements towards a position where a settlement is likely. The conciliator moves between the parties in an attempt to bring their positions closer together. Joint meetings provide an opportunity for negotiations to proceed under an impartial and independent chairperson. They can also be the appropriate place for proposals for resolving the dispute. Joint meetings proceed by each side explaining its position, asking questions of the other and being questioned by the conciliator.

During the various meetings, the conciliator constantly looks for signs that the parties are moving to a settlement. If and when agreement has been reached, or appears to be close in side meetings, the parties can be brought together into a concluding joint meeting. This enables the terms of the settlement to be finalised, with the parties indicating their assent. Since conciliators are not party to any agreements reached, they do not sign the agreed document, except possibly as witnesses.

Conventional arbitration

ACAS is also empowered to appoint external arbitrators in trade disputes, under certain pre-conditions. These are:

- that the specific consent of the parties is obtained;
- that the likelihood of the dispute being settled by conciliation is considered;
- that generally any agreed procedures have been used and a failure to agree has resulted.

Most arbitrations are conducted by a single arbitrator from a list maintained by ACAS. This is a relatively simple, flexible and quick method of arbitrating. Boards of arbitration are used for major disputes and may be appointed at the request of the parties.

Requests for voluntary arbitration often come in the form of a joint application from the parties, including their names, addresses and agreed terms of reference. ACAS then appoints a suitable arbitrator and this is confirmed as a signed minute of appointment. Each side is allowed time to prepare and exchange statements. Hearings are held on the employers' premises or at an ACAS office. The parties are notified in writing of all the details, with a request to send their written statements to the arbitrator and to exchange them before the hearing, since the submission and exchange of statements is a normal feature of the arbitration process.

Hearings are normally held in private and are conducted informally. The arbitrator usually meets both parties together and asks the claimant party to state its case in the presence of the other who is then invited to reply. The arbitrator then questions both parties and invites them to make any closing statements. The arbitration award is submitted to ACAS, about two weeks after the hearing, and is binding on both parties. Awards are confidential and are not published, unless the parties agree to this.

Pendulum arbitration

Pendulum arbitration, known as 'final offer arbitration' or 'last offer arbitration' in the USA, is a relatively new process in Britain (Wood 1985). It is an arbitration process particularly associated with new-style collective agreements (see Chapter 9) and normally requires the arbitrator to choose the 'final offer' of the employer or the 'final claim' of the union side in the negotiation process. The rationale for pendulum arbitration derives from the fact that new-style negotiating procedures normally distinguish between conflicts of rights and conflicts of interests. Rights relate to the application or interpretation of agreements, whilst interests relate to matters not covered by agreement (e.g. new claims on terms and conditions of employment).

In essence, the negotiating procedures and procedures to avoid disputes in new-style agreements are based on the rights of the parties, incorporated in the recognition agreement. The intention is normally to reconcile the few remaining conflicts of interest on substantive issues through in-company negotiation. Where differences of interest persist, pendulum arbitration is used. This is claimed to encourage collective bargaining in the last resort, to keep bargaining claims within reasonable limits and to provide a means for resolving impasses (Burrows 1986).

In pendulum arbitration, the management side states its case and its 'final offer' and the union side states its case and its 'final claim' to the arbitrator. The arbitrator might try by persuasion to bring the two sides closer together but eventually has to settle for one side's case or the other's. There is no 'splitting the difference'. It is argued that one of the benefits of this approach to arbitration is that little face is lost by either side. This is because their original positions are less far apart than in conventional arbitration, with even the losing side ending up not that far from its stated position. Another advantage is claimed to be that, whilst one side is entirely satisfied with the arbitrator's award, the other side does not feel that it has lost so much ground as with conventional arbitration.

Mediation

Voluntary mediation in trade disputes is half-way between conciliation and conventional arbitration. Mediators proceed by way of conciliation but are also prepared to make their own formal proposals or recommendations. These may be accepted as they stand or provide the basis for further negotiations leading to a settlement. Since it provides more positive intervention, mediation tends to constrain the parties more than conciliation does. But it is more flexible and less decisive than arbitration.

As with arbitration, in mediation ACAS may appoint a single mediator or a board of mediation. The three pre-conditions, listed above, need to be observed and the formulation of the terms of reference requires careful drafting. Written statements are exchanged and sent to the mediator but the conduct of meetings differs from arbitration. Sometimes the mediator meets the parties in joint and separate meetings. In other cases, hearings proceed in the style of arbitration. In other cases, the mediator acts as the chair of a working party, making recommendations on any points which the parties themselves cannot agree. Where a settlement is reached by mediation, the mediator's final report records the terms of the agreement and no further action is required. In other cases, it may be necessary for ACAS conciliation officers to assist the parties further, if required.

Unilateral action and industrial sanctions

Having examined the main voluntary, bilateral and trilateral processes of conflict resolution and accommodation in employee relations, we now turn to unilateral action and industrial sanctions. Unilateral action and industrial sanctions in employee relations involve management and unions acting as discrete parties. Unilateral action by management or unions, and any industrial sanctions imposed by one side on the other, are voluntary and collective processes of conducting employee relations which differ from other processes in two main respects:

- they involve the ultimate application, by management or unions, of one-sided power in determining and applying employee relations rules;
- because of this power dimension, British law impinges more closely on these employee relations processes than on other voluntarist ones, such as collective bargaining, joint consultation, conciliation, arbitration and mediation.

The right to manage

The right of management to manage in organisations is, in all capitalist countries but in Britain, the USA and Japan especially, at the root of employee relations decision-making and controversy. The right to manage or unilateral management decision-making – otherwise known as managerial prerogative, managerial rights or managerial functions – is where management interfaces with employees, the trade union function, collective bargaining and the law, insofar as this supports and constrains the right to manage in private and public organisations.

The origins of the right to manage can be traced to the emergence of capitalist business organisations in the nineteenth century and the parallel growth of craft trade unionism. The early capitalist entrepreneurs claimed their right to manage on the basis of property ownership. Since they and their families owned the factories, mines, railway companies, shipbuilding yards and shipping lines that they directed, controlled and organised, then it was they alone, they claimed, who should have the right to employ, pay, deploy, discipline and, if necessary, dismiss the hourly paid and salaried 'black coated' workers employed in their enterprises.

The entrepreneurial class's advocacy and defence of the right to manage, moreover, was reinforced by the demands of the craft unions to settle the terms and conditions of employment of their members unilaterally, without reference to the employers, and to enforce pre-entry closed shops on the employers, to control the supply of labour into the labour market (Clegg, Fox and Thompson 1964). This right to manage was embodied in the common law duty requiring workers to obey all reasonable and legitimate instructions given to them by their 'masters' or their supervisory agents. It was also incorporated into statute law by making companies solely accountable to corporate shareholders and stockholders and, unlike in Germany and France after the second world war, by not providing workers with a collective legal status, through, for example, statutory works councils and enterprise committees (Bercusson 1986).

Today, the right to manage is largely based on different claims for managerial authority (Storey 1980 and 1983). In essence, management justifies the right to manage on the grounds of economic efficiency, technical expertise and professional competency. The arguments run along these lines:

- it is management's responsibility to achieve organisational efficiency and success in the interests of those to whom they are accountable;
- it is management alone who have the knowledge, skills and abilities to carry out the tasks of effective managing;
- it is essential, if the organisation is to remain profitable, viable and cost-effective, that managers have the autonomy and authority to take and implement corporate decisions, including employment ones, without interference from internal or outside parties.

It is these sorts of ideas and interests which have led British employers to resist a statutory minimum wage, the European Community Charter of Fundamental Social Rights for Workers (Commission of the European Communities 1990) and the Social Chapter of the Treaty of Maastricht 1991.

The contemporary justification of the right to manage is both an attractive and a flawed concept. It is attractive because it makes economic sense to argue the necessity of management leadership and know-how in creating, administering and coordinating effective organisations. It is flawed, however, because the right to manage can never be absolute in enterprises for four main reaons:

- in practice, managerial authority has to be counterbalanced by the consent of those governed even by unilateral management rules;
- where employees are organised into trade unions, the right to make unilateral management decisions is constrained by collective bargaining;
- the law provides a floor of legal rights for employees (see Chapter 4);
- the right to manage is not a static concept, either organisationally or societally. What was a managerial right yesterday can become a workers' or a union's right today and what are workers' rights today can regress to managerial rights tomorrow. It depends on the balance of power in the employment relationship, as affected by market factors, trade union organisation, public policy and the law.

It is clear that the right to manage and to take management decisions unilaterally is a difficult employee relations process to examine definitively. It is also clear that since the early 1980s the right to manage has been strengthened. Even where employers recognise trade unions, 'right-to-manage' clauses are now being put in recognition and procedural agreements and 'status quo' clauses are being omitted. The latter provide that actions proposed by management cannot be implemented, if disputed by workers, until agreement has been reached or the procedure for avoiding disputes exhausted. Recent right-to-manage clauses state, for example, 'that the Union recognises the right of the Company to plan, organise, manage and decide finally upon the operations of the Company'. Another example, in the public sector, states that 'The [employers' federation] and the signatory Unions recognise that it is the right and responsibility of the institutions to manage their domestic affairs in the context of this Agreement' (Polytechnic and Colleges Employers' Forum 1989).

However complex the concept of the right to manage is, unilateral management rules normally take the form of what used to be called 'works rules' but are now normally referred to as 'company rules'. These are usually included in employee handbooks, along with background information about the employer, other employment matters, personnel policies and employee relations procedures, and they become incorporated into individual contracts of employment (Marks 1978). The right to manage is also closely linked with management use of employee involvement processes such as briefing groups, quality circles, total quality management (TQM), profit-related pay and employee share ownership (see Chapter 10).

Union rules

The union equivalents of the right to manage are union rules and custom and practice (C and P). Union rules are subsumed in:

- union rule books;
- union policies determined at their national policy-making conferences;
- operational policies determined amongst union activists locally.

Unilateral union-made rules are imposed on management where unions are strong and well organised at employer and workplace levels. C and P are unwritten and informal rules regulating employment and work at enterprise level. They are generally unilaterally determined, with management having no say in making them but tacitly accepting them. Some C and P, however, takes the form of 'shared understandings' between management and unions, which management accept but are unwilling to legitimise formally.

Formal union rules affecting employee relations at employer and workplace levels, deriving largely from union rule books, cover a wide range of working arrangements. They are traditionally associated with craft unions, such as those in the printing, skilled engineering and metal trades. With the relative decline of skilled manual occupations and the craft unions in recent years – largely due to technological change, market pressures on employers and new product markets – unilateral union rules are less important now than they were in the past (see Chapter 6). This has resulted in multi-skilling, job flexibility and union mergers. However, examples of such rules cover:

* the training of apprentices;
* the closed shop;
* job demarcation;
* working arrangements;
* 'manning' levels;
* working with other unions.

C and P rules are established by trade unionists either where such rules have been traditionally accepted by management without challenge, in order to maintain industrial peace, or where management rules – or joint rules – have lapsed and management turns 'a blind eye' to them, because it has lost control of them. Examples include:

* time-keeping;
* working practices;
* worker behaviour.

Workers may be required to finish at an agreed time on a Friday afternoon, for example, but C and P dictates that, within the last hour of work, workers who have completed their current job tasks may 'job and finish' and leave the employer's premises, before the official finishing time.

C and P are used as precedents by trade unionists either when arguing with management for a solution to conflicts about new employment rules or in applying existing rules to new situations. As such, C and P rules are jealously guarded by workgroups and unions. Management is only likely to challenge them when organisational efficiency is threatened, enterprise effectiveness is at risk and trade union power is weak. This was the case in many organisations in the 1980s and early 1990s.

Industrial action

Both management and unions are prepared, in certain cases, to use industrial sanctions against one another in order to achieve their employee relations goals. These sanctions, known as industrial action, involve disruption of normal working and can take a number of forms. On the employers' side, the lockout is the best known. But other sanctions open to employers include:

- withdrawing union recognition;
- withdrawing union facilities;
- transferring workers to less pleasant jobs;
- tighter workplace discipline;
- taking away bonuses;
- reducing overtime;
- changing working arrangements unilaterally.

On the union side, industrial sanctions include (see also Chapter 11):

- going slow;
- working to rule;
- banning overtime;
- working without enthusiasm;
- stoppages of work.

Sanctions are the means of last resort, for both sides, since they involve economic and social costs to both parties. Where employers take industrial action against their workers, the economic and social costs may be lost sales revenue or, in the public sector, withdrawn public services. The cost to workers is lost pay and benefits and possibly lost job security.

In participating in industrial action, unions, union leaders and employees are constrained by the law. In outline, the law seeks to regulate industrial action in a number of ways. This is done through a combination of:

- judge-made law, both criminal and civil;

- legislation;
- codes of practice, such as for picketing.

First, trade unions and individuals organising and taking part in industrial action may be liable for certain civil wrongs or 'torts' in circumstances which are not protected by statutory 'immunities'. There is no legal 'right to strike' in Britain, as in most of Western Europe, but immunities provide legal protections for unions and individuals taking part in lawful industrial action, providing the acts are done 'in contemplation or furtherance of a trade dispute'. Second, the law seeks to impose limits on physical manifestations of industrial conflict, such as picketing, occupations and sit-ins (Simpson 1986; see also Chapter 4 below).

Industrial action also affects the legal rights and obligations of employer and employee under the contract of employment. This is because the common law tends to treat all forms of industrial action by employees as breaches of contract, since they violate the employee's central obligation under the contract to work for the employer. This breach of contract is important in two respects. First, it may provide one of the ingredients of the economic torts for which trade unions may be liable. Second, it may entitle the employer to take disciplinary action against individual employees.

In theory at least, employers can respond to industrial action by individual employees in several ways (Mesher and Sutcliffe 1986):

- they may dismiss the employees, though dismissal letters often contain offers of re-engagement providing the workers return to work by a given date;
- it is common for employers to claim that the employees have dismissed themselves;
- it is possible to sue individual employees for damages, as they have repudiated the employment contract, though this is rare in practice;
- with a complete stoppage of work, the employer is entitled to stop the employee's pay, but problems may arise where there is partial stoppage, as in working to rule.

Legal enactment

The traditional ways of conducting employee relations in Britain are voluntary joint regulation, though collective bargaining between employers and unions, or voluntary employer regulation, through individual bargaining between employer and employee. Until the 1960s, legal enactment or legal regulation played a relatively minor role in employee relations, with the general thrust of state policy being non-interventionist (see Chapters 4 and 7). It was largely the common law that regulated the contract of employment (Lewis 1986). And it was the so-called emancipatory legislation provided by the Trade Union Act 1871, the Conspiracy and Protection of Property Act 1875 and the Trade Disputes Act 1906 that regulated relations between employers and trade unions, industrial conflict and trade union activity (Lewis 1976). Both employers and unions, unlike in most other industrialised countries, preferred voluntarism and the abstention of the judges and the courts in employee relations to legal interventionism.

The first indications of the growing influence of legal regulation in British employee relations emerged with the Contracts of Employment Act 1963 and the Redundancy Payments Act 1965. The Industrial Relations Act 1971, though repealed in 1974, was followed by further employment legislation enacted by Labour governments in the 1970s and by Conservative governments in the 1980s and early 1990s. The main legislation is currently incorporated in:

- Equal Pay Act 1970;
- Equal Pay Amendment Regulations 1983;
- Health and Safety at Work etc. Act 1974;
- Employment Protection Act 1975;
- Sex Discrimination Act 1975;
- Race Relations Act 1976;
- Employment Protection (Consolidation) Act 1978;
- Transfer of Undertakings (Protection of Employment) Regulations 1981;
- Wages Act 1986;
- Trade Union and Labour Relations (Consolidation) Act 1992;
- Trade Union Reform and Employment Rights Act 1993.

Some of these legal provisions regulate individual employee relations by providing statutory employment protection rights for employees and statutory union membership rights for trade unionists. Others provide statutory rights for trade unions. And others regulate collective employee relations such as industrial conflict and trade union activities (see Chapters 4, 7 and 11). The main statutory rights are summarised below.

Employment protection rights

Individual employees have over 20 statutory rights, subject to qualifying conditions, as illustrated in Exhibit 9.

Exhibit 9: *Main employment protection rights*

These include the right to:

- join or not to join a union;
- not be refused employment on the grounds of union membership;
- not be dismissed, or have action short of dismissal taken, because of trade union membership;
- written particulars of the main terms of the contract of employment;
- an itemised pay statement;
- not have unlawful deductions made from wages;
- guarantee payments when not provided with work by an employer on a normal work day;
- medical suspension payments;
- statutory sick pay;
- equal treatment in terms and conditions of employment, irrespective of gender;
- time off work for ante-natal care, maternity pay and maternity leave for female employees and, after giving birth, to return to work;
- time off work for public duties;
- not be discriminated against on the grounds of sex, marital status or race;
- not be dismissed in connection with medical suspension;
- minimum periods of notice;
- a redundancy payment when a job disappears;
- time off to look for work in a redundancy situation or to arrange training;
- payment from the Secretary of State in the event of employer insolvency;
- not be unfairly dismissed;
- a written statement of the reasons for dismissal.

If an employer infringes any of these statutory rights, an employee may make a claim to an industrial tribunal (IT). ITs have the power to make awards, including compensation, and enforce certain rights where an employer has acted unlawfully (Lewis 1990).

Union membership rights

In addition to their statutory rights as employees, trade union members have a number of rights relating to union membership. These are illustrated in Exhibit 10.

Exhibit 10: *Main membership rights of trade unionists*

These include the right to:

- not be unreasonably excluded or expelled from a union;
- compensation for being unreasonably excluded or expelled from a union;
- elect union executive committees, union presidents and general secretaries by secret ballot;
- secret ballots endorsing official industrial action;
- secret postal ballots for union political funds;
- not be unjustifiably disciplined by a union for failing to take part in official industrial action;
- apply to the High Court for an order that a union has taken industrial action without a ballot;
- stop deductions of union subscriptions at source.

Where trade union members claim that any of these rights have been infringed by a union, they may take their complaint to one of the following agencies, depending on the nature of the complaint: an industrial tribunal, the Certification Officer or the Commissioner for the Rights of Trade Union Members.

Trade union rights

Independent trade unions recognised by employers, the officials of independent recognised unions and members of recognised independent unions all have a series of statutory rights (Farnham 1990). These are illustrated in Exhibit 11.

Exhibit 11: *Rights of independent, recognised trade unions and time-off provisions*

These include the right to:

- appoint safety representatives and to establish safety committees at work;
- consultation on pensions in firms contracted out of the state earnings related pension scheme;
- consultation on collective redundancies involving 10–99 employees, within 30 days or less, and 100 or more employees within 90 days or less;
- information and consultation in business transfers including their reasons, timing and implications and the measures which the employer proposes taking in relation to employees;
- disclosure of information for collective bargaining purposes requested by trade union representatives;
- secret ballots on employers' premises for industrial action, union elections and related matters;
- public funds for secret postal ballots, from the CO, including postal costs, the cost of stationery and the printing costs of voting papers and envelopes;
- time off with pay for officials undertaking trade union duties and training;
- time off with pay for safety representatives and training;
- time off without pay for union members undertaking trade union activities and representing the union.

Worker participation in Western Europe

Employee relations in Western Europe have two main characteristics distinguishing them from those of Britain. First, there are frequently multiple systems of employee representation. These include collective bargaining, employee representatives on company boards and plant-based works councils. The second feature of European employee relations is their far greater reliance on legal enactment in regulating both collective relations between employers and unions and individual relations between employers and employees than is the case in Britain.

Co-determination at corporate level

Worker participation with management in corporate decision-making at board level takes place, in its most advanced form, in Germany. The form of co-determination in Germany depends upon company size, the legal structure of the company and the industry in which it is located. In essence, board-level worker participation is facilitated through two-tier boards. These consist of a supervisory board (*Aufsichsrat*) and a management board (*Vorstand*). The supervisory board is legally charged with appointing the management board, or its managing directors, and with overseeing its activities. Employee representatives sitting on the supervisory board have the same rights and duties as shareholder representatives. This, it is assumed, will result in entrepreneurial decisions which serve the joint aspirations of both shareholder and employee interests. Employee representatives may request information from the management board on all aspects of the business, including proposed corporate policies, profitability and sales. The management board is the legal employer, represents the company legally and is responsible for conducting the organisation's business operations.

In companies employing over 1,000 employees in the coal, steel and iron industries, supervisory boards consist of equal numbers of employee and shareholder representatives, though this is a declining sector of employment. Under the Works Constitution Act 1952, companies with over 500 employees but under 2,000 are required to have a supervisory board, a third of whose members are employee representatives.

In organisations with over 2,000 employees (whether joint stock companies, limited liability companies or limited partnerships based on share capital), supervisory boards consist of equal numbers of employee and shareholder representatives. The size of the supervisory board varies according to company size but some seats are reserved for trade unions that have members in the organisation, and for managerial employees. This means that 'workers', as a group, do not have full parity of representation on the supervisory board. In smaller firms, the employee representatives are directly elected by employee groups and in larger companies, with up to 8,000 employees, there are electoral colleges. The most important roles of the supervisory board are to appoint the management board and supervise management (Berghan and Karsten 1989).

In Sweden, by comparison, the approach to co-determination is based on collective bargaining rights. Its source is the Act of Employee

Participation in Decision Making (MBL) 1977. It is an expansion of earlier rights of trade unions to negotiate with employers. Employers are obliged to take the initiative in negotiating with trade unions at company level before decisions on major issues are made. These include closure, reorganisation and expansion of operations. The Act also requires employers to keep local unions informed about how company operations are progressing and about the guidelines for company personnel policy.

The MBL also presumes and encourages the signing of collective agreements on co-determination. The so called 'residual right' to industrial action means that unions are entitled to resort to industrial action if their requests for co-determination agreements, presented in connection with pay negotiations, are not met. The law also gives the unions priority of interpretation in most types of disputes. This is a major strengthening of employee influence, since most disputes of interpretation do not result in negotiations, and the unions have immediate enforcement of their interpretation. It is management which has to request negotiations in these circumstances, with negotiations being referred to national level if necessary or the unions being sued by the employer in the Labour Court (Forsebaick 1980).

Works councils at plant level

Works councils are widespread in Europe. They are prominent in France, Germany and the Netherlands. Basically, a works council is a body, established in law, normally organised at enterprise level, consisting of elected employee representatives with certain rights and responsibilities in their dealings with management and the employer.

In France, there is a multiplicity of representative bodies that have been set up in response to specific social and political pressures, at particular times. Employee delegates (*délégués du personnel*), which were instituted by the Popular Front in 1936, deal with individual employee grievances covering wages, conditions of employment and legal agreements. They are elected by the whole workforce in organisations employing over 10 employees, by a system of proportional representation, though in practice most of them are elected on a union slate. Workplace union branches (*sections syndicales*), established in 1968, can appoint their own stewards, collect dues, use notice boards and organise monthly meetings. In some firms, these branches have offices and other facilities.

Works committees in France (*comités d'entreprise*), set up in 1945 after the Liberation, deal with workplace consultation. They can be established in all firms employing at least 50 employees. They have the legal right to be informed and consulted on issues such as the number and organisation of employees, their hours of work and employment conditions. Managements have to submit an annual written report to the works committee covering the business's activities, profits or losses, allocation of profits, investments and salaries. Agreement by the works committee is required on arrangements for profit-sharing and changes in individual working hours. Works councils may create subcommittees to examine specific problems and, in companies with at least 50 employees, health, safety and improvement of working conditions committees are compulsory. Firms with at least 350 employees have to set up an employment-training committee and those with at least 1,000 have to set up an economic committee (Goetschy and Rojot 1987).

In Germany, works councils are directly elected by the workforce at establishment level, though in multi-plant companies a central works council can be formed by delegation from individual works councils. They may be elected in any establishment with at least five employees and must be recognised by the employer. White-collar workers, blue-collar workers and trainees are eligible for election but executive employees, who have their own employee representative committees, are excluded. The size of the works councils increases with the size of establishment, and representation of employee groups is in proportion to their numbers in the establishment. The members of the works councils are released with pay for their council activities, entitled to relevant training for their roles and protected by law against dismissal by the employer. Works councils in Germany have a wide range of functions (Berghan and Karsten 1989). Basically, works councils exist to protect the interests of workers in the plant. At the same time, works councils and the employers are expected to work together in a spirit of mutual trust, and in cooperation with the trade unions and employers' associations, for the good of the employees and the plant. Under Article 37 of the Works Constitution Act 1972, works councils have 'to see that effect is given to Acts, ordinances, safety regulations, collective agreements and plant agreements for the benefit of employees' and make 'recommendations to the employer for action benefiting the plant and staff' (Berghan and Karsten:

page 108). Works councils in German companies have the right to co-determination in matters outlined in Exhibit 12.

Exhibit 12: *The rights and responsibilities of works councils in Germany*

These cover:

- the conduct of employees in the plant;
- daily working times and distribution of working hours;
- the reduction or extension of hours normally worked;
- the time, place and form of payment of remuneration;
- establishing the general principles of leave arrangements and the preparing of leave schedules;
- introducing and using technical devices designed to monitor the behaviour or performance of employees;
- preventing workplace accidents and occupational diseases;
- the form, structure and administration of social services in the plant, company or combine;
- assigning and vacating accommodation rented to employees;
- establishing the principles of remuneration and introducing new remuneration methods;
- the fixing of job and bonus rates and comparable performance related remuneration;
- the principles for suggestion schemes in the plant.

Where agreement is not reached on these matters, a conciliation panel takes the decision and its award replaces agreement between the works council and the employer. Employers have to gain the consent of works councils for individual measures of personnel policy, such as staff grading or regrading, and vocational training. Works councils also have to be heard where employees are dismissed for the dismissal not to be void in law.

European Works Councils

Since the early 1970s, there have been a series of initatives within the EC to legislate for more systematic employee participation structures within the corporate sector. The draft European Works Council Directive, published by the Commission of the European Communities in January 1991, was the latest in a line of controversial proposals for EC employee participation measures over the last 20 years (Commission of the European Communities 1991). To date, only those measures requiring information disclosure and consultation on specific issues by employers have been adopted by the Council of Ministers (CoM). These include the directive on collective redundancies 1975, the directive on transfers of undertakings 1977 and the framework directive on health and safety 1989. Proposals for Euro-legislation on a European company statute in the early 1970s, on company law reform from the early 1970s until the early 1980s and on the Vredling measures in the early 1980s have been continually blocked within the EC's decision-making institutions.

The 1991 European Works Council Directive proposed the establishment of a statutory European Works Council (EWC) – or a similar arrangement – in every Community-scale undertaking, or group of undertakings, where it was requested by employees or their representatives. It now appears unlikely to be adopted on a mandatory basis. This is because of the difficulty of getting unanimous support for it amongst EC member states. The expectation is that progress on the issue is likely to be approached on a voluntary basis.

The proposal for EWCs was that mandatory councils would be required in:

- those undertakings employing at least 1,000 employees within the EC in each of two or more member states;
- those groups of undertakings with at least 1,000 employees, and with at least two group undertakings in different member states, each employing at least 100 members within the EC.

The scope, composition, competence and mode of operation of the EWCs was to be agreed between the management of the undertaking or group and a special negotiating body of employee representatives. Where the special negotiating body decided to discuss the setting-up of a EWC with management, but agreement had not been reached within a year, certain minimum requirements were to apply. The minimum requirements limited the competence of the EWCs to matters concerning the undertaking, the group as a whole, or two or more establishments or group undertakings in different member states.

EWCs would have had the right to meet central management annually and be informed of the undertaking's or group's progress and prospects. They would also have had the right to be consulted on management proposals likely to have serious consequences for the interests of employees. These matters included mergers, closures, relocations, organisational change and new working or production methods. For these purposes, the EWCs were to be able to request an additional meeting with management, if necessary.

EWCs were to have had a maximum of 30 members, drawn from existing employee representatives, or specially elected ones where none existed. The operating expenses of the EWCs were to have been met by the undertaking or group concerned. The original directive provided that members of the EWC would not have had to reveal any information of a confidential nature and that information could have been withheld where it would substantially have damaged the interests of the undertakings or groups concerned.

Hall (1992) argues, on the issue of the legal compulsion underpinning the establishment of EWCs, that the approach was inconsistent with the then government's emphasis on minimising employers' legal obligations in their dealings with employees and unions. Britain would therefore have been required to fill in the gaps left by the existing reliance on voluntary trade union recognition by employers. A fear of the employers is that mandatory EWCs could have potentially been the vehicle for developing European-level collective bargaining within multinational companies. Indeed, it can be expected that collective bargaining strategies in Britain will be influenced by the provision of European-level corporate information.

From the union point of view, the EWC proposal presented, on the one hand, a valuable opportunity for those unions seeking employer recognition. On the other hand, alternative channels of employee representation might have emerged which could have inhibited union organisation (Trades Union Congress 1991). It is also likely, since mandatory EWCs would have been relatively small bodies, that trade unions could have had problems agreeing representatives in multi-union situations and where they represented more than one establishment or company.

The social dimension

At a meeting of the European Council in Strasbourg on 8 and 9 December 1989, the heads of state or government of the EC member states, except that of the United Kingdom, adopted the Community Charter of Fundamental Social Rights of Workers, known in short as the 'Social Charter' (SC). The signatories intended the SC to be a statement of the progress already made in the social field in the EC and a preparation for new advances in it. In the preamble, the heads of state also underlined the priority attached to job creation, social consensus as a factor in economic development and rejection of all forms of discrimination or exclusion. The SC demands a series of initiatives to develop workers' rights, with the responsibility for these initiatives lying with the EC itself, member states and the 'social partners', that is employers and trade unions.

Accordingly, the Commission of the European Communities drew up an action programme for parts of the SC to be implemented at Community level. The programme covers 90 areas whose aims are to develop the social dimension of the single market, thus increasing the economic and social cohesion of the 12 member states. In some areas, falling within the competence of member states or the social partners, but arising in similar terms in all countries of the EC, the Commission has initiated non-binding measures encouraging some convergence of efforts, whilst respecting national practices.

The SC identifies and defines 12 areas where the fundamental social rights of workers are to be advanced and protected (Commission of the European Communities 1990). The aim of the SC is to set out the principles on which the European pattern of labour law, and the European concept of society and the place of labour within it, are based. They basically cover the social rights illustrated in Exhibit 13 (see also Chapter 4).

Exhibit 13: *The European Community Social Charter*

This sets out rights covering:

- the improvement of living and working conditions;
- freedom of movement;
- employment and fair remuneration;
- social protection and appropriate social assistance;
- freedom of association and collective bargaining;
- vocational training;
- equal treatment of men and women;
- information, consultation and worker participation;
- health protection and safety at work;
- the protection of children and adolescents;
- pensions and a decent standard of living for elderly people;
- the integration in working life of disabled persons.

After the Treaty of Maastricht 1991, the principle of qualified majority voting was extended to the field of social policy. This means that decisions within the CoM can be taken without the unanimous agreement of all member states. These matters include:

- improvements in the working environment;
- working conditions;
- the provision of information and worker consultation;
- equal opportunties;
- the integration of persons excluded from the labour market.

The UK government was unable to support these Treaty amendments. This means, when the Treaty comes into effect, that the protection offered by the SC does not apply to workers in Britain.

Assignments

(a) Why has there been a shift to personal contracts of employment in some organisations? Examine the pros and cons of personal contracts for employers and management.

(b) Identify the bargaining level(s), for a named bargaining unit, at which collective bargaining takes place in your organisation. Explain the likely influences on why collective bargaining takes place at the level(s) identified. What other bargaining units, if any, are there in the organisation? Identify the bargaining agents in each case and outline the bargaining scope, in terms of procedural and substantive agreements, for each bargaining group.

(c) Make a presentation describing and analysing the procedural agreements, between management and the unions, in your organisation.

(d) Read Marchington (1988) and make sure that you fully understand his four models of joint consultation. Using his framework, describe and analyse the joint consultative arrangements in your organisation. How are they linked, if at all, with the collective bargaining machinery in the organisation/industry?

(e) Your organisation's annual pay negotiations with the unions representing manual workers have broken down. Examine the circumstances in which the management side would resort to: (1) conciliation, (2) arbitration, (3) mediation, (4) industrial sanctions. Indicate the pros and cons of using each of these processes.

(f) Read Lewis (1986: pages 3–43). To what extent have British employee relations become juridified in recent years? Give reasons for your conclusion.

(g) Argue the case for introducing a (non-statutory) 'works council' in the establishment where you work. Provide a draft constitution for such a body and indicate the sorts of issues which would have to be addressed if the council was to operate effectively.

(h) Read Hall (1992). (1) Identify and analyse the developments and pressures which have shaped the current proposal for EWCs. (2) Examine the reasons why the British government and employers are opposed to the proposals incorporated within the EWCs proposal. What would have been the consequences for British transnational companies, operating in Britain, Germany and the Netherlands, if, say, the European Works Council Directive had been adopted, using the 'qualified majority' principle?

References

ADVISORY CONCILIATION AND ARBITRATION SERVICE 1979. *The ACAS Role in Conciliation, Arbitration and Mediation*. London: ACAS.

ADVISORY CONCILIATION AND ARBITRATION SERVICE 1983. *Collective Bargaining in Britain: its Extent and Scope*. London: ACAS.

BERCUSSON, B. 1986. 'Workers, corporate enterprise and the law'. In Lewis, R. (ed.) 1986. *Labour Law in Britain*. Oxford: Blackwell.

BERGHAN, V. and KARSTEN, D. 1989. *Industrial Relations in West Germany*. Oxford: Berg.

BURROWS, G. 1986. *No-Strike Agreements and Pendulum Arbitration*. London: IPM.

CLEGG, H. 1976. 'Pluralism in industrial relations'. *British Journal of Industrial Relations*. XIII (3).

CLEGG, H., FOX, A. and THOMPSON, A. 1964. *A History of British Trade Unions since 1889: Volume I 1889–1910*. Oxford: Oxford University Press.

COMMISSION OF THE EUROPEAN COMMUNITIES 1990. *Community Charter of the Fundamental Social Rights of Workers*. Luxembourg: Office of Official Publications of the European Communities.

COMMISSION OF THE EUROPEAN COMMUNITIES 1991. *Amended Proposals for a Council Directive on the Establishment of European Works Councils in Community-Scale Undertakings or Groups of Undertakings for the Purposes of Informing and Consulting Employees*. Luxembourg: Council of Ministers.

FARNHAM, D. 1990. *Personnel in Context*. London: IPM.

FARNHAM, D. and HORTON, S. (eds) 1993. *Managing the New Public Services*. Basingstoke: Macmillan.

FLANDERS, A. 1964. *The Fawley Productivity Agreements*. London: Faber and Faber.

FORSEBAICK, L. 1980. *Industrial Relations and Employment in Sweden*. Uppsala: Swedish Institute.

GOETSCHY, J. and ROJOT, J. 1987. 'France'. In BAMBER, G. and LANSBURY, R. 1987. *International and Comparative Industrial Relations*. London: Allen and Unwin.

GUNNICLE, P. and FLOOD, P. 1990. *Personnel Management in Ireland*. Dublin: Gill and Macmillan.

HALL, M. 1992. 'Legislating for employee participation: a case study of the European Works Councils Directive'. *Warwick Papers in Industrial Relations*. Number 39.

INCOMES DATA SERVICES 1991. *Industrial Relations*. London: IPM.

KOCHAN, T., KATZ, H. and MCKERSIE, R. 1986. *The Transformation of American Industrial Relations*. NY: Basic.

LEWIS, D. 1990. *Essentials of Employment Law*. London: IPM.

LEWIS, R. 1976. 'The historical development of labour law'. *British Journal of Industrial Relations*. March.

MCCARTHY, W. 1966. *The Role of the Shop Steward in British Industrial Relations*. (Royal Commission Research Paper 1). London: HMSO.

MARCHINGTON, M. 1988. 'The four faces of consultation'. *Personnel Management*. July.

MARCHINGTON, M. 1989. 'Joint consultation in practice'. In SISSON, K. (ed.) 1989. *Personnel Management in Britain*. Oxford: Blackwell.

MARGINSON, P., EDWARDS, P., MARTIN, R., SISSON, K. and PURCELL, J. 1988. *Beyond the Workplace: Managing Industrial Relations in Multi-Establishment Enterprise*. Oxford: Blackwell.

MARKS, W. 1978. *Preparing an Employee Handbook*. London: IPM.

MESHER, J. and SUTCLIFFE, F. 1986. 'Industrial action and the individual'. In LEWIS, R. (ed.) 1986. *Labour Law in Britain*. Oxford: Blackwell.

MILLWARD, N. and STEVENS, M. 1986. *British Workplace Industrial Relations 1980–84*. Aldershot: Gower.

MILLWARD, N., STEVENS, M., SMART, D. and HAWES, W. 1992. *Workplace Industrial Relations in Transition*. Aldershot: Dartmouth.

PALMER, S. 1990. *Determining Pay*. London: IPM.

PARKER, P., HAWES, W. and LUMB, A. 1971. *The Reform of Collective Bargaining at Plant and Company Level*. London: HMSO.

POLYTECHNIC AND COLLEGES EMPLOYERS' FORUM 1989. *Recognition and Procedure Agreement creating the Polytechnics and Colleges National Negotiating Committee*. London: PCEF.

PORTSMOUTH AND SOUTH EAST HAMPSHIRE HEALTH AUTHORITY 1991. *Contract for Senior Managers*. Portsmouth: PSEHHA.

RICO, L. 1987. 'The new industrial relations: British electricians' new-style agreements'. *Industrial and Labor Relations Review*. 41(1), October.

SHIRAI, T. 1983. *Contemporary Industrial Relations in Japan*. Wisconsin: University of Wisconsin Press.

SIMPSON, B. 1986. 'Trade union immunities'. In LEWIS, R. (ed.) 1986. *Labour Law in Britain*. Oxford: Blackwell.

STOREY, J. 1980. *The Challenge to Management Control*. London: Kogan Page.

STOREY, J. 1983. *Management Prerogative and the Question of Control*. London: Routledge and Kegan Paul.

TRADES UNION CONGRESS 1991. *Unions and Europe in the 1990s*. London: TUC.

WOOD, J. 1985. 'Last offer arbitration'. *British Journal of Industrial Relations*. XXIII (3), November.

Chapter 4

The environmental context of employee relations

The roles of the state, its government agencies and the law are crucial in influencing the structures, patterns and processes of employee relations. The government's economic policies and its legal policies on trade unions, the regulation of industrial conflict and employment protection rights have major implications for employee relations (see Chapters 1 and 7). Where economic policy focuses on creating the economic conditions necessary for full employment (Keynesianism), it strengthens union bargaining power in the labour market and the workplace, whilst weakening that of management. Where economic policy focuses on containing price inflation primarily through the instruments of reducing public expenditure, encouraging free market forces and using changes in interest rates to influence economic activity (monetarism and supply-side economics), this strengthens employers and management in their market relations with trade unions and their managerial relations with employees.

Similarly, where there is an 'abstentionist' legal policy supportive to trade union organisation, which encourages collectivist approaches to employment policy on the part of employers, the role of trade unions in employee relations is both legitimised and reinforced and limitations are placed on the right to manage. Where legal policy is 'restrictionist' and is aimed at weakening trade unions and encouraging individualism in employee relations, the power of management is strengthened and that of employees, collectively and individually, is weakened.

A further extension to political interventionism in employee relations is the 'social dimension' of the single European market. Ever since the EC was created, there have been a series of attempts by the European authorities not only to expand the internal European market but also to extend the coverage of its social policies to employees, citizens and their families in the member states. These social initiatives, whilst important to workers and individuals, have not always met with the approval of recent British governments or management organisations such as the CBI.

Economic management

Economic management is the actions taken by government to influence economic performance within the macro- and micro-economy. With the demise of classical *laissez-faire* in the mid-nineteenth century, governments became steadily more interventionist in economic affairs – but not in employee relations which were dominated by voluntarist values. This was in response to a series of political, social and democratic pressures. Political interventions in economic affairs by the state were also influenced by significant events, such as the first and second world wars. These marked discontinuity with the past in terms of increased levels of government expenditure but also pointed to the future in terms of more government involvement and intervention in the economy. During each of these wars, government expenditure rose rapidly, both absolutely and relatively, only to decrease again when hostilities had ceased, but not to prewar levels (Farnham and Horton 1993). These incremental increases in government intervention in the economy were paralleled by searches for appropriate methods of economic management to accompany them.

Economic management in Britain since the end of the second world war, in 1945, can be divided broadly into two periods. First, there was the era of Keynesianism which was the dominant economic orthodoxy supported by successive governments between 1945 and the mid-1970s. Second, there is the period of monetarism and supply-side economics which has dominated government economic policy since the mid-1970s. Both approaches to economic management have implications for the parties to employee relations, employee relations processes and their outcomes.

Keynesianism

The economic ideas associated with John Maynard Keynes (1936), most commonly referred to as Keynesianism, emerged out of the experiences of industrial depression, high unemployment and social deprivation during the 1930s. In the years immediately following the second world war, Keynesian economic policies became the new conventional wisdom of both academic economists and social democratic politicians in Britain and Western Europe.

Until Keynes's writings, economic theory was mainly concerned with the determinants of the general price level. Keynes, instead, focused on the determinants of the level of output in the economy, stressing the importance of aggregate demand. It is aggregate demand, he argued, that determines the level of employment, with a given population and existing technology. This contrasted with the prevailing economic orthodoxy of the time – classical economic theory – which attributed high unemployment to excessive real wages and high interest rates. According to classical theory, if money wages were reduced, and interest rates were cut, employment would increase because firms would employ more labour – at lower wage rates – and because increased savings would lead to greater investment spending.

In Keynes's *General Theory*, he argues that far from increasing employment, wage cuts, by depressing aggregate demand, reduce it. This is because the level of employment is determined, not by the level of wages, but by the level of aggregate demand. This, in turn, depends on the level of consumption, investment and government expenditure in the economy. He also argues that full employment occurs at a unique level of investment and unless there is some mechanism to ensure the 'correct' level of investment, full employment does not occur spontaneously. The orthodox view, in contrast, was that investment adjusts to the full employment level automatically, via the interest rate. But in Keynes's analysis, there is no automatic adjustment mechanism through the interest rate, so there is no certainty of creating full employment. In Keynes's system, the equality of savings and investment in the economy is achieved, not by changes in the interest rate, but by changes in the level of aggregate demand. It is government intervention in the economy, largely through its fiscal policy, that results in full employment, if current demand, including investment spending, fails to produce it.

Fiscal policy

The Keynesian emphasis in economic management is on creating the economic conditions necessary for achieving four policy objectives. These are:

- full employment;
- price stability;
- balance of payments equilibrium;
- economic growth.

The aim underpinning all Keynesian policy is that of achieving the level of aggregate demand commensurate with full employment. The policy instruments used by government for this purpose are largely fiscal (Donaldson and Farquhar 1988). This means that when unemployment is rising, due to falls in consumption or in investment spending, fiscal policy is used to inject spending power into the economy by cutting taxes and/or raising public expenditure. The latter is achieved by increasing the public sector borrowing requirement (PSBR), which is the amount by which government revenue falls short of government expenditure in a given expenditure cycle. These 'countercyclical' fiscal measures aim to increase aggregate demand and, in consequence, lead to a higher demand for labour by employers, thus reducing unemployment.

One problem of full employment is that it results in increased collective bargaining power by the trade unions in the labour market (Robinson 1937). In the private sector, unless the unions restrain their wage bargaining claims, or employers resist them, this leads to rising money wages, not necessarily matched by rises in labour productivity or falls in unit labour costs. These wage rises contribute to a wages–prices spiral by inducing: companies which have conceded 'unearned' wage increases to their workforces to raise the prices of their products in 'soft' product markets; other bargaining groups to seek higher wages for themselves in 'soft' labour markets; and these companies, in turn, to pass on the cost of their wage increases to their customers.

In the public sector, wage rises achieved in private industry act as benchmarks for trade union negotiators. This puts pressure on public sector employers to provide comparable wage levels to those in the corporate sector. These can only come out of increases in productivity, taxes or the PSBR. Tax increases are unpopular with government and the electorate; productivity increases may be resisted by the unions and their members; and the effects of increases in public borrowing are likely to be inflationary, especially where financing the PSBR takes the form of injecting new currency into circulation from the banking sector. Further, public sector borrowing raises interest rates through the increased sales of bonds, thus making borrowing by companies more expensive, with possible adverse effects on private investment.

Governments using Keynesian demand management techniques have two possible policy prescriptions to deal with these economic pressures. One is to deflate the economy through fiscal measures. This is done by cutting back purchasing power through raising taxes and/or cutting public spending. This raises unemployment, strengthens the hands of management negotiators at the wage bargaining table and weakens trade union bargaining power. But it can also result in trade union militancy, slow economic growth and reductions in exports. The result is a 'stop-go' economic cycle, only relieved by the reversal of government economic measures when unemployment and economic recession have brought stabilising pressures to bear on prices and the balance of payments. Reflation, in turn, leads to increases in public spending, renewed growth, falling unemployment, rising wages and rising prices and, eventually, to further attempts at deflation and price stability, thus completing the stop-go economic cycle once more.

Incomes policy

The second policy prescription available to governments pursuing Keynesian economic measures is an 'incomes policy', to complement fiscal policy. An incomes policy is where the government attempts to control wage inflation by intervening in the pay bargaining process between employers and trade unions (Panitch 1976). There are three main types of incomes policy:

- pay freezes;
- statutory norms;
- voluntary norms.

Pay freezes have been used for short periods in Britain on a number of occasions since the war. They prohibit the implementation of pay settlements during the period of the freeze. They therefore disrupt established internal pay differentials, and external pay relativities, between those who have implemented a settlement immediately before the freeze and those who have been constrained by it.

A *statutory pay norm* traditionally follows a pay freeze. This further defers the re-establishing of traditional wage differentials and relativities, as well as contributing its own distortions to the wages structure. A statutory pay norm imposes a zero increase, or a small ceiling, on all wage settlements. Settlements in excess of the statutory norm are usually only permitted where one of a number of criteria for exceptional treatment is satisfied. These may include:

- to reward work groups for rises in productivity;
- to help employers respond to labour shortages;
- to help the low paid;
- to restructure distorted pay differentials.

Statutory pay norms are also accompanied by a restriction on the number of pay settlements that any single negotiating group can achieve in a year, normally only one every 12 months. Statutory norms may be specified in terms of either a percentage pay increase or some absolute money sum to be added to existing pay levels. In practice, pay norms come to be regarded as the 'going rate' or target rate of increase for most negotiating groups. Where the sum specified is an absolute money sum, this results in a narrowing of percentage wage differentials. The specification of the norm in absolute terms in a succession of incomes policies in Britain in the early 1970s was a main reason for the substantial erosion of occupational wage relativities at that time.

Voluntary pay norms usually involve specifying a maximum permissible level of wage settlements but, unlike statutory policies, they do not have legal force. For this reason, there is normally less compliance with them. And such policies are only effective where government can exert its own direct control over wage levels, as amongst public sector employees.

Incomes policies have suffered from a number of shortcomings. First, it is suggested that they merely defer rather than cancel large wage increases, because once the policy is off, employee groups try to catch up lost ground. Second, where the norm relates to basic wage rates, earnings drift (or rises in weekly earnings in excess of negotiated wage increases) emerges to compensate for this, causing resentment among those who remain constrained by wage policy norms. Third, incomes policies tend to ossify the wages structure, preventing differential rates of change in money wages amongst competing job sectors. Fourth, there is the issue of policing incomes policies. In Sweden, in the 1960s and 1970s, both management and unions policed incomes policy voluntarily, without government intervention. In Britain, in contrast, state agencies such as the National Board for Prices and Incomes and the Pay Board were used in the late 1960s and early 1970s, but with varying degrees of success.

The new Keynesianism

Since the election of the first Thatcher government in Britain in June 1979, and the first Reagan administration in the USA in November 1980, Keynesian approaches to economic management have been largely rejected by both British and American governments in favour of market liberal policies, associated with monetarism and supply-side economics (see below). The market liberal emphasis in economic policy is on rational individuals pursuing their own self-interest in the market place, with the minimum of government intervention, supported by sound monetary policy to control inflation and by economic measures aimed at improving the ability of producers to supply goods and services to the market, efficiently and cost-effectively. The market liberal critiques of Keynesianism in Britain were fuelled by the onset of 'stagflation', that is rising inflation and rising unemployment, and by the failures of successive incomes policies in the 1960s and 1970s.

The economic experiences of the 1970s and 1980s have modified Keynesian thinking (Shaw 1988). First, few Keynesians would still argue that unemployment always represents a problem solely of effective demand without taking account of the supply side of the economy. Second, few Keynesians would argue today that an overall increase in public spending would continue to reduce the level of unemployment, without conceding that the problem is not just one of demand but also of training in human capital. Keynesians are now aware of the need to target public expenditure, by using it, for example, to produce a better-trained workforce, able to produce goods and services to meet consumer demand in the market place. Third, Keynesians are also aware of regional variations in unemployment, of unemployment in the inner cities and of the long-term unemployed. Structural unemployment, for example, is due to declining industries, economic change, new technology and global competition. All these problems require different solutions.

Keynesians now also accept that increasing aggregate demand in the classical Keynesian way will not deal with the problems of unemployed ethnic minorities, of women entering the labour market when there are no child-care facilities or of the unskilled, lacking training, qualifications and work experience. Unlike some of the market liberals who see these problems in micro-economic terms, Keynesians still see them as of macro concern, justifying a more interventionist approach by government in economic management.

Monetarism and supply-side economics

The mid-1970s marked a watershed in economic policy in Britain, as the decade ended in a break with the postwar settlement of full employment, Keynesianism and the welfare state. The wider economic contexts of the 1970s also provided new challenges for government policy-makers. First, there was the replacement of fixed exchange rates, agreed at Bretton Woods in 1944, by countries floating their own domestic currencies in 1973. Second, the spirit of policy cooperation internationally was replaced by foreign competition and freer markets as countries used the mechanism of interest rates to deal with the dual problems of inflation and balance of payments deficits. Third, rises in oil prices in the early 1970s and late 1970s produced very difficult challenges in economic management for governments of the major industrial countries (Keegan 1984).

Keynesian economics had become associated with interventionism and big government, whilst monetarism and supply-side economics were becoming associated with rational individualism, the market and less government. Mullard (1992: page 248) relates the demise of Keynesianism in Britain 'to the failure of UK governments to establish both a Keynesian economic and political agenda similar to that established elsewhere in Europe.' It is monetarism and supply-side economics that have dominated British and American economic management since the mid-1970s.

Monetarism

Monetary policy is concerned with the measures taken by government to influence the price and supply of money in the economy, through changes in the rate of interest. Clearly, in a free, deregulated money market, government can attempt to control either the supply (quantity) of money in circulation or its price, but not both. The growth in importance of monetary policy as an instrument of macro-economic management in recent years is explained to a large extent by the apparent failure of fiscal policy in the 1970s to resolve the problem of stagflation. Monetarist economists explain this failure in terms of excessive government spending, financed by spiralling budget deficits, not only through borrowing – from the banking and non-banking sectors – but also increasingly as a result of printing new money (Friedman and Schwarz 1963; Friedman 1991). Both of these lead to increases in the money supply in excess of the amount needed to finance the transactions that arise from growth in the physical output of the economy.

Monetarists argue that if the money supply is allowed to grow faster than the economy's output, then firms and households find themselves holding larger money balances than they want. This surplus of money balances is then spent on goods and services, leading to an increase in aggregate demand which it is beyond the capacity of the economy to supply. According to monetarists, this results in a general rise in prices. Additionally, any upward pressure on prices also fuels expectations of future inflation. This results in higher wage demands from trade union negotiators and an ensuing wages–prices inflationary spiral. A related consequence of excessive monetary growth, it is argued, is unemployment, as the competitiveness of firms declines and workers 'price themselves out of jobs'. In monetarist analysis, unemployment will only fall, in the longer term, if the productive efficiency of the economy is increased and inflationary expectations reduced.

The monetarist analysis of the role of money in the economy is based on the quantity theory of money. This relates monetary growth to the rate of inflation. The monetarist prescription is to allow the money supply to grow at a constant rate equal approximately to the growth in national output (the money supply rule). Money supply in excess of this, it is believed, is likely to result in inflation. Monetarists also believe that there are strong links between changes in the money supply and changes in interest rates, when interest rates (or the price of money) are determined in a free market. This is based on the assumption that people's willingness to hold assets in the form of money balances is relatively sensitive to the rate of interest.

Monetarists also argue that the rate of interest is a main determinant of investment decisions. The reasoning is that a fall in interest rates makes some investments profitable, which were previously unprofitable, and therefore aggregate investment should increase. Conversely, when interest rates rise, aggregate investment should fall. Aggregate investment, therefore, is inversely related to the rate of interest.

In the 1980s, monetary policy in Britain reflected the predominance given by governments to the importance of money in determining economic performance. In March 1980, the newly elected government unveiled its anti-inflation policy, with the announcement of its first medium-term financial strategy. Sterling M3 (broadly defined as notes, coins, current and deposit accounts in UK banks, and private sector holdings of sterling bank certificates of deposit) was the targeted money supply. However, achieving the desired growth in M3 in the following years proved problematic (Smith 1987). And in 1987, the Chancellor of the Exchequer quietly announced the end of targeting broad money in the Budget that year. This decision came after more than a decade of unsuccessful targeting. The main reason for this policy failure was the dramatic deregulation of the financial services sector in the 1980s, with the consequent acceleration in the rate of financial innovation in money markets.

With the abolition of exchange controls and with financial deregulation in Britain, governments felt it necessary to fall back on interest rate policy to restrain the rise of credit in the economy. But high interest rates, in turn, proved difficult to sustain over long periods for economic and political reasons. Moreover, from the mid-1980s, interest rates appeared to be set more with a view to influencing the level of the exchange rate rather than with a view to constraining growth in the money stock. Interest rates alone seem to be inadequate in restricting monetary growth sufficiently to squeeze out inflation. As such, their use is viewed as a blunt policy instrument.

It is further argued that monetarist measures to reduce inflationary pressures are likely to have a number of negative consequences for businesses (Ellis and Parker 1990). First, high interest rates, since they attract foreign currency into the economy, and cause the external value of the currency to rise, tend to hit exporters. Similarly, as the value of the domestic currency rises, domestic producers suffer as imported goods gain a price competitive advantage over home produced ones. Second, high interest rates, coupled with a high exchange rate, tend to decrease aggregate demand for domestically produced goods. This is likely to squeeze profits, to increase stocks of unsold goods and to result in more borrowing to finance this. Third, firms may not be able to survive a combination of high interest rates and a high exchange rate, since these have implications for employment, investment and the productive capacity of the economy.

Supply-side economics

Keynesian and monetarist macro-economic policies are both concerned with influencing the level of aggregate demand in the economy. Keynesian economics operates primarily through fiscal measures, whilst monetarist economic policy seeks to control growth in the supply of money and interest rates. The branch of economics which focuses on the micro-economic factors determining aggregate supply is referred to as 'supply-side' economics. The aggregate supply of an economy consists of the amount of total real output that producers are willing and able to produce at various prices in the short term.

Supply-side economists argue that the key to reducing unemployment and inflation lies in improving the ability of the economy to supply goods and services to the market efficiently and cost-effectively. In practice, most supply-siders also favour a sound monetary policy to keep down inflation so as to provide a favourable economic climate for employment and production. Recent supply-side economics differs from earlier attempts at *dirigiste* industrial policy in its emphasis on creating an economic environment conducive to private enterprise and free markets, rather than state planning, government intervention and investment subsidies. Supply-side measures are therefore aimed at creating an economic environment in which there are incentives for individuals to work and for firms to invest, produce goods or services and employ workers. The role of government is not to plan industry and manage demand but to liberalise markets, reduce taxes and public spending and deregulate the labour market.

The primary objective of supply-side policies is to create the economic conditions necessary for fast growth, low inflation and full employment. In essence, supply-side economics is concerned with increasing aggregate supply so that more demand can be accommodated, without inflation. The supply-side measures pursued by Conservative governments in Britain since 1979 have involved:

- reducing taxation and creating incentives to work and invest;
- privatising public industries;
- using the law to restrict union power in the labour market.

Improving economic incentives

After 1979, a number of major tax changes were introduced by governments to act as incentives to work, invest and encourage private enterprise. These are illustrated in Exhibit 14.

The unanswered questions which remain are whether pre-1979 taxes damaged the British economy and whether the changes introduced since then have improved incentives to work, invest and save and encouraged economic growth or not.

Exhibit 14: *Major tax incentives since 1979*

These include:

- reductions in the marginal rate of income tax on high earned incomes and the introduction of a uniform rate of tax on earned and unearned incomes;
- reductions in the basic rate of income tax;
- reductions in the rates of corporation tax on profits;
- increases in income tax thresholds, taking more people out of paying tax;
- introduction of technical changes to taxation legislation, to alleviate the impact of capital gains tax;
- introduction of tax exemptions and other incentives for investment in plant, buildings, enterprise zones, share options and personal equity plans.

Privatisation and deregulation

These measures involve:

- selling off state monopolies to private shareholders;
- introducing market competition into the remaining public services;
- introducing more competition into the private sector.

Underpinning them is the assumption that market competition is the key to higher productivity, wider consumer choice and lower prices. First, a wide range of public industries was sold off and denationalised by government after 1979, starting with Associated British Ports, British Aerospace, Enterprise Oil and Jaguar Cars (Farnham and Horton 1993). Second, more competition was introduced into the Civil Service, local government and the National Health Service (NHS), through compulsory competitive tendering. This requires these sectors to compete with external contractors for the provision of certain services such as cleaning, catering and some professional services. Third, more competition was introduced into the private sector through reforming some monopolies and removing restrictive practices, such as in the Stock Market, legal services and the supply of spectacles.

Improving labour market flexibility

Another supply-side policy goal of Conservative governments in the 1980s and 1990s was to make the labour market more competitive to enable wages to find their free market levels. Governments believed that real wages were not responsive enough to labour market factors and saw the unions as a prime cause of this. They were convinced that unions destroy jobs by raising wages above levels that employers can afford. They therefore enacted measures attempting to curb trade unions and their bargaining power through a series of trade union laws: the Employment Acts of 1980, 1982, 1988, 1989, 1990 and the Trade Union Act 1984. This legislation was subsequently consolidated, with other trade union legislation, as outlined in Figure 5, into the Trade Union and Labour Relations (Consolidation) Act 1992.

Figure 5: *Legal sources of the TULRCA 1992*

Conspiracy and Protection of Property Act 1875
Trade Union Act 1913
Industrial Courts Act 1919
Trade Union (Amalgamations, &c.) Act 1964
Industrial Relations Act 1971
Trade Union and Labour Relations Act 1974
Employment Protection Act 1975
Trade Union and Labour Relations (Amendment) Act 1976
Employment Protection (Consolidation) Act 1978
Employment Act 1980
Employment Act 1982
Trade Union Act 1984
Employment Act 1988
Employment Act 1989
Employment Act 1990

Another of the government's aims was to reduce 'involuntary' unemployment, by making the labour market more flexible and thus enable all those seeking employment to be in work. It was also felt that the structure of employment and levels of social security benefits distorted the labour market. Governments therefore attempted to make the trade-off between receiving social security payments and working less favourable to remaining unemployed. These measures included:

- indexing benefits to retail prices, rather than to earnings;
- reforming social security payments;
- making the obtaining of benefits more difficult for school leavers;
- abolishing earnings-related supplements, based on the previous level of earnings at work.

Legal policy

The state and the law are never neutral in employee relations. The state, through the application of the law, is the ultimate source of authority and power in society and employee relations are not excluded from its influence. Figure 6 illustrates how the law regulates relations between the primary parties to the wage–work bargain (through the contract of employment and employment protection rights), between unions and their members (through the contract of membership and union membership rights) and between the secondary parties (through voluntary collective agreements, trade union rights and the law on trade disputes).

Figure 6: *The law and employee relations*

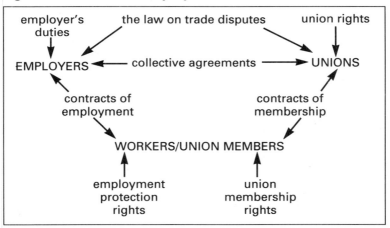

The key to understanding the role of the law in employee relations is identifying its emphasis and impact at particular times. These include:

- whether the law focuses on legal rights or legal freedoms for the parties to employee relations;
- whether it is abstentionist or interventionist in employee relations processes;
- whether it prioritises individual or collective patterns of employee relations;
- whether it affects the balance of bargaining power between employers and employees and between management and unions in the labour market;

- whether it seeks to regulate intra- and inter-union affairs;
- whether the law counterbalances management power by supporting union and employee interests or reinforces this power.

The law is a dynamic and iterative process and its outcomes depend on the legal sources regulating employee relations, the decisions of the courts and whether Parliament enacts Conservative or Labour government policies.

The sources of English employment or labour law are:

- legislation;
- codes of practice;
- the common law.

Legislation or statute law is determined by Parliament, whilst delegated legislation is actioned through statutory instruments, which are normally subject to approval from Parliament or from the CEuC and CoM. Codes of practice, such as those from ACAS, the Health and Safety Commission and the Equal Opportunities Commission, are guidelines to good employment practice, similar to those of the Highway Code for road users. The common law or case law is based on judicial decisions in the courts, which form binding precedents on lower courts. These legal decisions are based on certain legal principles identified by the judges.

The employment contract and statutory employment protection rights

The individual legal relationship between employer and employee, embodied in the contract of employment, is the cornerstone of British employee relations. The contract of employment originated in the common law and the law of 'master' and 'servant' in early capitalism. Today, the contract of employment is still largely regulated by the common law and the rules of contract built up by the judges. In theory, the contract of employment, made orally or in writing, is determined between two equal parties, employer and employee. As a legal relationship, it is one whereby the employer agrees to provide employment, wages and conditions to the individual employee who, in return, provides effort and skills in carrying out the job's tasks, is expected to take reasonable care in fulfilling the duties of employment and accepts the legal constraints of employment, such as not acting in conflict with the commercial interests of the employer.

In practice, the legal equality between an employer, normally a corporate body, and an employee, who is an individual, is a fiction. This is because once employed, employees put themselves under a common law obligation to obey all reasonable and lawful instructions given to them by the employer in carrying out their work tasks. This in reality is an act of subordination. As Kahn-Freund (1977: page 7) comments:

> There can be no employment relationship without a power to command and a duty to obey, that is without this element of subordination in which lawyers rightly see the hallmark of the 'contract of employment'.

An element of cooperation can be built into the employment relationship, and the power to command and the duty to obey can be ameliorated, but the ultimate power of command by management remains. A crucial legal issue is how far the courts interpret the contract in order to preserve the employer's power to command and management's right to manage.

A complementary legal issue is how far statute law, enacted by Parliament, offsets employer and managerial power under common law, by providing a series of workers' or employment protection rights for employees, thus redressing, to some degree at least, the inherent economic, social and common law imbalances in the relationship between individuals and their employer. The majority of these statutory rights are not incorporated into the contract of employment itself. The statutory right not to be unfairly dismissed, for example, is separate from the employee's common law contractual rights to wages, work and cooperation from the employer. And the right not to be unfairly dismissed, along with other statutory employment rights, does not become part of the contract. As Wedderburn (1986: page 5) points out, there are certain common law rights enshrined in the employment contract and enforceable by civil actions in the ordinary courts and, on the other hand, 'a separate, minimum "floor of rights" for individual workers gradually added to over recent years by statutes and enforced largely by civil claims in the industrial tribunals.' Claims for 'wrongful' dismissal – sacking without notice or payment in lieu of notice – used to go to the ordinary courts, whilst claims for 'unfair' dismissal, for unfair reasons and carried out in an unreasonable way, which are based on employment protection legislation, were settled in ITs. Now both types of claim are determined by ITs.

The statutory floor of employment protection rights extends into many areas of employment law, including:

- unfair dismissal;
- redundancy payments;
- discrimination on the grounds of gender, ethnic origin and nationality;
- union membership;
- maternity pay and maternity leave;
- minimum periods of notice;
- security of earnings.

This floor of legal rights was created in Parliament by governments sympathetic to the view that there should be a basic level of employment protection, below which no employee should fall. It was a level, moreover, over and above which trade unions could negotiate superior conditions through collective bargaining.

In the 1960s and 1970s, statute law sought to weaken employer power and strengthen that of employees by extending the floor of employment protection rights, underpinned by a system of ITs with legal remedies for those claiming that their rights had been infringed by law-breaking employers. Since the 1980s, although the case must not be overstated, the law has tended to strengthen employer power and to weaken the legal position of employees by making adjustments to the statutory floor of employment protection rights. Both unfair dismissal and maternity rights were restricted, especially for workers in small businesses. In 1980, the qualifying period for unfair dismissal claims by employees was increased from six months' continuous service to one year. In 1985, it was further extended to two years for newly appointed employees. Guarantee payments in cases of short-time working were reduced, limitations were placed on social security payments – by phasing out earnings-related benefits – and deductions were made from the supplementary benefit payments to families of striking workers. This is because governments since 1979 have believed in using market forces and competition to contain inflation and achieve prosperity, with changes in employment law mirroring these economic policy changes.

It may be inferred, therefore, that the content of the contract of employment has changed significantly since the 1970s, largely because of the new framework of statutory rights provided for employees by Parliament. These rights complement rather than replace the common law of the contract. As Napier (1986) argues, the role of the common law is two-fold. First, it acts as a legal backcloth and provides a set of rules in those situations unregulated by specific statutory measures or where the legal remedies which exist are inadequate or restricted in their application. Second, it plays a crucial role in the operation of the statutory floor of employment rights themselves. This is because Parliament has used certain contractual terms and concepts in defining the statutory rights of employees in the workplace.

Statutory union membership rights

A statutory floor of rights for trade union members has been enacted and extended in recent years. Some of these statutory rights, enacted under Labour governments, provide a set of positive rights for individuals to associate into unions, to be active within them and not to be dismissed on the grounds of union membership or for taking part in trade union activities. Others, enacted by Conservative governments since the 1980s, provide negative rights to abstain from union membership, or the right to dissociate. And a third set, also enacted since the 1980s, provides positive rights for union members to participate in or restrain union decision-making on specific issues (see Chapter 3).

The right to associate

Traditionally, there was no legal right for individuals to join trade unions in Britain, unlike in most other countries in Western Europe. This was because of the philosophy of legal abstentionism or voluntarism in British employee relations. This specifically excluded the law from intervening in relations between employers and unions, in trade disputes and in supporting or preventing individuals joining trade unions.

The case for legal protection of the positive right to associate was put by the Donovan Commission (1968), largely in terms of the reform and extension of collective bargaining. If, as Donovan concluded, voluntary collective bargaining was the best method of conducting employee relations, then a necessary condition for this was effective trade union organisation amongst the workforce. The

Commission therefore recommended that any condition in a contract of employment prohibiting union membership should be void in law and that dismissal for union membership should be deemed to be unfair. After the repeal of the Industrial Relations Act 1971, by the Trade Union and Labour Relations Act 1974, statutory rights to time off work for trade union lay officers and safety representatives were established, as well as the rights not to be dismissed, or subject to action short of dismissal, because of union membership or union activity.

The right to dissociate

The right to dissociate from union membership is related in part to opposition to the practice of the closed shop. A closed shop is any agreement or arrangement between an employer and union(s) which requires employees to be a union member as a condition of employment. Pre-entry closed shops limit jobs to those who are members of a specified trade union, whilst post-entry closed shops require those recruited by an employer to join an approved, recognised union within a set period after starting employment.

In the Employment Act (EA) 1980, protections were given for the first time to individuals against dismissal for non-union membership in a closed shop in the case of strongly held personal convictions. This derived from the government's objections to the closed shop in principle. As the Department of Employment (1981: page 66) stated:

> The Government's view of the closed shop is clear: it is opposed to the principles underlying it. That people should be required to join a union as a condition of getting or holding a job runs contrary to the general traditions of personal liberty in this country. It is acceptable for a union to seek to increase its membership by voluntary means. What is objectionable, however, is to enforce membership by means of a closed shop as a condition of employment.

Subsequent legislation first increased the protection and compensation of employees if they were dismissed because of a closed shop, under the EA 1982. The EA 1988 then made post-entry closed shops unenforceable, removed trade union immunity from any industrial action taken to enforce a closed shop and provided legal protection against dismissal for non-union membership, by making dismissal or discrimination against employees refusing to join a union automatically unfair.

Under the EA 1990, pre-entry closed shops became void in law, thus effectively making all forms of closed shop arrangement unlawful.

Another example of the right to dissociate was incorporated in the EA 1988. The TULRCA 1992 now provides protection for union members against what the law describes as 'unjustifiable discipline' by their unions. This upholds the right of individual trade members not to participate in lawful trade dispute, even where the action has previously been legitimised in a properly conducted industrial action ballot, and not to be disciplined by their union for failing to take part in the industrial action with which they disagree.

Intra-union rights

Membership participation in the internal affairs of trade unions has traditionally been provided under the union rule book and, where the rule book was infringed, there was the right to seek its enforcement through the courts. In the 1980s, governments increasingly held the view that the law needed to be changed in order to democratise the trade unions and make them more accountable to their members. A government green paper (Department of Employment 1983: page 37) stated that there was much public concern about the need for trade unions to become more democratic and more responsive to the wishes of their members and that 'society, including individual trade unionists themselves, is entitled to ensure that union power is exercised more responsibly, more accountably and more in accordance with the views of their members.'

It was this analysis which led to the passing of the TUA 1984. Its provisions, now incorporated in the TULRCA 1992, are:

- the right for union members to have the opportunity to participate in regular ballots to decide whether or not their union should undertake political activity, through union political funds and the political levy, at least once every 10 years;
- the right for trade union members to elect all voting members of their union's executive by secret ballot, at least once every five years;
- the right to participate in secret ballots before a union takes organised industrial action against an employer.

A further green paper (Department of Employment 1987: page 2) went on to argue that there was more to be done, stating:

It is the view of the Government that, having embarked on the process of giving proper and effective rights to union members, it should ensure that those rights are fully developed so that they provide the ordinary member with the effective protection that he or she is entitled to enjoy in a free society.

Accordingly, the EA 1988, also now incorporated in the TULRCA 1992, extended the rights of union members:

- to elect all the principal union officers by secret postal ballot;
- to take part in political fund review ballots by secret postal ballot;
- to restrain their union from calling on them to take part in industrial action not supported by a properly conducted secret ballot;
- not to be unjustifiably disciplined by their union;
- to inspect their union's accounting records.

The office of the CRTUM, created by the 1988 Act, has the power to support individual union members, by giving them advice and paying their costs, when making complaints against their union.

The law and trade disputes

Whether the issues are substantive or procedural in nature, employees who are organised into trade unions are likely to take collective industrial action or industrial sanctions against their employer when alternative forms of conflict resolution, such as collective bargaining, conciliation or arbitration, have failed to resolve the differences between the parties. Employee industrial action involves a range of possible activities taken unilaterally by unions and their members against an employer. These include working to rule, banning overtime and stoppages of work, with concomitant legal implications (see Chapters 1, 3 and 7).

Breach of contract

A central legal issue arising from most forms of industrial action taken by employees is that they commonly breach their contracts of employment, by violating the employee's common law obligation to work for the employer under the terms of the contract. But the law is complex in this respect and there are areas of legal uncertainty. Where, for example, working to rule focuses on working strictly in accordance with the terms of the contract of employment, this is not normally taken to be a breach of the contract. Where working to rule refers to the employer's works rules, this too is unlikely to involve a breach of contract in the first instance, since this is within the implied terms of individual contracts of employment. Where overtime is not normally a contractual requirement, a union ban on overtime would also not normally be taken to be a breach of contract by individual employees.

Where, however, an employer unilaterally changes the works rules, employees would normally be expected to conform with them, in all circumstances, since they become incorporated into individual contracts of employment as implied terms. Where working to rule refers to the union rule book, this too is likely to be in breach of contract, since the terms of the contract are likely to be ignored by employees 'working to rule' in this manner. Similarly, where overtime is contractually required, an overtime ban would be in breach of contract. It is in the cases of stoppages of work that the law is most clearcut, since such actions are obviously in breach of the employee's common law obligation to work for the employer and not to impede the employer's business.

All forms of industrial action have profound legal implications for individual employees, since the judges tend to see any industrial action as a challenge to the legitimate authority of the employer to employ labour and to deploy it, as embodied in the contract of employment. The employer's capacity to coerce through its economic power is not seen as problematic by the courts but as a legitimate property right. As outlined above, under common law, all forms of industrial action are treated in essentially the same way, as breaches of contract by the employee.

This means, first, that breach of contract may provide one of the ingredients of the economic torts (see below) for which trade unions may be liable. Second, it may entitle the employer to take disciplinary action against individual employees. Third, although continuity of employment is not broken by employees taking strike action, any such period does not count towards continuous service for the purposes of claiming employment protection rights.

Economic torts

A second legal issue arising from industrial sanctions taken by unions and their members against employers is that of 'economic torts'. Because the economic interests of employers and other organisations are damaged by collective industrial action, certain torts (civil law 'wrongs') may be committed in the process of conducting strikes, overtime bans and work to rules. The most common economic tort is that of inducing breach of contract.

The inducement may be direct or indirect. Direct inducement takes place when an outsider to the contract persuades one of the contracting parties to break the contract. The necessary elements of the tort are that the inducer must act intentionally, there must be evidence of inducement and the inducer must know or have the means of knowing of the existence of the contract, although that party need not know its actual terms. An example of direct inducement would be if a union official were to persuade union members to go slow or to refuse to work mandatory overtime. The official would then have induced a breach of the employment contract. The employer could obtain an injunction to end or prevent the inducement and/or obtain damages relating to any commercial loss it has suffered as a result of the breach of contract. The employer could sue both the official and the union itself.

Indirect inducement is more complicated. This occurs whenever a person (A) persuades a second person (B) to act unlawfully, with the intention of inducing a third person (C) to break a contract entered into with a fourth person (D). Because the inducement is indirect there is a further key requirement that the inducement must be obtained by unlawful means. For example, a union official (A) may persuade members (B) to break their employment contract with their employer (C), to prevent it supplying goods under a commercial contract with (D). The means of achieving the intended breach between (C) and (D) involves inducing a breach of the employment contract between (B) and (C) – in other words, the commission of an unlawful act. All the key requirements are present, and the fourth party (D) may bring an action for damages and/or seek an injunction against both the official and the union.

The tort of intimidation differs from inducing breach of contract in that it is concerned with threats rather than action itself. Intimidation occurs whenever there is a threat to commit unlawful action. Unlawful has been widely defined and includes, as well as criminal acts, tortious acts and breaches of contract. So a threat by a union official that members will strike in breach of contract unless wages are increased would amount to intimidation. As with inducing breach, there may be direct or indirect intimidation. Both intimidation and inducement can occur in the same dispute. First there may be a threat of unlawful action such as strike (intimidation) followed by the strike action itself (inducement).

Legal immunities

A third legal issue arising from industrial action is the common law liabilities of those organising or participating in industrial action and the statutory protections, or legal immunities, provided during stoppages of work and other sanctions. Unlike in other Western European countries, there is no legal right for workers or their unions to take industrial action in Britain. The situation differs in countries like France, for example, where the Constitution guarantees the individual worker the right to strike, and in Germany, where strikes are lawful, provided that they are in furtherance of improvements in working conditions and do not break a collective agreement (Department of Employment 1981). This means that in these countries workers and their unions are legally authorised, through systems of positive legal rights, to take industrial action against employers, subject to certain statutory conditions and qualifications.

In Britain, the law has taken a quite different path from that in other countries (Wedderburn 1986). Here the law governing industrial action and trade disputes starts with the common law. It is this which provides the basic legal principles which underlie subsequent statute law. The statutes governing strikes and other forms of industrial action have defined a system of 'legal immunities'. These protect those organising and taking part in industrial action from the civil (and possible criminal) liability arising from the imposition of industrial sanctions on employers. Without legal immunities, most industrial action would be illegal and trade unions, their officials and their members would be liable to civil actions for damages, and even criminal prosecution, every time they were involved in a strike, unless due notice, under the terms of the contract of employment, were given by the employees to the employer.

Legal immunities do not abolish civil wrongs (or 'torts'), or criminal liability, but they suspend liability in the circumstances of a trade dispute. Where these immunities are reduced, the common law liabilities are restored. Where they are extended, the common law liabilities relapse. If there were no immunities, then unions and individuals would be at risk of legal action by employers every time they organised a strike. The history of trade union law in Britain over the past 20 years reflects the differing views of Labour and Conservative governments about the role and scope of immunities in regulating industrial conflict. In general, Labour governments have strengthened immunities and Conservative ones reduced them.

To be protected in law, industrial action by unions and their members must: (1) fall within the legal definition of a 'trade dispute'; and (2) take place 'in contemplation of furtherance of a trade dispute' – the so called 'golden formula'. It is the golden formula which provides the basis for legal immunities. A trade dispute is now defined in law by Section 218 of the TULRCA 1992 as any dispute between 'workers and their employer' which relates 'wholly or mainly to':

- terms and conditions of employment;
- engagement or non-engagement of workers or termination or suspension of employment;
- allocation of work or the duties of employment;
- matters of discipline;
- membership or non-membership of a trade union;
- facilities for trade union officials;
- machinery for negotiation, consultation or other procedures, including trade union recognition.

In contrast to earlier legislation, secondary disputes (between workers and employers other than their own), inter-union disputes and political disputes are no longer incorporated within the statutory definition outlined above.

Legal immunities, as provided by Section 219 of the TULRCA 1992, were incrementally limited during the 1980s by amendments to the law through the Employment Act 1980, 1982, 1988, 1990 and the Trade Union Act 1984. In outline, immunity in law is now only provided where:

- the industrial action is between an employer and their direct

employees, with all secondary or sympathy action being unlawful;
- a properly conducted industrial action ballot has been conducted by the union, authorising or endorsing the action; and
- peaceful picketing is limited to the workers' own place of work.

Immunity is specifically removed where industrial action is taken to impose or enforce a closed shop or where the action is unofficial and not repudiated, in writing, by the union. Where the 'golden formula' does not apply, it is relatively easy for an employer to show that one of the economic torts is being committed and to obtain an interlocutory injunction on that basis. Moreover, since the EA 1982, trade unions are now treated as ordinary persons. This means that they can be sued if responsible for unlawful industrial action (see Chapters 7 and 11).

The social dimension of the single European market

In recent years, the single market programme of the EC has led to the expansion of a social dimension within the Community. This includes employment-related policies and objectives relating to improved living conditions in general. This commitment to social progress is not new in Western European politics. It has been a feature of national and supra-national politics in EC member states for many years. Issues such as comprehensive social security schemes, employee protection, job security and paid leave from work have been a much more important feature of Western European states than in the USA and Japan.

Another feature of Western Europe is the protection given to individual employees' rights to organise and take part in industrial action and the legal regulation of employee relations. In addition, politics in Western Europe has had a strong corporatist dimension, with the 'social partners' – employers and unions – having a formalised consultative role in national policy-making. According to one student of Europe, 'social policy in the widest sense is very much a hallmark of politics in Western Europe, regardless of country or government. Social policy is indeed a European invention' (Holmstedt 1991: page 39).

Employment and social policy

EC policies on employment and social issues do not form a coherent or comprehensive programme but a patchwork of different policy areas. They include legislation, action programmes and funding and cover such diverse subjects as health and safety, equal opportunities and training. The rationale for EC legislation in the field of employment is three-fold. The first is to harmonise provisions in member states to produce a 'level playing-field' for enterprise. The second is to facilitate freedom of movement of people within the EC and this requires some regulation and protection of workers' rights. A third reason is the need to create a community that is relevant to the people of Europe as well as to its entrepreneurs and business sector.

In the area of health and safety, for example, which is already covered by extensive legislation, the CEuC is proposing a long list of future legislation. In other areas, in contrast, such as trade union rights and collective agreements, recommendations rather than legislation are proposed and the CEuC is taking no coordinated action but leaving matters to governments, without seeking to enforce minimum safeguards.

This lack of cohesion in EC policies on employment and social policy is a consequence of the EC political institutions not being the machinery of an integrated, nation state, nor even of a federal one, but having very circumscribed political powers. The EC institutions are limited to framework legislation and pilot projects, without the powers of command that national, regional or local administrations have. Political power is still largely the prerogative of national governments. Despite the political difficulties attached to harmonising provisions in the area of labour law and employee relations, however, the CEuC has been active in developing draft legislation in this field for many years.

The roots of the social dimension of the EC run deep. The Treaty of Rome stated a commitment to common action on economic and social progress, as did the European Coal and Steel Community, which had extensive powers to fund and promote improvements in the working and living conditions of coal and steel workers. The European Economic Treaty contains a number of Articles authorising Community institutions to take action in various areas of social policy. The European Social Fund provides funding for retraining or settlement allowances for workers threatened by loss of employment. The Social Action Programme of 1974 laid the foundation for all future action in the social sphere for two decades. Many of the new proposals for legislation and action in this area which are being launched, as part of the single market programme, have their roots in the 1974 Action Programme (see below).

The single market programme has brought a new momentum to the development of the EC's social policy. Its roots lie in the belief that achieving support for a single market from both sides of industry, and all major political parties, requires parallel efforts in the social field. The single market programme includes measures to complete the traditional aims of Community legislation, such as full freedom of movement for people. It also commits member states to encourage improvements in social policy. And there is a general commitment to strengthen the EC's economic and social cohesion, especially by reducing disparities between the various regions and the backwardness of the least favoured regions. Freedom of movement, health and safety, and reform of the structural funds are included in the Single European Act 1987, as are various programmes to combat unemployment and to emphasise the need for social progress towards a 'people's Europe'.

The European Community Charter of Fundamental Social Rights of Workers

Discussion about the social dimension of the single European market has led to the adoption of the Social Charter by the various member states, except the UK (see Chapter 3). The Charter is intended as a bill of rights for European citizens in the social sphere, although it is no more than a series of recommendations on minimum standards. What it provides, in effect, is a collection of targets for Community action and minimum standards for member states to achieve.

The CEuC action programme on the Social Charter provides the framework for action in the employment and social fields for the next decade. The Commission is, for example, proposing to make the European labour market operate more smoothly. It is proposing action on employment contracts, collective redundancies and the regulation of working time. It wants action on equitable wages, minimum standards for national social security systems and protection for pregnant women at work. The provisions on health and safety at work contain the largest number of proposals, with the intention of establishing a safety, hygiene and health agency. Although the CEuC is not proposing any initiatives under the controversial chapter on freedom of association and collective bargaining, it does intend taking initiatives on employee consultation and participation.

The Social Charter proclaims the major principles underlying the following declared rights of individuals in the EC. In outline, these rights can be summarised as follows (Commission of the European Communities 1990):

- *Freedom of movement.* Every worker shall have the right to freedom of movement throughout the EC and to engage in any occupation or profession in accordance with the principles of equal treatment and access.
- *Employment and remuneration.* Every worker shall be free to choose their occupation and all employment shall be fairly remunerated, with workers having a wage sufficient to enable them and their families to have a decent standard of living.
- *Improvement of living and working conditions.* This principle states that the completion of the internal market must lead to an improvement in the living and working conditions of workers in the EC. Workers shall have a right to a weekly rest period and to paid annual leave. The conditions of employment of every worker shall be stipulated in laws, a collective agreement or a contract of employment, according to the arrangements applying in each country.
- *Social protection.* Every worker shall have a right to adequate social protection and shall enjoy an adequate level of social security benefits. Persons unable to enter the labour market must be able to receive sufficient resources in keeping with their circumstances.
- *Freedom of association and collective bargaining.* Employers and workers shall have the right to associate and their organisations shall have the right to negotiate and conclude collective agreements together. The dialogue between the two sides at European level must be developed. There shall be a right to strike and the utilisation of conciliation, mediation and arbitration machinery should be encouraged.
- *Vocational training.* All workers must be able to have access to vocational training and to benefit from it throughout their working lives. There should be leave for training purposes to improve skills or to acquire new skills.
- *Equal treatment for women and men.* Equal treatment must be assured and equal treatment for women and men must be developed. Equality of access should be provided to employment, remuneration, working conditions, social protection, education, vocational training and career development.

- *Information, consultation and participation of workers.* These principles must be developed along appropriate lines and shall apply especially in companies operating in two or more member states. These processes should be implemented particularly during: technological change; corporate restructuring; collective redundancies; and when transfrontier workers are affected.
- *Health protection and safety at the workplace.* Every worker must enjoy satisfactory health and safety conditions in the working environment. The need for training, information, consultation and the participation of workers in this area is stressed.
- *Protection of children and adolescents.* The minimum age of employment must be no lower than the minimum school leaving age. The duration of work must be limited, night work must be prohibited and initial vocational training must be an entitlement.
- *Elderly persons.* All retired workers must be able to enjoy resources affording them a decent standard of living. They must also be entitled to sufficient medical and social assistance.
- *Disabled persons.* The disabled must be entitled to additional concrete measures aimed at improving their social and professional integration.

The Social Action Programme

The Social Action Programme is a set of legal proposals from the CEuC to provide ways of enforcing the Social Charter's principles. Most of the major proposals are for legal instruments which, once adopted, are applicable to all member states. Other proposals are for studies or communications which may then lead to legislative proposals. The main proposals are illustrated in Exhibit 15.

Exhibit 15: *Main proposals of the Social Action Programme*

These are:

- a directive on special employment relationships involving part-time and temporary work;
- a directive on working time laying down certain minimum requirements about rest periods, holidays, night work, weekend work and systematic overtime;
- a revision of the 1975 Directive on collective redundancies;
- a directive on the protection of pregnant women and women who have recently given birth;

- a third equal opportunities programme;
- a directive on the protection of young people at work;
- a recommendation on financial participation of workers;
- a directive on the establishment of European company councils for informing and consulting with workers in European-scale enterprises;
- an instrument on access to vocational training;
- a range of directives on health and safety issues;
- an opinion on the criteria for an equitable wage;
- a communication on the development of collective bargaining, including collective agreements at European level.

Assignments

(a) Consider the situation where unemployment has risen to three million and inflation to 4 per cent. What would be a Keynesian economic response to this and how would this affect wage bargaining in your organisation? What would be a supply-side economic response to this situation and how would this affect wage bargaining in your organisation?

(b) Examine the reasons for introducing incomes policies, the forms they take and the conditions necessary for them to be effective. Compare and contrast how (1) a named public sector organisation might respond to a wages freeze; (2) a multi-plant manufacturing company negotiating with trade unions might respond; and (3) a small non-union company with 25 employees might respond. Provide a rationale for your answer in each case.

(c) Present a report summarising what 'unfair dismissal' is and the legal remedies available to those whose claim for unfair dismissal is upheld by an industrial tribunal.

(d) Union membership agreements are now unlawful. What action would you take, as a newly recruited personnel manager, if the chief executive of your company asked you to continue enforcing, on behalf of the company, an informal, closed shop arrangement with the unions?

(e) Read Simpson (1986: pages 161–92) and outline the development of trade union immunities in Britain and how the law on immunities has changed since 1980.

(f) What are the cases for and against employers supporting the Social Charter?

References

COMMISSION OF THE EUROPEAN COMMUNITIES 1990. *The Community Charter of Fundamental Social Rights for Workers*. Brussels: CEuC.

DEPARTMENT OF EMPLOYMENT 1981. *Trade Union Immunities*. London: HMSO.

DEPARTMENT OF EMPLOYMENT 1983. *Democracy in Trade Unions*. London: HMSO.

DEPARTMENT OF EMPLOYMENT 1987. *Trade Unions and Their Members*. London: HMSO.

DONALDSON, P. and FARQUHAR, J. 1988. *Understanding the British Economy*. Harmondsworth: Penguin.

DONOVAN, Lord 1986. *Royal Commission on Trade Unions and Employers' Associations 1965–1968: Report*. London: HMSO.

ELLIS, J. and PARKER, D. 1990. *The Essence of the Economy*. Hemel Hempstead: Prentice Hall.

FARNHAM, D. and HORTON, S. (eds) 1993. *Managing the New Public Services*. Basingstoke: Macmillan.

FRIEDMAN, M. 1991. *Monetarist Economics*. Oxford: Blackwell.

FRIEDMAN, M. and SCHWARTZ, A . 1963. *A Monetary History of the United States*. Princeton: Princeton University Press.

HOLMSTEDT, M. 1991. *Employment Policy*. London: Routledge in Association with the University of Bradford.

KAHN-FREUND, O. 1977. *Labour and the Law*. London: Stevens.

KEEGAN, W. 1984. *Mrs Thatcher's Economic Experiment*. Harmondsworth: Penguin.

KEYNES, J. M. 1936. *The General Theory of Employment, Interest and Money*. London: Macmillan.

MULLARD, M. 1992. *Understanding Economic Policy*. London: Routledge.

NAPIER, B. 1986. 'The contract of employment'. In Lewis, R. (ed.) *Labour Law in Britain*. Oxford: Blackwell.

PANITCH, L. 1976. *Social Democracy and Industrial Militancy: The Labour Party, the Trades Union and Incomes Policy 1945–74*. Cambridge: Cambridge University Press.

ROBINSON, J. 1937. *Essays in the Theory of Employment*. London: Macmillan.

SHAW, G. 1988. *Keynesian Economics: the Permanent Revolution*. Aldershot: Elgar.

SMITH, D. 1987. *The Rise and Fall of Monetarism*. Harmondsworth: Penguin.

WEDDERBURN, Lord 1986. *The Worker and the Law*. Harmondsworth: Penguin.

Chapter 5

Negotiation, grievances, discipline and redundancy

Marjorie Corbridge and Stephen Pilbeam

There are a number of basic personnel management activities that everyone managing employee relations becomes involved in at some time or other. Employees raise complaints and grievances with their managers, arising from their jobs, terms and conditions or the management decisions affecting them, and these need to be resolved. This necessitates managers using relevant grievance procedures, interview skills and appropriate judgement to ensure that such issues are dealt with fairly, quickly and efficiently. Similarly, managers who are concerned about the job performance, behaviour or effectiveness of their staff may take disciplinary action against them and this might even result in terminating their employment contract and dismissing them. Disciplinary action by managers has legal and procedural implications and it also necessitates appropriate interpersonal and professional skills on their part. Procedures need to be applied, legal requirements to be adhered to and management competency to be demonstrated. Where organisations are being restructured, skill mixes changed or market demand for a product – or citizen need for a service – falls, job losses can occur and a redundancy programme has to be implemented and managed.

It is the basic employee relations issues and activities associated with the handling of grievances, dealing with discipline and managing of redundancy that are addressed in this chapter. The essential principles underpinning negotiating activity are also examined briefly, because negotiating is something that all managers are involved in, not just personnel people. A more detailed analysis and examination of formal collective bargaining, however, is provided in Chapter 9.

The basics of negotiation

Negotiation is a process whereby two or more interested groups seek to

136

reconcile their differences through attempts to persuade the other group to move from their initial position, with the overall aim of reaching an agreement. Implicit in this process is an intention and a willingness to compromise in pursuit of an agreement which, although it may be less than ideal, is acceptable to all the groups involved. The precise definition of acceptability is subject to many influences and the contingencies of the negotiating situation, not least of which is the balance of bargaining power between the negotiating groups.

Negotiations pervade organisational life and essential negotiating skills developed within an employee relations framework are transferable to other areas of management. More flexible organisational structures, often with a reduced emphasis on hierarchical relationships, necessitate effective negotiation between teams, groups, and individuals on an intra-organisational basis. This is also reflected in the public sector where the recent development of purchaser and provider relationships, both internal and external, heightens demand for effective negotiation skills. The basis of any negotiating cycle therefore, whether formal or informal, is to reconcile conflicting viewpoints through concessions, compromise and exchanges between the parties involved. A useful framework to analyse the negotiation process is to identify three distinctive and sequential elements within it: preparation, negotiation and implementation. Negotiation also incorporates certain skills such as tactical adjustment, listening skills and some basic competences.

Preparing for negotiation

Thorough and careful preparation is arguably the key to successful and effective negotiation. The definition of clear objectives is essential because it enables each team to distinguish between the important and the less significant issues it wishes to address and it serves to clarify and synchronise the expectations of negotiators. A by-product of good planning is the development of effective working relationships and cohesion within the negotiation team.

A starting point in negotiation is the identification, clarification and consideration of the issues involved. Until a common understanding is achieved, it is inappropriate to make any strategic or tactical decisions. This exploration of the issues needs to be accompanied by information gathering activity. This activity is largely self-explanatory but involves accessing appropriate information sources. These include any facts surrounding the issue, employer information pertinent to the negotiation, including statistical material and company rules, and agreements. It also includes external information, for example, market rates in the case of pay negotiations and relevant legislation. There needs to be an assessment of who should be involved in the negotiations and consideration is also given to the size of the negotiating team. The need for particular skills, knowledge and expertise in relation to the particular negotiation will indicate the possible composition of the negotiating team.

The allocation of roles within the negotiating team is of critical importance and is perhaps best addressed by answering the following questions. Who is to be the leader? Where will the locus of decision-making lie? What control mechanisms are necessary to ensure a co-ordinated approach? Should a lead negotiator, observer and note-takers be allocated in advance? Who will have the authority to call adjournments? In essence, the decisions revolve around creating a cohesive team with members who are able to present a united front, or at least avoid overt disagreement in dealing with the other side. The negotiation process starts in the preparation stage because one of its purposes is to enable intra-group negotiation to take place before the actual negotiations with the other interest group or party. The achievement of intra-group consensus gives confidence to the negotiating team. It also reduces the possibility of exposing the team's weaknesses, or any apparent dissonance within it, which might have a negative impact on its negotiating position, during the negotiations.

In assessing the potential strength of the other side, negotiators need to take account of the skills, experience and expertise of the other team. In parallel with this, an important judgement to make is the level of commitment to the issue likely to be exhibited by the other side, coupled with its significance for them. The validity and logic of their arguments needs to be assessed and the power balance, as defined by the ability to impose unilateral action or take sanctions against the other side, is crucial. All these factors contribute to identifying the comparative strengths of negotiating positions and are prerequisites to the determination of strategy and tactics. The negotiating team also needs to focus upon the outcomes it seeks in relation to its pre-determined objectives. This process is facilitated by identifying the team's optimum and minimum acceptable outcomes. These polar points can be refined by considering what the team *would like* to achieve, what it *intends* to achieve, and what it *must* achieve (Kennedy *et al.* 1984). Some writers describe these as the ideal settlement point, realistic settlement point and fall back position (Atkinson 1980). Whatever analytical tool is used, the principle remains the same: defining the negotiating parameters as a focal point for the negotiating team. These parameters allow some flexibility, provide a framework for negotiating and give direction to the negotiation activity. Such decisions, or more accurately expectations, are not, of course, disclosed to the other side. But they are the subject of probing and speculation by the other party during the negotiation process.

It is useful to try to perceive and evaluate your side's expectations from the standpoint of the other side. Thus an associated aspect of the preparation element is to try and estimate and anticipate the parameters and expectations of the other group. A natural progression is to seek to predict the responses and arguments likely to occur and to plan appropriate counter-responses and counter-arguments. This predictive process can be over-arched with an assessment about the potential strategies available to the other side.

Decisions have to be made about the nature of the negotiations. Some are problem centred or integrative. Others are competitive or distributive. Which predominates, however, is determined largely by the negotiation issue (Walton and McKersie 1965). Integrative negotiation exists where the parties believe that cooperation and a problem-solving approach will produce a mutually acceptable outcome. The negotiations are more likely to be characterised by openness and a degree of trust between the parties. It is potentially a 'win/win' situation. In contrast, distributive negotiation is more likely to be perceived as a 'win/lose' situation because of the incompatibility of negotiation objectives between the parties and the behaviour within the negotiations which is likely to be influenced by this conflict perspective. There are rarely pure forms of either integrative or distributive negotiations. A more realistic strategy is to attempt to define the likely mix and develop an awareness of the oscillation and fluctuation during the negotiation process. Within these limits, there is advantage in appreciating that the purpose of negotiating is mutual benefit rather than the scoring of points by one side at the expense of the other. At this stage, it is useful to consider the implications of a failure to agree within the negotiation process together with what action may become necessary if this happens.

Whilst detailed preparation is vital, this should not predispose the negotiating team to developing a rigid position. Flexibility and the ability to manoeuvre within the negotiating process are essential and desirable characteristics. A further caveat is that the attitudes, personalities and relationships of the negotiators are likely to influence the negotiations independently of the strength of argument. Additionally, within each negotiating team the power, influence and accountability of the participants in relation to each other create an internal dynamic which should not be discounted. These factors suggest that the negotiation process should be viewed through an interactive and behavioural, rather than a purely mechanical, frame of reference.

Negotiating

An awareness of what can be described as the negotiating cycle offers valuable insights to the manager. This cycle involves a number of phases which, although initially sequential, often oscillate in order to reflect the ebb and flow of the negotiations which are also likely to be punctuated by adjournments and side meetings. The three phases can be described as arguing, proposing, and exchanging and agreeing (see Chapter 9).

Arguing

This formative phase begins with the opening statements and supportive arguments from the negotiating parties. The party presenting first has considerable influence in setting the tone of the negotiations. The initial negotiating positions are established by the rejection of demands and demonstrations of inflexibility. This phase is highly ritualistic, testing and challenging, but affords an opportunity to test the commitment and to identify the tactics of the other side.

Proposing

Having established their relative positions, the negotiators enter an exploratory phase in which each side seeks to discover some potential for flexibility and movement away from the other side's initial statements. This incorporates offers and concessions of a highly conditional nature. It is characterised by probing and encouraging the other side to reveal their real expectations whilst concealing your own. Suggestions are made rather than definitive proposals and there is a summarising of positions, coupled with attempts to move forward to find common ground between the two sides. It is a delicate phase with progress dependent upon allowing the other side to concede certain points without necessarily losing face. Concession may be implicit and disguised by the appearance of not having given way. Triumphalism is to be avoided as it may set back the negotiations to the arguing phase. A patronising approach is also likely to have negative consequences.

Emotional language can undo a fragile, emerging or embryonic agreement. As well as avoiding emotionally charged words, personal attacks and put downs, negotiators need to focus upon the positive and constructive rather than the negative and destructive, in terms of language and approach. It is also important during this phase to listen actively, observe behaviour and make appropriate judgements to enable movement to the next phase of the negotiations to take place.

Exchanging and agreeing

This phase is about exchanging concessions and consequently it moves the negotiations towards agreement. This assumes an overlap in the predetermined expectations of the parties involved. Clearly, if there is too wide a gap between negotiating positions, exchange is unlikely to occur. However, if concessions are made, a degree of convergence characterises the negotiations as the parties seek areas of common agreement. The exchange process has a momentum of its own. The expectation of concluding the negotiation can result in concessions by either side which may have been unthinkable earlier in the negotiations. Experienced negotiators may seek to exploit this situation, although they may pay a price for this if any exploitation becomes apparent to the other side.

As it becomes evident that compromise is possible, the negotiations move quickly to the agreement phase. The exchange process is checked, precise statements are made and potential misunderstandings are addressed. A written record serves the purpose of promoting common understanding of the outcomes to the parties.

Implementation

Ultimately negotiation has little benefit or value to those involved unless the negotiated outcomes are converted to action. This action has two aspects. The first is the effective communication with and dissemination of information to those affected by the agreement. The second is the devising of a programme of implementation which includes allocating responsibility and setting time-scales. A part of the implementation strategy is to evaluate the outcomes of the negotiations in relation to the agreed objectives and an assessment of negotiating performance. This evaluation will have implications for future negotiations.

Where, however, there is a failure to agree, this largely unsatisfactory outcome prompts a reassessment of the options available and an evaluation of whether or not agreement remains a viable proposition. If agreement appears unlikely, an examination of the alternatives becomes necessary. These may include an imposition of terms by one party, should it have the power to do so – although there are clearly implications for the relationship between the parties if this course of action is pursued. Alternatively, the parties can consider the value and practicability of third-party intervention, either internal or external to the organisation, in order to conciliate, mediate or arbitrate according to the situation (see Chapter 3).

Tactics and skills

In general, making concessions in negotiation without gaining something in return is to be avoided. Where a concession is unavoidable, a tactic used is to attempt to attach some conditions for acceptance. These conditions should be injected into the negotiations prior to an indication of a willingness to concede because they are then likely to stand more chance of being accepted. Once given, concessions cannot be withdrawn without inflicting some damage on the negotiation process and losing good faith. On the same basis, final offers must be final offers or credibility is affected.

Whilst it is potentially attractive to separate out the negotiating items within a set of negotiations, this presents a constraint on exchanges and concessions later. A wider perspective incorporating the whole package, whilst not necessarily as easy to manage as a segmented approach, is ultimately likely to be more balanced and fruitful. Threats and posturing, as well as creating uncertainty, are also legitimate tactics within a ritualistic framework. 'Trickery', however, may be destructive, and can affect not only the immediate negotiations but also all future negotiations by eroding trust between the parties.

Adjournments are a valuable tactic for negotiators but their value and scope goes beyond the tactical level. The skilled use of adjournments can have a significant impact upon the progress of the negotiations. Some potential uses of adjournment are shown in Exhibit 16.

Exhibit 16: *The uses of adjournment during negotiation*

These include:

- to consult privately when it is apparent that there is divergence or disagreement within the negotiating team;
- to discuss privately when a new argument becomes evident;
- to generally evaluate progress or lack of it;
- to allow an opportunity to consult with others;
- to consider whether or not to reject an offer;
- to take a break in order to regroup or relieve fatigue;
- to allow a cooling-off period if breakdown appears to be a probability;
- to consider the breaking off of negotiations or unilaterally withdrawing, when the negotiations have turned sour;
- to afford an opportunity for off-the-record communication between negotiation teams.

Frequent adjournments can be disruptive and may suggest a weakness of argument or lack of cohesion or coordination on the part of the side asking for them. They can also be an irritant to the other party if they are too frequent, unless this is perceived to be a desirable tactic. It is advisable to set a time limit for reconvening the negotiations in order to focus effort and ensure that the negotiations are not unnecessarily protracted. This time-scale must be realistic, as failure to adhere to an agreed resumption time can be a source of considerable antagonism, with consequent implications for the tenor of the negotiations when resumed. This latter point is more likely to apply in the case of adjournments during negotiations in process. It is less likely where a formal adjournment until another day is agreed.

The importance of listening skills in negotiation warrants special attention. It is self-evident, although not always appreciated, that most information can be gathered and obtained through listening actively.

Exhibit 17: *Active listening skills*

These include:

- concentrating on what is being said;
- observing and interpreting associated body language;
- encouraging through appropriate verbal and non-verbal responses;
- seeking clarification;

- using pauses through conscious attempts to avoid jumping in;
- using appropriate questioning techniques and valuing the importance of open questions;
- drawing appropriate and accurate inferences from what may be coded language.

Further, there is a good argument for allocating some team members to exclusively listening roles or even allocating observers to listen to specific members of the other side. Examples of active listening skills are indicated in Exhibit 17.

Clearly natural ability features as a variable in determining competence. However, there are elements of competence that can be developed through exposure to negotiations, training and experience. Some of the necessary inter-personal and analytical skills are indicated in Exhibit 18.

Exhibit 18: *Interpersonal and analytical skills in negotiation*

These include:

- oral communication;
- interpreting non-verbal cues;
- awareness and control of one's own body language;
- active listening;
- sensitivity to people and situations;
- ability to think on one's feet and articulate appropriately;
- creative thinking;
- persuasiveness;
- awareness of power relationships;
- problem-solving;
- judgement;
- assertion;
- quality of presentation;
- information processing and evaluation;
- teamwork and group dynamics;
- recognition of the ritualistic nature of negotiation and its implications.

These competences require underpinning by relevant theoretical knowledge to avoid superficiality and to encourage understanding. Effectiveness as a negotiator is founded on these competences and is enhanced or diluted by the approach or attitude adopted.

Stress in negotiation

Linked with the development of negotiating competences is the concept of negotiation stress which is likely to influence the degree of competence exhibited in negotiations. Arguably stress is a natural facet of negotiation but there are many potential sources of stress. First, there is the pressure associated with the need to achieve the predetermined negotiation objectives in the face of opposition. Additionally, in the case of team negotiations, there is the desire to be perceived as making an effective contribution to the team effort. Second, personal credibility is at risk in negotiation. Personal performance may enhance or diminish this and has implications not only for the next negotiation but also for the negotiator's general organisational reputation. The stress derives from wanting to preserve individual credibility and reputation. Third, the negotiating process itself is fertile ground for stress. This may be produced by the environment, the disparity in objectives, the emotional context, general fatigue or being the object of personal inference or attack. The skill for the negotiator is to recognise this possibility and to adopt appropriate compensating and personal adaptation strategies. To the list of general competences can be added the ability to manage stress.

Grievances

A grievance is an expression of perceived dissatisfaction or injustice that an employee feels towards the employer. It is based on the procedural right of individuals at work to express their dissatisfaction with any aspect of their work situation. Whilst disciplinary procedures allow the employer to express and try to resolve dissatisfactions it may have identified with the employee, in a grievance the employee is highlighting an issue of dissatisfaction with the employer. Many work situations have the potential to cause dissatisfaction and often the expression of a formal grievance is triggered by a particular event.

Salamon (1992) points out that the terms dissatisfaction, complaint, grievance and dispute may be regarded as overlapping segments of a continuum based primarily on the manner and formality of the presentation of employee dissatisfaction. These range from personal dissatisfaction to informal complaints, to formal grievances, to collective disputes. Not every employee dissatisfaction or complaint results in a grievance or a dispute. Whether it does or not depends on the employee's presentation of it and the employer's response to it and whether it is resolved to the satisfaction of the employee. The way in which the dissatisfaction is presented to management can range from an informal discussion to the formal presentation of the issue using the grievance procedure. The progression from the informal to the formal machinery may be seen as a failure to resolve the situation at the informal level or to deal with it or explain it to the satisfaction of the aggrieved individual.

The culture of an organisation has a major effect on the way in which grievances are received and handled. In a unitary or neo-unitary organisation there are assumptions that there are common values and common objectives and that management's right to manage is accepted by all (Farnham and Pimlott 1990). Therefore conflict within the organisation is seen as dysfunctional. Individuals may feel inhibited from raising a formal grievance because of the effect it may have on their career prospects and for fear of being labelled 'a trouble maker' or a 'deviant'. In a pluralist organisation, conflict is seen as inevitable and it is assumed that employees have a right to question management decisions and management's application of policies and procedures. Employees therefore normally accept that they have a right to raise grievances where they feel that this is necessary and the formal grievance procedure is likely to be more commonly used.

The need for formal mechanisms for resolving conflict is taken for granted, certainly in pluralist employee relations. Indeed the requirement in law on the part of the employer to have a grievance procedure was first included in the Industrial Relations Act 1971 and it is now incorporated in the Employment Protection (Consolidation) Act 1978. The grievance procedure therefore forms part of the written terms and conditions of employment. The subjects of grievances vary. They can range from issues affecting one individual with no organisational implications, to issues affecting a group of workers which challenges management decisions and with the potential to escalate to a dispute before being finally settled.

Grievance procedures

Grievance procedures provide the formal means for the presentation and resolution of employee dissatisfaction. Exhibit 19 indicates the basic elements to be incorporated within grievance procedures.

Exhibit 19: *The basic elements of a grievance procedure*

These are:

- management should agree with the recognised trade unions the procedure for raising grievances and for settling them promptly and effectively;
- there should be a formal procedure;
- if there are separate procedures for grievances and disputes these should be linked;
- an individual grievance should be settled as near to the point of origin and as quickly as possible;
- the procedure should be in writing.

Grievance procedures should set out the stages through which a grievance is heard within the organisational hierarchy. This recognises the authority and responsibility of the parties at the different levels within the organisation and allows for a structured approach to the situation. The stages also define the time-scale for the resolution of the problem. This, in theory, allows for a review of the decision at each stage. The number of stages in a procedure is, to some extent, determined by the structure of the organisation but in practical terms three to four stages are most appropriate. Any more than this can lead to a procedure that is unwieldy, slow and potentially confusing in the way it operates.

There are usually three levels for hearing grievances: departmental, functional and senior level. The departmental level provides the first hearing of the grievance through the line manager of the aggrieved person. The functional level – the next hearing of an unresolved grievance – involves the line manager's manager or the functional manager. And the senior level – the third (usually final) hearing of an unresolved grievance – is with a member of the senior management team or the managing director or chief executive. There may also be provision for an external review of the grievance or dispute, although this is more common in the disputes procedure, with many organisations providing for third-party intervention such as through ACAS or an employers' association. An example of a grievance hearing structure is provided in Figure 7.

Figure 7: *Grievance hearing structure*

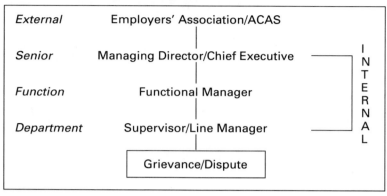

The time-scale for the resolution of a grievance from receipt of the written grievance to its settlement must be clearly defined and the aim should be to settle the grievance in the shortest possible time. The outcome of the grievance must be notified to the aggrieved person in writing, with a statement of their right to take the grievance to the next stage of the procedure if they are dissatisfied with the reviewing manager's decision. The grievance procedure should identify, if possible, the type of issues that can be raised within it. This should not be used as a means of restricting the use of the procedure. There are problems, such as personality clashes, that really cannot be resolved using a grievance procedure but only through effective communication and management. The procedure is used for such issues as implementation of national or local agreements, terms and conditions of employment, allocation of pay, overtime and so on. An example of a grievance procedure is shown in Figure 8.

There is one area of potential grievance that needs careful handling and may be best dealt with within a different procedure. Discrimination and harassment are highly sensitive and may in fact be perpetrated by the immediate line manager. Normal procedure for grievances is through the line manager, therefore there must be a facility for the resolution of these problems outside the usual reporting structure. It may be possible to have named people for the reporting of this type of incident or they can be dealt with through a separate harassment procedure.

Figure 8: *Example of a grievance procedure*

Grievance procedure

Management respects the right of employees individually or collectively to present grievances to management. It is in the interests of all that there are established formal procedures for handling these complaints.

a) Stage 1 – If you are unhappy about any aspect of your employment* you should raise the issue with your immediate supervisor or line manager. You will receive a response to your grievance within *three* working days.

b) Stage 2 – If the issue is not resolved to your satisfaction you may progress the matter in writing to your functional manager who will respond to you within *five* working days.

c) Stage 3 – If the matter is still unresolved you may take your complaint to a Senior Manager who will arrange a meeting within a further *ten* working days.

You have the right to be accompanied at any or all of these meetings by a representative or work colleague.

* Health and safety matters and incidents of racial or sexual harassment may be raised if you wish with the Safety Officer/Personnel Manager respectively.

Grievance interviews

The importance of management taking any grievance seriously must be emphasised. If any employee feels strongly enough to use the formal grievance procedure to raise a complaint then that person has the right to a fair and respectful hearing. However, as was discussed earlier, there are dissatisfactions and complaints that are raised outside the formal process. Again it is important that issues raised outside the formal procedure are treated with care as that will reduce the likelihood of the formal procedure being needed. Indicators of problems are high levels of labour turnover, absenteeism and problems with morale. Although these may indicate different problems, they should never be ignored.

The grievance interview requires the skills of any interview situation. This includes the need to:

- *Provide an appropriate physical environment free from interruptions.* It is important that the employee feels that the situation is being taken seriously, therefore a room where the complaint can be heard, in private, free from telephone and personal interruptions must be made available. The employee must be given prior notice of the date, time and venue of the interview and of their right to be accompanied by a union representative or a colleague if that is within the procedure.
- *Listen to, and hear, what is being said by the aggrieved individual.* Any interview requires good active listening skills and appropriate body language and eye contact are important if the aggrieved individuals are to feel that they are being listened to.
- *Ask appropriate questions in a non-threatening way.* In order that the manager understands the nature of the grievance and how the aggrieved feels, the situation causing the complaint must be presented in full by the employee. This may need careful probing and questioning so that all of the facts can be identified or clarified. It should be done in a calm and non-threatening way so that the employee feels that speaking openly will not disadvantage the case. It is often worth identifying what outcome the aggrieved is looking for, because it is not uncommon for the situation to require negotiation. Compromise may be the only way forward.
- *Prepare.* The nature of any grievance is that it is initiated by the employee. There may therefore be little that the manager can do to prepare for the first interview. The facts of the case need to be identified and it is at the second and subsequent stages that management's preparation is mainly undertaken. However, the written grievance should be read carefully and any information that the manager feels may be relevant should be gathered.
- *Analyse the facts and take a decision.* Having heard all the facts of the case, consulted the relevant policy and looked at any possible situation that may have set a precedent, the manager is then able to take a decision on the outcome of the grievance. Whilst there may be a need to discuss the case with a personnel manager or another manager, for advice, care must be taken that this does not jeopardise the fairness of treatment of the employee. The manager is taking the decision in the framework of the policies and procedures of the

organisation and therefore contributing to its 'case-law'. The decision may set a precedent that others will have to follow, therefore any management interpretation must be one that the employer can live with. The decision should be communicated in writing to the employee within the procedural time-scale. If further time is needed to allow for a full investigation of the situation then agreement should be sought with the employee for the time-scale to be extended. This ensures that the employer does not attract further complaint of not adhering to the agreed procedure.

Any individual grievance ends with an outcome that is ultimately accepted by the individual or the procedure is exhausted. However, the situation should not end there. It is important, as stated previously, that the decision is communicated clearly to the employee and that both parties understand exactly what has been agreed. There is also benefit to the employer in monitoring grievances both in terms of issues that are raised and outcomes that are agreed. It may be that some of the employer's terms and conditions of employment need to be re-written in a more easily understood form or that training needs to be given to explain the implementation of policies. Issues that are constantly giving rise to grievances may highlight a communication problem.

Discipline

Discipline is action instigated by management against an employee who fails to meet reasonable expectations in terms of behaviour, conduct or adherence to rules. A professional approach argues for an emphasis on problem-solving, coupled with a preventative and constructive perspective as this is likely to encourage a positive response from the employee. It also maximises the opportunity for acceptance of the problem, correction of the behaviour and reconciliation of the parties. Discipline can therefore be viewed as a conflict-resolving mechanism within the employment relationship, with an emphasis on improvement and remedy rather than punitive measures. Where encouragement, guidance or training do not result in improvement to an acceptable standard, punishment may however be necessary. Sanctions against the employee can act as a deterrent to the individual behaviour or conduct and, by example, for the work group as a whole. However fairness, equity and consistency in approaching discipline is likely to minimise disagreements and to benefit employee relations within the organisation.

Disciplinary rules and procedures

Disciplinary rules are necessary for promoting order and avoiding ambiguity and inconsistency in employee relations. By setting standards, rules determine acceptable and unacceptable employee behaviour. Disciplinary rules are usually formulated by management but need to be perceived as reasonable by employees and employee representatives if they are to be effective. In addition, rules legitimise management authority and enable management to obtain compliance to instructions in the interests of organisational effectiveness. Whilst disciplinary rules are organisationally specific, they encompass obligations incurred under statute, for example health and safety at work, and also reflect acceptable behaviour within a wider societal sense, for example, values associated with honesty, propriety and non-violence. Management has the responsibility for ensuring that disciplinary rules are clear, accessible and understood. This has implications for the appropriate use of language and the means of communication. This may include prominent display, word of mouth and incorporation into an employee handbook and other documents. Above all, rules should be designed on the principle of voluntary compliance rather than on the rationale of imposed retribution.

If disciplinary rules set standards, disciplinary procedures provide a means of ensuring that these standards are met and a method for dealing with a failure to meet them. A disciplinary policy incorporates rules and a procedure for dealing with transgressions and may include a general statement regarding the employer's attitude towards discipline. This general statement may indicate that a precursor to formal disciplinary action will be counselling or an informal 'word in the ear'.

An overriding assumption in managing discipline is that disciplinary procedures should conform to the laws of 'natural justice'. These principles have emerged from ideas of equity, due process and model legal practice. They include the basic principles indicated in Exhibit 20. The incorporation of these principles into disciplinary procedures is likely to enhance the perceived equity of procedures and strengthen compliance with the rules. Any perceived unfairness may create resentment and militate against compliance. In order to command

Exhibit 20: *The principles of natural justice*

These incorporate:

- knowledge of the standards or behaviour expected;
- knowledge of the alleged failure and the nature of the allegation;
- thorough investigation should precede any allegation;
- the opportunity to offer an explanation and for this explanation to be considered;
- the opportunity to be accompanied or represented;
- a fair and impartial hearing;
- a penalty should be appropriate to the offence, taking account of any mitigating factors;
- the opportunity and support to improve behaviour should be provided, except when misconduct goes to the root of the contract;
- appeal to a higher authority or a more senior manager.

respect and support, and to operate effectively, disciplinary procedures / CMC.
must also be accepted as fair by managers.

According to ACAS (1987: page 55) disciplinary procedures should:

(a) Be in writing.

(b) Specify to whom they apply.

(c) Provide for matters to be dealt with quickly.

(d) Indicate the disciplinary actions which may be taken.

(e) Specify the levels of management which have the authority to take the various forms of disciplinary action, ensuring that immediate superiors do not normally have the power to dismiss without reference to senior management.

(f) Provide for individuals to be informed of the complaints against them and to be given an opportunity to state their case before decisions are reached.

(g) Give individuals the right to be accompanied by a trade union representative or by a fellow employee of their choice.

(h) Ensure that, except for gross misconduct, no employees are dismissed for a first breach of discipline.

(i) Ensure that disciplinary action is not taken until the case has been carefully investigated.

(j) Ensure that the individuals are given an explanation for any penalty imposed.

(k) Provide a right of appeal and specify the procedure to be followed.

Although the ACAS Code of Practice is not legally binding upon employers, it can be taken into account by an industrial tribunal if it is considered to be relevant to the case. Further, if disciplinary rules are formulated principally by management and require compliance by employees, then there is a strong case for disciplinary procedures being decided by consultation or negotiation with employees or their representatives, if they are to have moral authority and to command respect.

Any disciplinary procedure should be incremental and should provide for a range of progressive sanctions against employees. The starting point is an informal oral warning, usually given by the supervisor, with the aim of resolving the issue at the lowest possible level. The first stage of the formal procedure may be a recorded oral warning administered by the line manager or personnel officer. The oral warning should make clear the consequences of a failure to improve or occurrences of further offences. The next stage of the procedure should be a written warning which, depending upon the severity of the case, may or may not be a final written warning. The final step may be either action short of dismissal, including disciplinary transfer, or reduction in status and responsibility, or termination of employment. The importance of following a procedure was highlighted by *Polkey* v. *A E Dayton Services* (1987 IRLR 503) where a dismissal was found to be unfair because of a procedural failure. Failure to follow a fair procedure is, therefore, not only bad practice but may also affect the legitimacy of the dismissal itself.

Disciplinary interviews

The importance of thorough investigation in disciplinary matters cannot be over-emphasised. Before disciplinary action is taken there must be a *prima facie* case of misconduct or breach of rules or unacceptable standards of work. It may be appropriate to suspend the employee during the investigation, particularly in cases of apparent gross misconduct. However, an unwarranted suspension will be to the detriment of the problem-solving approach and to the perception of equity referred to earlier. The investigation should include the collection of both verbal and written evidence and it is important to maintain impartiality at this preliminary point. Checking the employee's record is also essential and may contribute to the decision whether or not to proceed. If the evidence suggests that disciplinary action is justified, the employee should be informed and a suitable time and place arranged. The right to be accompanied or to be represented by a union should be made clear to the employee.

The disciplinary interview is potentially an emotional encounter and requires sensitive handling by the interviewer. Professionalism and good interpersonal skills are crucial. Clearly an introduction of those present and the reasons for attendance should precede the interview. The employer should explain the purpose of the interview and where it fits into the formal procedure. The complaint should be clearly stated, going through the evidence and concentrating on the facts. Employees should be given the opportunity to respond and explain their case by presenting their side of the argument, including any relevant special circumstances relating to the case. If it is apparent that there is no case to answer the interview should be terminated and no further action taken.

If the employee does not offer an acceptable explanation or justification for the action, a discussion should follow during which the problem is clarified and recognition and acceptance of responsibility for the situation is encouraged. It is then possible to seek to identify and explore possible improvements. Progress in partnership together, with the employer lending appropriate support, training and encouragement, is likely to resolve the matter to the satisfaction of all concerned.

If disciplinary action seems necessary, due consideration of all the circumstances is best achieved by adjourning the interview. During the adjournment, proper weight must be given to the employee's explanation and any special factors that have emerged or are known. Employers are able to act upon a reasonable belief based on the available facts; there is no need to prove the allegation beyond reasonable doubt. The decision or outcome of the disciplinary interview should be clearly and unambiguously communicated to the employee as should the right of appeal if there is dissatisfaction with the decision.

This description of the interview process belies the skills required. The very nature of the potential conflict works against a smooth process despite the emphasis on thorough preparation and professionalism. The interviewer can be confronted with a range of responses from aggression or distress to passiveness, on the one hand, and from outright rejection to total denial that there is a case to answer, on the other. It is important in these circumstances to be able to remain calm and rational and demonstrate a professional approach. The information-gathering nature of the interview requires good questioning skills and active listening. The ability to weigh the balance of probabilities and then decide on appropriate action are skills that can determine the success or otherwise of the disciplinary process.

The result of the interview needs to be formally communicated to the employee, with copies to the shop steward if appropriate. Clearly, this demands effective writing skills, not only because of the need to have an accurate record for the personal file, but also to ensure full communication and comprehension. Performance or conduct should be monitored and reviewed, and the employee either told of a satisfactory outcome or the next stage of the procedure invoked. Warnings, except in extreme cases, should be 'spent' after a predetermined period. This also is in the interests of justice so that the employee has the opportunity to 'wipe the slate clean' in due course.

The law and dismissal

Protection against unfair dismissal originated in the Industrial Relations Act 1971 and was consolidated in the Employment Protection (Consolidation) Act 1978. This gives an employee a limited job property right and some protection against unreasonable behaviour by the employer ending in loss of employment. The employer is in no way denied the freedom to dismiss individuals, in fact the legislation ensures that employers can legitimately dismiss employees for 'fair' reasons in 'reasonable' circumstances (Employment Department 1991). However, employment protection legislation serves to encourage good employment practice and endeavours to persuade employers to act reasonably and fairly in the circumstances. The legislation enhances the role of ACAS as a conciliator and this has a significant impact upon the number of cases which are settled or withdrawn before reaching an industrial tribunal. The legal remedies for employees are best viewed as a back stop (see Chapter 2).

Employees who are contractually employed for 16 hours or more a week are protected against unfair dismissal after two years' continuous service unless they have reached retirement age. Part-time employees working between eight and 16 hours a week require five years' continuous service. Employees with fixed-term contracts are not protected against non-renewal of their contract if they have waived their rights in writing. There is no service requirement in certain cases of dismissal relating to trade union membership or activities and allegations of sex or race discrimination. The Trade Union Reform and Employment Rights Act 1993 aims to strengthen protection against dismissal on grounds of pregnancy.

Dismissal takes place when either the employer terminates the contract, with or without notice, or the employee resigns by reason of the employer's behaviour and the employee considers the employer to have repudiated the contract by its actions or behaviour. Constructive dismissal, as this is known, may consist of a serious single act which is deemed to have destroyed the contract or alternatively it may constitute a series of smaller incidents which cumulatively add up to a claim. In law, dismissals must be fair and reasonable in the circumstances. Dismissal may be fair for reasons related to:

- the conduct of the employee;
- the employee's capability or qualification;
- redundancy;
- a statutory duty which prevents employment being continued;
- some other substantial reason of a kind that justifies dismissal.

Whilst these reasons provide convenient categories, it is the substantial merits of each incident or case that determine whether or not the dismissal is for a fair reason. The reasonableness of each decision relates to whether the dismissal is based upon sufficient factual evidence, whether the correct procedures have been followed and whether dismissal is justified.

An employer does not have to prove fault beyond reasonable doubt but to demonstrate that a reasonable belief was held at the time and that dismissal was justified by the information available following proper investigation. As part of the investigation, it is reasonable to expect the employer to talk to the employee as well as listen to and consider any explanations provided by the employee. This procedural importance makes it essential that dismissals are well documented. Fair reasons for dismissal require that a distinction is drawn between general misconduct, which is dealt with within the incremental framework of a disciplinary procedure, and gross misconduct which may justify summary dismissal for one occurrence. Gross misconduct may include drunkenness, theft, violence, breach of confidence and serious and wilful refusal to conform to the legitimate instructions of the employer. Alleged or suspected gross misconduct does not obviate the need for thorough investigation or the opportunity for employees to offer an explanation for their behaviour, but the serious nature of these offences goes to the root of the contract and destroys it. There is a duty on the part of the employer to ensure that what may constitute gross misconduct, and its potential consequences, are clearly and unequivocally communicated to the employees.

The capability of the employee may be in question if there is a failure to achieve a satisfactory standard of work or of job performance. If this is a failure to exercise competence, this may constitute misconduct. However, if the issue is one of incompetence or relative incompetence, the employer needs to point out the shortfall, specify the standard expected, indicate the consequences of a failure to meet the standard and give the employee reasonable time to improve. Within this process, there is an implicit obligation for the employer to provide reasonable and necessary support, training and guidance to the employee.

Incapability through ill health requires particularly sensitive handling and a distinction needs to be drawn between frequent short-term absences and long-term ill health. The issue is whether the employee is able to give continuous and effective service and each situation requires consultation with the employee and medical practitioners before deciding upon a course of action. The availability of alternative work needs to be considered, although there is no obligation upon the employer to create an alternative job. However, the organisation's resources are taken into account by ITs in making a decision. The age of the employee, the length of service, the likelihood of a return to health and the impact of the absence upon the organisation are all factors to be taken into account.

Redundancy occurs when all or a relevant part of an employer's business closes or the requirements for a particular type of work cease or diminish. Selection for redundancy requires employers to act reasonably and from genuine motives. There is a legal requirement to consult employees and their representatives (see below).

Dismissal for the reason that a statutory duty prevents employment continuing relates to situation where it would be unlawful for an employee to continue working in the position for which they were contractually employed. Although this appears straightforward, the experience is that dismissal on these grounds is rarely justified.

Some other substantial reason is included as a fair reason for dismissal to give ITs some scope to accept a dismissal that is for reasons which do not conveniently fall into one of the other four categories discussed above. Described by some as an 'employer's charter', it includes dismissals relating to third-party pressure to dismiss, personality conflicts, relationships between employees and business reorganisation. In the latter category, decisions by ITs point towards the needs of the business generally overriding the interests of the individual if it can be justified on commercial grounds. This entails an assessment of the balance of advantage to the employer through reorganisation against the disadvantage to the employee. This does not challenge the requirement to achieve change through consultation, persuasion and agreement.

Remedies for unfair dismissal

Where ITs find that there has been no unfair dismissal the matter ends, subject to any appeal by the applicant on a point of law. In cases where a tribunal is satisfied that dismissal is unfair, it has powers to order reinstatement or re-engagement of the employee. Reinstatement involves a return to the employee's previous job and acting as if dismissal had not taken place. Re-engagement involves a return to a comparable or otherwise suitable position. In considering the alternatives of reinstatement and re-engagement, ITs consider the applicant's wishes and any representation made by the employer relating to practicability. An employer cannot be compelled to take back an employee, but refusal to do so may result in an award of additional compensation to the employee.

An alternative to reinstatement or re-engagement, and the most commonly exercised power of ITs, is the award of compensation to the unfairly dismissed employee. This consists of a basic award which is based upon length of service and calculated on the same basis as redundancy payments. The tribunal may also make a compensatory award to take account of the employee's current and future financial losses arising from the dismissal, although the employee has an obligation to mitigate this loss by actively seeking other work. The compensation awarded by ITs takes account of the contribution by the employee to the dismissal and the award may be reduced in proportion to that contribution.

Preparing for ITs

An employee, the applicant, with a complaint, normally completes an

IT1 form and indicates the grounds for the claim and the relief being sought. After an assessment of the entitlement to claim by the Central Office of Industrial Tribunals, it is sent to the employer, the respondent, via the regional office. The employer is obliged to respond on form IT3. Clearly the response by the employer has to be preceded by several considerations and points of decision, the first of which is to decide whether to concede or to contest the claim. This decision takes account of:

- an appreciation of the legislation which may be relevant to the case;
- the skills required for the case and whether legal representation is necessary;
- a judgement on how well the case has been handled within the organisation in relation to documentation and the conduct of those involved;
- the likely consequences and cost of the decision to proceed. Importantly what is the applicant likely to achieve if successful and will it be better to seek an informal settlement?

If it is decided to contest the claim, it is necessary for the employer to gather the relevant documentation for consideration and also identify and consult the relevant witnesses and parties to the dismissal. This leads to a review of the situation, with consideration being given to the role of ACAS, who can intervene at the request of either side or on its own initiative. A pre-hearing assessment may be appropriate as a means of testing commitment and providing guidance on the merits of the case of both parties (Employment Department 1990).

ACAS may contact the applicant, or the applicant's representative, with a view to reducing the difference between the employer and employee and seeking to identify areas of consensus as a way of progressing towards an acceptable resolution. If, despite these efforts, the case goes to a tribunal the preparation required relates to proper and accurate presentation of the evidence. In addition, a coordinated and cohesive approach by those involved is essential, together with the determination of a strategy appropriate to the case, although chairpersons of ITs are not generally sympathetic to surprises or court room antics. Employers have no grounds for concern if they have acted reasonably, followed the principles relating to natural justice, have ensured that disciplinary action is taken according to agreed procedure by skilled interviewers, have documented the case appropriately and prepared thoroughly for the tribunal.

Redundancy

Prior to the 1960s, the concept of a right of ownership in a job would have seemed incredible to the average British worker. The right of the employer to decide who to 'hire and fire' was seen as absolute and embodied in the right to manage. The need to shed labour in an economic downturn was seen as inevitable and the worker had no power or legal protection in this situation. The first legislation directed at redundancy was the Redundancy Payments Act 1965 which set out the definition of redundancy and the compensation payment that the redundant workers were entitled to when their job disappeared. Payments were made from a now-defunct state redundancy fund. In the context of the political and economic situation of the time, it can be seen as a way of encouraging more mobility of labour in a situation of relatively low unemployment by discouraging employers from hoarding labour during periods of economic downturn.

The law and redundancy

Redundancy is one of the 'fair reasons' for dismissal identified in the Employment Protection (Consolidation) Act 1978. It occurs when employees are dismissed in the following circumstances (Advisory Conciliation and Arbitration Service 1988: page 4):

> where the employer has ceased, or intends to cease, to carry on the business for the purposes of which the employee was employed; or
>
> where the employer has ceased, or intends to cease, to carry on the business in the place where the employee was so employed; or
>
> where the requirements of the business for employees to carry out work of a particular kind have ceased or diminished or are expected to cease or diminish; or
>
> where the requirements of the business for employees to carry out work of a particular kind, in the place where they were so employed, have ceased or diminished or are expected to cease or diminish.

The law provides for redundancy payments for the loss of employment which is 'wholly or mainly' attributable to redundancy. There are, however, some employees who are excluded from this legislation.

These are:

- employees with less than two years' service after the age of 18;
- employees who have reached retirement age;
- employees working less than eight hours per week or working 8–16 hours with less than five years' continuous service;
- employees on fixed-term contracts of two years or more who have waived their right to claim redundancy payment.

The legislation allows for payment based on age and length of continuous service. This is illustrated in Table 1.

Table 1: *Statutory redundancy payments provisions*

Age	Payment
18–21	1/2 week's pay
22–40	1 week's pay
40–64	11/2 weeks' pay
64–65	reduced by 1/12 per month

Entitlement is calculated on completed years of service subject to a maximum of 20 years. From the age of 64, entitlement is reduced by 1/12 for each month of service beyond that age. The redundant employee has a right to a written statement of how the payment has been calculated. Any employee disputing the calculation of a redundancy payment may take their case to a tribunal up to six months after the employment has been terminated.

The TULRCA 1992 places a duty on employers to consult with recognised trade unions and to notify the Employment Department of the numbers of workers to be made redundant. The minimum statutory periods for consultation are as follows:

- where 10–99 employees are to be made redundant in one establishment within a 30 day period or less, the consultation must take place at least 30 days before the first redundancy;
- where more than 100 employees are to be made redundant in one establishment within a 90 day period or less, consultation must take place at least 90 days before the first redundancy;
- where there are less than 10 employees, or the redundancy is spread over a longer period management is required to consult at 'the earliest opportunity'.

Specific information that must be provided includes:

- the reason for the proposed redundancy;
- the numbers and types of employees to be made redundant;
- the total number of employees of this type employed;
- selection criteria to be used;
- the implementation plan and the period of redundancy.

Management are required to consult with the unions and listen to any representations made to the employer by the unions. However, there is no legal obligation to come to any agreement with the unions. Failure to consult can lead to the imposition of a protective award which requires employers to pay employees their normal pay for the period called 'the protected period'.

Redundancy policy

Management must plan ahead for redundancy, in terms not only of numbers to be made redundant but also by having an agreed redundancy policy prior to a redundancy situation arising. If a policy is in place, then the employer and the employees are not dealing with the details under stress or in emotive situations. The recognised trade unions or staff associations should be involved in determining both the policy and the redundancy procedure. The agreed policy should be supplemented by a procedure or implementation plan that identifies the process of handling the collective redundancies.

The redundancy policy should be a part of the package of employment policies that any 'good' employer has at its disposal. Any employer that is fearful of having a policy for redundancy because of its possible adverse effects on staff and the concern of employees that it may become a self-fulfilling prophesy is doing both itself and its workers a disservice. The policy should include:

- an opening statement about the maintenance of employment levels and the need for job security together with a recognition that the requirements for labour are not static and therefore change will take place over time;
- consultation arrangements;
- steps that the company will take to reduce the need for redundancy;
- the selection criteria;
- details of redundancy payments;

- details of redeployment procedures and related payments;
- a statement of the appeals procedure;
- redundancy support systems such as outplacement, counselling, and training.

Selecting for redundancy

The area most likely to give rise to claims for unfair dismissal is the criteria used for deciding who goes and who stays in a redundancy situation. Selection criteria must be stated in the redundancy policy and management must ensure that they are applied in an even-handed way. Any employees claiming unfair selection for redundancy can claim unfair dismissal at a tribunal provided that they are covered by the legislation. Care must be taken in the determination of selection criteria that discrimination does not take place. Selection based on part-time workers is likely to be seen as infringing the Sex Discrimination Act 1975, as part-time staff are usually women. The employer must also show that the new work patterns are needed to fit in with the organisation's requirements. Selection based on trade union membership is automatically unfair.

Non-compulsory redundancy

Voluntary redundancy. An increasingly acceptable method of selection in redundancy is voluntary redundancy. This requires employees to volunteer to be made redundant and for the employer to select individuals from that list. Problems can arise, however, if there are more volunteers than the employer wants to lose as any selection the employer makes must be fair. Also voluntary redundancy can be an expensive option for the employer, as commonly the longer-serving members of the workforce come forward and they attract higher redundancy payments. A further problem that can arise is that an imbalance of skills and experience develops in the organisation. This means that the employer must carefully work out the profile of the workforce that it needs to maintain its work activity, efficiently and effectively.

Early retirement. Early retirement can be redundancy. This may also be an expensive option as it requires a long-term financial commitment on the part of the employer. However, it can help in terms of workplace morale. Unfortunately, it can leave a skewed age structure, with little natural retirement for a few years, and this can lead to difficulties in career progression.

Compulsory redundancy

Last in first out (LIFO). This option is usually favoured by the trade unions. It is easiest to apply and is easy to understand. However, it can provide organisational problems in deciding whether, for example, it is to be applied on a company-wide basis or a departmental basis. In the former case, it can give rise to skill mix difficulties, if the latter, then the employer must make sure that internal transferees are excluded. The fairness of selecting long-service employees on LIFO, simply because they have been recently transferred to a new department, may well be open to question.

Skills or qualifications. The employer is likely to see the retention of a balanced workforce as the main priority in a redundancy situation. Here selection on the basis of skills or qualifications is appropriate. Again the importance of objectivity must be stressed and the profile of the required workforce should be decided before any individual decisions are made.

Efficiency or work performance. Management may decide to select employees on the basis of efficiency, which may include attendance and time-keeping. There are potential problems with this approach as it requires records that are absolutely accurate. Poor application of this criterion can lead to claims that the reason for dismissal is not redundancy but other factors.

Providing support

The announcement of redundancy in any organisation gives rise to feelings of anxiety and insecurity amongst the workforce. There is a need to communicate the issues, procedures and criteria with employees in general. There is no right time to communicate a redundancy situation and some may argue that it is best delayed as long as possible. This is fine if it does not give rise to rumour, as this will lead to a loss of trust and confidence in management and may well lead to greater problems in the long term. When the general announcement is made, the individual employees who are affected by the redundancy should then be seen by their manager. Managers need to have the skills to handle what may be one of the most difficult interviews they ever have to conduct. They must be prepared for the 'who', 'what', 'why' and 'how' questions and be given the information to answer them accurately and confidently. The interviews need to be handled in a confident and assertive way but also with empathy. Not all managers feel able to do this. Alternatives available to the employer in a redundancy situation are:

• to handle the whole process within current resources;
• to handle the redundancies using permanent managers (usually personnel managers) and appoint temporary staff to free up those managers;
• to use the services of outplacement consultants.

Outplacement

The term outplacement is defined by Eggert (1991: page 3) as 'the process whereby an individual or individuals compelled to leave their employer are given support and counselling to assist them in achieving the next stage of their career'. The aim is to facilitate the transition from the redundant job to the next employment. It usually consists of practical support such as job search, individual assessment programmes and employee counselling. Internal skills may be enough to handle small numbers of redundancies. Large-scale redundancies, however, often require additional support, either in the form of outplacement consultants, which are increasing in number, or through the Job Centres. This depends on the numbers involved and arrangements can be made at the place of employment to provide assistance to redundant workers. Outplacement specialists have the knowledge and skills to assist in a variety of situations. Senior and middle managers being made redundant need a different approach from manual workers, but all need careful handling, financial advice, possibly retirement programmes and skill development programmes. The use of psychometric tests to assist in identifying the skills and aptitudes of individuals can be of positive value. Many long-term employees may never have stood back and assessed their work and individual abilities. Sometimes the 'opportunities' which redundancy provides can be very fulfilling for the outplacement staff when they see the redundant worker move through the stages of disbelief and shock to success and hope in a new job role.

Counselling

Counselling redundant workers is increasingly recognised as a positive benefit by employers. In a redundancy situation, it is not only the employees under notice of redundancy who feel under stress and suffer anxiety. Those staying on are also likely to be concerned about their long-term prospects. Their job security has obviously been threatened and whilst they may feel relieved that their name was not on the redundancy list, they may none the less feel that this situation could be shortlived. The provision of counselling services is obviously needed and may be required for both those going and those staying. However, individuals respond differently to redundancy depending on several factors such as age, financial situation, personality, gender and length of service. Counsellors should be able to assess individuals and identify their different responses on a personal basis.

Assignments

(a) Observe or participate in a negotiation in your organisation.
   (i) Analyse the negotiation process in terms of the skills required. To what extent were these skills evident and how effectively were they utilised?
   (ii) Did adequate planning take place?
   (iii) Was it possible to detect movement through the 'phases' of negotiation?

(b) Identify a situation where you have been required to negotiate on a one-to-one basis.
   (i) Describe the situation.
   (ii) Was there a successful outcome?
   (iii) What contributed to the success or otherwise of the outcome?

(c) Identify a situation at work where you will have to negotiate on a particular issue.
   (i) Decide upon your *ideal settlement*, *realistic settlement* and *fall back position*.
   (ii) After the negotiation review the outcome in relation to your expectations.

(d) Body language or non-verbal cues make a vital contribution to the communication process. Keep a confidential log of body language which you observe in your organisation.

   (i) How does body language manifest itself?
   (ii) What do you interpret from the signs?
   (iii) How does it help or hinder the communication process?

(e) Attend an industrial tribunal and observe an unfair dismissal case.
   (i) Write a brief report on the proceedings and the outcome.
   (ii) Was a proper procedure followed by the employer?
   (iii) Comment upon whether the employer acted 'reasonably in the circumstances'.
   (iv) Discuss whether and to what extent the employee contributed to the dismissal.
   (v) Using the laws of natural justice outlined earlier in this chapter, examine each one in relation to the case and comment upon whether they have been adhered to.

(f) Obtain a copy of disciplinary procedures from two or more organisations.
   (i) Discuss to what extent they include the features recommended by the ACAS Code of Practice.
   (ii) Compare and contrast the disciplinary procedures, identifying strengths and weaknesses.

(g) Interview a manager who is experienced in disciplinary interviews.
   (i) Using open questions identify the skills required for effective disciplinary interviews.
   (ii) Write a brief report on your findings.

(h) Interview a number of managers in your organisation who may have some potential for involvement in grievance matters.
   (i) Question them about their understanding of the grievance procedure.
   (ii) Comment upon whether any training is warranted.

(i) Investigate the number of grievances you have had in your organisation over a specific period.
   (i) Analyse the subjects of the grievances and the outcomes of the hearings.
   (ii) Write a brief report on your findings paying particular attention to any organisational implications.

(j) Critically evaluate your organisation's redundancy policy. Comment on the effectiveness of the selection criteria identified in the policy.

(k) What support does your organisation offer to employees who are being made redundant. Evaluate the effectiveness of this and make recommendations for support for remaining staff.

References

ATKINSON, G. 1980. *The Effective Negotiator*. Newbury: Negotiating Systems Publications.

ADVISORY CONCILIATION AND ARBITRATION SERVICE 1987. *Discipline at Work*. London: ACAS.

ADVISORY CONCILIATION AND ADVISORY SERVICE 1988. *Redundancy Handling*. London: ACAS.

DEPARTMENT OF EMPLOYMENT 1987. *Redundancy Consultation and Notification*. London: ACAS.

EGGERT, M. 1991. *Outplacement*. London: IPM.

EMPLOYMENT DEPARTMENT 1990. *Industrial Tribunals Procedure*. London: ED.

EMPLOYMENT DEPARTMENT 1991. *Individual Rights of Employees: A Guide for Employers*. London: ED.

Employment Protection (Consolidation) Act 1978.

FARNHAM, D. and PIMLOTT, J. 1990. *Understanding Industrial Relations*. London: Cassell.

KENNEDY, G., BENSON, J. and MCMILLAN, J. 1984. *Managing Negotiations*. London: Business Books.

SALAMON, M. 1992. *Industrial Relations – Theory and Practice*. London: Prentice Hall.

WALTON, R. and MCKENZIE, R. 1965. *A Behavioral Theory of Labor Negotiations*. NY: McGraw-Hill.

Part Two

Managing
Employee Relations

Chapter 6

Employee Relations Management in Context

Sylvia Horton

Employee relations management takes place within both an internal and external context, and these affect the employee relations strategies, policies and practices of employers. The internal context is one over which managements have some control and is determined by the size, functions, structure, social composition and managerial philosophy of the organisation they manage. The external context is beyond the control of management, at least in the short to medium term, and is therefore a given. The external environment can be analytically separated into zones or sub-systems including the economic, technological, social and political. Empirically, they are interrelated but they each affect the ways in which organisations are managed, particularly in the area of employee relations.

The economic context

Britain is an advanced industrial society located in what is classed as the 'first world'. It had a Gross National Product (GNP), at market prices, of £574 billion in 1992 and, in terms of GNP per capita, it ranked eighth in the member states of the EC and sixteenth in the world league of high-income economies. These positions are lower rankings than it has had in the past and reflect a declining relative world economic position. During the last two decades, in particular, dramatic changes have occurred both in the international economy and in the domestic economy. First, there has been a major restructuring of international markets, with third world countries developing their own manufacturing industries and becoming important exporters of manufactured and semi-manufactured products to the economies of Europe, North America and Australasia. Second, the first world economies have been de-industrialising and concentrating on developing service and non-manufacturing industries. Thus the international flow of goods, patterns of trade and money flows are in a state of flux. Third,

173

Table 2: *Changing sector distribution of employment in the UK for selected years, 1971–92*

	1971	%	1979	%	1981	%
Manufacturing	8,065	(36.43)	7,253	(31.29)	6,222	(28.42)
Services	11,627	(52.52)	13,580	(58.60)	13,468	(61.52)
Other	2,447	(11.05)	2,340	(10.09)	2,203	(10.06)
All industries	22,137		23,173		21,892	

Source: *Social Trends* 22, 1992.

the collapse of the former communist regimes in Eastern Europe, and their movement towards open market economies, has extended the scope of the international economy by opening up new opportunities for trade. But it has also destabilised the world political order. Britain's economy has been affected by these international trends and by changes in its national patterns of production and consumption.

Domestically, the British economy has been characterised by changes in its structure, in the geographical location of industry and in the methods and patterns of work (Allen and Massey 1988). Table 2 shows the changing sectoral distribution of employment in the UK over the past 20 years. There has been a long-term shift from primary to service industries, as old traditional industries have contracted and new ones have emerged. The most significant change in recent years has been the decline in the proportion of the labour force employed in the manufacturing industries and the increase in the service sector. Between 1971 and 1992, the numbers employed in manufacturing fell by over 40 per cent, whilst those in service industries rose by a third. In 1990, employment in manufacturing accounted for 23 per cent of all employees. A year later it fell below five million for the first time since 1959 (Central Statistical Office 1992) and then to 4.5 million in mid-1992. The trend continues downward.

The changes in employment have not been uniform, however, and throughout the last two decades there have been fluctuating and relatively high levels of unemployment as shown in Figure 9. The numbers unemployed rose above one million in 1976, above two million in 1981 and passed three million in July 1985. The number peaked at 3.2 million in July 1986 and proceeded to fall sharply to 1.5 million in early 1990. Since then it has risen rapidly to over three million again at

									(000s)
1983	%	1986	%	1990	%	1991	%	1992	%
5,525	(26.22)	5,227	(24.44)	5,138	(22.43)	4,793	(21.56)	4,589	(21.09)
13,501	(64.08)	14,297	(66.8)	15,945	(69.63)	15,744	(70.82)	15,644	(71.89)
2,042	(9.69)	1,863	(8.71)	1,817	(7.93)	1,692	(7.61)	1,524	(7.00)
21,067		21,387		22,899		22,229		21,758	

the beginning of 1993. One of the most significant trends has been in the numbers of long-term unemployed, that is those out of work for more than one year. One-third of the 2.9 million registered unemployed in October 1992 had been out of work for at least 12 months and more than 50 per cent for six months or more. The composition of the long-term unemployed consists of unskilled manual and skilled craft workers, older workers, women, the young between 16 and 25, and blacks. But there is a growing number of unemployed amongst professional and managerial groups. Unemployment is highest amongst the young. In 1992, nearly one in five males and one in seven females under 19 were unemployed (Central Statistical Office 1993).

Figure 9: *Unemployment in the UK 1971–92*

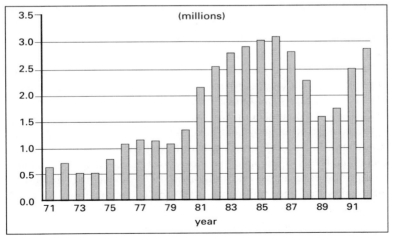

The changes in the importance and size of manufacturing have been accompanied by changes in the spatial distribution of economic activity within Britain. As manufacturing has contracted, the traditional industrial regions of Wales, the north-east, Lancashire and the Midlands have lost jobs. A census published in 1987 showed that 94 per cent of the jobs lost in manufacturing between 1979 and 1984 had been lost in the north. Although the expansion of the new service industries is not confined to the south, the latter has gained most from the rise of new industrial sectors and the growth in the service industries. There is an inverse relationship between de-industrialisation and tertiarisation and, as a result, inequalities between British regions have tended to increase. However, the regional impact of the recession in the early 1990s was felt more in the south, with more than a quarter of all unemployment concentrated in the south-east.

The changing structure of the economy has also been reflected in the occupational distribution of the labour force. The working population grew from 24.9 million in 1971 to 28.8 million in 1991. Approximately 90 per cent of the increase was accounted for by 3.5 million women entering the labour force. In 1990, there were 11.5 million economically active women representing 43 per cent of the workforce, compared with 16.1 million men. Most women were employed in the service sector. Between 1971 and 1990, there was an expansion of white-collar and professional jobs and a decline in blue-collar ones, with, by 1990, just under a half of men and two-thirds of women in non-manual occupations. The fastest growing area, for both men and women, has been managerial and professional occupations.

Whilst de-industrialisation is associated with job losses, it has also been accompanied by increases in productivity and output throughout much of the period under review. In particular, between 1980 and 1990, manufacturing productivity grew at an annual average of almost 5 per cent. This was the result of increased investment, the introduction of new technology and changes in the patterns and structure of the work process. On the one hand, many jobs have been de-skilled but, on the other, there has been a move to multi-skilling. Employers have generally sought to increase the flexibility of their workforces and to make use of a range of employment modes from full-time 'core' employees to 'peripheral', part-time and temporary workers, so as to control labour costs. In 1990, 75 per cent of employees worked full time and 25 per cent part time. The increase in part-time employment was largely accounted for by the increase in the number of women in employment. Of the 11.5 million women in employment in 1990, 5.2 million held part-time and 6.3 million full-time jobs, whilst 13.3 million men were in full-time and only 1.5 million in part-time ones. Women, therefore not only have provided the major source of the expanding labour force but also now fill 86 per cent of the part-time jobs. One in four women, but only one in ten men, is in part-time work (Central Statistical Office 1992; 1993).

Theories of economic change

There are a large number of writers who have sought to explain what has been happening both in the British economy and in its international context. As Hirst and Zeitlin (1991) observe, there is widespread agreement that something dramatic has been happening to the international economy over the past two decades. This includes:

- rapid and radical changes in production technology and industrial organisation;
- a major restructuring of world markets;
- consequent large-scale changes in the policies of economic management at the international, national and regional levels.

But there is a great deal of confusion about how to characterise these changes, the mechanisms at work, and the policy implications for different economic and political groups. The main competing theories can be grouped under the headings of 'Fordism', 'flexible specialisation', 'regulation theory' and 'post-industrialism'.

Fordism

Fordism is used to describe both an epoch and a form of production which dominated that epoch. During the first two decades of the twentieth century a series of innovations in manufacturing led to the large-scale mass production of commodities, using highly specialised machinery, extensive division of labour and assembly line processes. Labour was highly fragmented, generally semi-skilled or unskilled, and located primarily in factories. The factories produced long runs of standardised products, at relatively low unit costs.

Fordism is also associated with scientific management principles.

Frederick Winslow Taylor (1947), the father of scientific management, demonstrated that where employers adopted a rational scientific approach to production, this would maximise productivity, output and efficiency. This entailed the separation of planning, organising and controlling from the activities of executing and producing. In other words, it was the job of management to scientifically plan production, including the work process, and the job of workers to execute and carry out the work assigned to them. Through time and motion studies, and a careful analysis of the tasks involved in completing an activity, the 'one best way' of doing it could be identified. These ideas were extended to labour and led to scientific approaches to recruitment and training to ensure that management had the right quantity and quality of labour to do the job. The result was not only standardisation and bureaucratisation within organisations but also the emergence of an 'expert' managerial cadre claiming managerial prerogative and the right to manage within the workplace (Rose 1988).

Fordism is also associated with a particular pattern of consumption. Mass production requires mass consumption if it is to be sustained. It also requires market stability. This could only be achieved if purchasing power was sufficient to consume all that was produced. Mature Fordism came to be identified with a period of government regulation known as Keynesianism (see Chapter 4). This is where governments sought, through macro-economic policies, to manage the level of aggregate demand and maintain high levels of employment.

Finally, the Fordist system of work was reflected in particular social and economic patterns of employment. Full-time male employment was the norm, with workers' families dependent on a single income and on a 'social wage' provided by the state. The nuclear family consumed standardised commodities and standardised collective goods and services provided by a bureaucratic state (Jessop 1989a). Conflicts over the industrial and social wage were resolved by political processes within industry and at a national political level. Trade unions sought to increase their members' wages and improve employee relations through collective bargaining, whilst the two main political parties used parliamentary democracy to resolve conflicts over the size and distribution of the social wage.

The challenge to Fordism

Fordism did not characterise the whole of industry, either in Britain or in other economies. But in Britain between 1945 and the mid-1970s, it was the dominant mode of production. Fordism provided the basis for the full employment, economic growth and rising living standards of the postwar era, as well as the expansion of the welfare state. As several writers point out (Jessop 1989a; Hobsbawn 1968; Weiner 1981), the prosperity of the period concealed the underlying weaknesses of the British economy and its relative decline internationally. The structural weaknesses had their origins in the nineteenth century. But the problems also stemmed from the inability of governments to develop policies for dealing with under-investment, strong trade unions and import penetration whilst, at the same time, they adopted universalist social welfare programmes and heavy defence expenditure.

The changes that are occurring in Britain today can be seen as a change from traditional or classic Fordism to a 'new Fordism' or 'post-Fordism'. A new economic era and dominant economic mode is replacing it but there is no agreement as to what form Fordism is taking. There is, however, some agreement about the factors influencing this transformation and those causing the structural crisis of Fordism. First, there is the inability of Fordism to constantly deliver rising productivity, economic growth and prosperity. Fordism appears to have reached its economic and productive limits. Constantly rising returns to scale have been frustrated by the failure of demand to keep pace with supply. Saturated markets, changes in tastes and fluctuating purchasing power have all contributed to a decline in production. Latter-day Fordism was also plagued by employee relation problems, absenteeism and alienated workforces. These stemmed from the mass production labour process, the highly bureaucratised method of control and centralised monitoring systems.

Allied to these domestic factors was the instability of world markets and the increase in global competition. The latter has also contributed to the breakdown of international price-fixing and the emergence of globalised free markets for products, raw materials and finance. Political instability in the Middle East, which led to the oil crisis in 1974, seems to have been a turning point in the fortunes of classical Fordism. There are those who argue that the response has been pragmatic and reformist: Fordism has been 'modernised' and extended into 'neo-Fordism'. Others argue there has been a fundamental break with Fordism and a move to a post-Fordist period.

Neo-Fordism and post-Fordism

Neo-Fordism focuses on the changes which have taken place in the labour process, including the introduction of new technologies, increased automation and new modes of employment and working practices. Technological innovations such as computer-integrated manufacturing systems and electronic offices have led to reductions in the labour force, the employment of multi-skilled technicians and greater flexibility in production methods. At the same time, new working practices and the introduction of participative working groups, such as quality circles and team briefing, have introduced flexibility into socio-technical systems in the workplace (see Chapter 10).

These new technologies and new working practices have not only increased flexibility and production but also led to geographical decentralisation. This decentralisation has been both domestic and international. As Allen *et al.* (1992) point out, the neo-Fordist scenario is one in which traditional Fordism is being exported to third world countries with cheap labour supplies and new potential markets. At home, the use of the new technologies and increased automation have led to a new highly skilled technical elite and to a de-skilled peripheral workforce. But mass production is still widespread and employee relations are still rooted in the capitalist dynamics of class conflict.

Post-Fordists, in contrast, argue there is a qualitative shift taking place in the economic system which is transforming a mass production, mass consumption system into one of flexible specialisation and fragmented consumption. Murray (1989) argues that across sectors of the economy, there have been changes in product life and product innovation, with shorter flexible runs and a wider range of products on offer. There have been changes in stock control, using 'just-in-time' management processes, and in design and marketing, in response to increasingly diverse patterns of demand. In contrast to neo-Fordists, who stress job de-skilling and increased centralisation of management control, post-Fordists highlight re-skilling and multi-skilling, and less hierarchical work environments that extend employee involvement and employee control of the work process.

Neo- and post-Fordists share a common emphasis on the role of flexible manufacturing systems and the development of work processes designed to provide for speedy responses to market demand and to ensure high-quality products. They also both place emphasis on the demise of Keynesianism and the emergence of neo-liberal economic strategies designed to deregulate markets, encourage free enterprise and free trade (Jessop 1989b; Sabel 1982). Both also emphasise the globalisation of supply and demand and the market. Coombes and Jones (1988) distinguish between neo- and post-Fordists, principally on the basis of how they perceive technology. Neo-Fordists see technology as being used primarily to save labour and improve the quality of production. So although task structures and modes of management may differ from conventional Taylorism, they are not significantly different in terms of either horizontal or vertical division of labour. Post-Fordists, in contrast, perceive technology as the trigger for the production of new products and the basis for the transformation of the production process itself.

Flexible specialisation

Flexible specialisation theory has much in common with the Fordist school but its distinctive approach is the focus on the movement away from mass production to small batch production or craft production. Mass production is defined as the manufacture of standardised products in high volumes, using special-purpose machinery and predominantly unskilled labour. Craft production or flexible specialisation, conversely, is defined as the manufacture of a wide and changing array of customised products, using flexible, general-purpose machinery and skilled, adaptable workers (Hirst and Zeitlin 1991). According to flexible specialisation theory, the market and technological conditions necessary for Fordism and its labour process no longer exist. A new style of production, rooted in new technologies, is emerging and with it new relationships between managers and workers. Flexible specialisation emphasises flexibility in a number of areas. These include responsiveness to the market, to pressures on costs and to the workforce.

Lash and Urry (1987) see flexible specialisation as emerging from three causes:

- changes in technology;
- changes in taste (which break up mass market demand);
- competition from third world producers.

Technology is seen as an independent causative agent, with flexible specialisation being a reactive response to complex and niche markets in organising production. Producers must cut costs by minimising the holding of stocks and operating with the minimum levels of inventory. The introduction of new technology in the work process offers scope for multi-skilling and enhancing employee control of the work process. But it also facilitates greater managerial control and it is questionable whether the changes most benefit workers or managers.

Hirst and Zeitlin (1991) draw attention to two other features of flexible specialisation. First, it is a system of network production in which firms are aware that they do not know precisely what they have to produce and that they must count on the collaboration of workers and sub-contractors in meeting the market's eventual demand. Second, and linked to this, it creates a complex set of practices at company level, involving relationships with sub-contractors, other firms and the sectoral and district institutions supporting and sustaining the system of production.

Thompson (1989) sees flexible specialisation as a strategy that firms may follow. Flexibility may take a number of forms. Numerical flexibility is concerned with enhancing the firm's ability to adjust labour inputs to fluctuations in output. Functional or internal flexibility is concerned with adjusting and deploying the skills of the employees to tasks required by the changing production methods, technology and workload. And pay flexibility is allied to these and is concerned with adjusting labour costs to changing market conditions (Atkinson 1985; Wood 1989).

A central debate for the flexible specialisation school is whether a dual labour market is emerging, in which the core group of workers benefits from flexible specialisation, with its multi-skilling and employee involvement practices (see Chapter 10), whereas the peripheral group of part-time, sub-contract labour is de-skilled and without secure employment. A second debate revolves around how widespread flexible specialisation is. Atkinson (1985) concludes that in the mid-1980s, whilst flexibility had become an important theme in corporate thinking, few British firms had explicitly and comprehensively reorganised their labour force on that basis. Since then there has been an increase in flexible specialisation, especially in the public sector, where government policies of deregulation, contracting-out and privatisation have resulted in new strategies along the core-periphery model (see Chapter 7; Pollert 1987). Failure to introduce flexible specialisation within both the private and public sectors has often been attributed to a skills shortage amongst managers and workers.

Regulation theory

A more radical analysis of contemporary economic change can be found amongst regulationist theorists (Aglietta 1979; Boyer 1986 and 1987; Lipietz 1985, 1988, 1992). These scholars, mainly French sociologists based in Paris, have much in common with the flexible specialisation theorists but they adopt a broader concept of Fordism. For them, it is more than a production system and a particular labour process: it is a specific regime of capital accumulation, or a paradigm of production and consumption in which the economy is regulated in a particular way. Their approach is to focus on the way that the economy is regulated as a key to understanding economic activity, stability and change. They argue that the mode of regulation acts as a support system for the economy and 'pulls together and directs the wide variety of actions taken by firms, banks, retailers, workers, state employees.'

Regulation takes place at two levels – the national and the international. The mechanisms within each national economy regulate labour and capital, on the one hand, and different types of capital on the other. These controls include the system of management, the labour process, the system of wage payments, the role of market forces in determining prices and wages and the policies of the state towards incomes control and welfare provision (Harris 1988). At the international level, it is the international monetary system which is the key regulator.

Regulationists argue that it was the breakdown of both the internal and the international regulators in the 1970s which provided a turning point for the economies of the West generally and for Britain in particular. Keynesianism was the mode of regulation compatible with Fordism, holding it together for a generation and resulting in a distinctive period of economic growth. By the 1970s, however, a crisis of capitalism was emerging with which the old regulatory system failed to cope. Regulationists trace the structural crisis of Fordism, first, to the Fordist labour process and the inability of mass production methods, for both technical and social reasons, to realise further productivity gains. In addition, insufficient demand for everything that was or could be produced resulted in a fall in profits. The second cause was a change in the global level of demand and an increase in world competition. Capital had to search for new sources of profit and so structural reorganisation became necessary. The regulationist school sees the explanation for the changes in the economy in the inherent contradictions of capitalism and its tendency towards a falling rate of profit.

Post-industrialism

It was Daniel Bell (1973) who first identified what he thought were the characteristics of a new emergent economic system, the 'post-industrial society'. These were:

- the change from a goods-producing to a service economy;
- the emergence of a new professional and technical class;
- the central role of theoretical knowledge as the source of innovation;
- the creation of new information-based technologies.

Bell did not envisage that these developments would completely replace the industrial society of previous periods, but they would be sufficiently radical to justify the new title of 'post-industrial'. The post-industrial society would be one in which most people would be employed in service industries, manufacturing and manual work would decline, and white-collar and professional workers would become a new occupational elite. Society would be dominated by information and information technologies, which would transform organisational structures and processes as well as the location and content of work. In the post-industrial society, information would become the key commodity. Post-industrial society would, therefore, be an 'information society'.

Bell saw profit and production as the motivating force – the 'axial principle' – underlying the dynamics of change for the industrial society. The driving force behind post-industrial society would be knowledge and information. It would be the generation of knowledge and information and the new information technologies which would be the motors of economic growth. Bell was optimistic about the liberating effects of information technologies that would lead to the increasing automation of work processes and to high productivity. People would work less and enjoy more leisure. Those jobs not automated would require re-skilling and offer scope for job enlargement. Post-industrial society would guarantee sufficient wealth to raise standards of living for all and to reduce the class conflicts endemic in the industrial era. There would, Bell predicted, be an 'end of ideology' as all societies moved to the post-industrial stage of development. In his later writings, Bell recognised that one of the consequences of the high growth rates and liberating effects of automation in post-industrial society might be to weaken the 'work ethic', as people pursued hedonistic life styles and chose leisure rather than work and income. He saw this as a source of potential conflict and tension within the new 'information, service society'.

Toffler (1980) describes the post-industrial society as a 'third wave' after the 'first wave' agricultural and the 'second wave' industrial societies. New sciences and knowledge and new technologies would transform the economy structurally, geographically and socially. The new 'information society' would be characterised by desynchronisation, decentralisation, matrix structures, multiple command structures, networking, new life styles and prosumers. Whilst second wave industrial societies sought out predictability and principles compatible with mechanical causality, third wave societies would be governed by a perception of things as inherently and unavoidably unpredictable. In this type of society, order emerges out of chaos and chance dominates change. Toffler, like Bell, was optimistic about the post-industrial society. He predicted that information and communication would be the main means of integrating society and empowering the individual.

A less optimistic view of post-industrial society is presented by the French theorist Alain Touraine (1974). He describes the emerging society as a programmed society in which knowledge and information and 'technocracy' would dominate. However, unlike Bell, Touraine does not envisage an end of ideology and social conflict but a new class conflict between those who control information and its uses and those who do not. In the future, he argues, the root of conflict between social classes would not be ownership and control of property but access to information and its uses.

Two further writers, both in the Marxist tradition, are often grouped together in the same school as Bell and Toffler. However, both Castells (1989) and Gorz (1982) tend to distance themselves from the post-industrial emphasis. Castells states that the new information-based society is no more post-industrial than the industrial society was post-agrarian. It represents a further stage in the evolution of capitalism in which new technologies have enabled companies to operate in new ways. In particular, new information technologies now traverse continents, space and time, shrinking the world and markets and enabling flexible and fragmented multinational corporations to emerge. Similarly, within organisations, core 'information workers' now function alongside a peripheral workforce of low-skilled workers, thus segmenting the organisation and polarising the 'knowledge elite' and the supportive mass.

Gorz agrees with Castells that the new information technologies are altering the structure of work and producing a core of secure, well-paid workers on the one hand and a peripheral workforce, which is poorly paid and lacking any job security, on the other. In addition, he sees increased automation as creating 'jobless growth' and a rising pool of unemployed. Gorz describes the new class structure as consisting of a securely employed professional class, a 'servile' working class, increasingly alienated and totally instrumental in their attitude to work, and a swelling underclass of unemployed. For Gorz and Castells, the 'new industrial society' is characterised by growing inequalities.

All the post-industrial theorists agree that there has been a shift from manufacturing to a service-based economy in Western economies. Knowledge, information and communication technologies are both enabling and driving this transformation. The result is a changing social and power elite, with the old class structures giving way to new social formations. Bell and Toffler are optimistic about the outcomes of change, whilst Castells, Gorz and Touraine point to the differential benefits within a new class formation.

Conclusion

This brief summary of the main theories describing and explaining industrial change over the last two decades points to certain environmental factors which are influencing organisations and their production, marketing and employee relations strategies. These are:

- the changing industrial structures, modes of production and movement to flexible specialisation;
- the globalisation of markets, the spread of multinational corporations and geographical relocation;
- the emergence of new occupations, the dual labour market and changes in the class structure;
- the demise of Keynesianism and its associated patterns of internal and external regulation, and the emergence of new neo-liberal economic policies and state regulation;
- the transition from mechanical and electronic technologies to new information technologies.

It is impossible to separate out the interacting forces and to identify a single causal factor but a necessary condition of the changes would appear to be information technology.

Information technology

Technology is the application of knowledge to aid human production. There are many types of technology and it is advances in technology that have generally accompanied major waves of economic change. Toffler (1980) states that in all societies the energy system, the production system and the distribution system are interrelated parts of a 'techno-sphere' which has its characteristic form at each stage of social development. Fossil fuels provided the energy for industrial societies and a new technology spawned, first, steam-driven and, later, electromechanically driven machines. These were then brought together into interconnected systems to create factories, mass production and Fordist structures.

The new technologies are rooted in 'information technology' (IT). IT in its strictest sense is the science of collecting, storing, processing and transmitting information (Forester 1985: page xiii). It is the result of a convergence of the three separate technologies of electronics, computing and communications, and the invention of the silicon chip. Naisbitt (1982) points to the launching of the Russian satellite Sputnik in 1957 as the trigger for a technological and communications revolution which has transformed the world. From the late 1960s, a series of scientific and technological inventions converged to constitute a new scientific paradigm. Castell (1989) points out that the sequential scientific discoveries of the transistor (1947), the integrated circuit (1957), the planar process (1959) and the microprocessor (1971) mean that this new technological paradigm has characteristics which differentiate it from earlier paradigms. In the past, technology transformed processes rather than produced goods or services. The new IT is not only transforming processes bu also producing information as an output. Unlike earlier technologies, IT is also pervasive. The IT revolution is not confined to the economic sphere of production. It is also fundamentally changing the social, cultural and political spheres of our society at an accelerating rate.

Applications

Computers are found in homes, schools, hospitals, offices and shops as well as factories. Microchips control domestic appliances, programmed learning, machinery, banking cash points, telephones, aeroplanes and satellites. No type of commercial, service or public organisation has been left untouched. Although the pace of change varies between sectors and organisations, because of lack of investment, labour resistance, poor management or market factors, the changes over the last 20 years amount to a revolution in every aspect of life. In particular, there has been an exponential growth in telecommunications. Microelectronics has made possible the intelligent digital network, satellite communications, cable TV, cellular radio and videotex. All of these are transforming the way people work, where they work, how they receive entertainment, how they shop, how they conduct their financial relationships, the way they are educated and how they communicate with others.

Another dimension of the IT revolution is the international consequences of communication satellites. These make possible the creation of a 'global village'. The international financial market can be accessed from any financial centre in the world. Trader dealings take place continuously throughout a 24-hour period and a financial movement in any one country can send shock waves around the globe. Satellites also make possible the exporting of jobs and the fragmentation of the production process. Component parts can be produced in one area of the world, where labour is cheap, and transported for assembly into a finished product nearer the main market. Multinational corporations can have their headquarters in one country and their production units spread throughout the world and still communicate on a daily basis. Thus modern communications enable organisational flexibility.

Historically, new technology has been met with resistance, as it has threatened traditional occupations and skills. Yet in reality, new technology has resulted in the creation of jobs and led to increased production, increased wealth and higher standards of living. Optimists claim that new jobs will compensate for the losses, as in the past (Sleigh *et al.* 1979), whilst pessimists argue that job losses will be greater than the gains (Barron 1978).

Effects

What have been the effects of the new technology on employment patterns and work processes? As indicated in the previous section there are different views on the changes taking place but there is general agreement that IT offers scope for:

- relieving the boredom of repetitive assembly line work;
- job enrichment and job enlargement;
- new forms of work organisation with flatter hierarchies;
- transforming old-style employee relations;
- involving workers directly in the decision-making process;
- transferring the work base from the office to the home.

All of these opportunities have been seized upon more or less by British industry, although the first stage of the transformation from an industrial to an information society has been to apply the new technology to existing work processes. New industries have emerged, including a computer hardware and software industry. This is setting the pace of the IT revolution as it makes possible new ways of doing things and new things to do. Computers are eliminating jobs and restructuring organisations as 'informatisation' is developed. Computers make it possible to dispense with clerical systems and to create electronic offices. They are replacing brain power by storing, retrieving, sorting and transforming data into information at phenomenal speeds. In medicine and the law, 'expert systems' are replacing people in taking decisions based on information fed into the machine.

Nilles (1985: page 202) draws a comparison between the microcomputer and the car, and the telephone line and the highway. In industrial society, cars transported workers via the highway to factories and offices. Today it is information which is transported instead of the worker. 'In principle the telecommuter has access to anyone with a computer and with near-zero transit time.' Work styles are being changed significantly through telework and telecommuting. However, as Nilles points out, while telecommuting may facilitate geographical mobility, offer flexible patterns of work and solve the problem of urban congestion, it may erode employee loyalty, corporate identity and corporate integration. An alternative view is that telecommuters are becoming part of a peripheral workforce and home-working the sweat shops of the twenty-first century.

It is very difficult to predict the future use and the outcome of the application of new technology, because of the interrelatedness of the variables in a modern economy. Technology cannot be divorced from a whole range of factors that affect how it develops and the effect it has on work and society. For example, the impact of technology depends on: investment in a telecommunication grid; the reliability of transmissions; and the compatibility of systems both internally and externally. The present technological revolution is more wide-ranging than any in the past. It can erode jobs in every sector and job losses appear to be a significant event of the 1990s. But job losses are due not only to new technology but also to over-production, increased competition and falling profits. Business strategy has been to look at ways of reducing labour costs and of increasing flexibility which may actually save jobs in the long term.

Miles (1989) suggests that there is not simply one information society but many different possible information societies.These depend on the social choices that are made about the use and application of technology. These decisions are taken in both the public and the private domains and are reflected in public policy and business strategy. There is some debate about the nature of the technological changes taking place and the social processes facilitating this change. Miles and his colleagues (1988) identify three perspectives. One viewpoint is the 'transformist' perspective. This argues that there is a synergy between the properties of IT and emerging post-industrial values. The application of IT speeds up value change, which in turn facilitates further application of IT. Professional groups within society who are at the forefront of IT and those societies further down the post-industrial route provide leadership and act as the vanguard of change. Technology appears in this perspective as a driving force which it is difficult to resist.

The second, 'continuist', perspective is more sceptical about the rate of change and its revolutionary effects. It points to the incremental nature of the change process, including technological change, and to the differential use of the more advanced forms of IT. The adoption and diffusion of IT is slow and pragmatic. The continuists point to the limited changes which have taken place in work processes and in ways of life in the last two decades and the failure of computers to live up to expectations. Change in the future is likely therefore to be gradual, disjointed, incremental, pragmatic and unpredictable.

The third, 'structuralist', perspective shares with the transformist view the perception that IT represents a revolutionary technology, but rejects the idea that it is leading to a new social order. Structuralism sees IT as more likely to facilitate a further development of industrialism or super-industrialism than to lead to its being superseded. In structuralism, elements of continuity and transformation are merged. Technological determinism is rejected in favour of a view of technological development as resulting from social factors on both the supply and demand sides, often called 'technology push' and 'technology pull'. New knowledge and innovations provide the potential for change but are not all used. There has to be an awareness of them and they have to be perceived to be relevant and appropriate. Whether they are or not depends on management strategies, market conditions and public policies. Equally, a demand for new technology and ways of solving social problems stimulate technological innovation. Thus technology push and technology pull are not exclusive. They feed on each other, but both depend on the structural context of organisations and markets.

There is, therefore, some difficulty in predicting or forecasting technological change. Miles identifies the potential for IT applications in the different parts of the economy and points to three likely persistent trends:

* employment is likely to continue to shift from primary and secondary sectors to the tertiary sector;
* service, administrative and professional occupations will increase relative to traditional manual and production jobs;
* lifetime working hours will decrease.

In addition, Miles identifies continuing trends and a number of possible future impacts of IT on organisational structures and management including:

* using IT to link operations over long distances;
* decentralising operations and management activities;
* facilitating greater coordination and strategic control;
* providing growing competitive advantage for firms;
* using IT for scenario building;
* highlighting the importance of information as a commodity;
* making information management a key function in firms.

The impact of IT on consumer goods and services and on social behaviour is again difficult to predict, but there is likely to be a continuing adaptation of IT to new functions, the development of new IT applications and a greater diffusion of IT-based commodities and services. Education, health and legal services are being transformed, as IT enables individuals to access knowledge and information in the home, at resource centres and at terminals in public places. The 'dark' scenario of the impact on society predicts social isolationism, privatism, increased alienation and breakdown of values. The 'bright' view is one of increased freedom and empowerment, more social time, more communication, more self-service and more and better services, particularly for the sick, the elderly and the disabled. The crucial issues are whether the information society will lead to a more integrated and socially equal community or whether it will lead to new forms of inequality and inequity.

The social context

British society has changed more rapidly during the last half-century than at any time in its past. There have been significant changes in its population, social structures, the role of women, social attitudes, culture and the dominant ideas influencing its politics. These are linked to changes in its economic system and in technology but are themselves variables in the total equation of change.

Demography

Britain's population was 57.6 million in 1992, having grown slowly from 50 million in 1951. It will continue to grow to 60 million by 2030 when it is anticipated that deaths will exceed births and it will start to fall. There were 28.1 million males and 29.5 million females in 1992. The birthrate tended to fall in the postwar period, although there was a baby boom in the late 1940s, another in the 1960s and a third in the early 1990s. These fluctuations are reflected in the age structure of the population, which is also affected by migration and life expectancy. There are also differences in the birth rates of ethnic groups within Britain. In 1991, the total period fertility rate for women born in Britain was 1.8 and 2.5 for women born in the New Commonwealth. The latter had fallen from 3.8 in 1971 and there is a growing convergence between these two groups. One significant trend has been the percentage of births outside marriage, which increased from 8 per cent in 1971 to about a third in 1991. There are significant differences between different ethnic groups. Only 1.2 per cent of births are outside marriage amongst women born in Pakistan and Bangladesh, 47.8 per cent amongst those born in the Carribean and 34.1 per cent amongst those born in Africa.

Table 3: *Age and sex structure of the UK population for selected years, 1951–91*

	Under 16	16–39	40–64	65–79	80–over	All Ages (=100%) (millions)
Mid-year estimates						
1951	—	—	31.6	9.5	1.4	50.3
1961	24.8	31.4	32.0	9.8	1.9	52.8
1971	25.6	31.3	29.9	10.9	2.3	55.9
1981	22.2	34.9	27.8	12.2	2.8	56.4
1991	20.3	35.2	28.7	12.0	3.7	57.6
Males	21.4	36.5	29.1	10.7	2.3	28.1
Females	19.3	34.0	28.3	13.3	5.1	29.5
Mid-year projections						
2001	21.3	32.6	30.5	11.4	4.2	59.2
2011	20.1	30.0	33.7	11.7	4.5	60.0
2021	19.5	30.5	31.9	13.6	4.5	60.7
Males	20.2	31.6	32.1	12.7	3.4	30.0
Females	18.7	29.5	31.6	14.5	5.7	30.7

Source: *Social Trends* 23 1993

Within the overall population, there have been significant changes in its structure, as shown in Table 3. The declining birth rate has resulted in a fall in the 0–16 age group from over 14.3 million in 1971 to 11.6 million in 1990. This gave rise to talk of a 'demographic time-bomb' in the 1990s, when it was claimed that there would be too few school leavers to meet industry's demand for labour. The onset of recession in 1990 averted the problem. At the other end of the age structure, the number of people over 65 is growing both absolutely and relatively. Their numbers were almost five times greater in 1991 than in 1901 and had grown by 3.5 million between 1951 and 1991. This group is expected to increase by another 2.5 million by 2025. In 1901, it represented 8 per cent of the population; in 1951, 11 per cent; and in 1991, nearly 16 per cent. By 2031, it is estimated that it will reach 14.6 million, a rise of nearly 40 per cent over 1990 (Central Statistical Office 1993).

The labour force is traditionally drawn from the 16–64 age group. This rose from 33.5 million in 1961 to 36.8 million in 1990 but is expected to stabilise up to the end of the century. The economic activity rate varies between men and women, with men forming the larger part of the labour force. Women, however, now form an ever larger proportion, with a constantly rising participation rate, whilst that of men continues to fall. Between 1981 and 1992, 10 per cent of married women of working age joined the labour force. Over a half of all women of working age are now economically active. Because of the ageing profile of the population in general, there will be a shift towards the higher age groups. In 1986, only one in four of the labour force were under 24. By 2001, only one in six will be under 24 and over one-third of the working population will be over 45. Because of the higher birth rates of the ethnic minorities, they will represent a growing proportion of the younger working population.

From the 1950s, there was a net influx of Commonwealth immigrants, first, from the West Indies, then, from the Indian sub-continent and, in the 1970s, from east Africa. Since then, there have been a series of laws to restrict immigrants from the New Commonwealth and their numbers have fallen. In 1990, of 52,000 immigrants less than half were from the New Commonwealth and most of those were dependents of people already settled in Britain. There are now 2.9 million people from ethnic minorities born either in Britain or overseas who represent about 5 per cent of the population. The number has doubled since 1971, when they constituted 2.3 per cent of the total. The largest minorities are from India (30 per cent), the West Indies (21 per cent) and Pakistan (16 per cent). Smaller communities are drawn from Bangladesh, Africa and the Arab countries, each of which constitute about 5 per cent.

According to the Department of Employment Labour Force Survey (1990), 43 per cent of the present ethnic minorities were born inside the UK, half of those being of West Indian origin. There are significant differences in the age structures of the ethnic minorities. Most are below 30 and only 5 per cent are over 60. They still have the highest birth rates but, as stated above, these are falling. The pattern of past immigration has resulted in Britain becoming a multiracial society with a rich mix of religions and cultures. The ethnic minorities are not distributed evenly throughout the country. They are concentrated in the large cities, often in ghetto areas. They also tend to be found in the lowest-paid jobs and are more likely to be unemployed than white people.

The pattern of migration has been changing during the 1980s, with more migrants coming from or moving to Europe. But in the late

1980s, there was a dramatic increase in the numbers seeking political asylum, a rise from 4,000 in 1986 to 45,000 in 1991. This reflected the general political instability throughout the world, the upheavals in Eastern Europe and the opportunism of some people who sought the economic advantages of living in Britain. In response, the government introduced an Asylum Bill in 1992 to tighten up immigration control. The fact that only 4,680 applications were processed in 1991 and there were nearly 69,000 cases outstanding also deterred people from applying. Controls are likely to be more difficult to enforce with the introduction of the European single market since January 1993.

Almost 80 per cent of the population live in urban areas and of the remaining 20 per cent most commute to urban areas to work. There has been a slow but continual migration of population from the north to the south throughout the century and Scotland experienced an absolute population decline from 1961 to 1989, though since then there has been a small net influx. The overall pattern is one of net migration from the north-east, Northern Ireland, the north-west and Wales to the south-east of England. In the late 1980s, the major growth areas were, in addition to the south-east, East Anglia and the south-west. Other significant trends have been suburbanisation, with people moving out of the metropolitan areas to smaller towns and dormitory areas, and the growth of retirement centres concentrated mainly around the coast. Geographical mobility is also an increasing social feature of the UK, with one million people moving between regions in 1989 (Central Statistical Office 1992).

Social structure

The period between 1945 and the late 1970s was one of relative affluence and social progress. A postwar consensus amongst the major political parties on welfare-Keynesianism, an expanded public sector and high levels of employment and consumption led to rising standards of living for all. There was increased immigration to meet labour shortages and more women entered employment and the labour market. New occupations, and in particular new professions, emerged in the expanded welfare state. These changes resulted in greater social mobility, a more multicultural society and a more complex social structure. The class structure began to change as the working class became more affluent, white-collar jobs increased and wealth became more evenly distributed. The boundaries between the classes became blurred, as a result of social mobility, merging life styles and similar patterns of consumption.

Class and occupation

The debate about the changing class structure revolves around the extent to which the traditional working class is being absorbed into the middle classes and whether a new working class has emerged. The concept of working class is itself problematic, since in modern society most people work for a wage or salary. Traditionally, the working class has been associated with blue-collar manual occupations which are skilled, semi-skilled or unskilled. This distinguishes it from white-collar workers, the professions and the self-employed who constitute a middle class. In 1951, about two-thirds of the working population and their families were in manual occupations. Between the 1971 and 1981 censuses the proportion of employed people in manual work fell from 62 to 56 per cent for men and from 43 to 36 per cent for women (Halsey 1986: page 31). By 1992, only about one-third of the labour force had manual jobs and an increasing proportion of those were females and from ethnic minorities. The traditional working class is therefore smaller than it was and its composition has changed. This is the result of:

- a contraction of the industries in which manual workers were traditionally found – shipbuilding, coal, iron and steel, docks, transport and textiles;
- restructuring, automation and the introduction of new technology in industries such as printing and car manufacture;
- the transfer of production to countries with cheaper labour and the closure or contraction of British plants.

The middle classes or white-collar occupations, in contrast, grew in the postwar period and now constitute the largest group. They consist of the service group of employees, the professions, managers and the growing number of self-employed. This 'new' middle class is highly fragmented and heterogeneous. It consists of three sub-strata:

- an upper middle class which includes the higher professions, senior civil servants, senior managers and those holding senior technical positions;

- a middle middle class which includes the lower professions and middle management and technical grades and the old middle class of small business owners and farmers;
- a lower middle class of those in clerical and supervisory positions, minor professionals and para-professionals and white-collar shop-workers.

The middle class has become numerically and socially the most significant social stratum.

The upper class consists of a small number of interconnected families which own a disproportionate amount of wealth, control and own large parts of industry, land and commerce and hold the top positions in business, politics and the other insitutions, thus making up the 'Establishment'. This class is economically dominant and operates through networks which are national and international. Scott (1982: page 114) states 'the core of the class consists of those who are actively involved in the strategic control of the major units of capital of which the modern economy is formed.'

Those who argue that the old class system is coming to an end point to the relatively open and fluid boundary between the upper middle class and the upper class. This enables pop stars, inventors and successful business people to become millionaires, ministers and members of the House of Lords. Equally, they point to the 'new working class' which is now more skilled, more educated and more affluent than the 'old working class', with life styles and consumption patterns in common with the professional middle classes. Social mobility and the changing status attached to new occupations is levelling the distinctions and blurring the differences. A closer analysis, however, gives rise to an alternative perspective.

Lockwood (1958) views class membership as largely a function of an individual's market and work situation. The market situation consists of income, degree of job security and opportunity for upward mobility. The work situation, on the other hand, refers to 'the set of social relationships in which the individual is involved at work by virtue of his position in the division of labour' (page 15). The latter is reflected in the degree of autonomy, independence and control that an individual has over work and the skills which the work requires. The working class is distinguishable not only by the market situation that workers occupy but also by the work situation, in which manual workers have little control and no autonomy over the work process.

Though there continues to be a difference between the working and middle classes based upon income and types of work, status and qualifications, the changing nature of the work process in many clerical, managerial and professional occupations is leading to a loss of autonomy and job control which is blurring the distinction amongst the classes. Many white-collar, lower middle class workers are being proletarianised (Crompton and Jones 1984). This proletarianisation of the middle classes is also reflected in a more instrumental attitude towards work. Another significant factor is that many clerical jobs have become feminised and this has led to a relative decline in the rewards and status of office work. So it could appear that there is a downward merging of the classes rather than an upward mobility.

Class, income and wealth

Class is more than a group of people with similar jobs or market position. Class is associated with common life styles, culture, consumption patterns and a command over resources which gives power and status, thereby extending freedom of choice to those comprising it. The class structure reflects the distribution of power within society, the differential access to resources and relative life chances.

Between 1945 and 1975, there was some evidence of an increase in the equality of personal income. The Royal Commission on the Distribution of Income and Wealth (1979) showed that there had been some marginal change, with the share of the top 10 per cent falling from 29.4 per cent of total income in 1959 to 26.6 per head in 1974–75. Over the same period, the share of the top 1 per cent had fallen from 8.4 per cent to 6.2 per cent. However, the bottom 50 per cent only increased their share from 23.1 to 24.2 per cent. So although there was a redistribution amongst the top third of income earners, in general income distribution remained relatively stable. Personal income after tax showed a small degree of equalisation, due mainly to progressive taxation and welfare state redistributive social policies. As Table 4 shows, this trend has been reversed since 1979 and inequality has increased. In 1977, the bottom fifth of households accounted for 4 per cent of disposable income and 9 per cent of post-tax income. The top fifth accounted for 43 and 37 per cent respectively. In 1988, the figures were 2 per cent and 7 per cent for the bottom one-fifth and 50 and 43 per cent for the top fifth.

Table 4: *Quintile shares of household income in the UK 1977–88*

	Bottom fifth	Next fifth	Middle fifth	Next fifth	Top fifth	Total
Equivalised original income						
1977	4	10	18	26	43	100
1979	2	10	18	27	43	100
1981	3	9	17	26	46	100
1983	3	8	17	26	47	100
1985	2	7	17	27	47	100
1987	2	7	16	25	50	100
1988	2	7	16	25	50	100
Equivalised gross income						
1977	9	13	18	24	37	100
1979	8	13	18	24	37	100
1981	8	12	17	23	39	100
1983	8	12	17	23	39	100
1985	8	12	17	24	40	100
1987	8	11	16	23	43	100
1988	7	11	16	23	43	100
Equivalised disposable income						
1977	10	14	18	23	36	100
1979	9	13	18	23	36	100
1981	9	13	17	23	38	100
1983	10	13	17	23	38	100
1985	9	13	17	23	38	100
1987	8	12	16	23	41	100
1988	8	11	16	23	42	100
Equivalised post-tax income						
1977	9	14	17	23	37	100
1979	10	13	18	23	37	100
1981	9	13	17	22	39	100
1983	9	13	17	22	39	100
1985	9	13	17	23	39	100
1987	8	12	16	22	43	100
1988	7	11	16	22	44	100

Source: Central Statistical Office, from *Family Expenditure Survey*

Employee Relations

Table 5: *Distribution of wealth in the UK 1976–89*

		1976	1981	1986	1989
					Percentages and £billion
Marketable wealth Percentage of wealth owned by:					
Most wealthy	1%	21	18	18	18
Most wealthy	5%	38	36	36	38
Most wealthy	10%	50	50	50	53
Most wealthy	25%	71	73	73	75
Most wealthy	50%	92	92	90	94
Total marketable wealth (£ billion)		280	565	955	1,578
Marketable wealth less value of dwellings Percentage of wealth owned by:					
Most wealthy	1%	29	26	25	28
Most wealthy	5%	47	45	46	53
Most wealthy	10%	57	56	58	66
Most wealthy	25%	73	74	75	81
Most wealthy	50%	88	87	89	94
Marketable wealth plus occupational and state pension rights (historic valuation) Percentage of wealth owned by:					
Most wealthy	1%	12	10	10	11
Most wealthy	5%	24	23	23	26
Most wealthy	10%	34	33	34	38
Most wealthy	25%	54	55	57	62
Most wealthy	50%	78	78	81	83
Marketable wealth plus occupational and state pension rights (latest valuation) Percentage of wealth owned by:					
Most wealthy	1%	13	11	10	11
Most wealthy	5%	26	24	24	26
Most wealthy	10%	36	34	35	38
Most wealthy	25%	57	56	58	62
Most wealthy	50%	80	79	82	83

Source: *Social Trends* 22, 1992

The distribution of wealth has changed slightly more over the post-war period but again the change has been a redistribution within the top 50 per cent which still own over 90 per cent of disposable wealth. As Table 5 shows, the top 1 per cent still own 18 per cent of marketable wealth, whilst the bottom 50 per cent still have only 6 per cent. The distribution does not change significantly when the value of dwellings is excluded but does change slightly more when occupational and state pensions are included. The most wealthy 1 per cent then own only 11 per cent, whilst the least wealthy 50 per cent own 17 per cent. Wealth, then, continues to be very unevenly distributed, even more so than income, and since 1979 the gap has widened.

Townsend (1979) suggests that in the late 1970s some 25 per cent of households were in relative poverty. Official statistics published in 1992 show that those living on less than half the country's average income – the nearest thing to the poverty line – rose from five million in 1979 to 12 million in 1989 (Department of Social Security 1992). Those with less than half the average income, after housing costs, had increased from 9 per cent in 1979 to 22 per cent in 1992. Furthermore, one in four children lived in poverty, compared with one in ten in 1979. In 1993, 30 per cent of the population were estimated to be at or below the official poverty line. Some of those were in work on low wages, others included the unemployed, the sick, the elderly, the old, one-parent families and the ethnic minorities.

This burgeoning strata of poor has been described as a new 'underclass' (Dahrendorf 1987) and a neo-proletariat (Gorz 1982). This underclass is distinct from the traditional working class because it is marginalised, both economically and politically, and tends to be apathetic and fatalistic or to constitute a criminal subculture, functioning outside the norms and institutions of society. The growth in the underclass is clearly a consequence in part of the economic changes taking place in Britain: the declining requirement for manual workers and the creation of a dual labour market, with high-paid core workers and low-paid peripheral ones. On the other hand, government policies of rolling back the welfare state, reducing social benefits and welfare support, and abolishing wages councils, have also contributed.

Class and consumption

Class based upon occupation, income and wealth is an objective perception but people's own subjective perceptions and how they assign themselves is often very different. People's self-assignment is more often based on patterns of consumption and life style than on market or job position. It is this that has led some writers to suggest that class rooted in production relationships is no longer the most significant social division. They argue that it is changing consumption patterns that explain contemporary political alignments, not economic class (Dunleavy 1980; Hamnett 1989; Saunders 1978; 1984).

Saunders distinguishes between 'collective consumption' and 'private consumption'. The former refers to those goods and services provided by the state and available to the public as a citizen right. Private consumption refers to the purchase of goods and services, by individuals, through the market. There was a great increase in collective consumption after 1945, with the spread of the welfare state. Collective provision of health, education, housing and other community services was associated with a rising standard of living for all and was an important factor in the *embourgeoisement* of the working classes. Greater personal affluence since the 1960s enabled the working class to consider home ownership and consumer durables similar to those enjoyed by the middle class. In terms of material life styles, there was a convergence here too. However, there was little private consumption of merit goods, such as health and education, except amongst the upper class. Both the middle and working classes received universal services from the state.

Since 1979, there has been a notable shift within both the working and middle classes towards private consumption. Successive Conservative governments encouraged this, first, with the sale of council housing and tax incentives to take out private health insurance and educational convenants. Later changes to the expenditure and organisation of public services persuaded people to look more to the market and to privatised consumption. This change has had certain consequences, particularly for those whose market position is weak. As Saunders (1984) argues, it is now consumption patterns that are every bit as important as occupational class in understanding patterns of power, privilege and inequality, in explaining the kaleidoscopic nature of the modern social structure and in accounting for the changing political alignments that have resulted from many years of Conservative, market-centred governments.

The present class structure consists, then, of an underclass, the new working class, and the salariat and technocrats who largely make up a new middle class. An upper class still tops the social strata, upheld by institutions like the monarchy, the House of Lords, the aristocracy and the honours system. It is divided today between those traditional conservatives, who are often referred to as 'one nation Tories', and the *nouveaux riches* who are 'entryists', part of the business elite and often market liberals. The power and functions of the upper class remain the same, since they combine ownership of property and wealth with strategic control of industry and other major institutions. They are, however, becoming increasingly invisible and globalised.

The enlarged middle classes are the fastest growing and the most heterogeneous group. They range from the traditional higher professions and the salariat of managers and administrators to the new professions and technocrats, the para-professionals and the small shopkeepers and self-employed. The reconstituted working class is located above the underclass and consists of manual and low-level clerical workers who are distinct both from the apathetic underclass and the middle class. Those in the new working class are described by Goldthorpe and Lockwood (1968) as affluent but not bourgeois. In contrast with the traditional working class, which was class conscious and politically committed to the trade union and labour movement, the new working class has more instrumental attitudes towards work, unions and politics and they are more privatised in their social lives. They prefer to amass material things, own their own homes and spend time with their families. In the work situation, however, they have little control, are the most vulnerable to economic change, are affected by de-skilling and have the weakest market position. Their numbers are being expanded as the market situations of lower grade technical, office and shop workers change. Braverman (1974) argues that technological change downgrades these workers and relegates them to the status of a proletarian working class, whilst upgrading others who gain access to a higher class. The new working class lacks homogeneity but is less heterogeneous than the 'new' middle class.

Gender

Class is not the only basis of inequality in Britain. Another social division cutting across class is gender. Gender differences are socially constructed and reflect the different social expectations and roles which are attached to men and women in society. Just as the changes taking place within the economy are affecting the class structure so they are affecting gender relationships especially, but not exclusively, at work.

Employee Relations

In 1901, women accounted for only 29 per cent of the workforce and most were confined to unpaid domestic work within the home. Two world wars saw women called in as a reserve army of labour to do the jobs left by the men mobilised into the armed forces. There was a return to normality after 1918 but in 1945 the welfare state opened up many new jobs for women and, since then, they have formed an increasingly important proportion of the labour market. Women accounted for 44 per cent of the labour force in 1992 and this was expected to rise to 50 per cent by the turn of the century. Over 50 per cent of all women between 16 and 60 are now in employment. This figure is the second highest in the EC, with only Denmark, at 61 per cent, currently higher.

The pattern of women's employment is different from that of men in a number of ways. First, women are concentrated in four main areas of employment. These are:

- clerical and administrative work;
- catering, cleaning and hairdressing;
- retailing;
- the caring services, including nursing, teaching and social work.

These four areas account for 80 per cent of all female employment. Women's opportunities for work have depended on the growth and expansion of these sectors. After 1945, the expansion of the welfare state and, in the 1970s and 1980s, the growth of service industries, provided jobs. In addition to horizontal gender segregation, there is also a vertical segregation. Women's jobs are not only different from men's but also concentrated in the lower levels of the occupational hierarchy. Far fewer women than men are found in managerial positions, even in those organisations where women are a majority of workers, such as in the NHS. Overall, women constituted only 20 per cent of managers, 8 per cent of general managers and 2 per cent of company directors in 1990.

In addition to occupational segregation, women are also found disproportionately in part-time jobs. Part-time paid work was virtually unknown before 1939 but has become an increasingly evident feature of the labour market since then. Both during and after the war, governments exhorted employers to provide part-time jobs for women and it set an example itself. The increase in women in work over the last 20 years has been almost entirely accounted for by part-time employment. In 1971, there were 5.5 million full-time and 2.8 million part-time workers. In 1981, the figures were 5.3 and 3.8 million, and in 1987, 5.4 and 4.3 million respectively. In 1992, 86 per cent of all part-time jobs were filled by women. Full-time workers are more likely to be women without children, without dependent children or professional women. Part-time workers are more likely to be married women with dependent children. 'Part-time employment is particularly appropriate for married women because it enables them to continue to shoulder their dual role – caring for their families and adding to the family income without radically disturbing the gender divisions of labour within the home' (McDowell 1989: page 165). Women fill most of the part-time jobs and 40 per cent of temporary full-time work.

Women's position in the labour market is also reflected in their earnings. In 1992, their gross hourly earnings were 75 per cent of men's but their take-home pay was only 66 per cent of the average male income. This is due to both horizontal and vertical segregation, the fact that they are in part-time and temporary jobs and that they work less overtime. In 1990, 29 per cent of men worked more than 50 hours a week, in contrast to fewer than 5 per cent of women (Jowell *et al.* 1990). Women therefore are more likely to be in low-paid, low-status, part-time jobs with low levels of responsibility. This has a significant effect on women's career structures and career development.

The reason for this position of women in the labour market is partly a result of social expectations and early socialisation but largely a consequence of the structure of the family and the structure of employment itself. Traditionally, the structure and organisation of employment have been based upon male working and career patterns which take no account of women's role in child-bearing and child-rearing. A continuous working day, week, year and work life are incompatible with the dual role of women in society. Consequently, if women wish to return to work after the birth of a child, they tend to look for part-time employment. An interrupted career inevitably limits the opportunities for promotion and career advancement. This results in the relatively small number of women in managerial levels or at the top of the professions. Operating in a patriarchy has meant endemic discrimination of women in all spheres of social activity. Women are under-represented not only in the higher positions of employment but also in politics, the churches, the media and all other major social institutions (Randall 1987; Rees 1992; Witz 1992).

In the 1970s, equal opportunities legislation paved the way for changes in the status of women and has led to some improvement in their economic, political and social conditions. There are a growing number of women in the professions, they constitute 50 per cent of graduates and are breaking into the male bastions of the higher civil service, the academic world, the police and the media. There is evidence that fewer women are returning to part-time employment after childbirth and many more employers are providing creches, flexitime, annual hours and term-time only contracts to both attract and retain women. A Business in the Community initiative, Opportunity 2000, launched in 1991 and supported by 141 employers employing 25 per cent of the workforce, is committed to taking positive action to change the culture of their organisations and to promote equal opportunities for women. Many have set targets for women in management (Business in the Community 1992).

In stark contrast to these positive actions, in the dual labour market which is emerging, as a feature of economic reconstruction, women provide the majority of the peripheral workforce. They are also in those clerical occupations which Gorz (1982) and others see as being proletarianised and they constitute a reserve army of labour which enables employers to adopt numerical flexibility strategies. Women have traditionally been reluctant to join trade unions and are therefore more receptive to calls for individualised systems of employee relations.

The contraction of the welfare state and of the occupations traditionally associated with the social services affect women disproportionately. The government's community care policy has implications for women in their traditional role as carers of the frail and elderly. As service industries shed labour during the recession in the 1990s, it was women who were most affected. The changing economic situation offers women employment opportunities but it also exposes women's generally weaker market situation. In addition, women are faced with pressures resulting from the changes in gender roles that are taking place within the family and in society generally.

Culture and change

National culture consists of the ideas, values, attitudes and beliefs which influence the way that people perceive the world and themselves in it. It fashions their behaviour, how they relate to others and how they interpret and understand their experiences. Socialisation during childhood, through the primary agencies of the family, kinship and school, has a major influence on the formation of perceptions, attitudes and beliefs. Halsey (1986: page 97) describes the nuclear family of parents and dependent children as 'the reproductive social cell of class, status and of culture'. However, socialisation continues throughout life, and secondary agencies such as the workplace, trade unions, the churches, the army, peer groups and the media may reinforce or challenge earlier influences. People change as a result of their own experiences and their observations of their changing environment.

Change

Society is constantly changing, but there is normally a cultural lag. People are often resistant to change because it threatens their security, their understanding of their world and their status within it. Change is accompanied by uncertainty and threats, although it can also offer opportunities. Older people are usually the most resistant to change, because they have invested so much in the past. Younger people find change easier to cope with, if only because they lack the reference points of the older generations. Also, a rejection of traditional values is seen by the young as a necessary step in asserting their independence.

Britain has experienced rapid change over the last half-century. Halsey (1986) paints a picture of pre-1945 Britain as consisting of a classic industrial economy, a family-centred social structure and a centralised democratic polity. This was the essential triangle within the social order. Men worked and women ran the homes, the economy produced and the family reproduced, and the state protected and administered. After 1945, the social order began to change. The state assumed many of the responsibilities of the family in education, health and the care of the elderly, whilst it supplemented family incomes with benefits and supported the old and the unemployed.

The family began to change as more women, especially married women, entered paid employment. The size of families declined as contraception enabled women to control their fertility. Marriage itself became less stable as women enjoyed greater economic independence, secular values replaced religious ones and changes in the law made divorce easier. More men became economically inactive, whether by retirement or unemployment, and began to assume domestic responsibilities. This challenged conventional gender roles. More people continued their education beyond school leaving age and a more highly educated population emerged. Changes in the economy led to changes in occupation and a higher GNP led to higher personal incomes.

People worked less and had more leisure time. State expenditure on the welfare state increased, resulting in a rising social wage, more public sector employment and a larger proportion of GNP being spent by government.

From the mid-1970s, the social order began to change again, coinciding with the economic transformation identified earlier in this chapter. In particular, this resulted in:

- changing patterns of employment;
- an increase in unemployment, especially amongst the young and those over 50;
- more women in work;
- more people in education and training;
- cuts in public expenditure and the privatisation of public industries and public services;
- a contraction of employment in the public sector.

The period was one of economic instability, political turbulance and continuous change.

Family relationships with the state and with the economy have also changed. The family now produces and consumes. As women increasingly work, men have assumed domestic roles of parenting and homeworking. Work and leisure have become intertwined as people 'do-it-themselves'. Divorce rates have risen to the highest in Western Europe, with one in three marriages ending in divorce. Serial monogamy has increased and complex networks of unconventional extended families have emerged at the same time that conventional kinship networks are weakened by social and geographical mobility. Further changes in the family have arisen from child-centred, hedonistic approaches to child-raising. Traditional authority relationships have given way as 'familial controls over upbringing were attenuated'. Halsey (1986: page 113) describes a situation in which traditional culture is weakened by these multiple forces of change and, amongst the younger generation, fashionability, hedonism and a desperate individualism serve as substitutes for a securely held morality. The state is withdrawing from its provider role in some areas and families are having to reassume responsibility. Education is increasingly seen as the vehicle for social mobility and is no longer restricted to the young. Adult education and training are being used as major vehicles for changing attitudes to those of an enterprise culture.

Social attitudes

Britain's immediate history, like its past, is characterised by both continuity and change. Continuity is usually associated with stability, tradition and consensus, whilst change is associated with instability,
conflict and dissent. How far the changes since the 1970s have
affected social beliefs, values, and culture is difficult to assess. One
way to monitor people's attitudes is through regular surveys over time.
This has been done since 1983 by Social and Community Planning
Research (SCPR) which carries out an annual British Social Attitudes
Survey (BSAS). This provides a moving picture, portraying how
British people see their world and themselves and, through their eyes,
how society itself is changing. Over a period of several years, these
surveys have focused on people's attitudes towards: the economy;
public spending and the role of government; changes in the family;
and the moral climate. The evidence is that public attitudes have
changed and, when plotted against class, gender and age, the results
provide a picture of where cultural transformation is accompanying
economic change and where traditional attitudes are persisting.

The eighth BSAS (Jowell *et al.* 1991) reveals that Britain is divided,
although on most issues attitudes are not polarised. Class provides the
social roots of economic convictions but there is almost as much
disagreement within each class as there is amongst the classes.
Polarisation where it exists tends to occur on moral issues, such as
gender roles and homosexuality. These issues are not high profile at
the moment and therefore do not pose a threat to social stability but
they may do in the future.

In spite of the attacks on the welfare state, especially from the political right, there is still a widespread public attachment to it. Table 6
shows responses during the 1980s to be consistent. Ninety-eight per
cent supported government provision of health care and 97 per cent
supported a decent standard of living for the elderly. Attitudes towards
the unemployed were more divided, although 68 per cent in 1985 and
60 per cent in 1990 thought the government should provide jobs for
those wanting them. The vast majority of people appear willing to pay
more on taxes for health and education and to pay more or to support
existing taxes to fund pensions, policing and unemployment. There
clearly is a widespread consensus on the welfare state and on a positive role for government in dealing with unemployment.

However, there are different interests amongst the classes. Working

210 *Employee Relations*

Table 6: *Social attitudes towards government policy and the welfare state 1985 and 1990*

Percentage who say it should definitely or probably be the government's responsibility to:	1985	1990
. . . provide health care for the sick	98	98
. . . provide a decent standard of living for the old	97	97
. . . provide decent housing for those who can't afford it	n/a	90
. . . provide a decent standard of living for the unemployed	81	77
. . . provide a job for everyone who wants one	68	60
. . . give financial help to university students from low-income families	n/a	90
. . . reduce income differences between rich and poor	69	71
. . . provide industry with the help it needs to grow	92	91
. . . keep prices under control	91	87

Source: Jowell, R. *et al.* (eds) *British Social Attitudes: the 8th Report*

class people are especially likely to regard 'the provision of jobs, unemployment benefits and housing for poorer groups as essential government responsibilities, to name social security as a priority for extra spending and to criticise unemployment benefit as being too low' (Jowell *et al.*: page 32). The middle classes, who tend to be the main beneficiaries of the universal services, are fortunate in having all-class support for those services such as health, education and to a lesser extent pensions of which they make the most use.

Strong support for the welfare state is matched by positive support for government intervention in the economy. In 1990, for instance, 82 per cent of the public supported controls on credit, 72 per cent were in favour of import controls and 83 per cent supported Keynesian policies of public investment to reduce unemployment. However, on the issues of unemployment benefit and redistribution of income there was some disagreement. Whilst 71 per cent supported some redistribution of income, approximately 25 per cent disagreed and 6 per cent disagreed strongly. On unemployment payments, only 37 per cent thought the government should spend more, with 45 per cent favouring the same expenditure and 18 per cent less.

There is almost as much disagreement about attitudes towards gender roles as about redistribution. In 1965, nearly four in five women felt that mothers of the under-fives should stay at home. By 1980, that proportion had fallen to around three in five. By 1987, it had dropped further to well under a half (Brook *et al.* 1989). In 1990, only 27 per cent of the public thought that a woman's job was to look after the home, whilst 55 per cent disagreed. However, when asked whether family life suffered if the woman worked, 47 per cent agreed, 17 per cent were neutral and 36 per cent disagreed. Four in five women between the ages of 18 and 24 felt that it was not the woman's job to look after the home, whilst more than half of women over 65 took the opposing view. Men differ far less in their attitudes to gender roles than women, although there is a class difference. with graduates and more educated males tending to adopt more liberal views (Jowell *et al.* 1991).

The conclusions drawn by Heath and McMahon (1991) from the eighth BSAS were that Britain is divided to a greater or lesser extent. There is disagreement about the economic issues of redistribution of wealth and unemployment. Whilst there is consensus on specific aspects of the welfare state, such as health and pensions, it does not extend to other aspects, such as unemployment benefits, which are more closely related to economic issues. There is also widespread disagreement about moral issues such as extra-marital relationships and pre-marital sex. On most issues, attitudes are divided but not polarised. Polarisation exists, however, about attitudes towards homosexuality and gender roles. It appears that attitudes towards these two issues become more traditional with age and there is a distinct generation gap. Class does not appear to be the major division in British society today. Although working class people are less divided on economic issues than the middle classes are, there is no evidence of a consensus amongst them. Indeed, there is almost as much spread within classes as there is within the population as a whole. Class, therefore, does not appear to be as significant in defining social attitudes, indicating social status or determining political affiliation as it was in the past.

The political context

Changes within society stemming from economic, technological and social forces give rise to conflicts. It is these conflicts which are at the root of politics. Politics is the process by which societies resolve and manage conflicts and disagreements about the allocation of resources, distribution of power and the making of the rules which regulate social behaviour. It is about who decides the rules, how the rules are made and what the rules will be. Not all social behaviour comes within the ambit of politics and there is both a private and public domain. That divide, however, is not fixed but is itself politically determined. The boundary between the public and the private domain became a major political issue in the 1970s and 1980s.

The British political system is primarily concerned with making and implementing the public policies and rules which govern society. In contrast to the market, where individuals themselves take decisions about what to produce and consume, politics is about the collective, authoritative allocation of resources whereby representatives of the people take decisions on their behalf. These decisions are binding and can be enforced by the legitimate exercise of power by the state agencies of the police and the courts.

Britain, like other Western states, is described as a liberal democracy. Liberal democracies have a number of distinctive features including representative governments chosen regularly through open elections by universal suffrage. Parties compete for power offering the electorate manifestos and policies from which they can choose. Civil liberties ensure freedom of speech, freedom of association, freedom of movement and freedom from arbitrary arrest. A free press enables not only the dissemination of ideas but also the opportunity to criticise, challenge and present alternative views to the government in office. An independent judiciary is designed to ensure that governments and public officials are subject to the law and that individual freedoms are protected. Above all, in a liberal democracy, government is limited rather than absolute. It is circumscribed by a constitution as to what it can and cannot do and the ways in which it can exercise its authority.

Governments are also constrained by the need to maintain support within the elected assembly to whom they are accountable, in theory at least. They also need to maintain the support of the electorate if they are to remain in office. They are also constrained by the need to ensure the acceptance of their policies by those who have to implement them.

Governments are further limited by the availability of resources, their involvement in international organisations, such as the EC, the UN and the General Agreement on Tariffs and Trade, and by their inability to control their own external environment.

Political systems only ever approximate political models like that of liberal democracy, and Britain is no exception. They evolve and change over time. The absence of a written constitution has enabled the British system to change more easily than most, although it is marked by continuity and tradition, as well as by innovation and modernity. Those same features are to be found in the British political culture as well as its political institutions.

Political change

One of the main characteristics of the British political system has been its dominance by two main political parties. In all general elections between 1945 and 1974, the Conservative and Labour parties never won less than 87 per cent of the vote and they dominated the House of Commons. Since then that pattern has changed. Table 7 shows that since 1974 there has been a marked decline in support for the two main parties and a realignment of the electorate. Third parties have taken approximately 20 per cent of the vote. Another trend has been a fall in the electoral turnout. These changes in the political system have coincided with the changes in the economy identified above.

One thesis (Crewe 1986; Butler and Kavanagh 1984) is that the changes in voting patterns reflect changes in the class structure. Traditionally, class appeared to be the dominant factor in the way people voted. The Labour party, created by the trade unions to represent working class interests in Parliament, has traditionally attracted the majority of the working class vote, although never all of it. The Conservative party, seen as the party of the privileged, propertied and business classes, has attracted the votes of the upper and middle classes and some working class deferential voters (Nordlinger 1967; McKenzie and Silver 1968). The two main parties have tended to present issues in class terms, although they have also claimed to be acting in the national interest. Although British politics has been structured in class terms, throughout most of the century substantial minorities, both of the middle and working classes, have voted against their supposedly natural class interests. About one-third of the working class have

Table 7: UK electoral statistics 1945–92

	Electoral Turnout %	Conservatives % votes	seats	Labour % votes	seats	Liberals[1] % votes	seats	Welsh & Scottish Nat. % votes	seats	Other % votes	seats
1945	73.3	39.8	213	48.3	393	9.1	12	0.2		2.5	22
1950	84.0	43.5	299	46.1	315	9.1	9	0.1		1.2	2
1951	82.5	48.0	321	48.8	295	2.5	6	0.1		.6	3
1955	76.8	49.7	345	46.4	277	2.7	6	0.2		.9	2
1959	78.7	49.4	365	43.8	258	5.9	6	0.4		.6	1
1964	77.1	43.4	304	44.1	317	11.2	9	0.5		.8	0
1966	75.8	41.9	253	47.9	363	8.5	12	0.7		.9	2
1970	72.0	46.4	330	43.0	288	7.5	6	1.3	1	1.8	5
1974 Feb	78.1	37.8	297	37.1	301	19.3	14	2.6	9	3.2	14
1974 Oct	72.8	35.8	277	39.2	319	18.3	13	3.5	14	3.2	12
1979	76.0	43.9	339	37.0	269	13.8	11	2.0	4	3.3	12
1983	72.7	42.4	397	27.6	209	25.4	23	1.5	4	3.5	17
1987	75.3	42.3	376	30.8	229	22.6	22	1.7	6	2.8	17
1992	77.7	41.9	336	34.4	271	17.8	20	2.3	7	3.5	17

1 1945–79 Liberals; 1983–7 Lib–SDP Alliance; 1992 Liberal Democrats

Source: Butler, D. and Kavanagh, D. *The British General Election of 1992*

regularly voted Conservative and about 20 per cent of the middle class have voted Labour.

Since 1974, the electorate appears to be fragmenting politically along unfamiliar lines. What is in dispute is 'whether class based support . . . has been undermined specifically by partisan dealignment, the disaggregation of economic interests, cognitive consumer voting, or the development of new sectoral cleavages' (Marshall *et al.* 1988: page 121). The case for and against class dealignment is most clearly presented by Crewe (1986) and Heath *et al.* (1987). Crewe claims that the Conservative share of the middle class vote, and the Labour share of the working class vote, have both declined to the point where class is insignificant because fewer people are voting along class lines than are not. Heath argues, in contrast, that there has been no significant class dealignment but rather the relative sizes of the classes have changed. The working class shrunk from 45 per cent of the population in the 1960s to 34 per cent in the 1980s and is still falling, although partisan alignment within the smaller working class is still high. Crewe accepts the contraction in the size of the working class but asserts that there has been a decline of working class consciousness and solidarity which explains their withdrawal of support for the Labour party. Heath, on the other hand, places the responsibility for the decline of the Labour party on its failure to present a viable alternative to the Conservatives. A more radical approach to explaining changes in voting patterns, linked to ideology and the media, is developed by Dunleavy and Husbands (1985).

Clearly, the main beneficiaries of the changes in voting patterns since 1974 have been the centrist and the nationalist parties. Their support is drawn equally from all classes and their images and ideologies are not class based. Their electoral support, however, has not been able to break the mould of British politics, because the electoral system does not translate votes proportionally into seats in the House of Commons, as shown in Table 7. Britain therefore remains an essentially two-party system, but one which has been dominated by one party since the Conservatives were re-elected to office in 1979. Whilst the debate about dealignment continues, the evidence from the BSASs since 1983 suggest that class is only one of the cleavages which influences political opinion and voting behaviour, albeit still a significant one. Another significant fact is that the beginnings of dealignment appear to coincide with major changes in the ideologies and policies of the main political parties. These, in turn, are responses to the economic and social changes occurring within society itself.

The postwar settlement

All governments elected between 1945 and the 1970s were broadly agreed on policy objectives, although there were differences of emphasis on means and priorities. This came to be called the postwar consensus. It comprised three interrelated elements:

- support for a mixed economy, incorporating Keynesian demand management;
- support for a welfare state, with universal services including health, education, housing, social insurance and old age pensions;
- acceptance of a social democratic framework within which people had both civil and social entitlements and rights.

Within this consensus, minority interests were acknowledged and major interests were incorporated into the policy-making process. In particular, industry and labour, represented by the CBI and the TUC, joined with government to form a tripartite structure for discussing economic policy (Farnham and Horton 1993).

The postwar settlement is seen by Gamble (1988) as the political context compatible with a regime of accumulation based on the Fordist principles of mass production and mass consumption. Commitment of all governments to the four economic goals of full employment, economic growth, low inflation and a stable currency – and the use of Keynesian economic techniques – ensured a high and constant level of aggregate demand and the transfer of many of the social costs of capital accumulation to public agencies. As a result, public expenditure increased, the public sector expanded and large public bureaucracies became the monopoly suppliers of both social services and public utilities. Initially, this could be funded by a constantly rising GNP. By the 1970s, however, the state was consuming almost 50 per cent of GNP and accounted for almost 30 per cent of the labour force (see Chapters 1 and 4).

In the 1970s, cracks began appearing in the political consensus, largely because Keynesian management of the economy, so apparently successful in the 1950s and early 1960s, was no longer working. Growth was slowing down, unemployment was rising, inflation was proving difficult to control and there were recurrent balance-of-payments

crises. Britain was losing its share of world markets and import penetration by its main competitors was encroaching on domestic markets.
Keynesianism as an economic strategy came under attack, but so too
did the welfare state (Dearlove and Saunders 1991). High public
expenditure on the welfare state was seen as a root cause of Britain's
economic problems, because it was sustained by high taxation, high
borrowing and high interest rates. All of these, it was claimed, discouraged investment, choked off consumption and led to economic
stagnation. There were many critics and critiques of the postwar settlement, both on the left and the right of the political spectrum, but it was
the New Right that came to the fore and exploited some people's fears
of a large-spending, social welfare state (Farnham and Horton 1993).

The New Right

The New Right advocated the primacy of the market over politics,
both as a means of producing and distributing goods and services in
society and as an institutional arrangement for providing social organisation and social control. It argued that markets offer freedom of
choice, result in the most efficient use of resources and give opportunities for inventiveness, creativity and enterprise. Politics, in contrast,
restricts, constrains, denies choice and results in inefficiency and a
misallocation of resources. New Right critics also challenged the welfare state as creating dependency, weakening individual responsibility,
denying people freedom of choice and empowering professional
interests.

These ideas came to dominate the Conservative party, especially
under the leadership of Margaret Thatcher, and they were evident in
the policies pursued by the three Conservative governments led by her
after the elections of 1979, 1983 and 1987. Although some changes of
emphasis can be seen in the governments led by John Major, there are
also strong elements of continuity within them. The stated goals of the
Conservative government elected in 1979 were to reverse Britain's relative economic decline, to improve the efficiency of the economy, to
create the conditions for continual economic prosperity, to reassert
Britain's role in the world and to 'destroy socialism'. The strategies
adopted were to 'roll back the state', reduce public expenditure, cut
taxation and state borrowing, privatise the nationalised industries and
deregulate the economy, including the labour market.

There were also attempts to introduce markets into the public sector and increase the efficiency of public organisations. Keynesianism was replaced by monetarism and supply-side economics, and the previous commitments to manage aggregate demand and maintain full employment were abandoned. The major economic priority became controlling inflation.

The government also sought to change the political culture and to wean people from supporting the welfare state to supporting 'popular capitalism' and an 'enterprise culture'. Property ownership was facilitated by the forced sale of council houses, by the sale of the public industries and by encouraging share ownership schemes and profit-sharing in the private sector. Compulsory competitive tendering (CCT) in local government, the NHS and the civil service broke down the barriers between the public and private sectors and deregulation afforded opportunities for businesses, old and new, to compete in bus transport, telecommunications, hospitals, residential nursing homes and ophthalmic services. Gradually CCT, or market testing as it became known, was extended throughout the whole of the public sector. Labour market deregulation was accompanied by attacks on the trade unions. A programme of legislation curbing the powers of trade unions sought not only to free up the labour market but also to undermine collectivism in favour of individualism at work (see Chapters 7 and 10).

There is a paradox which runs through both New Right ideology and Conservative government policies since 1979. This is described by Gamble (1988) as the 'free economy' and 'the strong state'. In order to free the economy and to move towards a market-dominated system, the state has had to be highly interventionist and to become highly centralised. The paradox also stems from the duality within the New Right thinking of a liberal strand, which argues for the free market economy, and a conservative strand, which is more authoritarian and interested in restoring social and political authority in society.

For well over a decade, successive Conservative governments sought to achieve the objectives stated in 1979. They took it as axiomatic that market decision-making is inherently superior to political decision-making and they have been committed to free markets, free enterprise and free trade, even though some economists argue that this has been a part cause of many of Britain's economic difficulties. They have consistently sought to bring inflation down, with mixed success, in the belief that a stable medium of exchange and store of value is essential for the market to function efficiently. In addition, low inflation improves Britain's competitive position in international trade. They have pursued supply-side economics by cutting income tax, although overall taxes increased during this period. Financial, product and labour markets have been deregulated and small businesses have been encouraged. The success rate of new businesses has been low, however, with less than 60 per cent surviving more than a year. The government was less successful in reducing or containing public expenditure which was the same proportion of GNP in 1992 as it had been in 1979. Neither did they consistently reduce the PSBR which in 1993, at a projected £53 billion, was higher than at any time since 1945.

Traditional and emerging patterns of employee relations management

Figure 10 sums up the main *traditional* and *emerging* economic, organisational, social and political contexts within which employers and managements have operated and are operating, especially but not exclusively in Britain. The elements within each of these contexts are derived from the analyses provided in the earlier parts of this chapter. These are obviously 'pure' typologies and, in the 'real world' of personnel management, the traditional and emerging contexts of employee relations management are rarely as clear-cut as Figure 10 implies. These typologies are identified and used merely as tools of analysis and for the purposes of description, rather than of prescription. What is clear, however, is that the traditional contexts, which were largely established in the immediate postwar period, no longer universally apply. The 1980s and 1990s, above all, were and are a period of immense change, uncertainty and transition, economically, socially, politically and organisationally. Whilst, in practice, elements of the traditional contexts remain, they are being challenged and counterbalanced by the forces of change, as indicated in the emerging contexts outlined in Figure 10.

These external contexts, in turn, are impinging on the patterns of employee relations management currently being practised in Britain, as shown in Figure 11. Traditional patterns of employee relations management, based on collectivism, managing relatively high levels of organised industrial conflict and 'personnel management' strategies, now co-exist with emerging patterns of employee relations management – sometimes in the same organisation, sometimes in different

Figure 10: *The contexts of British employee relations*

Traditional contexts	Emerging contexts
The Economy	
protected economy	open economy
strong national markets	globalised markets
industrialisation	de-industrialisation
strong manufacturing base	dominant service base
national ownership	multinational ownership
large public sector	smaller public sector
mass consumption	customised consumption
steady growth	variable growth
regulated labour market	de-regulated labour market
Work Organisation	
Fordist	post-Fordist
bureaucratic/hierarchic	organic/flat
mechanical technology	information technology
mass production	batch production
full-time employment	flexible employment
male employment	growing female employment
single skills and unskilled work	multi-skills and de-skilled work
task-based work	team-based work
The Social Structure	
young population	ageing population
nuclear family structure	multiple family structure
large working class	small working class
small middle class	large middle class
strong class identities	interest-based identities
class subcultures	diverse subcultures
growing equality	growing inequality
stable society	dynamic society
The Polity	
two-party system	multi-party system
partisan voting	issue-based voting
consensus politics	conviction politics
corporatist policy-making	governmental policy-making
national sovereignty	Europeanisation
strong collectivist/welfare state culture	strong individualist/enterprise culture
Keynesian policies	monetarist/supply-side policies
state support for collective bargaining	state support for individual contracts

Figure 11: *Patterns of British employee relations (ERL) management*

Traditional patterns	Emerging patterns
strong unions	weak unions
collective bargaining	employee involvement
jointly driven ERL	management-driven ERL
policy focused on groups	policy focused on individuals
collective agreements	personal contracts
standardised payments	payment by performance
narrow wage differentials	wider wage differentials
common employee benefits	packaged employee benefits
employment security	employment insecurity
high levels of organised industrial conflict	low levels of organised industrial conflict
personnel management strategies	human resources management strategies

organisations. The 'new employee relations' and the emerging patterns of employee relations management, in contrast, are based on individualism, low levels of organised industrial conflict and 'human resources management' strategies. There are clearly hybrid forms of employee relations management, which draw on elements of both the traditional and emerging models outlined in Figure 11. But the important factor to recognise is that the pattern which predominates, whether nationally or organisationally, evolves largely from the contexts which have been examined in this chapter. When these contexts change, as they inevitably do, so do the dominant patterns of employee relations management. No one pattern of employee relations management is either self-evident or axiomatic at any one time, or over time. It is a function of management choice, taking account of the economic, organisational, social and political contexts in which the employer operates.

Assignments

(a) What are the major changes that have occurred in the British economy since 1971?

(b) Read the latest edition of *Social Trends* and identify three major features that could be having an effect upon employee relations in your organisation.

(c) Read Cockburn, 'Women and technology: opportunity is not enough' in Purcell *et al.* (1986) and discuss the issues raised about the relationship between technology and gender.

(d) What are the main characteristics of pre-industrial, industrial and post-industrial societies? What causes a change from one to another?

(e) Read Murray, 'Fordism and post-fordism', in Hall and Jaques (1989) and argue the case for a new model of political economy.

(f) Divide into groups and examine one of the four theoretical perspectives of economic change in Britain – Fordism, flexible specialisation, regulation theory and post-industrial society. Discuss the similarities and differences amongst them and their implications for employee relations management.

(g) Consider the major differences between the old technologies and IT.

(h) Read Chapter 3 of Dearlove and Saunders (1991). What are the differences between: the party identification model; the issue voting – rational choice model; and the radical approach? Which seems the most able to explain the outcome of the 1992 election?

(i) What are the most significant observations of the latest British Social Attitudes Survey?

(j) Read Hayek, '1980s unemployment and the unions,' in Coates and Hillard (1986). Consider its validity in the light of the performance of the British economy in the 1990s.

(k) Read Allen *et al.* (1992: pages 357–368) and examine the 'modernist dilemma'.

(l) What evidence is there that the human resources control strategies that management adopt are changing in line with changes in the structure and organisation of work?

(m) Read Walby (pages 127–140) in Wood (1989). What light do recent developments in theories of flexibility shed on the major transformation in the gender composition of the workforce?

(n) Critically examine the optimistic view of the post-Fordist society presented in Piore and Sabel (1984).

(o) Read Chapter 7 of Miles *et al.* (1988). Debate the optimistic and pessimistic scenarios of the future effects of technology in the UK.

(p) What do you consider to be the main economic, social, technological and political factors affecting the management of employee relations in recent years?

(q) How would you categorise your organisation's current patterns of employee relations management?

References

AGLIETTA, M. 1979. *A Theory of Capitalist Regulation: the US Experience.* London: Verso.

ALLEN, J., BRAHAM, P. and LEWIS, P. 1992. *Political and Economic Forms of Modernity.* Oxford: Polity.

ALLEN, J. and MASSEY, D. (eds) 1988. *The Economy in Question.* London: Sage and the OU.

ATKINSON, J. 1985. 'Flexibility: planning for an uncertain future'. *Manpower Policy and Practice.* 1, Summer.

BARRON, I. 1979. *The Future with Micro-electronics Forecasting: the Effects of Information Technology.* London: Pinter.

BELL, D. 1973. *The Coming of Post-Industrial Society.* NY: Basic Books.

BELL, D. 1976. *The Cultural Contradictions of Capitalism.* NY: Basic Books.

BOYER, R. 1990. *The Regulation School: A Critical Introduction.* NY: Columbia University Press.

BRAVERMAN, H. 1974. *Labor and Monopoly Capital: The Degradation of Work in the Twentieth Century.* NY: Monthly Review Press.

BROOK, L., JOWELL, R, and WITHERSPOON, S. 1989. 'Recent trends in social attitudes'. *Social Trends 19.* London: HMSO.

BUSINESS IN THE COMMUNITY 1992. *Opportunity 2000 Information Pack.* London: Business in the Community.

BUTLER, D. and KAVANAGH, D. 1992. *The British General Election of 1992.* London: Macmillan.

CASTELLS, M. 1989. *The Informational City.* Oxford: Blackwell.

CENTRAL STATISTICAL OFFICE 1992. *Social Trends 22.* London: HMSO.

CENTRAL STATISTICAL OFFICE 1993. *Social Trends 23.* London: HMSO.

COCKBURN, C. 1987. 'Women and technology: opportunity is not enough'. In PURCELL, K., WOOD, S., WATON, A. and ALLEN, S. (eds). 1987. *The Changing Experience of Employment.* London: Macmillan.

COOMBES, R. and JONES, B. 1988. 'Alternative successors to Fordism'. Paper presented at the Conference on Society, Information and Space, Swiss Federal Institute of Technology, Zurich. Mimeo: UMIST and Bath University.

CROMPTON, R. and JONES, G. 1984. *White-Collar Proletariat.* London: Macmillan.

CREWE, I. 1984. 'The electorate: partisan dealignment 10 years on'. In BERRINGTON, H. (ed.). 1984. *Change in British Politics.* London: Frank Cass.

DAHRENDORF, R. 1987. 'The erosion of citizenship and its consequences for us all'. *New Statesman.* 12 June.

DEARLOVE, J. and SAUNDERS, P. 1991. *Introduction to British Politics.* Oxford: Polity.

DEPARTMENT OF EMPLOYMENT 1991. 'Employment labour force survey 1990'. *Employment Gazette.* 99. London: HMSO.

DEPARTMENT OF SOCIAL SECURITY 1992. *Households below Average Income 1979–1989.* London: HMSO.

DUNLEAVY, P. 1980. *Urban Political Analysis: The Politics of Collective Consumption.* London: Macmillan.

DUNLEAVY, P. and HUSBANDS, C. 1985. *British Democracy at the Crossroads*. London: Allen and Unwin.

FARNHAM, D. and HORTON, S. (eds). 1993. *Managing the New Public Services*. Basingstoke: Macmillan.

FORESTER, T. (ed.) 1985. *The Information Technology Revolution*. Oxford: Blackwell.

GAMBLE, A. 1988. *The Free Economy and the Strong State*. Basingstoke: Macmillan.

GOLDTHORPE, J., LOCKWOOD, D., BECHHOFER, F. and PLATT, J. 1968. *The Affluent Worker in the Class Structure*. Cambridge: Cambridge University Press.

GORZ, A. 1982. *Farewell to the Working Class*. London: Pluto Press.

HALSEY, A. 1986. *Change in British Society*. Oxford: Oxford University Press.

HAMNETT, C. 1989. 'Consumption and class in contemporary Britain'. In HAMNETT, C., McDOWELL, L. and SARRE, P. (eds) 1989. *The Changing Social Structure*. London: Sage and the OU.

HARRIS, L. 1988. 'The UK economy at a crossroads'. In ALLEN, J. and MASSEY, D. (eds) 1988. *The Economy in Question*. London: Sage and the OU.

HAYEK, F. 1986. '1980s unemployment and the unions'. In COATES, D. and HILLARD, J. (eds).1986. *The Economic Decline of Modern Britain*. Brighton: Wheatsheaf.

HEATH, A., JOWELL, R. and CURTICE, J. 1985. *How Britain Votes*. Oxford: Pergamon.

HEATH, A. and McMAHON, D. 1991. 'Consensus and dissensus'. In JOWELL, R., BROOK, L. and TAYLOR, B. (eds) 1991. *British Social Attitudes: the 8th Report*. Aldershot: Dartmouth.

HIRST, P. and ZEITLIN, J. 1991. 'Flexible specialisation versus post-Fordism: theory, evidence and policy implications'. *Economy and Society*. 20(1), February.

HOBSBAWN, E. 1968. *Industry and Empire*. NY: Weidenfeld and Nicolson.

JESSOP, B. 1989a. *Thatcherism: The British Road to post-Fordism*. Essex Papers in Politics and Government No 68. Department of Government: University of Essex.

JESSOP, B. 1989b. 'Conservative regimes and the transition to post-Fordism: the cases of Britain and West Germany'. In GOTTDINER, M. and KOMNINOS, N. (eds) 1989. *Capitalist Development and Crisis Theory: Accumulation, Regulation and Spatial Restructuring*. London: Macmillan.

JOWELL, R., BROOK, L. and TAYLOR, B. (eds) 1991. *British Social Attitudes: the 8th Report*. Aldershot: Dartmouth.

KING, D. 1987. *The New Right*. Basingstoke: Macmillan.

LASH, S. and URRY, J. 1987. *The End of Organised Capitalism*. Oxford: Polity.

LIEPITZ, A. 1985. *The Enchanted World: Money, Finance and the World Crisis*. London: Verso.

LIEPITZ, A. 1988. *Mirages and Miracles: The Crisis of Global Fordism*. London: Verso.

LIEPITZ, A. 1992. *Towards a New Economic Order*. Oxford: Polity.

LOCKWOOD, D. 1958. *The Blackcoated Worker*. London: Allen and Unwin.

McDOWELL, L. 1989. 'Gender divisions'. In HAMNETT, C., McDOWELL, L. and

SARRE, P. (eds) 1989. *The Changing Social Structure*. London: Sage and the OU.

MCKENZIE, R. and SILVER, A. 1968. *Angels in Marble*. London: Heinemann.

MARSHALL, G., NEWBY, H., ROSE, D. and VOGLER, C. 1988. *Social Class in Modern Britain*. London: Hutchinson.

MILES, I. 1989. *Information Technology and Information Society: Options for the Future*. Programme on Information and Communication Technologies (PICT). Policy Research Paper No. 2. ESRC: London.

MILES, I., RUSH, M., TURNER, K. and BESSANT, J. 1988. *Information Horizons: The Long-Term Implications of New Information Technologies*. Aldershot: Edward Elgar.

MURRAY, R. 1989. 'Fordism and post-Fordism'. In HALL, S. and JAQUES, M. (eds). 1989. *New Times*. London: Lawrence and Wishart.

NAISBITT, J. 1982. *Megatrends*. NY: Warner Brothers.

NILLES, J. 1985. 'Teleworking from home'. In FORESTER, T. (ed.). *The Information Technology Revolution*. Oxford: Blackwell.

NORDLINGER, E. 1967. *Working-Class Tories*. London: MacGibbon and Kee.

PIORE, M. and SABEL, C. 1984. *The Second Industrial Divide*. NY: Basic Books.

POLLERT, A. 1987. *The Flexible Firm: A Model in Search of Reality: or a Policy in Search of a Practice?* Warwick Papers in Industrial Relations, No 19. Coventry: Warwick University.

RANDALL, V. 1987. *Women and Politics*. London: Macmillan.

REES, T. 1992. *Women and the Labour Market*. London: Routledge.

ROSE, M. 1988. *Industrial Behaviour*. London: Penguin.

SABEL, C. 1982. *Work and Politics: The Division of Labour in Industry*. Cambridge: Cambridge University Press.

SAUNDERS, P. 1978. 'Domestic property and social class'. *International Journal of Urban and Regional Research*. 2.

SAUNDERS, P. 1984. 'Beyond housing classes'. *International Journal of Urban and Regional Research*. 8.

SAUNDERS, P. 1989. *Social Class and Stratification*. London: Tavistock.

SAUNDERS, P. and WILLIAMS, P. 1986. 'The new conservatism: some thoughts on recent and future developments in urban studies'. *Society and Space*. 4.

SCOTT, J. 1982. *The Upper Classes: Property and Privilege in Britain*. London: Macmillan.

SLEIGH, J. 1979. *The Manpower Implications of Micro-Electronic Technology: a Report*. London: HMSO.

TAYLOR, F. W. 1947. *The Principles of Scientific Management*. NY: Harper and Row.

TAYLOR-GOOBY, P. 1991. 'Attachment to the welfare state'. In JOWELL, R., BROOK, L. and TAYLOR, B. (eds) 1991. *British Social Attitudes: the 8th Report*. Aldershot: Dartmouth.

THOMPSON, G. 1989. 'Strategies for socialists'. *Economy and Society*. 18(4), November.

TOFFLER, A. 1980. *The Third Wave*. NY: Bantam Books.

TOURAINE, A. 1974. *The Post-Industrial Society: Tomorrow's Social History*. London: Wildwood House.

226   *Employee Relations*

TOWNSEND, P. 1979. *Poverty in the United Kingdom*. Harmondsworth: Penguin.

WALBY, S. 1989. 'Flexibility and the changing sexual division of labour'. In WOOD, S. (ed.) 1989. *The Transformation of Work*. London: Unwin Hyman.

WEINER, M. 1981. *English Culture and the Decline of the Industrial Spirit 1850–1980*. Cambridge: Cambridge University Press.

WITZ, A. 1992. *Professions and Patriarchy*. London: Routledge.

WOOD, S. (ed.). 1989. *The Transformation of Work*. London: Unwin Hyman.

WORLD BANK 1992. *World Development Report: Development and the Environment*. NY: Oxford University Press.

Chapter 7

The State and Employee Relations

The state consists of those institutions and offices of state which provide the machinery of government. In Britain, these include:

- the cabinet and government ministers who comprise the executive authority of the state;
- Parliament, which is a representative assembly that makes law, raises revenue and is a scrutinising body;
- central government departments, governmental agencies, public bodies, public enterprises and the local authorities which administer governmental policies;
- the state's agencies of law enforcement and adjudication such as the courts, tribunals and the police.

In contemporary capitalist states, like those of Western Europe, North America and Australasia, because relations between employers and employees have become part of the public domain, the state is also an employee relations policy-maker. Public policy in this area relates to the ways in which the state seeks to influence the parties, processes and outcomes of employee relations. The state acts in a number of roles including:

- as an actor in the labour market and in the determination of wages and employment;
- as a regulator of industrial conflict;
- as an employer;
- as a law maker and law enforcer.

It is these issues of state employment policy that are addressed in this chapter.

Early public policy: *laissez-faire* and the emergence of collective *laissez-faire*

An embyronic modern public policy on employee relations in Britain developed in the early nineteenth century and was rooted in the ideas of *laissez-faire*. *Laissez-faire* was based on the assumption that market decisions were preferable to political fiats in determining the alloca- tion, distribution and exchange of economic resources. As applied to the free labour market, *laissez-faire* policy meant that market freedoms took precedence over political decisions in determining the procedural arrangements and the substantive outcomes of the wage bargaining process. The state's role was a minimalist one of providing a frame- work of contract law within which the primary parties to the wage–work bargain conducted themselves. Wage-fixing was regarded as a private matter, between the individual 'master' and individual 'ser- vant', in which there was no role for the state or state institutions to intervene.

The state's attitude to trade unions in the early part of the nineteenth century was one of outright hostility and opposition. Unions were seen by both the state authorities and employers as 'criminal conspiracies' and illegitimate combinations acting 'in restraint of trade' (Pelling 1987). Unions, it was argued, distorted the workings of the free labour market and took away the freedoms of the primary parties to negotiate terms and conditions individually, in pursuit of their own advantage and self-interest. Accordingly, both Parliament and the judges declared unions to be criminal combinations. It was only after Parliament relaxed its outright ban on unions in 1824 and after emancipatory statutes were enacted – in 1859, 1871 and 1875 – that trade unions were relieved from the worst consequences of criminal liability. The judges then turned to the development of civil liability which, in turn, was only relieved by the Trade Disputes Act 1906 (see Chapter 4). This gave trade unions blanket immunity from liability in tort, pro- vided immunities to individuals inducing breaches of contracts of employment and legitimised peaceful picketing.

By the early twentieth century, trade unions were well established as collective wage-bargaining agencies, covering a number of well-organ- ised trades and industries (Clegg, Fox and Thompson 1964). But whilst Parliament had legitimated trade union activities, the state excluded itself from the joint wage-fixing process between autonomous employ- ers and independent unions – just as it had done in the individual wage bargain between master and servant and employer and workman. Collective agreements were negotiated voluntarily between the secondary parties to employee relations, they were legally unenforceable and there was no legally binding, national minimum wage. A policy of collective *laissez-faire* and 'voluntarism' – embodied in the concepts of 'free collective bargaining' and the exclusion of the judges and the courts from relations between employers and trade unions – began to replace individual *laissez-faire* as the dominant ideology underpinning British employee relations. It was a 'public' policy which suited government, employers and trade unions alike.

Gradually, however, the policy of collective *laissez-faire* incorporated a series of incremental, interventionist policies by the state. First, the state found that it could not stand aside when standards of cleanliness, overcrowding, ventilation and working conditions in factories and mines, especially those affecting women and children, were unsatisfactory, dangerous to health and safety or offensive to 'public morality'. Accordingly, there was the piecemeal enactment of a series of factory and safety legislation, starting as early as the Factory Act 1833, which aimed to deal with these matters on a trade-by-trade and industry-by-industry basis.

Second, the state also found that it could not stand aside when disruptive industrial conflict appeared to threaten either social stability within the community or the established political order. In 1896, the Conciliation Act was passed, enabling provision to be made for the registration of boards of conciliation and arbitration and for the Board of Trade to inquire into the causes and circumstances of a trade dispute, or nominate a person to do so, or appoint conciliators or arbitrators to try and resolve it. This was followed by the Industrial Courts Act 1919 which extended the provisions for voluntary arbitration in Britain beyond those embodied in the 1896 Act (Wedderburn and Davies 1969). This effectively provided the legal basis for state intervention in the regulation of industrial conflict until ACAS was created by the Employment Protection Act 1975.

Third, the state also found itself having to intervene to protect the terms and conditions of employment of those in the labour market unable to look after themselves and who were likely to be exploited in the wage-bargaining process by unscrupulous, greedy employers. There was particular concern about the so called 'sweated trades' at the beginning of this century. Sweating was associated with home workers who had very low wage rates, excessive hours of work and insanitary working conditions. It was the Trade Boards Acts 1909 and 1918, followed by Wages Councils Acts after 1945, which sought to remedy these abuses. These Acts set up wage-fixing bodies, comprised of equal numbers of employers and worker representatives with independent members, to establish minimum, legally enforceable, hourly wage rates and other conditions of employment for workers in trades and industries where wages were low and there was no collective bargaining. The intentions were, initially, to protect the low paid and, later on, to encourage the development of collective bargaining in unorganised industries (Bayliss 1959).

The employee relations consensus 1945–79

The interwar years, from 1919 to 1939, were a watershed in the development of public policy on employee relations, when deep economic recession and high unemployment resulted in hard labour markets, weakened trade unions and the strengthening of the right to manage in the workplace. However, with the steady growth in the scope and size of the state and of state activity in economic and social affairs in the twentieth century, government could no longer abstain from employee relations decision-making as it had done for much of the nineteenth century. This was especially the case during the first world war, the second world war and after 1945. During the two world wars, for example, the state developed active labour market and wages policies. These were necessary to ensure that labour was allocated and directed to essential industries and occupations, to maximise industrial output and to gain the collaboration of the unions and their members in the war effort.

The state built on these policies in the postwar period, after 1945. Besides the policy of being a 'model' and 'good practice' employer (see below) and, after 1965, of developing a statutory floor of employment protection rights (see Chapter 4), Britain's postwar governments up till 1979, with the major exception of the Heath government 1971–74, tried to develop a consensus on employee relations policy, acceptable to employers, trade unions, their members and the wider community. This policy comprised three interrelated elements:

- maintaining full employment in the labour market;
- searching for an incomes policy;

* supporting voluntary collective bargaining.

The attempt to achieve an employee relations consensus incorporated a policy, where trade union power was strong, based on *free collective bargaining*. This was modified at other times by a policy of *bargained corporatism* (see Chapter 1), when the state authorities tried to constrain union wage-bargaining power, in conditions of full employment, by making concessions to the unions and their members on social policy, economic policy and employment law. An attempt was made to move away from a liberal state organised on free market principles to a more corporatist state. Corporatism is where the state authorities try to integrate the interests of capital, labour and government through centralised political institutions so that wage, economic and related policy issues are discussed centrally (Schmitter and Lehmbruch 1979).

Maintaining full employment

Market *laissez-faire* economic policies in the interwar years resulted in mass unemployment, widespread poverty and social deprivation (Taylor 1965). The popular demand at the end of the second world war for 'full employment', which had been an economic reality from 1939 to 1945, was in part a reaction by the British people to the economic and social distress experienced by millions of them a decade earlier.

The rationale for full employment

With the extension of the political franchise and the gradual democratising of society during the twentieth century, the democratic imperative began to challenge the market imperative as the motivating influence on state policy in both ecomomic affairs and employee relations. After the second world war, the democratic imperative became even more pressing.

One impact of the democratic imperative was from below. It arose from the fact that a generation of workers emerged – from 1945 till the mid-1970s – with the expectation that governments would pursue, amongst other measures, a labour market policy of full employment. The power of the ballot box now meant that the electorate could replace any government failing to deliver the policy objective of full employment and the extension of a comprehensive welfare state. This political fact was not lost on government ministers and public policy-makers in determining their economic, employment and labour market priorities after 1945.

A second impact of the democratic imperative immediately post-1945 was from above. This derived from the demands of certain political reformers, social theorists and democratic forces, especially within the Labour party. They attacked the five prewar social evils of 'Want, Disease, Ignorance, Squalor and Idleness' and wanted 'full employment in a free society'. They not only accepted the principle but also wished to implement the policy of full employment in practice. Indeed, by the 1950s, full employment had become a bipartisan policy to which both major political parties, the Conservatives and Labour, were committed. The reasons for this bipartisanship were partly political. The realities of democratic politics meant that unless cabinets and ministers actively pursued full employment as a policy goal, neither they nor the government of which they were members would be re-elected at the next general election.

There were also intellectual reasons for governments supporting the policy of full employment, since the arguments supporting the full employment agenda had been put and won earlier by individuals such as Keynes (1936) and Beveridge (1944). For Beveridge (1944: pages 15–16) unemployment was an 'evil'. But the greatest evil of all 'is not physical but moral, not the want it may bring but the hatred and fear which it breeds.' In his view, to look to individual employers to maintain aggregate demand and full employment was absurd. They were not within the power of employers to determine. 'They must therefore be undertaken by the State, under the supervision and pressure of democracy, applied through . . . Parliament.'

By full employment, Keynes, Beveridge and their supporters did not mean 'no unemployment' at all but unemployment being reduced to a minimum and for as short a time as possible. This required government stimulating aggregate demand in the economy (Chapter 4) and ensuring that those seeking jobs would be certain that they would be re-employed after only a short period of being out of work. To facilitate the transition between jobs, the unemployed would receive unemployment benefit, whilst looking for new employment, and be provided with state funded employment services to assist them in doing this. Using combinations of fiscal and incomes policies, successive governments, both Conservative and Labour, fine-tuned the economy for some 30 years – 1945–75. This ensured, certainly until the early 1970s, that unemployment in Britain remained low at some 2–3 per cent of the working population or around 300,000 to 500,000 unemployed persons.

The consequences of full employment

The government's economic policy goal of full employment had three main consequences for employee relations. The first was that with the economy expanding, private sector employers were often faced with labour shortages, particularly of skilled, trained workers. Employers normally responded to this by bidding up wage rates, or by supplementing the earnings of their workforces locally, in order to compete in local labour markets with other employers. The result was 'wages drift' or a gap between nationally negotiated wage rates and what was actually earned by workers at workplace level. Furthermore, when government dampened down the economy, because of inflationary pressures, employers would hoard labour, rather than lose it to other employers. This was in the expectation that when the economy began to take off again, they would have the necesssary labour resources to enable them to deal with rising demand for their products or services.

The second, related consequence of soft labour markets was the increased wage-bargaining power provided to trade union negotiators. Local labour market shortages also undermined the regulative authority of national, multi-employer collective agreements. This resulted in the spread of plant or workplace bargaining, led from the union side by local, autonomous shop stewards, accountable largely to their members at plant level (see below). They often bargained toughly with local managers and were generally more willing than full-time union officers to threaten and use industrial sanctions in the wage-bargaining process. In consequence, during the 1960s, there was an increase in the number of unconstitutional strikes (in breach of agreed negotiating procedures) and unofficial strikes (not supported by the unions nationally). Governments became increasingly concerned about the economic efficiency and efficacy of British collective bargaining arrangements, processes and outcomes.

A third, knock-on effect of tough wage bargaining in the private sector was that these wage increases provided the benchmarks by which the public sector unions made their wage claims to the employers. This provided governments with a series of dilemmas. Resisting such wage claims could result in industrial conflict amongst the state's workforce, damage to the state's reputation as a fair employer or the loss of staff to the private sector. On the other hand, conceding such claims could result in: large rises in public spending, and therefore in taxation and/or public borrowing; wage-price-wage inflation; and state employers being seen as weak, ineffective parties in the wage-bargaining process, providing a bad model for private sector employers to follow.

Searching for an incomes policy

The potentially inflationary effects of collective bargaining in conditions of full employment led postwar governments to search for an industrial consensus on the levels of annual wage increases compatible with price stability, economic growth and balance-of-payments equilibrium. The first attempt was that of the Labour government in 1948, following an economic crisis during summer 1947. It issued a White Paper (Cmnd 7321, 1948) arguing for no general increase in money incomes, unless justified by labour shortages. The TUC, though initially sceptical, gave the policy its qualified approval, but its annual Congress in 1949 voted for an end to wage restraint and the policy ceased to have effect during 1950. The last attempt at an agreed incomes policy was at the beginning of 1979. The Labour government and the TUC published a joint statement which, whilst placing no limits on wage increases, expressed a joint commitment to reduce inflation to the level of Britain's overseas competitors over the following three years. With the return to power of a Conservative government, led by Margaret Thatcher, in May 1979, the policy lapsed.

Between 1950 and 1979, there were over 20 attempts to create a wage-bargaining consensus acceptable to employers and unions (ACAS 1980). Some were unilaterally initiated and imposed by government for given periods such as between 1966 and 1969 and, under the Counter Inflation Act 1972, between 1972 and 1974. Other attempts, for example in the mid-1960s, sought the voluntary support both of the unions, through the TUC, and of the employers, through the CBI. Yet others, such as the 'social contracts' between the Labour government and the TUC between summer 1975 and August 1977, were jointly monitored, government–union attempts at limiting wage increases for limited periods.

The nub of the incomes policy issue was trying to get a central agreement on annual wage increases. This involved developing a wages consensus amongst government, the unions and the employers, by which the economic outcomes of voluntary collective bargaining (increasingly conducted at company and factory levels in the private sector) would be broadly in line with annual increases in national productivity and output.

If wage negotiators could not be persuaded to agree to limit their members' money wage increases in line with rises in real productivity at factory level, this would have a number of effects. First, private sector employers which conceded such wage rises would have to increase their product prices to remain profitable. This would contribute to wage-price or cost-push inflation. Second, these wage increases, in turn, would provide benchmarks for other wage bargainers to follow in the private sector, especially those operating in the same external labour markets. Unless the outcomes of these wage bargains were in line with productivity increases, these too would add to wage-price inflation. Third, the rates of increase in private sector wages provided reference points for union negotiators in the public sector. Where these were conceded, without productivity strings being attached, these in turn would fuel wage-cost inflation, creating demands for even higher wage increases by wage bargainers in the next pay round.

In these circumstances, there were few incentives for union wage bargainers to restrain their members' wage claims for any substantial period. If union leaders failed to satisfy their members' wage expectations, their members might take unofficial industrial action anyway. Employers, too, were unlikely to be convinced of the merits of wage restraint by resisting the wage demands of their unionised workforces. They would generally want to avoid expensive and disruptive industrial action and would also be concerned that they might lose some of their labour force, if their company's wages were uncompetitive with those of other employers. And in any case, they were able to pass on rises in wages costs to their customers, in the form of higher product prices, in soft product markets. The only set of employers likely to resist excessive wage claims were public sector ones. They needed to set examples to the private sector and to keep public spending under control but they employed only a minority of the labour force.

It is clear, in retrospect, that in the period of the employee relations consensus, the one area of public policy where consensus proved to be elusive was in constraining wage bargaining 'in the national interest'. After 1965, the efforts were virtually continuous and a number of approaches were tried. These included voluntary and statutory pay norms (see Chapter 4) but none were successful in restraining wage increases for any length of time. With strong trade unions operating in conditions of full employment, various attempts by governments to adopt a policy of 'bargained corporatism' (see Chapter 1) failed to persuade union leaders, and their members, to accept any variant of public wage policy other than that of 'voluntary collective bargaining'. When national pay guidelines existed, national union leaders lacked the authority and control to get local shop stewards and full-time officers to comply with pay norms, other than in the short term. Unlike the Swedish and German experiences at this time, attempts at designing effective incomes policies in Britain failed miserably to deliver what was intended.

Supporting voluntary collective bargaining

State support for voluntary collective bargaining, or collective *laissez-faire*, as a process for determining the outcomes of the market relations between employers and employees, can be traced back to the late nineteenth century. Indeed the final report of the Royal Commission on Labour Laws (1894) had supported the growth of strong, voluntary organisations of employers and employees, industry-level collective bargaining and a role for government in helping to minimise and settle industrial disputes. It was during the period 1945–79 that this policy reached its apotheosis.

Whitleyism

The Whitley Committee (1916–18) reinforced state support for voluntary collective bargaining as a method of conducting employee relations. During the first world war, there had been a great expansion, reorganisation and flexibility expected in manufacturing industry, in response to the demands of the war economy. There had been a significant growth in the numbers and powers of local shop stewards who had challenged the authority of full-time union leaders, had used local bargaining to undermine national wage agreements and had made demands for 'workers' control' of industries and factories.

In the light of these pressures for change, the Committee recommended the establishment of standing joint councils of voluntary employers' associations and union organisations at industry, district and workplace levels. Whilst power was to be concentrated at national level, it was recommended that the machinery should concern itself with a wide range of issues. These included:

- determining wages;
- agreeing terms of employment;
- promoting efficiency;
- encouraging 'joint cooperation' between employers and workers at all levels.

To encourage the development of collective bargaining, the Committee further recommended the setting up of a permanent, voluntary arbitration body and inquiry machinery (Farnham 1978).

In the interwar years, Whitley councils were established in a number of private and public industries. These included the civil service, electricity, gas, building and printing – largely where collective bargaining had not existed previously (Charles 1973). With the encouragement of the Ministry of Labour and National Service, further joint industrial councils, or similar bodies, were established or re-established in the period immediately following the second world war. These included the NHS, local government, the railways and the water supply industry. Furthermore, with full employment, steady economic growth and rising union membership, the numbers of workers whose terms and conditions of employment were directly determined by collective bargaining increased, mainly through industry-level, multi-employer bargaining. By the mid-1960s, the Ministry of Labour (1965) estimated that upwards of 18 million employees, out of a workforce of 24 million, had their terms and conditions of employment determined by voluntary collective bargaining or statutory wage-fixing machinery.

The Donovan Commission

Between 1965 and 1968, the Royal Commission on Trade Unions and Employers' Associations (the Donovan Commission) undertook an examination of British employee relations, at a time when collective bargaining was being conducted in conditions of full employment and strong union bargaining power. Its report epitomised the support that the liberal state wished to give to voluntary collective bargaining. It concluded (Donovan 1968: page 50) that:

> Collective bargaining is the best method of conducting industrial relations. There is therefore wide scope in Britain for extending

both the subject matter of collective bargaining and the number of
workers covered by collective agreements.

Donovan's anlaysis concentrated on what was happening in private
manufacturing industry. The Commission identified the central defects
in British employee relations at that time as the disorder in
employer–union relations, pay structures and collective bargaining procedures within factories. This was the result of the conflict between
formal, industry-wide bargaining at multi-employer level and informal,
factory bargaining at company or plant level. The formal system pur-
ported to settle the terms and conditions of employment of workers.
But in practice it was fragmented, competitive, wage bargaining within
factories between managers and shop stewards, outside the control of
employers' associations and national trade unions, which determined
actual earnings. This bargaining provided local additions to national
wage rates, such as piecework, bonus and overtime payments. In the
Commission's view, moreover, companies lacked effective internal
procedural arrangements to curtail unofficial and unconstitutional
industrial action by their workforces.

The Commission's main recommendations (pages 262–64) for the
reform of collective bargaining were:

- collective agreements should be developed within factories to regulate actual pay and procedural matters at this level, whilst industry-
  wide agreements should be limited to those matters which they
  could effectively regulate;
- at corporate level, boards of directors should develop comprehensive
  collective bargaining machinery and joint procedures for the settlement of grievances, discipline, redundancy and related issues;
- companies with over 5,000 employees, including the public sector,
  should be required to register their procedural agreements with the
  Department of Employment and Productivity;
- a Commission on Industrial Relations (CIR) should be established
  which (a) would investigate and report on problems arising out of
  the registration of procedural agreements and (b) would consider
  problems referred to it concerning companies not large enough to be
  covered by the registration arrangements.

The Royal Commission also argued that new measures were needed
to encourage the extension of collective bargaining in Britain. Its main

recommendations here were:

- any stipulation in a contract of employment that an employee was not to belong to a trade union should be void in law;
- the CIR should deal with problems of trade union recognition, where employers refused to negotiate with unions;
- wages councils legislation should be amended to encourage the development of voluntary collective bargaining machinery;
- legislation under which an employer was required to observe relevant terms and conditions for an industry should be amended;
- unilateral arbitration should be available on a selective basis, where it could contribute to the growth or maintenance of sound collective bargaining machinery.

Donovan's prescriptions for change epitomised the state's support for the development of voluntary collective bargaining in Britain and for extending its scope. Whilst voluntary reform proceeded on a piecemeal basis after Donovan, its proposed programme of legislation to promote voluntary collective bargaining was not acted upon immediately. This was because the Labour government that had established the Commission lost the general election of 1970 and, even before then, it had difficulty getting its post-Donovan White Paper accepted by the TUC and Parliamentary Labour Party (Jenkins 1970). The Heath government which replaced it was committed to major reforms of the law on employee relations. Although the Industrial Relations Act 1971 claimed to promote the principle of collective bargaining freely conducted between workers' organisations and employers, in fact, it sought to extend the influence of the law on employer and union behaviour but markedly failed to do so (Weekes *et al.* 1975). Its principles challenged those of the employee relations consensus and, largely as a result of this, the vast majority of employers and unions ignored the Industrial Relations Act 1971. They continued to conduct their employee relationships as they always had done, through voluntary collective bargaining.

The Employment Protection Act 1975

With the Labour party re-elected to office in 1974, state support for the reform and extension of voluntary collective bargaining continued and, in retrospect, reached its highest point. It was facilitated by the

Employment Protection Act (EPA) 1975, the Employment Protection (Consolidation) Act (EPCA) 1978 and related legislation. Part I of the EPA 1975 focused on the machinery for promoting the improvement of employee relations, within which ACAS had a pivotal role, whilst the EPCA 1978 consolidated the employment protection rights of individual employees, including those of trade unionists. In establishing ACAS, the EPA 1975, section 1(1), stated:

> [ACAS] shall be charged with the general duty of promoting the improvement of industrial relations, and in particular of encouraging the extension of collective bargaining and the development and, where necessary, reform of collective bargaining machinery.

The legislation drafted to do this was aimed at:

- *Encouraging trade union membership and activities.* Employees were given statutory protection from being prevented or deterred by employers from joining or taking part in the activities of an independent union or being compelled to join a non-independent union. Where employers infringed these provisions, employees had the right to go to an industrial tribunal.
- *Providing statutory time off work for those involved in trade union duties.* Officials of independent, recognised trade unions were given the right to time off work with pay for undertaking certain union duties, such as approved training, and time off without pay for certain union activities. Where these rights were infringed by employers, individuals could make a claim to an industrial tribunal.
- *Facilitating trade union recognition by employers.* Under the Section 11 procedure of the EPA 1975 (repealed by the Employment Act 1980), independent trade unions could approach ACAS where an employer refused to recognise them. It was ACAS's duty to examine the issue, consult with the parties, conduct inquiries and to report its findings. Where ACAS recommended recognition and an employer refused to comply with it, the Central Arbitration Committee (CAC) could make an award on terms and conditions, which became incorporated as implied terms in the contracts of employment of individual workers. This was a form of compulsory arbitration but there was no legal enforcement of union recognition.
- *Obliging employers to consult with and provide information to recognised independent unions.* Independent recognised trade unions were provided with statutory rights to be consulted on proposed col-

lective redundancies and occupational pensions. They were also entitled to be provided with information by employers where it would be in accordance with good practice to disclose or where it would assist in the conduct of collective bargaining. There was, additionally, a statutory duty on employers to consult with independent recognised unions on health and safety matters. These included: the appointment of safety representatives; the appointment of safety committees; and the provision of information to safety representatives.

* *Providing legal procedures for extending terms and conditions of employment where unions were not recognised.* Schedule 11 of the EPA 1975 (repealed by the Employment Act 1980) enabled claims to be made to ACAS by independent unions (or employers' associations) that an employer was observing terms and conditions of employment less favourable than the recognised terms and conditions or, where there were no recognised terms and conditions, less favourable than the general level in any trade, industry or district. Failing settlement by ACAS, the CAC, if it found the claim to be well founded, could make an award for the appropriate terms and conditions to be observed as implied terms in the contracts of employment of workers. This too was a form of compulsory arbitration.

Public policy since 1979: the challenge to collective *laissez-faire*

After 1979 governments rejected Keynesian economic theory and Beveridge social welfare principles (see Chapter 4). This had considerable implications for public policy on employee relations, which shifted from one focused on *voluntary collective bargaining*, in conditions of full employment and strong trade unions (with attempts at *bargained corporatism* through 'social contracts') to a policy of *neo-laissez-faire*. It is a policy rooted in market liberal economic principles and weak trade unions (see Chapter 1).

The *employee relations consensus* emphasised:

* state intervention in the labour market;
* state support for employee relations collectivism, whilst using the law as a 'prop' to promote collective bargaining;

- excluding the courts and the judges from intervening in the internal affairs of trade unions and the regulation of industrial conflict.

Neo-laissez faire, in contrast, emphasises:

- deregulating the labour market;
- individualising employee relations, with the legal props to collective bargaining being loosened or removed and legal restrictions on trade unions being enacted;
- depoliticising the trade unions.

The policy instruments used have included: legislation; economic measures; government example in its own spheres of responsibility; and the creation of the Commission for the Rights of Trade Union Members (Farnham 1990).

The theoretical and moral underpinnings of economic, social and employee relations policy since 1979 have been rooted in market economics and liberal individualism, or 'market liberalism'. Market economics assumes that supply and demand in the market place, acting through the price mechanism, are preferable to political rationing by politicians in deciding what to produce in an economy, how to produce it and how goods and services are to be distributed amongst the population. Liberal individualism pinpoints the individual, not interest groups or pressure groups, as the prime decision-making authority, with the freedoms and natural rights of the individual being inalienable and non-negotiable. Free markets lead to economic efficiency and equity, it is argued, whilst free-thinking individuals in doing what is best for themselves maximise economic welfare generally.

The market economic model makes three assumptions about the relationship of the market to the individual:

- that individuals act rationally in pursuing their own self-interest in the market place;
- that the free play of impersonal, decentralised market forces is the best way of increasing the prosperity and welfare of the individual and of the wider community;
- that the individual consumer is sovereign in the market place because of freedom of consumer choice and market competition amongst producers.

For market liberals, because the individual is central to economic decision-making, and because it is assumed that he/she knows what is best for him/herself, the role of government is limited to providing an economic and constitutional framework for individuals to pursue their own self-interest. The state only intervenes to protect the individual's rights to property, liberty and access to free markets. Market liberal – or neo-*laissez faire* – economic, social and employee relations policy, in short, aims at optimising market efficiency, minimising government intervention in private affairs and protecting individual rights against vested interests.

Deregulating the labour market

There is some debate whether there is 'a' labour market in Britain or a series of 'segmented' labour markets. Market liberal macro-economists emphasise the contexts of the general labour market, whilst market liberal micro-eonomists try to explain how rational agents in disaggregated labour markets produce different responses to changes in wage levels and unemployment. The macro-economists focus on how factors independent of the labour market – such as inflation, the exchange rate and mortgage tax relief – are likely to influence wages and unemployment; the micro-economists try to evaluate the influence of institutional factors affecting them. To simplify the market liberal analysis, this section focuses on the micro-issues of labour market policy, rather than the macro-issues.

The micro-issues

Labour market deregulation has been a central plank of government policy since 1979. Given that labour services are commodities which are bought and sold by rational employers and rational workers in the market place, market liberals argue that levels of wages and employment are determined by the forces of supply and demand in the market. In a free labour market, the quantity of labour supplied equals the quantity demanded at the market wage. Unemployment is symptomatic of labour market rigidity and means that the price of labour is too high, so that wages need to be adjusted downwards if the labour market is to clear. Where there are barriers to a freely operating labour market, it is necessary to deregulate it to make it more competitive. This, it is argued, is in the interests of economic efficiency and individual freedom.

One cause of unemployment and labour market rigidity identified by market liberal economists is institutional. Where, for example, employers have to take account of the costs of compensation for unfair dismissal, they are deterred, it is claimed, from increasing demand for new employees. Extending employment protection rights thus has the overall effect of bringing about a fall in labour demand and increasing unemployment. Second, fiscal factors, such as changes in taxation and social security, are also claimed to increase unemployment. This is because higher taxes reduce labour supply, whilst higher social security payments result in people being unemployed longer, with more time being spent in job searches.

A third cause of unemployment, in the view of market liberals, is collective action by workers organised into trade unions. Unionised workers are viewed as restricting labour supply and limiting access to jobs for non-union workers who are likely to drive wage rates down. A rise in demand for unionised labour results in higher wages but not in higher employment, because the supply of labour is fixed in the short term. Indeed, market liberals argue that trade unions actually contribute to higher unemployment because they restrict labour supply, whilst union wage rates do not reflect changes in labour supply or labour demand. More than that, the unionised sector is the benchmark for the whole economy, setting wage norms for other workers to follow. In the non-unionised sector, in contrast, labour supply is seen as being responsive to changes in wage rates. And an increase in labour demand there will be reflected in both higher wages and higher levels of employment.

The policy presciptions

According to market liberals, government can reform and deregulate the labour market by improving the supply side of the market. It can do this in four ways. First, it can reduce the time spent unemployed and in job searches by reducing the rates of social security payments. Second, government can increase labour supply by reducing personal taxation rates. These two measures aim to increase incentives to work, so that more people make themselves available for employment and join the labour market. A third measure is removing wages councils and minimum wages legislation, since these are likely to increase the price of labour to employers thus resulting in a fall in labour demand. The fourth way in which government can act is by reforming trade union immunities. The aim here is to make it more difficult for trade unions to take lawful industrial action, without incurring severe financial costs in doing so. All these measures were, to varying degrees, adopted by Conservative governments during the 1980s and 1990s by a series of legislative and economic initiatives.

Individualising employee relations

The necessary conditions for employee relations collectivism are:

- freedom of association for workers to join trade unions;
- 'free' trade unions independent of employers and the state;
- employer recognition of trade unions;
- bargaining in good faith.

Since 1979, one plank of public policy has aimed at the decollectivisation of employee relations, with employers being encouraged to use more individualist methods of determining and implementing the wage–work bargain. This policy, stemming from the precepts of market liberalism, has taken three main forms, with government attempting to:

- weaken union organisation;
- strengthen the right to manage;
- discourage union militancy.

Weakening union organisation

Whilst freedom of association and independent trade unions continue to exist in Britain, union organisation has been weakened dramatically since 1979, in at least three respects. First, union density, normally expressed as the percentage of the potential workforce who are union members, has fallen drastically, especially in the private sector (see Chapter 8). This is largely as a result of structural reorganisation of the economy and high levels of unemployment during the 1980s and 1990s (Daniel and Millward 1984; Millard and Stevens 1986; Millward *et al.* 1992). Smaller employment units and the reduction in size of the manufacturing sector have adversely affected union organisation. High unemployment also weakens union bargaining power with employers and makes the retention of union members more problematic and the recruitment of new members a more difficult task for union organisers (Martin 1992).

Second, as a result of a series of changes in employment law since 1980, closed shop agreements, or union membership agreements (UMAs), between employers and trade unions are unlawful. A UMA is any arrangement by which employees are required to be members of a union as a condition of employment. Pre-entry closed shops are where jobs are restricted to individuals who are already members of the appropriate union, whilst post-entry closed shops require employees to join a specified union within a set period of starting work. Where individuals claim that their legal right not to belong to a union is infringed, they have a right to make an application to an industrial tribunal and seek compensation.

Outlawing the closed shop has weakened union organisation. UMAs covered some quarter of the employed workforce in the late 1970s (Dunn and Gennard 1984). Although it is difficult to calculate the extent of the closed shop currently, and despite the continuance of some informal closed shop arrangements, current legislation has both ended the enforcement of the practice and debilitated union organisation.

Third, other legal measures, originally incorporated in the Employment Act (EA) 1988 and the Trade Union Act (TUA) 1984 and now embodied in the Trade Union and Labour Relations (Consolidation) Act (TULRCA) 1992, as amended, provided rights for union members to elect union executive committees and union leaders by postal ballot, at least once every five years. These legislative changes in union election procedures, outlined in a Green Paper in 1983, stemmed from the government's desire to ensure that trade union members are truly representative of their memberships. Because the unions had not reformed themselves voluntarily, the government claimed that it 'had reluctantly come to the conclusion that some legislative intervention is necessary' (Department of Employment 1983: page 16). Another interpretation of these provisions, however, is that they are seen by government as a further means of weakening collective links amongst trade unionists, and between union members and the union, thus loosening union cohesion and collective solidarity (see Chapter 8).

Strengthening the right to manage

The right to manage is that area of corporate decision-making which management considers to be its alone and is not constrained by collective bargaining or the law (see Chapter 3). The boundaries of the right to manage are the interface between unilateral management control and the ability of employees, individually or collectively, to influence or counterbalance those decisions most affecting their working lives. Given government commitment to the enterprise culture and the free market economy since 1979, one policy goal has been to strengthen the right to manage. Its rationale is to provide managers, in both the private and public sectors, with more autonomy in organisational decision-making and to restrict union activity and collective action. It is aimed at enabling employers to react more swiftly to changing product markets, to obtain greater flexibility from their human resources and to have more control over worker productivity. Companies and public sector organisations, in turn, should then become more efficient, effective and competitive, thus boosting the economy, economic growth and employment.

The pressure for employers to recognise unions for collective bargaining purposes has been considerably weakened since 1979. One of the first measures taken by the government was to repeal, in the EA 1980, the Section 11 procedures embodied in the Employment Protection Act (EPA) 1975. This means that ACAS no longer has a statutory duty to investigate and make recommendations on union recognition. ACAS's only remaining duty is to conciliate on trade union recognition claims, on a voluntary basis. The number of requests for this has fallen dramatically in the past decade (ACAS Annual Reports).

The powers of wages councils to set wage rates for those aged under 21 and other conditions were abolished by the Wages Act 1986, which limited wages councils to setting minimum adult hourly rates and overtime rates. Subsequently, the Trade Union Reform and Employment Rights Act 1993 abolished wages councils completely. Fair Wages Resolutions (see below) have been rescinded and the comparable terms and conditions procedure – Schedule 11 of the EPA 1975 – has been repealed. Where 10–99 employees are to be made redundant, the minimum period for trade union consultation has been reduced. Further, union-only or union recognition clauses in commercial contracts are now void in law. It is also unlawful to discriminate against or victimise contractors on these grounds.

All the above public policy changes have enabled employers to be more flexible and autonomous in determining the terms, conditions and working arrangements of their employees. The emphasis is on strengthening the right to manage, at the expense of employee and union rights, and weakening the legal props to collective bargaining.

Discouraging union militancy

Changes in collective labour law since the 1980s have aimed at reducing union ability to take part in lawful trade disputes (see Chapter 4). Legal immunities, the legal definition of a trade dispute and industrial action ballots are at the root of the issue. Where employees take industrial action, they are normally in breach of their contracts of employment. Under common law, it is unlawful to induce people to break a contract, to interfere with the performance of a contract or to threaten to do so. Without legal immunities, unions and their officers could face legal action for inducing breaches of contract when organising industrial action. Legal immunities provide protections for unions and individuals so that they cannot be sued for damages for inducing breaches of contract when furthering industrial action in certain circumstances (see Chapter 1). The Employment Acts 1980 and 1982, however, withdrew immunities from certain types of industrial action, opening up the possibility of unions and individuals having injunctions issued against them, or being sued, where their actions are unlawful. These legal provisions are now incorporated in the TULRCA 1992.

The law also provides that those organising industrial action are only protected when acting 'in contemplation or furtherance of a trade dispute'. To remain within the law, those calling industrial action must be able to show that there is a dispute and that the action is in support of it. Lawful disputes are those between workers and their own employers and must be concerned with matters 'wholly or mainly' connected with terms and conditions, negotiating machinery and so on. The following types of disputes are now *unlawful*:

- inter-union disputes;
- 'political' disputes;
- disputes relating to matters occurring overseas;
- disputes with employers not recognising unions or employing non-union labour;
- 'secondary' or 'sympathy' disputes between workers and employers other than their own.

Where unions act unlawfully, they lose their legal immunity (see Chapter 11).

Unions are also required to ballot union members involved in a

The State and Employee Relations
249
trade dispute, before authorising the action. Under the TUA 1984 (now incorporated in the TULRCA 1992), it became a condition of legal immunity that, before organising industrial action, the union holds a secret ballot in which all those about to take the action are entitled to vote. The action is only lawful where a majority of those voting support it. The EA 1988 went further by providing union members with the right to apply to the courts for an order restraining their union from inducing them to take industrial action without a properly conducted ballot. The Trade Union Reform and Employment Rights Act 1993 requires unions to give seven days' notice to the employer of their intention to hold an industrial action ballot, which must normally be a full postal ballot and be independently scrutinised. Where an unlawful act is authorised by a union official, or by a committee to which such officials report, the union is liable unless it disowns the unlawful act in writing.

The effect of removing legal immunities from certain industrial action is to provide those damaged by the action, such as employers or union members, with the right to take civil proceedings against the union, or in some cases the individual, responsible. The remedies are:

- seeking an injunction to prevent or stop the action; or
- claiming damages from the union for conducting unlawful action.

Under the TULRCA 1992 and the Trade Union Reform and Employment Rights Act 1993, union members have the statutory right not to be unjustifiably disciplined by their union. It specifies the actions which count as discipline and the conduct for which discipline is justifiable. Unjustifiable discipline for union members includes:

- refusing to take part in balloted industrial action;
- crossing a picket line;
- refusing to pay a levy for supporting a strike or other industrial action;
- failing to agree or withdrawing from an agreement with an employer regarding deductions of union dues;
- working or proposing to work with members of another union or with non-union members;
- working or proposing to work for an employer who employs non-union members or members of another union.

Depoliticising trade unions

Union political activity, though difficult to define in practice, has always been a sensitive and ambivalent issue for the Conservative party to deal with. On the one hand, the Conservatives want the votes of trade union members in local, national and European elections. On the other hand, there are many in the Conservative party who are distinctly hostile to unions on not only political but also economic grounds. The political objections of many Conservatives to the trade unions are to the close political affiliations of some unions to the Labour party. Trade unions affiliate members to the Labour party, sponsor Labour Members of Parliament and participate in Labour party decision-making. The economic objections of many Conservatives to the trade unions are that they distort the working of the free labour market, inhibit economic efficiency and weaken management authority in the workplace.

The underlying assumption of recent public policy-makers in seeking to depoliticise the trade unions is that the economic and political roles of trade unions can be dissociated. This analysis accepts the unions' economic role as legitimate, up to a point, but asserts that their political role needs to be circumscribed, by law. This is necessary, market liberals argue, on the grounds that it makes politicians democratically accountable to their constituents, not to special interest groups such as trade unions, and secondly that the unions can concentrate on their more rightful and more legitimate role of protecting their member's employment interests in the labour market. Depoliticising the unions could also facilitate an ideological change on the part of the unions and their members, enabling them to identify more closely with the goals of a dynamic effective capitalism, operating in a competitive enterprise culture.

Political strikes

The definition of a trade dispute in the TULRCA 1992 now requires trade disputes to 'relate wholly or mainly to' the subjects listed. This raises doubts about the lawfulness of any dispute having political elements. This change in the legal definition of a trade dispute, in seeking to exclude those with a political element, effectively restricts some types of actions aimed at defending or improving terms and conditions of employment. An example is where workers decide to take industrial action in protest at their industry or organisation being privatised.

Political fund review ballots

The TULRCA 1992, as amended, requires unions with 'political objects' and political funds, which are normally used to support the Labour party and to conduct political campaigns, to ballot their members, at least once every 10 years, on whether they wish their union to continue to spend money on political matters. Ballots must be by post and are subject to independent scutiny. The scrutineer has access to a union's membership register and must inspect the register or a relevant copy where it is felt appropriate to do so. The distribution, counting and storage of voting papers must be undertaken by independent scrutiny. If these ballots are not held, the authority to spend money on political objects lapses.

Privatisation

Privatising substantial parts of the public sector, and contracting out certain services in public sector organisations, has transferred large numbers of workers out of public employment (see below). This means that the government is no longer their employer. These businesses cannot therefore call upon government to increase public spending to finance their wage settlements with their employees. They are now required to have regard to market and financial considerations when responding to terms and conditions claims. This takes wage determination in these sectors out of politics, thus in effect depoliticising their wage bargaining process.

Settling trade disputes

Since 1979, successive governments have publicly rejected any role in industrial peacekeeping. Government ministers have abstained from directly intervening, by conciliating or mediating, in intractable trade disputes, even in the public sector, no matter how bitter the disputes have been. This approach assumes that dispute resolution must be left to the direct employers and trade unions to settle themselves. The outcome can then be determined by strong employers relying on market forces to generate financially prudent wage settlements and a sense of economic reality amongst the workforce and their union leaders in the wage bargaining process.

Rejecting corporatism

Public policy since 1979 has resulted in governments excluding the TUC from industrial policy-making. Governments have refused to consult directly with the TUC on economic, employment or social policy decisions and they have abandoned top-level meetings with TUC officials. A succession of government Green Papers on trade union law reform, for example, was not used for consultative purposes but as draft legislation which was enacted subsequently in virtually the form in which it had been presented. Indeed, the only remaining corporatist body, the National Economic Development Council, was formally wound up in 1991.

The state as an employer

As the role of the British state expanded during the twentieth century, so the number of people employed by state agencies also increased. An outline summary of the structure of state employment by major sectors, since 1961, is provided in Table 8. From this, it can be seen that state employment rose steadily until 1979, when it reached a peak of almost eight million employees, on a headcount basis. By 1991, it had fallen to under six million – the level it had been in 1961. Between 1961 and 1991, employment in the nationalised industries fell by over 1.5 million, whilst increasing in other public corporations by some 60,000. In central government, employment in the NHS doubled between 1961 and 1991, fell in the armed services and in the civil service but increased by 140,000 in other central government organisations. In local government, total employment increased by almost 400,000 between 1961 and 1991, with rises in all the main local authority services but especially in education and the social services.

The state as a model and good-practice employer

One of the traditional roles of the state in employee relations, from the late nineteenth century till the late 1970s, was to be a 'model' and 'good-practice' employer. Although the concepts overlap, they may be distinguished analytically. As a 'model' employer, the state adopted what it deemed to be progressive employment practices, such as encouraging union membership and recognising trade unions, in order to enhance 'best practice' in the public sector and to act as an example

Table 8: *Numbers employed in the public sector 1961, 1974, 1979 and 1991*

				(thousands)
	1961	1974	1979	1991
Public corporations				
Nationalised industries	2152	1777	1849	516
NHS trusts	—	—	—	124
Other	48	208	216	107
Total	2200	1895	2065	747
General government				
Armed services	474	345	314	297
NHS	575	911	1152	1092
Civil service	672	705	738	580
Other	69	179	183	208
Total	1790	2140	2387	2177
Local authorities				
Education	785	1453	1539	1416
Social services	170	272	344	414
Construction	103	135	156	106
Police	108	160	176	202
Other	703	762	782	810
Total	1869	2782	2997	2948
Grand Total	5860	6817	7749	5872

Source: derived from *Economic Trends*

for the private sector. As a 'good-practice' employer, in contrast, the state adopted certain of the employment practices of the best private sector companies, such as wages comparability, so as to be able to recruit, retain, reward and motivate high-quality staff in the public sector. As a 'model' employer, the state played a 'lead' role in employee relations, whilst as a 'good-practice' employer, the state had a 'following' role (Farnham and Horton 1993).

The model employer concept of the public sector can be traced back some 100 years. In 1893, for example, the House of Commons passed a resolution stating that 'no person in Her Majesty's Naval Establishments should be engaged at wages insufficient for proper maintenance.' It added that 'the conditions of labour as regards hours, wages, insurance against accidents, provisions for old age, sickness, etc., should be such as to afford an example to private employers throughout the country' (White 1933: page 156). Examples of model employment practices adopted by public sector employers after 1945, and earlier in some cases, include:

- job security;
- jointly agreed employee relations procedures with the public sector unions for handling grievances, discipline, dismissal and redeployment;
- equal opportunities and equal pay;
- occupational pensions;
- training and career development;
- the recruitment of disadvantaged workers.

To varying degrees, these model practices applied across the public sector. When compared with private employers, the public sector demonstrated a rich pattern of relatively homogeneous, consistent and standardised employment practices, aimed partly at influencing 'bad' practices in the private sector (Beaumont 1981).

A prime example of a model employment practice was in relation to 'fair wages' principles, linked with union membership. The Fair Wages Resolutions of the House of Commons (1891 and 1946, but rescinded in 1983) obliged private contractors, supplying goods to public organisations, to pay 'fair wages' to their employees and to recognise their rights to be union members. The principle underlying these resolutions was that it was the government's duty to use its bargaining position with private contractors to ensure that they observed at least minimum standards of fairness in the terms and conditions of employment provided to their employees. The outcome of collective bargaining was acknowledged to be the relevant standard of fairness to be met by the contractors' terms and conditions of employment (Beaumont 1992). These arrangements, it was believed, would eliminate unfair wage-cutting amongst government contractors and influence the development and growth of union organisation and collective bargaining in these parts of the private sector.

One facet of being a good-practice public employer meant providing terms and conditions of employment comparable with those provided by the best private employers. As the Priestley Commission wrote regarding Civil Service pay (Priestley 1955: para. 172):

> We consider that the Civil Service should be a good employer in the sense that while it should not be among those who offer the highest rates of remuneration, it should be among those who pay somewhat above the average . . . the Civil Service rate should not be lower than the median but not above the upper quartile.

This principle of 'pay comparability' was incorporated in guidelines provided to the Civil Service Pay Research Unit, set up as a result of the Priestley Commission. It was a principle legitimised more generally in the public sector in the late 1970s by the Standing Commission on Pay Comparability (SCPC). Although abolished in 1981, the SCPC, set up by the Prime Minister, James Callaghan, in March 1979, had a distinctive role. Its remit was to examine the pay and conditions of employment of groups of public sector workers referred to it by the government, with the agreement of the employers and unions concerned, and to report on these. In each case, the SCPC had to make recommendations 'on the possibility of establishing acceptable bases of comparison with terms and conditions for other comparable workers and of maintaining appropriate internal relativities' (Standing Commission on Pay Comparability 1981: iii).

The related roles of the model and good-practice employer in the public sector were not always compatible. One example was public sector employers acting as leaders of wage restraint in their own sector, during periods of incomes policy, but at other times acting as followers of private sector wage levels in order to recruit and retain staff. However, providing a lead in some employment practices and in others following the best private employers were crucial elements in the employment policy of the state to its employees, certainly up to 1979.

The reasons for state employers adopting these policies were partly practical and partly ethical. First, they had the relative freedom to develop innovative employment policies and practices because they were unconstrained by the short-term pressures of profit-making and financial stewardship that acted on private employers. Second, such practices were seen as contributing to public sector efficiency by attracting the right staff, minimising industrial conflict and retaining a quality workforce. Third, the government considered that public employers had a social duty to provide examples of model and good employment practices which might be copied by less progressive private sector employers.

Converging with the private sector?

Since 1979, although the changes must not be exaggerated, public sector employment policies and practices have shifted as a result of government initiatives. Put briefly, rather than public sector employment practices being used by state employers to influence the private sector, a number of private sector employment practices – such as performance-related pay, personal contracts, the removal of wage-bargaining procedures and compulsory competitive tendering – are being introduced into the public sector. There is thus increasing convergence between the public and private sectors, but with the public sector following the lead of some leading private employers, rather than vice versa. These changes in employee relations policies and practices in public sector organisations are complementary to the changes in macro public policy – based on neo-*laissez-faire* principles – since 1979.

Compared with the private sector, the specialist personnel management function came into the public sector relatively late. It was not until the 1970s, partly as a result of local employee relations problems, that the establishment function, certainly in the Civil Service, NHS and local government, began to be superseded by specialist personnel managers. Although part of the management structure, personnel managers also saw themselves as mediating between employers and employees, and seeking to accommodate both the management needs for efficiency and fairness and the employee needs for fairness and job satisfaction. Since the 1980s and in the 1990s, this traditional personnel management role, in turn, is being challenged by an increasing emphasis on styles of management and employee relations more associated with those of the private sector – HRM.

There is a lively academic debate about the differences between personnel management and HRM (Guest 1987, Storey 1989, Torrington and Hall 1991). However, it is generally recognised that HRM differs from traditional personnel management in a number of ways:

- HRM focuses on employees as resources which, like other resources, need to be used efficiently.
- Employees are viewed as a key resource, with employers actively pursuing employee commitment to corporate goals and values. Only through a systematic set of policies on recruitment, rewards for performance, staff appraisal, training and development, and effective communication, it is argued, can commitment and excellence be achieved.

- HRM assumes that personnel management is the responsibility of all line managers rather than of personnel specialists.
- There is a preference for management communication with employees individually, rather than relying on collective forms of information exchange through trade unions.
- HRM assumes a unitary model of employee relations, in contrast with the pluralist model underpinning traditional personnel management.

A central focus of HRM, compared with traditional personnel management, is improving employee performance. This necessitates selecting the 'right' people to do the job, rewarding them accordingly, appraising their performance and training and developing them to do their existing and future jobs better and more efficiently. As in the private sector, public sector employers are responding to these issues in a number of ways (Farnham and Horton 1993).

Recruitment and selection

In parts of the public sector, responsibility for recruitment is being decentralised, innovations are reducing the time taken to recruit and better selection techniques are being introduced. 'Head hunters' and assessment centres are now being used and greater use is being made of psychometric testing, bio-data sifting and wider sources of potential recruitment. The latter is being achieved by opening up competition to top posts, recruiting from the private sector and using short-term contracts. Another recruitment and employment strategy, borrowed from the private sector, is that of implementing more flexible working arrangements (Management and Personnel Office 1987). These challenge the public sector model of lifetime employment, enabling public employers to reduce costs, improve productivity and compete with the private sector for some of their staff.

Rewarding performance

One of the most significant HRM innovations in the public sector since the mid-1980s has been the introduction of performance-related pay (PRP). PRP is an individualised form of payment providing for periodic rises in pay that reflect assessments of individual performance and personal value to the organisation. Such increases may determine the rate of progression through pay scales or be increments added to existing pay scales or lump sums. Copied from the private sector, PRP is predicated on the belief that rewarding 'high performers' by paying them more helps focus attention on achieving corporate objectives, improves performance and encourages 'a more decisive, competitive and entrepreneurial spirit' (Murlis 1987: page 27). PRP was first introduced into the Civil Service in 1985 and has been extended radically since then. In the NHS, the recommendations of the Griffiths Report (Department of Health and Social Security 1983) resulted in the introduction of PRP for general managers and, in the 1990s, there were plans to extend PRP to other professional groups.

Staff appraisal

With increased emphasis on improved performance in the public sector, staff appraisal systems are becoming widespread for many groups of staff. Based on private sector practice, staff appraisal was triggered in the NHS by the Griffiths Report and led to the introduction of an 'individual performance review' for some senior staff. The emphasis was on sharply defined individual responsibilities for achieving objectives, combined with the need to develop a stock of potential general managers from within the service. As in other parts of the public sector, staff appraisal is seen as playing a key role in redefining roles, generating clarity of purpose and building commitment to a new sense of corporate identity. Performance appraisal, together with staff development (see below), is being used by government as an instrument for inducing cultural change, measuring performance and introducing flexible reward systems in the public sector, based on private sector experience (Farnham and Horton 1993).

Staff development

Part of the drive to enlarge the training function in the public sector since the 1980s has derived from the need to provide staff with the skills and competences necessary for operating the new management systems being introduced. In the Civil Service, NHS and local government, many of these new systems are computer-based, and staff therefore need appropriate training.

New management development programmes have been introduced in the Civil Service, some of them offered jointly with private sector organisations. In the NHS, the National Health Service Training Agency was established in 1985 to provide health authorities with leadership and support 'as they develop, implement and manage education and training programmes to help achieve the goal of cost-effective high-quality health services' (Annandale 1986). In local government, a key role has been taken on by the Local Government Management Board, which resulted from a merger between the Local Government Training Board and the Local Authorities Conditions of Service Advisory Board. In an attempt to raise the quality of public service provision, public organisations are also using another 'big idea' borrowed from the private sector – 'total quality management' – and training their staff to implement it (see Chapter 10).

Relations with employees

The new employee relations in the public sector since 1979 have manifested themselves in a number of ways. Wage negotiating machinery was removed from nurses and the NHS professions allied to medicine in 1983, and from school teachers in 1987. As a result, about half the staff in the NHS have their pay determined by pay review bodies, and about 400,000 teachers in England and Wales now have no national wage bargaining arrangements. The principle of comparability of public sector pay with that of the private sector, as embodied in the Priestley Commission (1955), was effectively destroyed by the abolition of the Civil Service Pay Research Unit in 1981. Since then, the ability of the employer to pay, value for money and market forces have become the dominant criteria for determining collective pay increases in all parts of the public sector. National collective bargaining came under further attack in 1990 when the government signalled its intention to encourage decentralised wage bargaining in the public sector, modelled on private sector practice. Structural changes in the Civil Service, NHS and education provide the opportunity for changing bargaining structures (see Chapter 9), with likely changes in local government to follow. NHS trusts are free to set their own terms and conditions for staff, whilst 'Next Steps' agencies in the Civil Service are likely to break away from Whitleyism.

Compulsory competitive tendering

Compulsory competitive tendering (CCT) and 'contracting out' are not new to the public sector. But previously, under the Fair Wages Resolutions (FWRs), any private employer subcontracting to the public authorities had to ensure that its terms and conditions of employment were not less favourable than those existing in the public sector, or those which were the norm in the industry through collective bargaining. With the rescinding of the FWRs in the 1980s, there was a general deterioration of the terms and conditions for those workers covered by CCT arrangements.

Until the Trade Union Reform and Employment Rights Act 1993, there appeared to be no legal protection for such workers. The government claimed that the EC's Acquired Rights Directive, implemented in Britain through the Transfer of Undertakings Regulations 1981, applied only to commercial undertakings. In the European Court of Justice in 1992, however, the Redmond case confirmed that the Directive applies to employees in both the private and public sectors. This decision was incorporated in the 1993 Act. This means, in any transfer of undertakings, that: contracts of employment are transferred to the new employer, together with existing terms and conditions; collective agreements, where they exist, are transferred; union recognition is transferred; and dismissals that result from such transfers are automatically unfair.

Assignments

(a) Why did 'free collective bargaining', or collective *laissez-faire*, have such an appeal to employers, the unions and the state? Does it still do so?

(b) Read Wedderburn (1986) pages 21–25 and examine why legal immunities, rather than positive legal rights, became incorporated in the English legal system affecting employee relations.

(c) Critically examine the Donovan Commission's presumption (1968: page 54) that: 'properly conducted, collective bargaining is the most effective means of giving workers the right to representation in decisions affecting their working lives, a right which is or should be the prerogative of every worker in a democratic society.' What are some of the implications of this statement for managing employee relations?

(d) Read Farnham (1978) and analyse the main characteristics of Whitleyism as a model of employee relations practice.

(e) What have been the goals of neo-*laissez-faire* public policy on employee relations since 1979? Evaluate the effectiveness of this policy and examine some of its implications for employee relations management.

(f) Interview a number of public sector employees and find out why they joined public sector organisations. Ask them what they understand by the terms 'model' employment practices and 'good' employment practices, with examples of each. Ask them what they regard as the main differences between public sector employment practices and those of the private sector.

(g) What features of state policy on employee relations, since the 1980s, have influenced the emergence of 'human resource management' practices amongst British employers? How have these HRM practices manifested themselves?

References

ADVISORY CONCILIATION AND ADVISORY SERVICE 1980. *Industrial Relations Handbook*. London: HMSO.
ADVISORY CONCILIATION AND ARBITRATION SERVICE 1981–1992. *Annual Reports*. London: ACAS.
ANNANDALE, S. 1986. 'The four faces of management development'. *Personnel Management*. July.
BAYLISS, F. 1959. *British Wages Councils*. Oxford: Blackwell.
BEAUMONT, P. 1981. *Government as Employer – Setting an Example?*. London: Royal Institute of Public Administration.
BEAUMONT, P. 1992. *Public Sector Industrial Relations*. London: Routledge.
BEVERIDGE, W. 1944. *Full Employment in a Free Society*. London: Allen and Unwin.
CHARLES, R. 1973. *The Development of Industrial Relations in Britain 1911–1945*. London: Hutchinson.
CLEGG, H., FOX, A. and THOMPSON, A. 1964. *A History of British Trade Unions since 1889. Volume 1 1889–1910*. Oxford: Clarendon.
CMD. 7321 1948. *Personal Incomes, Costs and Prices*. London: HMSO.
DANIEL, W. and MILLWARD, N. 1983. *Workplace Industrial Relations in Britain*. London: Heinemann.
DEPARTMENT OF EMPLOYMENT 1983. *Democracy in Trade Unions*. London: HMSO.
DEPARTMENT OF HEALTH AND SOCIAL SECURITY 1983. *NHS Management Inquiry* (the Griffiths Report). London: HMSO.
DONOVAN, Lord 1968. *Royal Commission on Trade Unions and Employers' Associations: Report*. London: HMSO.
DUNN, S. and GENNARD, J. 1984. *The Closed Shop in British Industry*. London: Macmillan.
Employment Protection Act 1975.
FARNHAM, D. 1978. 'Sixty years of Whitleyism'. *Personnel Management*. July.
FARNHAM, D. 1990. 'Trade union policy 1979–89: restriction or reform?'. In

SAVAGE, S. and ROBINS, L. (eds). *Public Policy under Thatcher.* Basingstoke: Macmillan.

FARNHAM, D. and HORTON, S. 1993. 'Human resources management in the public sector: leading or following the private sector?'. *Public Policy and Administration.* Special edition, Spring.

GUEST, D. 1987. 'Human resource management and industrial relations'. *Journal of Management Studies.* 24(5).

JENKINS, P. 1970. *The Battle of Downing Street.* London: Knight.

KEYNES, J. M. 1936. *The General Theory of Employment, Interest and Money.* London: Macmillan.

MANAGEMENT AND PERSONNEL OFFICE 1987. *Working Patterns.* London: MPO.

MARTIN, R. 1992. *Bargaining Power.* Oxford: Clarendon.

MILLWARD, N. and STEVENS, M. 1986. *British Workplace Industrial Relations 1980–1984.* Aldershot: Gower.

MILLWARD, N., STEVENS, M., SMART, D. and HAWES, W. 1992. *Workplace Industrial Relations in Transition.* Aldershot: Dartmouth.

MINISTRY OF LABOUR 1965. *Written Evidence of the Ministry of Labour to the Royal Commission on Trade Unions and Employers' Associations.* London: HMSO.

MURLIS, H. 1987. 'Performance-related pay in the public sector'. *Public Money.* March.

PELLING, H. 1987. *A History of British Trade Unionism.* Harmondsworth: Penguin.

PRIESTLEY REPORT 1955. *Royal Commission on the Civil Service.* London: HMSO.

ROYAL COMMISSION ON LABOUR LAWS 1894. *Final Report of the Commission 1991–94.* (Chairman: Duke of Devonshire). London: HMSO.

SCHMITTER, P. and LEHMBRUCH, G. 1979. *Trends Towards Corporatist Intermediation.* London: Sage.

STANDING COMMISSION ON PAY COMPARABILITY 1981. *Final Report.* London: HMSO.

STOREY, J. 1989. *New Perspectives on Human Resource Management.* London: Routledge.

TAYLOR, A. J. P. 1965. *English History 1914–45.* Oxford: Clarendon.

TORRINGTON, D. and HALL, L. 1991. *Personnel Management.* London: Prentice Hall.

Trade Union Reform and Employment Rights Act 1993.

Trade Union and Labour Relations (Consolidation) Act 1992.

WEDDERBURN, Lord and DAVIES, P. 1969. *Employment Grievances and Disputes Procedures in Britain.* Berkeley: University of California Press.

WEEKES, B., MELLISH, M., DICKENS, L. and LLOYD, J. 1975. *Industrial Relations and the Limits of the Law.* Oxford: Blackwell.

WHITE, L. 1933. *Whitley Councils in the British Civil Service.* Chicago: Chicago University Press.

WHITLEY COMMITTEE 1917–18. *Reports.* London: HMSO.

Chapter 8

Management and Trade Unions

Voluntary collective bargaining, with management dealing with trade unions and employee representatives, on labour market and certain managerial isssues, remains a major employee relations process in Britain. The Workplace Industrial Relations Survey (WIRS) estimates that in 1990 the proportion of employees covered by collective bargaining was 54 per cent of all establishments in its representative sample. Although this was considerably less than the 71 per cent coverage identified in an earlier survey in 1984, in 1990 80 per cent of the establishments surveyed still recognised trade unions, compared with 89 per cent in 1984 (Millward *et al.* 1992).

The conditions necessary for effective collective bargaining to take place include:

- freedom of association for workers to organise into independent trade unions;
- the willingness of workers to join and participate in the activities of independent trade unions;
- the ability of the unions to recruit, retain and service their members effectively;
- employer recognition;
- a fair balance of bargaining power between employers and unions in the bargaining process.

To deal with trade unions effectively, therefore, managements need to understand the nature of trade unions, their employee relations activities, preferred methods of operating and the values and purposes for which they stand. They also need to be aware that whilst unions collectively share certain common principles and ideologies, each individual union, in turn, has its own institutional characteristics, employment policies and responses to employee relations problems.

In Britain, employer recognition of trade unions depends, to a large extent, on the ability and voluntary efforts of trade unions in recruiting, retaining and providing services to their members effectively. It also reflects the level of economic activity and structure of the economy at any one time. The willingness of employers to recognise trade unions is a function of:

- the balance of bargaining power between the secondary parties, when unions demand recognition for the first time;
- the perceived benefits of recognition to the employer in each case.

With the economy expanding and the demand for labour rising, union recognition is more easily achieved by the unions and more likely to be agreed to by managements. With the economy in recession and with excesss labour supply, union recognition is less easily achieved and more likely to be resisted by management. In these circumstances, derecognition may be a more attractive option for some employers to adopt.

Developments in trade unions

Membership trends

Union membership in Britain is in the form of a Pareto distribution. This means that there is a small number of very large unions and a large number of very small ones, with the small number of very large unions making up over 80 per cent of total union membership. In 1990, for example, the Certification Office listed 23 unions each having over 100,000 members and another 264 unions each with less than 100,000 members. The 23 largest unions comprised some eight million members and the 264 other unions only had about 1.8 million members distributed amongst them (Certification Office 1992).

Table 9 shows that in 1960 there were 15 major trade unions in Britain, with more than 100,000 members each, comprising a total of over six million members. By 1980, there were 26 such unions, totalling over 10 million members. In 1990 this had fallen to 24 unions of this size, including the Police Federation, which is not listed by the Certification Office, with a total of eight million members. In other words, total union membership in Britain's largest unions in 1990 was about two million members less than it had been in 1980. This total membership, however, was still some two million

Table 9: *Union membership in Britain's largest unions in 1960, 1980 and 1990*

			(000s)
	1960	1980	1990
Transport and General Workers Union (TGWU)	1302	1887	1224
Amalgamated Engineering Union (AEU)[1]	973	1166	702
General Municipal and Boiler-makers Union (GMBU)[2]	796	916	865
National Union of Mineworkers (NUM)	586	370	116
Union of Shop Distributive and Allied Workers (USDAW)	355	450	362
National Union of Rail Maritime and Transport Workers (NURMTW)[3]	334	167	101
National and Local Government Officers Association (NALGO)	274	782	744
National Union of Teachers (NUT)	245	272	218
Electrical Electronic Telecommunication and Plumbing Union (EETPU)[4]	243	405	367
National Union of Public Employees (NUPE)	200	699	579
Manufacturing Science and Finance Union (MSFU)[5]	*	491	653
Union of Construction Allied Trades and Technicians (UCATT)[6]	192	312	207
Confederation of Health Service Employees (COHSE)	*	216	203
Union of Communication Workers (UCW)[7]	166	203	203
Society of Graphical and Allied Trades (SOGAT)[8]	158	200	169
Iron and Steel Trades Confederation (ISTC)	117	104	*
Civil and Public Services Association (CPSA)[9]	140	216	123

Royal College of Nursing (RCN)	*	181	289
Banking Insurance and Finance Union (BIFU)	*	141	171
Association of Professional Executive and Computer Staff (APEX)[10]	*	140	*
National Communications Union (NCU)[11]	*	131	155
National Union of School Masters/ Union of Women Teachers (NAS/UWT)	*	156	169
Amalgamated Society of Boilermakers (ASB)[12]	*	124	*
Assistant Masters and Mistresses Association (AMMA)	*	*	139
National Graphical Association (NGA)[13]	*	116	130
Police Federation (PF)	*	112	180
National Union of Civil and Public Servants (NUCPS)[14]	*	109	114
	6332**	10066	8185

* Not applicable

** This total includes two other unions, the National Union of Agricultural Workers and the National Union of Garment and Tailoring Workers, with 135,000 and 116,000 members respectively in 1960.

1. Known as the Amalgamated Union of Engineering Workers in 1980; became the Amalgamated Electrical and Engineering Union in 1992, after a merger with the EETPU.
2. Known as the General and Municipal Workers Union in 1960 and 1980.
3. Known as the National Union of Railwaymen in 1960 and 1980.
4. Known as the Electrical Trades Union in 1960.
5. Known as the Association of Scientific Technical and Managerial Staff in 1980. It merged with the Technical Administrative and Supervisory Section of the AEU to form the MSFU in 1988.
6. Known as the Amalgamated Society of Woodworkers in 1960.
7. Known as the Union of Post Office Workers in 1971.
8. Known as the National Union of Printing Bookbinding and Paper Workers in 1960. Became the SOGAT in 1975 and merged with the NGA in 1991 to form the Graphical Paper and Media Union.
9. Known as the Civil Service Clerical Association in 1960.
10. Merged with the GMBU in 1989.
11. Known as the Post Office Engineering Union in 1960 and 1980.
12. Merged with the General Municipal Workers Union in 1982.
13. See note 8 above.
14. Known as the Society of Civil and Public Servants in 1980.

Source: TUC and Certification Officer *Annual Reports*

members higher than amongst similar unions in 1960.

Table 9 also shows that of the 15 largest unions listed in 1960, only three had smaller memberships in 1980. These were the NUM, NURMTW and ISTC. By 1980, these 15 largest unions had been joined by 11 others: MSFU (then known as ASTMS); COHSE; RCN; BIFU; APEX; NCU; NAS/UWT; ASB; NGA; PF; and NUCPS. The decline in the absolute and relative size of some of the old 'smoke-stack' unions, such as the NUM, NURMTW and ISTC, and the rise to greater prominence of 'white-collar' unions in the public and private services by 1980 reflected, in part at least, the changing industrial and employment structures in Britain during the 1960s and 1970s (Bain 1970).

Between 1980 and 1990, as also shown in Table 9, this trend continued. During this decade, whilst there was a decline in the absolute memberships of all the largest unions recruiting amongst manual workers (except the NGA), and even amongst some white-collar unions in the public sector, such as the NUT, NALGO and CPSA, there were rises in membership in other white-collar unions recruiting professional, technical and administrative workers in parts of the private and public sectors. The large unions gaining members during these years were: MSFU; RCN; BIFU; NCU; NAS/UWT; AMMA; and NUCPS. Some of this growth in the memberships of these unions can be accounted for by union mergers, such as those involving the MSFU. In other cases it arose from expanding recruitment opportunities for unions such as the RCN and BIFU or for the NAS/UWT and AMMA which were taking members from established organisations in their own sector, such as the NUT. Further evidence of the relative decline amongst some of the large private sector unions during the 1980s is provided by the absence of the ISTC, ASB and APEX from those organisations with over 100,000 members each in 1990. By this time, the ISTC's membership had fallen to around 40,000, the ASB had merged with the General and Municipal Workers Union in 1982 to form the GMBU and APEX, in turn, had merged with the GMBU in 1989.

It is likely that the trend towards more union amalgamations and mergers will continue into the 1990s. The AEU and EETPU amalgamated in 1992 to create the Amalgamated Engineering and Electrical Union, with over a million members. NUPE, NALGO and COHSE also merged to form the largest public sector union in the world, UNISON, with some 1.5 million members. And discussions are reported to have taken place between the TGWU and GMBU about

Table 10: *TUC membership, TUC affiliations and non-TUC membership 1978–91*

Year	Membership of TUC	Numbers of TUC-affiliated unions	Membership of non-TUC unions
1978	11,865,390	112	1,188,206
1979	12,128,078	112	1,084,276
1980	12,172,508	109	463,847
1981	11,601,413	108	709,821
1982	11,005,984	105	738,406
1983	10,510,157	95	789,722
1984	10,082,144	89	691,809
1985	9,855,204	91	963,745
1986	9,580,502	89	1,017,506
1987	9,243,297	87	1,236,853
1988	9,127,278	83	1,259,960
1989	8,652,318	78	1,391,288
1990	8,405,246	78	1,404,773
1991	8,192,664	74	not available

Source: TUC, *Annual Reports* and CO, *Annual Reports*

future working arrangements between them.

Another way of examining recent union membership trends is by analysing membership in unions affiliated to the TUC (see Chapter 2) and that in unions which are not TUC affiliated, as shown in Table 10. This shows, first, that total union membership in Britain peaked at an all-time high of 13.2 million members in 1979, comprising 12.1 million members in TUC-affiliated unions and just over a million in non-TUC unions. By 1990, the overall level of union membership had fallen to 9.8 million members, consisting of some 8.5 million in TUC-affiliated organisations and some 1.4 million in non-TUC unions. This represented a fall of 26 per cent in overall membership, a fall of 30 per cent in the membership of TUC unions and a rise of 30 per cent in the membership of non-TUC unions for the period 1979–90.

Second, between 1978 and 1991, the number of unions affiliated to the TUC declined from 112 to 74. This reduction in the number of TUC-affiliated unions is largely accounted for by the series of amalgamations and mergers taking place amongst TUC unions after 1980. Yet whilst membership in TUC-affiliated unions fell steadily during the 1980s and early 1990s, that in non-TUC unions grew slowly from 1981, after it had fallen dramatically by over 600,000 members between 1979 and 1980. The effect was that between 1981 and 1990, membership in non-TUC unions rose by almost 100 per cent from about 709,000 to 1.4 million.

Union structure

Union structure focuses on the recruitment and membership bases of trade unions, which are organised on occupational (or craft), industrial or general lines. Occupational, 'craft' or 'trades' unions are exclusive bodies and were the first type of employee organisation to emerge in Britain (during the nineteenth century). One of their main recruiting devices was the pre-entry closed shop (Gennard 1990). Today few occupational unions exist and those that do are relatively small in size. This is because of changing occupational boundaries, the widening scope of occupational classifications, the de-skilling of craftwork due to technological changes, the growth of multi-skilling and the break-down of traditional craft sectors of employment. Unlike industrial unions which recruit vertically within an industry, occupational unions recruit horizontally across industries.

Current examples of occupational unions include the British Actors' Equity Association, the British Medical Association, the British Airline Pilots' Association and the Professional Footballers' Association. The main structural feature of occupational unions such as these is that they recruit members selectively, on a job-by-job basis, irrespective of where they work. It is the worker's occupational status, job skills and qualifications or training which determine whether or not individuals qualify for membership of a particular occupational union, not the industry or the organisation which employs them.

Industrial unions recruit selectively but less exclusively than occu-pational unions. They seek members vertically from amongst all employment grades, normally including both manual and non-manual workers, within a single industry. The best examples of industrial-based unions are in Germany, where there are 16 industrial unions with about eight million members, all of which are affiliated to the DGB. These unions cover:

- the metal industry;
- public services;
- chemicals;
- postal services;

- construction;
- food, drink and tobacco;
- textiles and clothing;
- education and science;
- media;
- police;
- wood and plastics;
- agriculture;
- leather;
- mining and energy;
- rail;
- commerce, banking and insurance.

With the reunification of western and eastern Germany, demarcation disputes between certain industrial unions have emerged and it is likely that some reorganisation within the DGB will take place, such as between the chemicals and mining and energy sectors (Jacobi *et al.* 1992).

In Britain, in contrast, because of the continually dynamic and constantly evolving structure of industry, the difficulty of defining industrial boundaries with precision, and the growth of multi-occupational and multi-industry unions, there are very few single-industry unions left. The best remaining examples are the NUM and the ISTC, with the NURMTW and the Broadcasting and Entertainment Trades Alliance retaining some features of industrial unionism. Yet even in these cases, there are other unions competing for members in these sectors, thus weakening the exclusivity of the industrial union base.

General or 'open' unions, in contrast to occupational and industrial unions, are 'all-comers' organisations with four main membership characteristics. They draw their members:

- non-exclusively;
- from amongst both manual and non-manual workers;
- horizontally across industries;
- vertically within industries.

For a number of historical and structural reasons, general unions have become the dominant model of British trade unionism.

Because of the financial pressures on them, substantial membership leakages in the 1980s and changes in the economy, British trade unions have had to adapt their recruitment strategies and institutional structures to these circumstances. The essential issues facing British unions in recent years have been employer hostility, financial viability and membership retention. Consequently, most craft unions have opened up their boundaries to less skilled workers; industrial unions have continued to diversify their memberships – sometimes across industrial sectors; and general unions have sought to retain and extend their membership boundaries to maintain their influence and power in the trade union movement.

The net result has been a series of union amalgamations and mergers since the early 1980s. This has strengthened general unionism in Britain at the expense of occupational and industrial unions. These mergers have often been driven by the political allegiances of union leaderships or the search for stronger union membership bases, rather than by the desire to create rational union structures. There are three main consequences of this:

- There has been a shift towards the creation of a few 'super' unions whose membership boundaries overlap, resulting in competitive membership recruitment amongst them.
- These amalgamations and mergers have not mitigated the problems associated with multi-unionism at industry, employer and workplace levels and in dealings with employers.
- The role of the TUC has to some degree been weakened, since these larger unions feel less need for the services and support of an umbrella organisation at central level like the TUC and they are more critical of its coordinating functions.

Trade union policy

The essence of trade union policy is to protect the employment interests of their members, as individual workers, by dealing with employers collectively. As Hyman (1975: page 64) writes, the central purpose of a trade union 'is to pemit workers to exert, collectively, the control over the conditions of employment which they cannot hope to possess as individuals'. They do this largely 'by compelling the employer to take account, in policy- and decision-making, of interests contrary to [its] own.'

Any general analysis of union policy starts by examining their functions and roles as economic and political agents, acting on behalf of employees in their market and managerial relations with employers. Such an analysis clearly highlights the essential divergences between union policy and employer policy on many employee relations issues. Employer policy is normally aimed at achieving profitability, economic efficiency and management control of employee behaviour, achieved through corporate hierarchies. Union policy, on the other hand, is aimed at achieving 'fair' terms and conditions of employment, participation in corporate decision-making and power-sharing with management, achieved through collective bargaining, other employee relations processes and internal union democracy.

It is these differences in organisational rules and values, stemming from this dichotomy between purpose and method, which give rise to conflicts of interest in employee relations between employers and unions, where trade unions are recognised. This dichotomy also explains why some employers resist union organisation and recognition in their workplaces.

The labour market function

The classical analysis of the trade union function is provided by the Webbs. It was they who first described, analysed and evaluated the purposes and methods of trade unions. For the Webbs, unions exist to enforce 'Trade Union Regulations' on employers for the workers they represent. There is no 'Trade Union Rate of Wages' nor 'a Trade Union Working Day' but many different rates and hours of work which vary from occupation to occupation. (Webbs 1913: page 560) Trade unions are thus seen by the Webbs as bodies defending sectional economic interests, rather than working class interests as a whole. Whilst all unions have broadly similar purposes, and use largely the same methods to achieve them, each union has its own unique purposes and uses those methods most appropriate to its particular cirumstances.

Seven trade union regulations are identified by the Webbs. These are:

- the Standard [wage] Rate;
- the Normal [working] Day;
- Sanitation and Safety [at work];
- New Processes and Machinery;
- Continuity of Employment;
- the Entrance into a Trade;
- the Right to a Trade.

At the core of the Webbs' analysis is their conclusion that: 'in the making of the labor contract the isolated individual workman, unprotected by any combination with his fellows, stands in all respects at a disadvantage compared with the capitalist employer' (page 658). Whilst workers strive to get the best terms they can from their employers, the employers, in turn, 'are endeavouring, in accordance with business principles, to buy their labor in the cheapest market' (pages 658 and 184). Workers combine together, therefore, to be better able to enforce the regulations of their trade upon employers.

Unions use two 'economic devices' to do this: 'the Device of the Restriction of Numbers' and 'the Device of the Common Rule' (Part III: Chapter III). The device of the restriction of numbers is concerned with labour supply. It involves unions using apprenticeships, excluding new competitors from the trade and asserting 'a vested interest in a particular trade' in order to influence the labour market. In these ways, unions can make a better bargain with the employers, insisting on adequate wages, better conditions of employment and shorter hours of work for their members.

The device of the common rule is the enforcement of minimum standards of employment on employers below which no employer may fall. It is not a maximum standard, since some employers may provide terms and conditions better than the minimum. The Webbs go on to analyse the 'three distinct instruments or levers' used by unions to enforce the regulations of their trades. These are: 'the Method of Mutual Insurance, the Method of Collective Bargaining, and the Method of Legal Enactment' (page 150).

Mutual insurance

The method of mutual insurance is the provision of funds by trade unionists, through collective subscriptions, to insure their members' incomes against the economic misfortunes of unemployment, sickness and accidents. According to the Webbs, 'until Collective Bargaining was permitted by the employers, and before Legal Enactment was within the workman's reach, Mutual Insurance was the only method by which Trade Unionists could lawfully attain their end.' The existence of 'friendly [society] benefits' enables unions to maintain discipline over members breaking union rules and to enforce upon all members the decisions of the majority.

Where differences arise between an employer and its employees, unions using the method of mutual insurance can apply economic pressure on employers, through what the Webbs describe as the 'Strike in Detail'. This is the process, if an employer refuses to conform to the regulations of the trade, by which union members leave the employer's employment, one by one, and are sustained by 'Out of Work' benefit from the union. But, as the Webbs state, 'as a deliberate Trade Union policy, the Strike in Detail depends upon the extent to which the union has secured the adhesion of all the component men in the trade' and their capacity to pursue their common ends collectively (pages 166 and 169).

Collective bargaining

The method of collective bargaining enables joint machinery to be established between employers and unions to settle the employment rules within a trade (Part II: Chapter II). Collective bargaining prevents wage undercutting by both employers and employees, maintains 'industrial peace' and enables distinctions to be made between the negotiating arrangements for concluding new agreements and those for interpreting existing ones. Also:

> When the associated employers in any trade conclude an agreement with the Trade Union, the Common Rule thus arrived at is usually extended by the employers, as a matter of course, to every workman in their establishment, whether or not he is a member of the union (page 209).

Determining the common rules of the trade through collective bargaining is a very flexible union method, since agreements can be made at 'shop', 'district' and 'whole industry' level, with 'impartial umpires' or conciliators being available, acceptable to both sides, where collective agreement cannot be reached. For the Webbs (page 218), this joint method for settling the terms and conditions of employment, 'neither by the workmen nor by the employers [alone], but by collective agreement', was attracting 'a growing share of public approval' and support at the time. This was because of the compromises and concessions required of the two sides in the negotiating process and the benefits to both sides in adopting it.

Legal enactment

The method of legal enactment enforces the regulations of the trade through Act of Parliament. For the Webbs, legal enactment is a method about which trade unionists are ambivalent. On the one hand, before unions can get a common rule enforced by the state, they must convince the community at large 'that the proposed regulation will prove advantageous to the state as a whole, and not [be] unduly burdensome to the consumers.' Further, what Parliament enacts might not be the full measure asked for. On the other hand, Acts of Parliament apply uniformly to all districts, whether unions are strong or weak, and to all employers. Legal enactment, therefore, is 'the ideal form of Collective Bargaining, a National Agreement made between a Trade Union including every man in the trade, and an Employers' Association from which no firm stands aloof.'

The Webbs saw the TUC as the body for obtaining, by Parliamentary action, particular measures desired by its constituent unions. But, as the Webbs warned, once the TUC 'diverges from its narrow Trade Union function, and expresses any opinion, either on general social reforms or party politics, it is bound to alienate whole sections of its constituents' (Part II: Chapter IV).

Summary

For the Webbs, then, all trade union regulations are based on the assumption that, in the absence of common rules, the determination of terms and conditions of employment are left to the free labour market, placing workers at an economic disadvantage *vis à vis* employers.

> . . . this always means, in practice, that they are arrived at by Individual Bargaining between contracting parties of very unequal economic strength. Such a settlement, it is asserted, invariably tends, for the mass of the workers, towards the worst possible conditions of labor – ultimately, indeed, to the barest subsistence level – whilst even the exceptional few do not permanently gain as much as they otherwise would (page 560).

In the Webbs' analysis, the essence of trade union policy is to remedy and offset this imbalance in labour market power, through the use of appropriate economic devices and methods. For everything beyond 'the National Minimum', wage earners must depend on the method of collective bargaining. But for those regulations and rules based on enduring considerations, such as the health and efficiency of workers, legal enactment is to be preferred (pages 796–806).

The participatory function

It was Flanders who took the Webbs' analysis of union policy and the union function a stage further. In his view, the value of a union to its members is less in its economic achievements than in its capacity to protect their dignity. Whilst union members are interested in labour market regulation and how labour is managed, because these define their rights, status and security, they are also interested in making and administering employment rules and having a voice in shaping their own destiny. To secure membership allegiance and support, unions must provide services to their members and 'this is made possible by [union] participation in job regulation.' They do this primarily through collective bargaining. Yet since collective agreements are a body of jointly agreed rules, and the process of negotiation 'is best conceived as a diplomatic use of power, trade unions operate primarily as political, not economic, institutions' (Flanders 1968a: pages 238–40).

The constant underlying purpose of trade unions, then, is participation in job regulation. 'But participation is not an end in itself, it is a means of enabling workers to gain more control over their working lives' (Flanders 1968b: page 42). The issue which concerns Flanders is the slow rate of progress made by trade unions in advancing this social purpose, especially, when he was writing, under conditions of full employment. For him, one of the weaknesses of trade unions is that a lot of their energies are absorbed in the struggle for 'more money' for their members, whilst the struggle for their members' status in the workplace receives far less attention. In this view this is remediable, where unions refuse to accept any final definition of exclusive managerial functions: 'They have recognised that the frontiers of union control are shifting frontiers, that any decision that affects the life and well-being of their members can be their concern' (Flanders 1961: page 23). Participation by unions jointly with management in non-wage issues is clearly legitimate where their members' employment interests are affected.

Trade union practice

Trade union practice derives from trade union policy. Given the essential role of trade unions in providing the collective representation of employees in their relations with employers, trade union practices are directed towards any area of common concern to their members, their employment status or occupational interests. Union practices are reflected in the objectives, means and methods of trade unions. These vary by union and according to the circumstances facing any group of trade unionists at any one time. A number of contingent factors affect whether or not these objectives are achieved and whether or not the means and methods used are effective. These include (see also Chapters 6 and 7):

- the state of labour markets;
- employer policy;
- management style;
- the law;
- public policy.

Objectives

Exhibit 21: *The TUC's union objectives*

- improved terms of employment;
- improved physical environment at work;
- security of employment and income;
- industrial democracy;
- fair shares in national income and wealth;
- full employment and national prosperity;
- improved social security;
- improved public and social services;
- a voice in government;
- public control and planning of industry.

Because of the sectionalised nature of British trade unionism, it is very difficult to provide a definitive set of universal trade union objectives, applicable to all unions at all times, and it is significant that neither the Webbs nor Flanders tried to do so. A prescriptive analysis of the 'permanent objectives' of unions is provided by the TUC in its evidence to the Donovan Commission. The objectives distinguished by the TUC (1966) are of different kinds. Some are substantive, some procedural and others do not concern employment as such. They are seen as complementary to one another and as providing choice for unions, enabling them to place lesser or greater emphasis on any one or more of them at any given time. The union objectives outlined by the TUC are illustrated in Exhibit 21.

Of these 10 objectives, only the first four are direct employee relations objectives. The next three are macro-economic and the last four are political objectives. It is some measure of the difficult environment facing trade unions in the 1990s that only the first three of the above objectives are likely to be aimed at by trade unions in Britain currently.

A modified analysis of union objectives was provided by the TUC (1974: pages 6–7) a few years later. It is through the unions, the TUC argues, that employees set the key objectives for advancing their interests. These provide rights at work including:

- *Establishing terms of employment.* Bargaining with employers about pay, hours and working conditions, including equal pay, allowances, retirement and pensions, redundancy, safety and health, and training, for all workers who are employed, part-time as well as full-time.
- *Fair representation.* Representing members to ensure the implementation of all rights that flow from agreements and from the law – eg maternity pay; safety requirements; protection against unfair disciplinary action or dismissal; protection against race or sex discrimination.
- *Influencing employer decisions.* Working together with employers to ensure the future of the enterprise and to safeguard jobs, and to that end to improve productivity.

Over and above this, however, workers' standards of living depend on actions taken by governments. These include:

- how the government manages the economy;
- the priorities given to welfare and public services;
- how taxes are raised and used;
- what government does to ensure that unions are not at a disadvantage given the enormous power of many modern businesses.

The union role, then, is to protect and advance the standards of living of workers in any way which is appropriate.

Means and methods

For the TUC (1966: page 43), trade union 'means' are interdependent with trade union 'methods'. 'It is impossible to bargain without anything to bargain with. This is the distinction between trade union means and trade union methods'. The choice between means and methods is a practical one, with union practice reflecting the circumstances in which a particular group of workers finds itself. But the basis of trade union effectiveness is 'combination' and this involves a number of means. Exhibit 22 illustrates the union means, listed by the TUC.

Exhibit 22: *The TUC's union means*

These include:

- organisation;
- 100 per cent membership;
- national and local coordination;
- income;
- union competence.

Without high levels of membership, sound organisation and responsive leadership, a union's ability to perform its representative functions on behalf of employees is seriously impaired.

Union methods, in turn, are related to their objectives and means. The TUC argues that the dividing lines between the various methods are imprecise, they are diverse and their emphasis varies according to circumstances. The union methods which the TUC distinguishes are illustrated in Exhibit 23.

Exhibit 23: *The TUC's union methods*

These include:

- collective bargaining;
- joint consultation;
- autonomous job regulation;
- services for members;
- influencing government;
- political action;
- international activities.

The challenges to the unions

It is clear that by the 1990s the 'permanent objectives', means and methods of trade unions have been weakened by labour market factors, the employee relations strategies of some employers and government policy. Trade union practice is obviously affected by high levels of unemployment, when more emphasis is placed by some employers on soft forms of joint consultation or non-union forms of employee involvement, and when other employers use more direct methods – dealing with employees on an individual rather than on a collective basis (see Chapter 10). Union effectiveness also suffers when government policy is directed towards deregulating the labour market and excluding the unions from the political process. As a result, since the mid-1980s, trade union practice, membership recruitment patterns and membership attitudes have been adversely affected by a number of contextual and employee relations factors.

Contextual changes

The 1980s were a period of immense economic, technological, social and political change in the western world but especially in Britain (see Chapter 6). There have been significant changes in the social structure, with an ageing population, a larger proportion of women workers in the labour market and the weakening of traditional class allegiances. Working methods and working practices have been dramatically affected by technological change and the 'information technology' revolution has left very few occupational groups unaffected by its impact on employment, job tasks and the work environment (Daniel 1987).

For over a decade, there have been persistent and very high levels of unemployment and radical changes in the structure of the economy, with shifts in the balance between manufacturing and services, and the private and public sectors. The international economic environment has been continuously turbulent and unstable. Large flows of finance capital have been transferred across national frontiers, with the purpose of gaining the highest possible returns from it, resulting in the weakening of national employment bases and traditional patterns of employment. Further, the move towards a single European market has not resulted in the economic stability and economic potential expected of it by some British companies.

The election to power of four consecutive Conservative administrations, in 1979, 1983, 1987 and 1992, resulted in public policies on employee relations which are recognised as being unsupportive of the trade union function. The result has been a set of labour market policies, employment legislation and government strategies that have weakened union bargaining power, outlawed inter-union solidarity action and denied the unions any role in influencing public policy (see Chapters 3 and 7).

These changes have not generally benefited the trade unions. Many employment units have become smaller, mass redundancies have resulted in large membership leakages from the unions and recruitment of new union members from the 'new' service sector has proved to be problematic. The occupational structure, the nature of labour markets and the content of job tasks have changed, weakening traditional union membership bases and patterns of union recruitment.

Employer policies

With private sector employers facing increasingly competitive open markets, and the public sector being privatised or deregulated, there has been a shift towards employment flexibility. This has resulted in the growth of short-term contracts, part-time working and changing patterns of shift work. These new working arrangements are generally not conducive to employment stability and membership retention in the trade unions. According to the Workplace Industrial Relations Survey (WIRS) (1992: page 74), whilst there is little evidence of full union derecognition in Britain in recent years, which amounts to 'just over 1 per cent of all workplaces in 1990', its limited data on the timing of derecognition 'was suggestive of a growing phenomenon', with a substantial concentration of the practice in 1989.

The WIRS also concludes that although new consultative arrangements created by management normally supplement rather than replace collective bargaining, there is evidence of management initiatives 'aimed at increasing employees' involvement at work' which took place with 'increasing frequency throughout the 1980s' (page 362). In these circumstances, it is possible that some employees see the union role of participating in 'job regulation' as being less important, especially where managements adopt proactive employee relations practices of these sorts. Indeed, the TUC claims (1988: page 6), union influence is being further challenged in organisations because of

Employee Relations

trends 'such as the increasing management emphasis on winning the commitment of the individual employee ("human resources management") and the continued decentralisation of collective bargaining.'

Inter-union competition

Differences between unions arise from a number of factors. These include:

- membership recruitment;
- job demarcation;
- recognition and bargaining rights;
- wages policy;
- contribution levels and services to members.

In the majority of inter-union disputes involving TUC affiliates, the TUC has been the final arbiter through the device of TUC disputes committees. In the early and mid-1980s, however, the so called 'Bridlington Principles', which aim to regulate inter-union membership competition and poaching amongst affiliated unions, came under increasing stress. This was the result of:

- the pressure on unions to recruit new members in competing areas because of membership leakages after 1980;
- the multi-occupational and multi-industry structure of British unions;
- the emergence of 'single-union agreements' on greenfield sites that exclude other unions with members in the unit from employer recognition;
- controversy over the 'no-strike' provisions in such agreements.
(See TUC 1988.)

However, the pressures for inter-union competition are likely to become more intense, now that the Trade Union Reform and Employment Rights Act 1993 provides trade union members with a statutory right to decide for themselves which union to join, even in multi-union situations. This effectively removes the Bridlington arrangements for dealing with disputes over membership amongst TUC unions.

It was the issue of single-union or 'new-style' agreements that caused particular differences amongst TUC affiliated unions and led eventually to the expulsion of the EETPU from Congress in September 1988. The decision to expel the EEPTU from the TUC arose from a complaint by the GMBU, TGWU and USDAW that the EEPTU had acted in contravention of the TUC's Disputes Principles and Procedures by signing a single-union deal with Christian Salveson at its Warrington and West Cross depots. The disputes committee decided, on the evidence presented, that the complainant unions should have been consulted by the EEPTU, before it entered into a sole negotiating agreement with the company at the two depots. The EEPTU's failure to accept the decision of the committee placed it in direct conflict with Congress who heard the union's appeal on 5 September, which was lost (TUC 1989).

Trade union strategy

Trade union strategy is the ways in which unions adapt their policies and objectives and adjust their means and methods in response to economic and social factors, employer initiatives and the framework of public policy within which employers and unions operate. As voluntary associations promoting the employment interests of their members, trade unions are a mixture of 'movement and organisation' (Flanders 1968b). Members of a movement combine together because they share the same sentiments, values and ideas and want to achieve common goals collectively. To survive as organisations, however, unions must have effective means for translating their goals into practical outcomes for their members. By their very nature, unions have to be dynamic organisationally, whilst maintaining the values and ideas for which they stand. They 'need organisation for their power and movement for their vitality, but they need both power and vitality to advance their social purpose' (page 44). As indicated above, this dual measure of trade union effectiveness has been severely tested in recent years. The main responses of the unions to these challenges are discussed below.

The collective bargaining agenda

Objectives

Trade unions are developing a number of positive and developmental

responses to the economic, technological, social and political problems facing them and their members. The TUC (1991a: pages 12–13)
has outlined some of these main developments in what it describes as
the 'New Bargaining Agenda' of trade unions. It provides examples of
attempts by some unions to 'raise the negotiating horizon beyond
immediate pay concerns to embrace [a] wide range of longer-term
developmental considerations.' The emerging themes, identified by the
TUC, at which the unions are aiming, are illustrated in Exhibit 24.

Exhibit 24: *The bargaining agenda for TUC unions in the 1990s*

- building for the future in terms of job security, job creation, the attainment of full employment and the elimina-
  tion of under-employment;
- focusing on job development, training and career
  prospects to give more workers control over their working
  lives and to provide them with more satisfying, fulfilling
  and rewarding jobs;
- emphasising 'fair play' policies, such as: improving the
  jobs, careers, status and pay of low paid workers; upvalu-
  ing the jobs of women; providing equal opportunities for
  disadvantaged groups; and providing developmental
  opportunities for those doing part-time, temporary and
  sub-contract work;
- giving priority to environmental and quality of life objectives and essential working conditions, such as: health and
  safety; the working environment; leisure; sickness benefit;
  occupational pensions; and family provisions.

In the TUC's view, the more the unions talk about employee development issues of this sort, and about the devolution of management
responsibilities to their members, the more they will find themselves
questioning existing management prerogatives.

The GMBU and UCW (1991: page 1) have suggested a similar
'New Agenda' that Britain's unions should adopt in the 1990s. In their
view, 'it is essential that Britain's unions abandon traditional reactive
stances . . . set an Agenda which confronts the new issues of the 1990s
. . . [and take] collective bargaining into territory that we have barely
explored before.' They argue that unions need to work together with
employers and government to create successful industry, a strong

economy and a 'caring, sharing society'. In these unions' analysis, the new circumstances facing employers, unions and government in the 1990s are:

* the European Community;
* rising expectations amongst consumers and employees;
* the role of women in the workforce;
* environmental concerns;
* restructuring within industry.

The GMBU and UCW argue that this situation should involve a joint response by unions and employers, with government support, aimed at matching productivity levels abroad and at negotiating ways of working which ensure that new skills and new plant are brought to bear on the productivity gap separating Britain from its foreign rivals.

In response to these challenges, the GMBU and UCW want unions to talk 'to Britain's employers about how to achieve quality performance, cost and price competitiveness and a fairer society.' The collective bargaining agenda would include issues such as training, investment, new product development, work restructuring, equal opportunities and health and safety issues. 'The New Agenda would make the quality of output rather than the price of inputs the centrepiece of talks between trades unions and employers.' Pay would be on the bargaining agenda 'but work organisation, training and quality should form the focus' (page 8). Unions should press management to discuss how they intend to develop the talents of their workforces, the investment they propose to make and how they can encourage employees to ever higher standards of customer service.

The negotiating framework

The TUC identifies enterprise-level bargaining as the obvious focus for employee relations decision-making, although it does not rule out industry and sector bargaining for some matters. Indeed, the TUC emphasises the importance of national framework agreements for establishing minimum rates for jobs or a floor of pay below which no employee may fall. It also supports single-table bargaining so that the entire job and pay structure can be taken into account in union–employer negotiations. On a wider front, the TUC believes that there is need for coordination at a European level – 'initially in terms of exchanges of information on . . . performance comparisons and agreement on principles' (TUC 1991a: page 14). This international role is likely to expand in the future but, in the short term, is focused on agreeing bargaining objectives amongst European unions. There is also a case for establishing 'independent comparability arrangements', providing an agreed database for negotiators, especially but not exclusively for public sector unions.

Quality in the public services

With new approaches to public sector management being introduced into public organisations in recent years (Farnham and Horton 1993; Storey 1992), and increasing emphasis being placed on 'service quality', the TUC is becoming increasingly conscious of the need for the unions to address quality as an issue. It distinguishes three approaches to service quality in the public services (TUC 1992a). These are:

- 'quality management', which requires all members of staff to clarify their products and services, so as to identify their customers, and to be given measurable goals to achieve that are monitored on a regular basis (see Chapter 10);
- 'customer care', which clarifies the provider–user relationship by setting out the quality of service to be provided and the rights of redress;
- 'quality assurance', which attempts to improve the quality of standards through the application of the British Standards Institution quality assurance standard BS 5750.

Each of these demands union responses to the search for quality in the public services.

Union participation

The unions argue that most quality programmes are management driven, consequently they are not designed to accommodate union involvement. The TUC proposes, therefore, that if service quality is to be significantly improved, it requires more direct involvement of employees in decision-making about the way services are provided and managed. According to the TUC, a key challenge for the unions 'is to confront the call for more open communications, devolved self-management and active employee participation.' The unions claim that quality agendas are set by management, with the strategy for enhancing employee involvement designed and executed with minimum consultation of staff. Similarly, employee empowerment is often more concerned with the obligations and duties of individual employees rather than with collective rights and representation. 'The main objective is usually to tie the employee's performance more closely to [the] overall goals of the organisation.' What public service unions are arguing for is the benefits of a 'partnership approach to improving quality service', especially at workplace level, with the key to responsive and effective public services being a well-trained workforce (TUC 1992a: pages 20–22).

A Quality Work Assured (QWA) servicemark

The public service unions want to raise the union profile and articulate more precisely the commitment of staff to quality and what improving service quality means from the workers' perspective. They believe that it is important to grasp the language of service quality and to stress their commitment to partnership, openness, accessibility, flexibility and choice. But the unions also want to formulate a mechanism for identifying the quality component in service provision in relation to the quality of working conditions and the quality of the workforce. The aims of the TUC's QWA servicemark are to (TUC 1992a: page 26):

- increase citizen and customer awareness and evaluation of the conditions and way in which a service is provided;
- expose the competence and commitment of the workforce and management;
- illustrate best practice in terms of employee participation and involvement;
- identify the employer's commitment to training and equal opportunities;
- facilitate a close relationship and understanding between staff and service users;
- ensure compliance with health and safety and other employment legislation;
- increase employee awareness of good management practice;
- inform users of an employer's industrial relations record;
- help develop quality standards at work;
- widen choice and preference;
- inform users of staff behaviour and attitudes;
- identify labour costs for a public service.

It is hoped, in short, that the QWA servicemark will provide a benchmark by which quality of public service inputs and outcomes might be measured, for the benefit of both users and providers.

The union response

The key 'quality' objective identified for public service unions in the 1990s is to exert a positive influence on the development of public services to the benefit of users and producers. It is suggested that unions will have to work much closer together and that further consideration needs to be given, in managing quality, to union relations with management and service users. The unions are stressing the importance of education and training programmes to equip staff, and union officials, to deal with demands for high-quality services and to ensure that programmes of performance measurement and appraisal are implemented in a fair and systematic way. In campaigning for quality, the unions are arguing that their 'vision is a high-quality workforce producing high-quality services' (TUC 1992b: page 3).

Inter-union disputes

In 1988, the TUC amended its rules on inter-union relations and a new code of practice was approved by Congress to mitigate inter-union rivalry, as a result of the recommendations by a Special Review Body appointed after the 1987 Congress.

The amendments to 'Principle 5' provide that no union is to organise where another union has the majority of workers employed and negotiates terms and conditions, unless by arrangement with that union. Where a union has members, but not a majority and does not negotiate terms and conditions, another union seeking to organise should consult with the existing union. If there is no agreement, the matter should be referred by either union to the TUC. Where a disputes committee adjudicates, it will take into account:

- the efforts which the union opposing entry of another union is making to retain membership and the degree of organisation over this period;
- any existing collective bargaining arrangements;
- the efforts that the union seeking entry is making to secure majority membership;
- the provisions of the code of practice.

The code of practice, which is annexed to the TUC's Disputes Principles and Procedures, is designed to set standards for affiliated unions organising and seeking recognition with an employer on new sites. It requires affiliated unions that are negotiating single-union agreements to give prior notification to the TUC of their intention to do so. The code goes on to say that (TUC 1988: page 19):

> Unions must not make any agreements which remove, or are designed to remove, the basic democratic lawful rights of a trade union to take industrial action in advance of the recruitment of members and without consulting them.

Unions are also expected to cooperate with any procedures operated by the TUC and related bodies concerning inward investing authorities. This is to avoid inter-union competition which could damage the attractiveness of the area. When negotiating recognition agreements, which have implications for substantive agreements, affiliated unions are expected to take into account the general level of terms and conditions that are already agreed with the company and to take all possible steps to avoid undermining them.

Unions and Europe

British unions, acting primarily through the TUC and the ETUC, recognise that the evolution of the EC poses immense challenges for trade unions and trade unionists. For the unions, the essential challenge of EC policy is to make a reality of Europe's social dimension, so that worker and citizen interests are taken into account within the EC, as well as those of business. The TUC is participating with the ETUC to develop economic and social policies aimed at maximising prosperity and economic security for working people in the Community's member states (TUC 1991b).

Economic and monetary union (EMU)

The TUC and ETUC believe that the basic objectives of EMU must be to promote sustainable growth, full employment and stable prices. They want economic policies leading to greater convergence amongst member states in terms of industrial performance, job creation and living standards. Policy on EMU is illustrated in Exhibit 25.

Exhibit 25: *ETUC policy on EMU*

> - to strength EC regional policy and transfer resources to regions in economic difficulty;
> - to ensure that a new European central bank is made democratically accountable and that the social partners are regularly consulted through an advisory committee;
> - to use European institutions to create a European industrial relations area as part of the social dimension;
> - to make member states not complying with agreed economic and employment objectives lose EC financial assistance.

Institutional reform

The ETUC seeks a number of measures to make EC institutions more democratic and accountable. These include:

- creating an enhanced law-making role for the EuP;
- giving the EuP authority to move towards political union, in association with national governments;
- giving the EuP power to elect the president of the CEuC.

The ETUC's proposals for amendments to the European treaties are illustrated in Exhibit 26.

The Law and Trade Union Membership

The law now provides a series of statutory rights for trade union members (see Chapters 3 and 4). The first set of rights, to join and organise trade unions (the right to associate), emerged slowly and took place in two phases. Phase one removed statutory criminal prohibitions, with the state allowing workers and unions to use 'self-help' measures to achieve 'voluntary' employer recognition for collective bargaining purposes. Phase two was the creation of positive legal rights for trade unionists against employers. Workers in Britain now have the right to join an independent trade union and not to be dismissed, or have action short of dismissal taken against them, because of their trade union membership. Such actions by employers are automatically unfair in law and where individuals think these rights have been infringed, they may make a complaint to an industrial tribunal.

Exhibit 26: *Proposed amendments to the Community treaties by the ETUC*

Amendments are proposed:

- ensuring that social and employment policies are a basic EC activity;
- giving ethnic minorities and third country nationals equal rights;
- defining the undercutting of some terms and conditions of employment as unfair competition;
- restricting the exclusion from qualified majority voting to fiscal provisions only;
- extending qualified majority voting to:

  – job creation and employment protection
  – employment law
  – working conditions
  – equality of treatment
  – initial and continuing training
  – social security and welfare
  – health and safety at work
  – trade union law and collective bargaining
  – information and consultation of workers
  – working environment
  – the environment;

- strengthening regional policy.

The law also provides protections for those who do not want to join a trade union or a particular union (the right of dissociation). This makes it automatically unfair for employers to dismiss individuals where they refuse to belong to a union. This is a relatively new right which, apart from the period of the IRA 1971, has been built into public policy since the early 1980s (see Chapter 7). The strategy pursued has been to remove the legal props to the closed shop, built into the unfair dismissals legislation under the TULRA 1974 and 1976, and to provide a right for employees not to be union members, even where there is no closed shop arrangement. These rights are also enforceable through ITs, with the right of appeal to the EAT. Obviously, strengthening the right not to join a union can only be done at the expense of weakening the right to become a union member and the ways these rights are reconciled vary from country to country (von Prondynski 1987).

The legal relationship of unions to their members

A third and extended group of statutory rights provided to trade union members is to take part in trade union activities and trade union decision-making and to restrain certain trade union actions which are unlawful (intra-union rights). Traditionally, the 'freedom' for members to participate in union activities, and for unions to operate within boundaries of the law, was provided in the union rule book. These common law rights still exist and can be enforced in the courts, under the common law, where individuals consider that the rule book is not being applied by the union or its officials. Indeed, the CRTUM has powers to grant assistance to trade union members who complain that their union has failed to observe the requirements of the union rule book (Commissioner for the Rights of Trade Union Members 1988–1992; see below). However, the statutory rights of trade unionists in relation to their unions have been extended in recent years and these are summarised below.

Industrial action ballots

Union members have the right to participate in industrial action ballots when a union is contemplating, authorising or endorsing industrial action and it would be lawful for the union to organise such action, if the statutory requirements of the ballot are satisfied. The law also gives union members the right to apply to the courts, with the assistance of the CRTUM, for an order restraining a union from inducing them to take any kind of industrial action in the absence of a properly conducted ballot. Where appropriate, the courts will make an order requiring the union to take steps to withdraw any authorisation or endorsement of the action, and to leave its members in no doubt that it has been withdrawn. If the court order is not obeyed, anyone who sought the order can return to the court, asking that the union be declared in contempt of court. Unions in contempt of court can be fined and refusal to pay fines can lead to the sequestration of union assets (Department of Employment 1990; see also Chapters 4 and 11).

Union elections

Union members have the right to elect by secret ballot all members of the principal executive committee of their union, at least once every five years. Unions must keep a register of their members' names and addresses and ensure that the entries on the register are accurate and reasonably up to date. Registers can be inspected by an independent scrutineer, where this is felt to be appropriate. The distribution, counting and storage of voting papers must be undertaken by someone independent of the process. All candidates seeking election must be given the opportunity to prepare an election address and have it distributed at no cost to themselves. Elections must be under independent scrutiny, with the scrutineer being responsible for supervising the election and producing a report. If a union fails to comply with these statutory requirements, members can make a complaint to the CO or to the courts. The CO's procedures are less formal than those of the courts but court proceedings may be assisted by the CRTUM (see below).

Union political funds and political fund review ballots

Members of unions have the right to vote, by secret ballot, if their union intends to set up a political fund – and then in political fund review ballots, at least onve every 10 years. If a union with a political fund fails to hold a review ballot after 10 years, its authority to spend money on political objects automatically lapses. The rules for conducting political fund ballots must be approved as rules of the union and be approved by the CO. The CO only gives approval where: every member is entitled to vote; there is a postal ballot; and the ballot is subject to independent scrutiny. Where unions fail to comply with the balloting rules approved by the CO, members may complain to the CO or the courts. Union members also have the right to complain, to the CO or to the courts, if a union unlawfully spends money from its general funds on 'political objects'.

Misuse of union funds

Union members have the right to prevent the unlawful use of their union's funds or property. These include the right to seek a court order against union trustees in order to prevent them applying, or permitting the application of, union funds to any unlawful purpose. They also have the right to inspect their union's accounting records, accompanied by an accountant. Further, there is the right to prevent a union's funds or property being used to indemnify anyone for fines or other penalties imposed on them for any criminal offence or for contempt of court. Unions must also take all reasonable steps to provide their members, within eight weeks of sending the annual return to the CO, with a statement covering: income and expenditure; income represented by membership fees; salary and benefits paid to senior officers and the executive committee; and the report of the auditor(s) on the return.

Union membership registers

Union members have the right to ensure that their union maintains a membership register. Unions must allow any members who have given reasonable notice to check, free of charge, at a reasonable time, whether they are included in the register. They must also supply members with a copy of their register entry on request. Any complaints on these matters are dealt with by either the CO or the courts.

Unjustifiable discipline

Union members have the right not to be disciplined, by being expelled, fined or deprived of membership benefits by their union, where that discipline is unjustifiable. Discipline is unjustifiable in law where the individual's conduct is concerned with any of the reasons illustrated in Exhibit 27. Individuals who believe that they have been unjustifiably disciplined by their union may make a complaint to an industrial tribunal. If, after conciliation with ACAS, the tribunal finds that the complaint of unjustifiable discipline is well founded, it makes a declaration to that effect. An application for compensation may also be made to the EAT if the union does not lift the penalty imposed, with the award being 'just and equitable in all the circumstances.'

Enforcing union membership rights

The bodies with the responsibility for enforcing the rights of trade members are the courts, CO, ITs and, most particularly, the CRTUM. The role of the CO, for example, is to deal with complaints by union members that trade unions have failed to comply with one or more of the provisions which impose the duty on trade unions to hold secret postal ballots for electing members of their principal executive committees and to maintain an accurate register of their members. In 1991, for example, a typical year, the CO

Exhibit 27: *Unjustifiable union discipline*

It is unjustifiable for a union to discipline its members where they:

- fail to take part in or support any strike or other industrial action;
- show opposition to or lack of support for the above;
- fail to break, for any purpose connected with the above, any obligation imposed by a contract of employment;
- encourage or assist other individuals honouring their contracts of employment;
- assert that the union or its officials has broken, or is proposing to break, any requirement imposed by the union rule book or the law;
- encourage or assist other individuals in making, defending or vindicating such assertions;
- fail to agree to or withdraw from an agreement with an employer for the deduction of union dues;
- resign from the union, refuse to join another union, belong to another union or propose to do so;
- work or propose to work with members of another union or non-union members;
- work or propose to work for an employer who employs non-union members or members of another union;
- consult or seek advice from the CRTUM or the CO;
- refuse to comply with any penalties imposed by the union following unjustifiable disciplinary action;
- propose to do any of the above.

Table 11: *Applications to the CRTUM for assistance in legal proceedings 1991–92*

Membership right	Number of applications	Outcome
Industrial action ballots	1	Assisted
Union elections	9	2 assisted
Political fund rules and ballots	1	Not assisted
Unlawful use of union property/funds	3	1 assisted
Inspection of accounting records	0	–
Union membership register	0	–

dealt with only two complaints of this sort and there were no out-standing complaints at the end of the year (Certification Office 1992).

The role of the CRTUM is much wider. The Commissioner pro-vides material assistance to union members who are contemplating taking legal proceedings against their union in any complaint coming within her statutory remit. She also has the authority to grant assis-tance to union members who claim that their union has breached its rule book in certain matters. Table 11 analyses the assistance pro-vided by the Commissioner in the first category of applications, in 1991–92, and shows that she received only 14 applications, with assistance being provided in four instances.

Table 12 shows the number of applications for assistance received by the CRTUM in which union members complained that their union had failed to observe the requirements of their rule book. Of the 31 applications received, 10 were assisted by the Commissioner. Although the total number of applications received by the Commissioner is not large, it appears to be growing. She believes this is the case because (CRTUM 1992: page 3):

> . . . all concerned have realised, or are coming to realise, that I am an unbiased source of help which can be utilised should the need arise and when other attempts to resolve problems between

Table 12: *Applications to the CRTUM for assistance in union rule book issues 1991–92*

Rule book issue	Number of applications	Outcome
Appointment, election or removal of persons from office	13	3 assisted
Disciplinary proceedings	2	Not assisted
Balloting of members	7	2 assisted
Applications of union funds/property	2	1 assisted
Collection of industrial action levies	0	–
Constitution of proceedings of committees/conferences	7	4 assisted

unions and their members have failed. I will continue to work to ensure that those who need my help are aware of the assistance I can provide.

Union recognition

Recognition of trade unions by employers, for the purposes of collective bargaining on terms and conditions of employment, is a critical stage in the development of employee relations within an organisation. The act of recognition demonstrates a decisive level of acceptance by management of the union role in employee relations and represents a fundamental change in the nature of the employment relationship between employers and employees. It shifts from one based on unilateral management prerogatives, individualist employment practices and unitary personnel management principles to one based on joint regulation, collectivism and pluralism, in those areas covered by procedural agreements between the employer and the union(s) (see Chapter 3).

Table 13 shows the extent of union recognition in Britain, as a proportion of all establishments, for 1980, 1984 and 1990. From these figures, it is clear that whilst union recognition generally declined in the decade 1980–90, it is still more likely amongst:

- manual rather than non-manual workers;
- manufacturing rather than service establishments;
- public sector rather than private sector workers.

There is also a correlation between union recognition and size of establishment, with larger establishments being more likely to recognise trade unions than smaller ones. In periods of high unemployment, however, obtaining recognition from employers is increasingly a problem for the unions. As the General Secretary of the TUC asserted at its annual congress in 1991: 'Recognition and getting it is probably the single most urgent issue for us all' (TUC 1991c: page 294). Congress therefore reaffirmed its commitment 'to reaching new laws to help unions and members attain recognition from reluctant and hostile employers' (page 282). Discussion in this section focuses largely on union recognition in medium to large private sector establishments. It does, however, have implications for parts of the public sector, where, with the decentralising of management decisions and responsibilities – in hospital trusts, civil service agencies and the educational sector – new recognition issues are arising between the employers and unions.

Employee Relations

Table 13: *Union recognition in Britain 1980, 1984 and 1990*

	Manufacturing			Services			Percentage of all establishments		
							Public sector		
	1980	1984	1990	1980	1984	1990	1980	1984	1990
Manual workers	65	55	44	33	38	31	76	91	78
Non-manual workers	27	26	23	28	30	26	91	98	84
All workers	65	56	44	41	44	36	94	99	87

Source: WIRS 1992

Multi-union recognition

Multi-union recognition is the norm in British employee relations. This is because of the large number of trade unions in Britain, its trade union structure and its history of employee relations. These factors result in distinctive patterns of employee representation and bargaining structures in establishments where trade unions are recognised. Besides multi-union recognition, other features of employee relations where unions are recognised include multiple bargaining units and separate unions for manual and non-manual workers. In 1990, the WIRS estimates that:

- 2.5 unions, on average, were recognised in all establishments with recognised unions;
- about a third of establishments with recognised manual unions had two or more unions;
- over 50 per cent of establishments with recognised non-manual unions had two or more unions.

It also estimates that almost 60 per cent of establishments in the private sector had two or more bargaining units in 1990, with about a half of all unionised workplaces having 'manual-only' unions and some two-thirds 'non-manual-only' unions (Millward *et al.* 1992).

Union recognition in Britain is entirely a voluntary process. There is no statutory obligation on employers to recognise trade unions, even where there are high levels of union membership within an establishment or part of it. In the USA, in contrast, the National Labor Relations Act 1935 – as amended by the Taft-Hartley Act 1947 – provides a series of rights for American workers. These include the rights: to join unions and organise for collective bargaining purposes; to vote whether or not to be represented by a union by means of a secret ballot, enforced by the National Labor Relations Board; and to be protected from 'unfair labor practices', on the part of employers, which might interfere with their rights regarding trade union organisation (Kochan 1980). This results in more proactive employee relations policies by American employers than in Britain, leading to either union avoidance strategies or pre-emptive union recognition strategies, even though union recognition in the USA is the lowest in OECD countries. (Kochan *et al.* 1984).

The demand for recognition in Britain is usually a union-driven process. Recognition claims are made where a union, or a group of unions, with members within an establishment, approaches an employer to negotiate what is called a 'recognition and negotiating procedure' or, more simply, a 'recognition agreement'. In essence, a recognition agreement is one between an employer and the signatory union(s) which provides representational rights for a specified group of employees, through the agency of the union(s), in a defined bargaining unit, on agreed matters. This suggests, in all but a minority of cases, that British employers deal reactively with recognition claims made by trade unions, rather than initiating recognition agreements themselves. The employer then has to decide whether to reject, consider or accept a recognition claim on its merits. This is done on the basis of what management perceives to be in the best interests of the company and its employees.

In deciding whether to move towards a recognition agreement with the union(s), employers take a number of factors into account. These include: union strength and effectiveness, including their labour market position; employee attitudes and preferences; and employer policies and objectives. The risks of recognition and non-recognition are normally evaluated by management too, including the need to avoid industrial action, inter-union conflict, fragmented bargaining units and the loss of employer initiative in employee relations decision-making (Institute of Personnel Management 1977). Where, on balance, an employer decides to concede a union claim for recognition – and to negotiate an agreement – a number of decisions need to be taken between the parties in the interests of stable employee relations.

Determining the bargaining level

A crucial issue to be decided is the level at which collective bargaining is to take place. This is normally at employer level in single-site companies or, in multi-plant companies, at either central or site level. The factors influencing this decision include: what, if any, other bargaining arrangements already exist within the company; what comparative advantage management and unions see in bargaining at a particular level; the size and distribution of the potential bargaining group; the extent of union membership and potential membership; the organisational structure; the company's financial control system; and corporate personnel policies (see Chapter 9).

Determining the bargaining unit

Bargaining units are fundamental to collective bargaining and precise definition of a bargaining unit is important for a number of reasons. The bargaining unit:

- establishes rights of collective representation for individual employees in the unit;
- defines the area in which procedural and substantive agreements negotiated between the employer and the union(s) apply;
- enables employees to know with whom they are grouped for negotiating purposes.

In general, employers want bargaining units appropriate to their organisational structures and employment policies, whilst avoiding workforce fragmentation, and unions want bargaining units based on their recruitment policies and patterns of membership.

A number of factors affect the determination of bargaining units. These are typically grouped into three categories (Commission on Industrial Relations 1974: page 22):

> *(a) Factors relating to the characteristics of the work group*
> job skills and content; payment systems; other common conditions
> of employment; the training and experience of employees; qualifications and professionalism; and physical working conditions.

(b) Factors introduced by the presence of trade union member-
ship and collective bargaining arrangements

employee preferences of association; general employee wishes
towards collective bargaining; the maintenance of existing collective bargaining arrangements which are working well; and
membership of unions or staff associations.

(c) Factors based on management organisation and areas of
decision-making

the presence of procedures unilaterally operated by management;
management structure; promotion patterns; geographical location; and recruitment source.

Bargaining units, in short, have to be appropriate to the situation in
each case. This includes the circumstances of the workgroups concerned, existing collective bargaining arrangements and the needs of
efficient management.

The key issue to be resolved in determining recognition claims is
that of identifying the 'core group' of employees for recognition purposes, with the above factors being taken into account in doing this.
The core group of employees is the one with strong common interests,
around which a possible bargaining unit can be formed. For bargaining
units to be stable and viable in the long term, it is essential that they
are based on the common interests of the employees covered by the
collective bargaining arrangement. The core group is central in determining bargaining unit issues, since each unit needs to be based on at
least one core group with sufficiently strong common interests to support effective collective bargaining procedures.

Four questions have to be addressed when a core group, or groups,
is being considered for inclusion in a bargaining unit. These are its
potential in terms of:

• organisational coverage;
• geographical coverage;
• vertical coverage;
• horizontal coverage.

The first two questions are commonly linked together, as are the second two. This means that once a core group is identified, it can be
extended by including additional groups of employees within it, in one
or more of the four directions listed above. In this way, bargaining
units can be designated that cover as wide a common interest group as
possible. This avoids creating too many small bargaining groups,

which can result in fragmented negotiations and treating related groups of employees inconsistently.

Determining union bargaining agents

Employers normally prefer negotiating with a single union, rather than with several. Apart from the special case of 'single-union' recognition, however, which is discussed below, the majority of bargaining units contain more than one union within them. Two main factors influence the efficacy of the bargaining agents in union recognition claims: employee support for the unions, and the unions' effectiveness as negotiating bodies. Potential employee support can be assessed in terms of: actual union membership within the proposed unit; the number of employees supporting the union(s) claiming recognition; and the number who would be prepared to join the union(s) if recognition is agreed. Union effectiveness is the ability of the unions to organise members, maintain membership and represent members in dealings with the employer. Whilst some employers deal with staff associations, especially for some groups of non-manual workers, most, with few exceptions, prefer negotiating with *bona fide* unions. Union effectiveness can be assessed in terms of their: financial viability; experienced officials; research and legal expertise; and negotiating record.

Drafting the agreement

The types of clauses contained in a recognition agreement, negotiated with trade unions, are illustrated in Exhibit 28.

Exhibit 28: *Clauses in recognition agreements*

These include:

- names of the employer and the bargaining agent(s);
- a description of the bargaining unit and any sub-units;
- the terms and conditions that are negotiable;
- union membership and non-membership;
- the numbers of, constituencies of and facilities for union representatives;
- the negotiating procedures and procedures for handling grievances and avoiding disputes;
- other provisions;
- provisions for varying and terminating the agreement.

Single-union recognition

Single-union recognition is where a company recognises only one union for collective bargaining and related purposes. In some traditional collective bargaining arrangements, companies may recognise only one union per bargaining unit. But single-union recognition, in the sense that it is used here, provides for only one union bargaining agent, covering all employees with representational rights in the company. This practice is associated with what are called 'new-style' collective agreements or 'new-style' bargaining (see Chapters 3 and 9), although the newness of such activities is, in reality, questionable.

Management and single-unionism

The major difference between the process of single-union recognition and that of multi-union recognition is that it is management and commercially driven, not union driven, although the unions involved in single-union deals would dispute this. One of the first recorded single-union recognition agreements was between Toshiba Consumer Products (UK) and the EEPTU, at Plymouth in April 1981 (Bassett 1986). This agreement arose out of the closure of Rank Toshiba Ltd in 1980 and was negotiated when the new company was established as a single-site operation assembling colour television sets (Rico 1987). Since then, the numbers of such agreements have increased, but the number of firms and employees covered by them is still relatively small compared with those covered by traditional collective bargaining practices.

It is generally recognised that where managements negotiate and consult with trade unions, they often prefer to deal with one union rather than with many. The advantages of this include: having one representational channel for all employees through which all discussions are focused; avoiding inter-union competition and inter-union disputes within the workplace; and simplifying the bargaining structure within which the parties operate. Over and above this, some managements claim that single-union recognition is beneficial where a company is aiming at teamwork, quality and flexibility amongst its workforce – as in 'hi-tech', 'greenfield' site companies. In these circumstances, single-union recognition, with its emphases on harmonised terms and conditions of employment and a committed workforce, is seen as facilitating a common purpose within the company and good working relations between the company and its workers.

In the case of a greenfield site, the process of selecting an appropriate union by the employer is rooted in the management dictum: 'Talk to every union that could conceivably have an interest in representing your employees and then make a decision as to which union best fits . . . Those not selected will respect that decision' (Wickens 1987: page 133). Management's recognition objective is a clear one: to negotiate with one union, on terms, conditions and procedural issues, for all workers in the bargaining unit. This necessitates early discussions with the various unions wishing to represent the bargaining group, whether or not they already have members within the bargaining unit, with management emphasising that it alone will take the final decision as to which union will be invited to sign the draft recognition agreement.

That decision takes account of a number of factors. One is the attitudes and experience of the local union officials, who are normally invited to present their union's case for recognition, each arguing why their union is likely to give the 'best deal' to the company – the so-called 'beauty contest'. Even before this, it is customary for the company to investigate the backgrounds and policies of the unions, both locally and nationally, to 'make an assessment of the "comfort" factor which ranks very highly in the decision-making process' (Wickens 1987: page 134). These factors are likely to include the national and local politics of each union, the reputations of the local union officers and the unions' employee relations records. Information for this is gathered from local companies, employers' associations and media sources. In this respect, the experiences of employers with single-union recognition arrangements is particularly useful, as are those of companies that have not gone down this path – and the reasons why.

Another factor to consider is which union is likely to be the most acceptable to the employees within the bargaining group. Some judgement has to be made by the company about the potential willingness of employees to join the selected union. There are a number of indicators here: existing levels of membership; the respective membership bases of the competing unions; how these relate to the bargaining group; and the degree of occupational homogeneity within the bargaining unit. In some cases, the company surveys its employees, using a secret ballot to assess their preferred union and choice of bargaining agent.

Unions and single-unionism

Union attitudes to single-union recognition are ambivalent. In some sectors, single-union recognition has always been the norm; for example, in retailing and in parts of the white-collar Civil Service. In other cases – union recognition on greenfield sites – it is generally accepted that there are advantages in recognising the sense of having the entire workforce, in one establishment, in a single union in a single bargaining unit. On the other hand, there is hostility amongst some unions to the practice, incorporated in most single-union, new-style agreements, of including so called 'no-strike' or 'final offer' arbitration arrangements (Burrows 1986). These, it is claimed, remove the basic democratic rights of trade unions and their members to take legitimate industrial action against employers, when they deem this to be necessary, and they should be resisted.

The other concern that unions have with single-union agreements is to do with infringing the recruiting and negotiating freedoms of other unions with membership interests in the bargaining unit. According to the TUC (1988a: page 9), single-union agreements cause particular differences amongst unions where they:

(a) exclude other unions who may have some membership in the unit covered by the agreement; or exclude unions which previously held recognition or bargaining rights;

(b) exclude other unions who, while having no members in the unit concerned, have recognition agreements in other UK units operated by the same employer;

(c) represent an intrusion by one union into areas considered to be the province of an industrial union(s), or the exclusion by an industrial union of unions representing particular occupations;

(d) are agreed by one union, where another has been previously campaigning for membership perhaps over a long period;

(e) lead unions to compete with each other for employers' approval which encourages dilution of trade union standards and procedures.

It is these factors which led the TUC to amend its rules on inter-union regulations in 1988 (see above).

Derecognition

Though it is still a relatively rare employee relations occurrence, derecognition is nevertheless practised by some employers. It takes place where an employer partially or fully withdraws union negotiating rights from the union(s) in a particular bargaining unit, by giving notice of the intention to terminate an existing recognition agreement.

Full derecognition is where negotiating rights for a whole bargaining group are withdrawn – as was the case for school teachers in 1987, when the Burnham Committee was abolished by the government who replaced it with an interim pay advisory committee (Farnham 1993). In other cases, full derecognition takes place, as amongst white-collar staff in some insurance companies, where there is lack of support for the union or staff association amongst the staff concerned. Partial derecognition takes place where the employer unilaterally withdraws the number or coverage of the negotiating groups, and/or union negotiating rights, but at least one recognised union, and one bargaining unit, remains in the establishment or enterprise.

Claydon's analysis (1989) of derecognition is more sophisticated. He analyses derecognition in terms of a matrix and distinguishes between *breadth* and *depth* of derecognition. Breadth of derecognition can be 'general', 'grade-specific' or 'plant-specific'. There are five types of depth of derecognition:

- 'partial', where the union retains some bargaining rights;
- as 'a bargaining agent', where the union only retains rights to consultation and representation;
- 'collective', where the union can only represent members in individual grievances;
- 'complete';
- 'deunionisation', where union membership is discouraged.

The most common forms of derecognition appear to be collective 'grade-specific' and complete 'grade-specific'.

The reasons given by Claydon for derecognition include: external pressures; ownership, management and reorganisation; company objectives; and union organisation and industrial relations history – with corporate objectives probably lying at the heart of union derecognition. According to Claydon (page 219) it is 'greater pay flexibility, more flexible working practices, and heightened commitment', especially amongst managerial and staff grades, that are the main employer goals associated with union derecognition.

Assignments

(a) Read Millward *et al.* (1992: pages 57–77). (i) Identify union membership trends in Britain 1984–90 and (ii) examine the factors explaining these trends. How do these trends relate to your own organisation?

(b) Examine the latest *Annual Report* of the CO and explain the legal rules relating to union mergers and amalgamations. Report and comment on recent amalgamations and mergers in Britain and their implications for employee relations.

(c) From the TUC's last *Annual Report*, identify three key issues of concern to the TUC during this period and indicate how the TUC is attempting to address these issues.

(d) What are the main features of multi-unionism in Britain identified by the Workplace Industrial Relations Survey in 1990 (Millward *et al.* 1992: pages 77–85)? What sort of problems associated with multi-unionism occur in your organisation?

(e) Read the Webbs (1913: Part II – Chapter V). Analyse and comment on the role of 'the Standard Rate' as a trade union rule. How significant is the concept of the 'standard rate' for trade union negotiators today?

(f) Read the TUC (1991a: pages 21–28) and analyse the new bargaining agenda developments which it highlights. What are the conditions which are necessary for this agenda to be effective at employer level? How relevant are they within your organisation?

(g) Read the TUC (1992a: pages 30–47). What are the employee relations implications of the case studies outlined in the report? Comment on the survey of quality initiatives provided in Chapter 8.

(h) Examine the view put forward by Anderman (1992: page 248) that:

'The right to dissociate currently embodied in UK legislation has been introduced in recent years as part of a wider legislative programme designed to promote individualism at the expense of established collective structures . . . it calls into question the legitimacy of trade unions as collectivities enhancing the freedom of their members as individuals by the use of collective institutions.'

(i) An employer is in dispute with the union representing the technical staff who are taking strike action over a pay claim. One of the strike leaders, who has both a full-time and part-time contract, has been informed by her departmental manager – on the instruction of the chief executive – that he is not to renew her part-time contract. This is due for renewal at the beginning of next month for a further one year period. What do you do? And why?

(j) Provide some examples of individual conduct that the law would regard as reasons for unjustifiable union discipline, in the case of a lawful trade dispute. What would be some of the employee relations implications of such conduct for (1) management and (2) the union(s) in such cases?

(k) Read the latest *Annual Report* of the CRTUM. What sorts of applications did she receive during the past year and what were the outcomes?

(l) Read Kochan (1980) and outline the main provisions for union recognition in the USA under the Wagner Act 1935, as amended. How might such a set of legal arrangements be applied to Britain?

(m) Outline the steps to be taken by the employer in responding to a union recognition claim by factory workers in a non-union company, operating on a single site, with 250 employees in the factory, 150 administrative and supervisory staff and 50 technical staff. The union claims 'over 40 per cent membership' amongst the factory workers, '25 per cent' of administrative and clerical staff and 'substantial support' amongst the technicians.

(n) Read Wickens (1987: pages 127–61). Examine how the companies discussed in this chapter went about getting single-union agreements and why. What distinguishes the approach to management–union relations outlined in this chapter from (1) non-union companies and (2) companies with multi-union representation?

(o) Read Burrows (1986: pages 52–62) and examine and evaluate trade union attitudes to single-union deals.

(p) Read Clayton (1989: pages 214–22) and examine the reasons why employers use union derecognition strategies.

(q) An employer recognises a single trade union in a negotiating unit comprising its supervisory and shop floor staff. Management wishes to withdraw recognition arrangements for the supervisors and to put them on personal contracts and performance related pay. Outline a strategy how this might be done and examine some of its implications for employee relations in the company.

References

ANDERMAN, S. 1992. *Labour Law*. London: Butterworth.
BAIN, G. 1970. *The Growth of White Collar Unionism*. London: Oxford University Press.

BASSETT, P. 1986. *Strike Free: New Industrial Relations in Britain.* Basingstoke: Macmillan.

BURROWS, G. 1986. *No-strike Agreements and Pendulum Arbitration.* London: Institute of Personnel Management.

CERTIFICATION OFFICE 1992. *Annual Report of the Certification Officer 1991.* London: HMSO.

CLAYDON, T. 1989. 'Union derecognition in Britain in the 1980s'. *British Journal of Industrial Relations.* 27(2).

COMMISSION ON INDUSTRIAL RELATIONS 1974. *Trade Union Recognition: CIR Experience.* London: HMSO.

COMMISSIONER FOR THE RIGHTS OF TRADE UNION MEMBERS 1988–92. *Annual Reports.* London: Central Office of Information.

DANIEL, W. 1987. *Workplace Industrial Relations and Technical Change.* London: Policy Studies Institute.

DEPARTMENT OF EMPLOYMENT 1990. *Code of Practice on Trade Union Ballots on Industrial Action.* London: Central Office of Information.

FARNHAM, D. 1993. 'Human resources management and employee relations'. In FARNHAM, D. and HORTON, S. (eds) 1993. *Managing the New Public Services.* Basingstoke: Macmillan.

FARNHAM, D. and HORTON, S. (eds) 1993. *Managing the New Public Services.* Basingstoke: Macmillan.

FLANDERS, A. 1961. 'Trade unions in the sixties'. In FLANDERS, A. 1970. *Management and Unions.* London: Faber and Faber.

FLANDERS, A. 1968a. 'Collective bargaining: a theoretical analysis'. In FLANDERS, A. 1970. *Management and Unions.* London: Faber and Faber.

FLANDERS, A. 1968b. 'What are trade unions for?' In FLANDERS, A. 1970. *Management and Unions.* Faber and Faber.

GENNARD, J. 1990. *The History of the National Graphical Association.* London: Unwin Hyman.

GMB and UCW 1991. *A New Agenda: Bargaining for Prosperity in the 1990s.* London: GMB/UCW.

HYMAN, R. 1975. *Industrial Relations.* Basingstoke: Macmillan.

INSTITUTE OF PERSONNEL MANAGEMENT 1977. *Trade Union Recognition.* London: IPM.

JACOBI, O., KELLER, B. and MUELLER-JENTSCH, W. 1992. 'Germany: codetermining the future'. In FERNER, A. and HYMAN, R. (eds) 1992. *Industrial Relations in the New Europe.* Oxford: Blackwell.

KOCHAN, T. 1980. *Collective Bargaining and Industrial Relations.* Illinois: Irwin.

KOCHAN, T., MCKERSIE, R. and CAPELLI, P. 1984. 'Strategic choice and industrial relations theory'. *Industrial Relations.* 23(1).

MILLWARD, N., STEVENS, M., SMART, D. and HAWES, W. 1992. *Workplace Industrial Relations in Transition.* Aldershot: Dartmouth.

RICO, L. 1987. 'The new industrial relations: British electricians' new-style agreements'. *Industrial and Labor Relations Review.* 41(1), October.

STOREY, J. 1992. *Developments in the Management of Human Resources.* Oxford: Blackwell.

TRADES UNION CONGRESS 1966. *Trade Unionism*. London: TUC.

TRADES UNION CONGRESS 1974. *Trade Union Strategy*. London: TUC.

TRADES UNION CONGRESS. 1981–90. *Annual Reports*. London: TUC.

TRADES UNION CONGRESS 1988. *Meeting the Challenge*. London: TUC.

TRADES UNION CONGRESS 1991a. *Collective Bargaining Strategy for the 1990s*. London: TUC.

TRADES UNION CONGRESS 1991b. *Unions and Europe in the 1990s*. London: TUC.

TRADES UNION CONGRESS 1991c. *Annual Report*. London: TUC.

TRADES UNION CONGRESS 1992a. *The Quality Challenge*. London: TUC.

TRADES UNION CONGRESS 1992b. *Quality Work Assured*. London: TUC.

VON PRONDYNSKI, F. 1987. *Freedom of Association and Industrial Relations*. Dublin: Mansell.

WEBB, S. and B. 1913. *Industrial Democracy*. NY: Longmans.

WICKENS, P. 1987. *The Road to Nissan*. Basingstoke: Macmillan.

Chapter 9

Collective Bargaining

Voluntary collective bargaining is a major employee relations process in Britain (see Chapters 1, 3 and 7). As an employee relations strategy it was adopted by 51 per cent of the private manufacturing employers and 78 per cent of the public sector employers covered by the WIRS 1990. It is only in the private sector services that collective bargaining is underrepresented – according to the WIRS, 33 per cent of the establishments were covered by it. The coverage of collective bargaining reflects the patterns of union membership and union recognition within establishments. In the private sector, for example, the characteristics of workplaces particularly associated with collective bargaining include:

- high union density;
- larger enterprises;
- predominantly manual or predominantly non-manual workforces.

Conversely, the WIRS concludes, 'part-time workers are less likely to be covered by collective bargaining because they are more difficult for trade unions to organise' (Millward *et al.* 1992: page 93).

As an employee relations process, collective bargaining settles, by voluntary negotiations between representatives of employers and trade unions, the market and managerial relations between employers and employees. In other countries, however, such as in Europe and the USA, it is legally regulated, and collective agreements are legally enforceable between the parties. Collective bargaining is the major method used by trade unions in pursuing the employment goals of their members (see Chapter 8). In 1981, the International Labour Office (ILO 1986: pages 1–2) adopted Convention 154 which provides an operational definition of collective bargaining. This defines it as all negotiations between employers (or employers' organisations) and workers' organisations for the purposes of determining terms and conditions of employment and/or regulating relations between them. The ILO adds that 'not the least important objective of collective bargaining is that of avoiding violence as a means of resolving problems [between employers and employees].'

The basic economics of collective bargaining

In free labour markets, the price or wage of labour is established, in the short term, where the market between buyers and sellers is in equilibrium (Chapter 1). This is the market wage where the amount of labour demanded by the employers is equal to the amount supplied by workers. In practice, real life labour market characteristics are inconsistent with the perfectly competitive, free market model. This is because of (Adnett 1989):

- the heterogeneity of workers and jobs, resulting in persistent wage differentials amongst the workforce;
- imperfect and costly information, making it difficult for firms and workers to be fully aware of labour market conditions;
- the high costs involved in labour turnover for firms and job changing for workers;
- the existence of imperfectly competitive product markets;
- the behaviour of trade unions as wage bargainers with employers.

There is also the debate about 'segmented' labour markets. Those using this analysis argue that open labour markets are only found in the secondary labour market, characterised by labour-intensive, low-technology, low-paid industries. In the primary labour market, which is characterised by well-paid, high-status, secure jobs, firms operate structured internal labour markets (ILMs) which are often non-unionised. These structured ILMs are largely independent of competitive forces in the wider labour market. This requires firms to finance their own internal training programmes, partly because of the technological demands of jobs, thus encouraging them to reduce their labour turnover (Doeringer and Piore 1971). Because of these factors, the wages structure reflects custom and practice, rather than worker productivity or external market forces. It is social cohesion, rather than efficiency, which underlies the relative wage rigidity and seniority determined pay scales of ILMs (Doeringer 1986).

What, then, is the function of trade unions in the labour market? Basically, it is to offset the relative disadvantage in market bargaining power that workers have as individuals when negotiating wages and conditions of employment with employers. The employer is in a strong labour market position, if it negotiates separate wages deals with each of its workers individually, because it can undercut wages, especially in conditions of unemployment. The employer does this by only recruiting those workers willing to take the lowest wage offered. By joining the union, employees try to even up the wage bargaining disparity between themselves and the employer, thus remedying their labour market disadvantage.

Once it is recognised as a wage bargaining agent by the employer, the union aims to gain improvements in its members' terms and conditions of employment. It does this through its wages claims. Union wage claims are based on one or more of the following grounds:

- the rate of inflation;
- the profitability of the enterprise;
- increases in the labour productivity of its members;
- inter-occupational wage comparabilities;
- labour market shortages.

One way in which the union can achieve its wages objectives is by restricting the supply of labour to those who either are union members or who join the union once they are employed. If the employer can hire cheaper non-union labour, then the union will find it very difficult to protect the existing wage levels and conditions of work of its members. The classical method used by unions was to restrict labour supply through 'the device of the restriction of numbers' (the apprenticeship system) and the closed shop (Dunn and Gennard 1984). Current legislation, however, makes it very difficult for employers and unions to negotiate closed shop agreements – whether of the pre-entry or post-entry type.

The union effect on wage rates and employment, through collective bargaining, is outlined in Figure 12. In the absence of a union, the firm, operating in a free labour market, faces a downward sloping labour demand curve DD and a horizontal labour supply curve SS, since labour supply is fixed in the short term. This results in a market wage of W and an employment level of E. By restricting labour supply to the firm to amount R, the union can increase the market wage to U, thus trading off lower employment for higher wages for its members. How far the union goes in this direction depends on the

Figure 12: *The union effect on wage rates and employment*

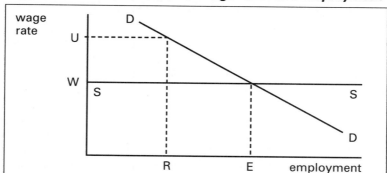

preferences and tastes of the union leadership and its members. It can try to maximise either the per capita income of those in employment or the total income of its members. What its wages policy is depends on the distribution of power and the structure of decision-making within the union.

Union wage bargaining power varies across firms and industries. In addition, the more inelastic labour demand is, in a firm or an industry, the larger is the wage differential for the workers. Since the demand for labour is a derived demand, which depends on the demand for a firm's output, there are differences in the wage rewards between firms and industries operating in different product markets. In industries in 'soft' markets, with little domestic or foreign competition, firms are likely to make substantial profits in buoyant market conditions, with the unions and their members benefiting from this.

In highly competitive industries with 'hard' markets, by contrast, if the union raises wages above the market level, firms will be driven out of business. It is only possible to raise wages above the market level where the union organises the whole industry. The result of this will be that firms will pass on wage increases, negotiated by the union for its members, to consumers in the form of higher product prices.

Union wage differentials can also arise from unpleasant conditions of work. Where unions operate in firms and industries with rising productivity, due to management-led changes in working practices, and this results in unpleasant working conditions, they try to negotiate compensating wage increases for their members. As a result, the employer obtains higher productivity, shareholders gain higher profits and union members are compensated for worsened conditions of employment. This practice is called productivity bargaining.

The nature of collective bargaining

It was the Webbs (1913) who provided the first detailed analysis of collective bargaining. They identify collective bargaining as one method by which unions enforce the common rules of the trade (see Chapter 8). They put forward the classical view of trade unions as primarily wage bargaining agents, whose role is to offset the inequalities of individual bargaining between employers and workers in the labour market. For Flanders (1968), collective bargaining is a power-centred rather than an economic process, with unions using their power to penetrate the management function by acting as institutions of 'job regulation' on any matter affecting the employment interests of their members (see Chapter 8). Dubin (1954), a sociologist, sees collective bargaining primarily as the industrial counterpart to political democracy, which provides a source of social stability, social order and social change in industry and society.

Kahn-Freund's (1954) penetrating analysis of collective bargaining, from a socio-legal perspective, argues that it is associated with the evolution of social norms to regulate social conflict in industry. The emergence of collective bargaining depends on the extent and forms of legal intervention by the state. For Marxists, collective bargaining is the process by which the working class, through experiencing industrial action, trade union militancy and employer exploitation, becomes politicised. Unions are the means of not only protecting the employment interests of their members but also furthering the class struggle between the wage earning 'proletariat' and profit seeking capitalists (Hyman 1975).

Bargaining: contract, law and governance

Chamberlain and Kuhn (1965) provide one of the most comprehensive and persuasive analyses of collective bargaining, by identifying three views of the process. These are 'the marketing concept', 'the governmental concept' and the 'industrial relations concept'. In outline, in the marketing concept, collective agreements act as a 'contract' between the parties to employee relations. In the governmental concept, they are a system of 'law-making', applied and adjudicated through collective bargaining. And in the industrial relations concept, collective agreements provide a method of 'industrial governance', whereby corporate decision-making focuses on 'jointly decided directives'.

The wage–work bargain

The marketing concept views collective bargaining as an exchange relationship. It is a means of contracting for the sale of labour, between employer and employee, through the agency of the union. The collective agreement acts as a contract for the buying and selling process which is strictly and definably limited, for a specified period. This view of collective bargaining is equivalent to that of the Webbs and is based on the assumption that the bargaining inequality in the labour market, between employer and employee, oppresses individual workers and needs to be remedied. Whether or not the substantive agreements arrived at establish an equality of bargaining power is irrelevant. What is important is the strict interpretation and application of the collective agreement. Its terms represent the bargain struck and its clauses are to be honoured for the period that it runs. In disputes over the contractual obligations of the parties, recourse may be made to the relevant procedural arrangements between the parties.

Industrial jurisprudence

The governmental concept of collective bargaining views it as a constitutional system in industry. It is a political relationship, in which the union shares industrial sovereignty with management over the workers and, as their representative, uses that power in their interests. The industrial constitution, written by management and union representatives, has legislative, executive and judicial elements. The legislative branch consists of the joint management–union committees which make and interpret agreements. Executive authority and the right to initiate decisions are vested in management, but within the framework of the industrial 'legislation' determined by the parties. Management has the right to manage, plan product development, change working methods and create personnel policy but it must act within the established 'rules'. Where differences between the parties cannot be resolved by negotiation, the judicial element of the industrial constitution is used. This involves the use of procedures to settle differences between the parties and, ultimately, the intervention of third parties to determine the issue, if necessary.

According to Chamberlain and Kuhn, the ethical principle underlying the governmental approach to collective bargaining is 'the sharing of industrial sovereignty'. It has two facets (page 124):

> In the first place, it involves a sharing by management with the union of *power* over those who are governed, the employees. In the second place, it involves a joint defense of the *autonomy* of the government established to exercise such power, a defense primarily against interference by the state. Both stem from a desire to control one's own affairs.

The sharing of power between management and union means that only employment rules which are mutually acceptable, and have the consent of employees, can be legitimised and enforced. Sovereignty is held jointly by management and unions in the collective bargaining process, resulting in participation by the union in job control. On the other side, sovereignty is also concerned with limiting the control of those, outside the employee relations constitution, who might wish to interfere in the autonomous collective bargaining process.

Chamberlain and Kuhn go on to distinguish between the 'constitutional law of industry' and its 'common law'. In the former, the collective agreement establishes the terms of the employer–employee relationship and individual cases are governed by these terms. In the firm's common law, developed through joint procedures for settling grievances and differences of interpretation of agreements, there are no written standards of control. 'It is the mutual recognition of the requirements of morality and the needs of operation which provides the basis of decision and ultimately the norms of action' (page 128). And these are often rooted in the social customs and unwritten conventions of the enterprise.

Industrial governance

The third concept of collective bargaining, the industrial relations concept, is a functional relationship. It is where the union joins with company officials in reaching decisions on matters in which both have vital interests. A system of industrial governance follows out of a system of industrial jurisprudence. The presence of the union allows the workers, through their representatives, to participate in the determination of policies guiding and ruling their working lives. Indeed, 'collective bargaining *by its very nature* involves union representatives in decision-making roles' (page 130). Since the nature of the bargaining process is appropriate to its own industrial setting, collective bargaining is a method of conducting industrial relations, using procedures for making joint decisions on all matters affecting labour.

The ethical principle underlying the concept of collective bargaining as a process of industrial governance is that those who are integral to the conduct of an enterprise should have a voice in making those decisions which are of most concern to them. This is the 'principle of mutuality' and is a correlate of political democracy. According to Brandeis (1934):

> collective bargaining is today the means of establishing industrial democracy – the means of providing for workers in industry the sense of work, of freedom, and of participation that democratic government promises them as citizens.

This view of collective bargaining implies that authority over workers requires their consent. And defining authority within the enterprise involves areas of joint decision-making through collective agreement. As conceptions of the corporate decisions affecting worker interests expand, so does the area of joint agreement. 'And as the area of joint concern expands, so too does the participation of the union in the management of the enterprise' (page 135). Ultimately, collective bargaining becomes a system of management.

Bargaining as a developmental process

These three views of collective bargaining are not mutually exclusive. They can be seen as stages in the development of the collective bargaining process and of the bargaining relationship between an employer and a union. As the scope of collective bargaining extends, there is a shift along the spectrum from the marketing, to the jurisprudential, to the industrial governance concepts. Similarly, as the scope of collective bargaining shrinks, there is a shift back towards the marketing concept.

These three approaches to collective bargaining represent different conceptions of what the bargaining process is about and they express normative judgements about it. Each stresses a different guiding principle and each influences the actions taken by the parties. For example, under the marketing concept, withholding data or distorting facts may be a legitimate negotiating tactic by the parties. Under the governmental concept, it may be difficult to determine whether specific data should be accessible to both parties, or confidential to one. Under the industrial relations concept, all relevant data becomes necessary to make informed, joint decisions.

The distinctions amongst these three approaches are not just academic ones but practical. The marketing approach emphasises the existence of alternative choices in any employer–union relationship, however limited these are. The governmental and industrial relations approaches emphasise the continuity of a given relationship and regard collective bargaining as a continuous process. Which approach is stressed is determined by the views adopted by the parties as to the nature of the bargaining process, the importance they place on particular bargaining outcomes and the balance of bargaining power between them.

Negotiating behaviour

A seminal but complex analysis of negotiating behaviour in the collective bargaining process is provided by Walton and McKersie (1965). They distinguish four sub-processes of negotiating activity, each with its own function for the parties to negotiation, its own patterns of behaviour and its own instrumental tactics. These are: distributive bargaining; integrative bargaining; attitudinal structuring; and intra-organisational bargaining. The originality of their study lies in its synthesis of the interaction and interrelationship amongst these four sub-processes.

The distributive bargaining model

Distributive bargaining is a conflict-resolving process, involving competitive bargaining behaviour between the negotiators. It is aimed at influencing the division of limited resources between them. It is central to management–union negotiations and is usually regarded as the dominant activity in their relationship. Distributive bargaining involves a 'win-lose' situation for the parties. In a wage negotiation, for example, what the management side wins, the union side loses. And what the management side concedes, the union side gains. In game theory, it is a 'fixed-sum' pay-off, with each side giving up something to achieve a compromise agreement.

In distributive bargaining, the collective bargaining agenda consists of 'issues' or areas of common concern in which the objectives of the parties are in conflict. Since distributive bargaining is the process by which each party attempts to maximise its own share of fixed, limited resources, the following sorts of issues are determined by it:

- wage levels;
- conditions of employment;
- working arrangements;
- staffing levels;
- union security;
- employee job rights;
- discipline;
- lay-offs.

But there is also a degree of mutual dependency between the parties. This is because settling conflict between them enables each side to benefit from the relationship. Both sides need to continue their relationship, rather than terminate it.

The bargaining range of the parties is bounded by upper and lower limits. At some upper limit of wage costs, the employer is forced to cease trading. At some lower limit, it loses the ability to retain its workforce. For any settlement point chosen by the negotiators, within this bargaining range, there are two possible outcomes. The parties may agree or disagree. Yet what negotiators demand, and what they actually expect, depends on their preferences or 'subjective utilities' for possible settlements. These also depend on their preferences or 'subjective disutilities' for avoiding strikes – and the potential costs of these. Negotiators have to evaluate various possible settlements by assigning probabilities to them. Their target and resistance points, in the bargaining range, reflect assessments of these utilities, probabilities and expected outcomes.

The integrative bargaining model

Integrative bargaining is a problem-solving process in which the negotiators seek a solution to a common employee relations problem. It takes place when the nature of the problem permits solutions which benefit both parties, or at least do not require equal sacrifices by both of them. It is the process by which the parties attempt to increase the size of the joint gain between them, without regard to the division of resources. The resolution of the problem, by negotiation, represents a 'win-win' situation for the parties. In productivity bargaining, for example, where management and the union try to get lower unit costs of production, through more efficient working practices, the gains in cost savings are shared. This results in more profits for the company, higher wages for the workforce and lower prices for the customers. In game theory, this is a 'positive sum' game, with benefits to both sets of negotiators.

The integrative collective bargaining agenda focuses on 'problems', rather than issues. These contain possibilities of greater or lesser amounts of value to both parties. Walton and McKersie argue that integrative bargaining potential is more normally found in qualitative rather than monetary employee relations issues. These include:

- providing individual job security, whilst increasing management flexibility;
- preserving jobs, whilst raising enterprise efficiency;
- expanding employment benefits, whilst limiting the employer's costs;
- facilitating union security, whilst providing management control, through closed shop or 'agency' shop agreements.

The integrative bargaining model comprises four main stages: identifying the problem; searching for alternative solutions and their consequences; ordering preferential solutions; and selecting a course of action. The conditions facilitating collective bargaining problem-solving depend on a number of factors. These include:

- the motivation of the parties;
- access to information by the parties;
- their having the communication skills to exchange this information;
- a supportive and trusting climate between them.

The tactics used by negotiators for optimising integrative bargaining outcomes focus on developing and inducing these conditions between the parties.

Mixed bargaining

It is rare, in practice, for the collective bargaining agenda not to include items which can be pursued only through some combination of distributive and integrative bargaining. Management–union negotiations present few pure-conflict situations and few problems allowing the parties total mutual gain. This results in 'mixed bargaining' which is a complex combination of the two processes, involving a variable sum, variable pay-off structure. Distributive bargaining assumes little or no variability in the sum available to the parties, whilst integrative bargaining assumes no difficulty in allocating shares between them. Mixed bargaining confronts both of these possibilities simultaneously, recognising that they are interdependent. It involves complex bargaining strategies and presents the parties with difficulties in identifying the preferred strategy. As Walton and McKersie write (page 179):

> The point . . . is that as bargaining comes to a showdown, what is purely integrative bargaining or what is beginning to move toward distributive bargaining becomes difficult to separate. Both sides are trying to converge on a point, but at the same time they are trying to protect their own self-interests.

The attitudinal structuring model

According to Walton and McKersie, an additional function of negotiating is that of influencing the relationships between the parties. These attitudes include friendliness or hostility, trust, respect, the motivational orientation towards each other – especially regarding competition or cooperation between them – and beliefs about each other's legitimacy. Negotiators take account of personal interaction in negotiations to produce attitudinal changes between them. Attitudinal structuring is a socio-emotional process used by negotiators to attain desired relationship patterns between themselves and to change attitudes during negotiations.

Walton and McKersie construct a model of the social-psychological forces affecting bargaining relationships. These include:

- the structural determinants of behaviour;
- attitudinal structuring activities;
- emergent relationship patterns;
- the consequences of these patterns.

They then develop a model of the attitudinal change process using two theories: cognitive balance theory and reinforcement theory.

The essence of cognitive balance theory is that individuals prefer consistency or balance amongst their cognitions, rather than dissonance. There is a psychological cost in holding discrepant cognitions. By introducing a discrepant cognition into another's awareness, the negotiator creates forces aimed at modifying existing cognitions, inducing a change in the target attitude and producing a change in negotiating behaviour.

Reinforcement theory assumes that people behave in ways which are rewarded, whilst avoiding behaviour which is punished. Negotiators therefore use rewards and punishments to shape the other party's behaviour. Where that party adopts cooperative patterns of behaviour, which are rewarded by his/her opposite number, it tends to develop more positive attitudes consistent with the new behaviour. In this case, a change in the target behaviour results in changes in negotiating attitudes.

The intra-organisational bargaining model

Intra-organisational bargaining is the process that takes place within the management side and union side, prior to and during negotiations. It seeks to resolve the conflicts over objectives, strategies and tactics within each bargaining organisation and to achieve internal consensus within them. Walton and McKersie analyse these conflicts in terms of the relationships between the chief negotiators and the groups they represent.

In examining the nature of internal conflict within bargaining organisations, Walton and McKersie focus on 'boundary role conflict' and 'factional conflict'. Boundary conflict results from the forces pulling chief negotiators in opposite directions; those forces arising from the internal expectations of their own groups and those arising from the other side's expectations during negotiations. Factional conflict arises from differences over negotiating objectives or the means of achieving them. The conditions under which internal conflict is likely to be most pronounced are where there are different preferences and feasibility estimates within the bargaining organisation. These, in turn, arise out of differences in underlying motivations, perceptual factors and emotional states of its constituents.

In response to boundary and factional conflicts, chief negotiators use a variety of behavioural techniques aimed at bringing the expectations of their constituent groups into line with their own. The problem arises from gaps between the expectations of the negotiators' groups and the negotiators' projections about the outcome and their judgements about the best way to bargain. 'The problem is resolved if expectations are brought into alignment with achievement, either *before the fact* of settlement or *afterward*, or if *perceived* achievement is brought into alignment with expectations' (Walton and McKersie 1965: page 303).

Chief negotiators have to make strategic choices about whether to modify, ignore or comply with the substantive and behavioural expectations of their groups, applying appropriate 'tactical assignments' to them:

- They may attempt to modify the aspirations of their group, ignoring their behavioural expectations. This is the most active strategy for achieving intra-organisational consensus.
- They may attempt to modify their group's aspirations, but less directly, by managing to comply with their behavioural expectations. This is a moderately active strategy.
- They may ignore, rather than change, their group's aspirations, whilst complying with their behavioural expectations, which is a passive strategy.

Synthesising the sub-processes

In synthesising the four sub-processes of negotiation, Walton and McKersie identify the 'commitment pattern' as the key aspect of distributive bargaining: 'openness in communication' in integrative bargaining; 'trust' in attitudinal structuring; and 'internal control' within the bargaining organisation in intra-organisational bargaining. Strategic and tactical issues arise, however, in the synthesising process. For example, whilst an 'early and firm commitment strategy' is preferable in distributive bargaining, it frustrates integrative bargaining, is likely to be negative for attitudinal structuring and could frustrate the other party's aim of achieving internal consensus in his/her bargaining organisation.

Similarly, a high degree of open communication is preferable for integrative bargaining and is consistent with efforts to improve relationships between the parties. However, anything but openness is required for distributive bargaining. It can also be problematic for intra-organisational bargaining, where negotiators often keep their organisations in the dark about bargaining developments or exaggerate their bargaining achievements.

Trust is a key element affecting attitudinal structuring. It plays a limited but essential role in distributive bargaining, has a more central role in integrative bargaining and facilitates intra-organisational bargaining. 'The fact is that trust appears to be an unmixed asset in [all] negotiations. There is little to commend a policy of distrust [in any respect]' (Walton and McKersie 1965: page 358). The amount of 'internal control' influences how negotiators attempt to resolve intra-organisational bargaining within the bargaining organisation: the more the control, the more the chief negotiator is able to persuade the group to adopt his/her views. However, whilst control is important for purposive attitudinal structuring, it has advantages and disadvantages for both distributive and integrative bargaining.

Bargaining power

Bargaining power is a central and important concept in collective bargaining. As Fox and Flanders (1969: page 250) comment: 'Power is the crucial variable determining the outcome [of collective bargaining] . . . [though] only when the group is able to mobilise sufficient power . . . does [employee relations] conflict become manifest.' Various theories have been proposed to explain bargaining power and its impact on negotiating outcomes.

One group of theories analyses how bargaining power is generated or created by the participants. The writers examining the 'causes' of bargaining power include Hoxie (1921), Pen (1952), Hicks (1932) and Dunlop (1950). Hoxie, for example, discusses the factors giving unions bargaining strength. Pen suggests a model of bargaining which incorporates the relative satisfactions of the parties in the bargaining process. He also considers how time brings about changes in the balance of power as economic conditions and public opinion shift. Hicks, an economist, sees wage bargaining power in terms of the levels of sacrifice made by the parties, to achieve specific advantage for themselves and those they represent. For Dunlop, bargaining power is determined primarily by the preferences of employers and workers, market conditions, negotiating skills and the ability to coerce the other party.

Atkinson (1980) argues that certain propositions can be derived from what these theorists have hypothesised about the generation of bargaining power. These are:

- What creates bargaining power can be appraised in terms of subjective assessments by individuals involved in the bargaining process.
- Each side can guess the bargaining preferences and bargaining power of the other side.
- There are normally a number of elements creating bargaining power.
- The volatile elements in creating bargaining power may be positive or negative. Positive elements provide inducements to adopt certain bargaining positions, whilst negative elements are the costs or disadvantages likely to be incurred by negotiators in not adopting certain bargaining positions.
- Bargaining power is dynamic and not static.

The second group of theories analysing bargaining power examines the consequences or the 'effects' of that power in bargaining relationships. Phelps Brown (1966: page 331), for example, estimates the differences made by collective bargaining to wage movements and identifies 'a positive association between those movements and collective bargaining.' Schelling (1963) suggests that bargaining power is, in the last analysis, the strength of the negotiator's position in the 'non-bluff' situation. And Stevens (1963: page 81) defines bargaining power as either 'power which is fully inherent in the original (pretactical play) pay-off matrix' or power which 'is (in part) tactically contrived by "moves" which rig the game.'

According to Atkinson (1980: page 11) the propositions following from these analyses of the effects of bargaining power are:

- The scarcer the resource in contention – and the greater the desire of the parties to possess it – the greater the importance of the strengths of the positions from which they make their demands.
- Bargaining power determines the position that can be adopted by each party, after all bluff has failed.
- The credibility of a negotiating position depends on whether the other side perceives that power to be real and that it will be used in support of a bargaining commitment.
- It is not total bargaining power which is important in the negotiating process but the '*area of imbalance*' between the two sides in the bargaining relationship.

Assessing bargaining power

A useful model for assessing bargaining power is provided by Atkinson. He links the definition of bargaining power provided by Chamberlain and Kuhn (1965: page 170) with the bargaining model provided by Levinson (1966). Chamberlain and Kuhn define bargaining power as the ability to secure another's agreement on one's own terms. A union's bargaining power, for example, is management's willingness to agree to the union's terms, with that willingness, in turn, depending 'on the cost of disagreeing with the union terms, relative to the cost of agreeing to them.' This definition assumes that negotiators adopt the course of action *least* likely to hurt them and the side they represent.

Your party's 'bargaining power', according to Atkinson, is indicated by *the disadvantages to your opponent of disagreeing with your proposal* relative to the *disadvantages to your opponent of agreeing with your proposal*. Conversely, their bargaining power is indicated by *the disadvantages to you of disagreeing with their proposal* relative to *the disadvantages to you of agreeing with their proposal*.

Both the disadvantages of disagreement and the disadvantages of agreement need to be examined in terms of the *costs* of the disadvantages to the party and the *likelihood* of the costs being incurred. Atkinson suggests that the costs for each element representing a disadvantage may be rated from 1 (a very low cost) to 10 (a very high cost). Similarly, the likelihood of the cost being incurred for each element may range from 0.1 (where the element has little chance of becoming a cost) to 1.0 (where the element is certain of becoming a cost).

Combining the costs and likelihoods for each element gives a total weighting for the disadvantages of disagreeing and of agreeing with a bargaining proposal. Where agreement with the proposal incurs *more* weighting (costs) than disagreement does, bargaining power rests with *the party to whom that proposal is made* (for that proposal alone). Where agreement with the proposal incurs *less* weighting (costs) than disagreement does, bargaining power rests with *the party making the proposal*.

Applying the bargaining power model: an example

A hypothetical example of how the above model can be used to assess bargaining power is shown in Figure 13. In this case, the model is being used to provide guidance to the management negotiators, in determining their immediate response to the annual wage claim of the unions representing the manual workers in their company. The basic question facing management is where bargaining power rests and why.

Let us examine a situation where the unions are claiming an across-the-board wage increase of 7 per cent and a shortening of the working week from 37.5 hours to 35 hours. The factors to be taken into account by management in making their response include: inflation is 4 per cent and falling; the going rate for local wage increases is 2–3 per cent; unemployment locally is low but rising; and demand for the company's products is rising. The unions have balloted, and received support, for a 'work to rule' if the wage claim is not satisfied.

Figure 13: *An illustrative use of the bargaining power model*

Disadvantages to management of disagreeing with the unions' claim			
Element	**Cost**	**Likelihood**	**Total**
work to rule	8	1.0	8.0
lost orders	8	0.9	7.2
some workers might leave firm	7	0.4	2.8
			17.0
Disadvantages to management of agreeing with the unions' claim			
Element	**Cost**	**Likelihood**	**Total**
increased unit costs of production	10	1.0	10.0
settlement higher than 'going rate'	7	1.0	7.0
could set a precedent	8	0.5	4.0
			21.0

In this example, agreement by management with the unions' bargaining proposal is likely to incur more weighting (or costs) to management than disagreement. This indicates that bargaining power rests with management for this proposal. In this case, however, the balance of power is relatively marginal. This illustrates both the strengths and weaknesses of this approach to assessing bargaining power. On the one hand, when individuals make such assessments:

• they are clearly subjective;
• reassessments are necessary as bargaining proceeds, in the light of new information;
• it is difficult to quantify 'bargaining power'.

On the other hand, this approach:

• identifies the elements contributing to bargaining power in different situations;
• provides a basis for analysing a bargaining position;
• helps to formulate a bargaining strategy and prepare a case.

Employer bargaining strategy

In deciding to recognise trade unions for collective bargaining purposes, employers also have to determine a strategy as regards the bargaining level on which they will negotiate with the unions (see Chapter 8). Post-recognition, a reassessment of bargaining levels may also be necessary. A number of strategic choices of bargaining levels is available: multi-employer, single employer and enterprise bargaining or a combination of these levels (see Chapter 3). The level or levels at which collective bargaining takes place is a vital management task and a crucial element of an employer's bargaining strategy. As Towers (1992: page iii) concludes, it has implications for the process of bargaining and the distribution of power between the parties. 'It affects the content of collective agreements and has important ''knock-on'' effects for the role and status of the personnel function and trade unions.' The bargaining level is also significant in the control of labour costs and for national economic policy objectives.

Bargaining trends

Table 14 shows the most important bargaining level for determining the most recent pay increase for manual and non-manual employees in private manufacturing, the private services and the public sector in

1984 and 1990. It is limited to those employers that bargained with unions in these sectors and relates only to the most important *pay*-bargaining level. In many instances pay-bargaining for these groups of employees took place at more than one level, whilst in some cases non-wage issues were also determined at the 'most important' pay-bargaining level. Despite its limitations, however, Table 14 indicates some important trends in pay-bargaining levels since the mid-1980s.

The most striking feature of Table 14 is the predominance of multi-employer-level pay-bargaining in the public sector. This was true for both manual and non-manual bargaining groups, even though there was a slight decline in the proportion of non-manual employees covered by it in 1990, compared with 1984. There were declines in the importance of multi-employer-level pay-bargaining for both manual and non-manual employees in the private services between 1984 and 1990, though its importance appeared to grow amongst non-manual employees in private manufacturing.

By 1990, single-employer-level pay-bargaining was the major feature of the private sector services, for both manual and non-manual employees. Correspondingly, between 1984 and 1990, the importance of single-employer-level pay-bargaining had declined in private manufacturing. This was accompanied by the growth in importance of enterprise-level pay-bargaining for manual employees in private manufacturing between 1984 and 1990 and by the relatively high proportion of non-manual employees in this sector who were covered by enterprise-level pay agreements in both 1984 and 1990.

The decline in multi-employer-level pay-bargaining in the private sector is part of a long-term trend which can be traced back to the 1950s and which accelerated in the early 1980s (Confederation of British Industry 1988). Even where multi-employer bargaining persists, its content progressively excludes pay. The trend towards decentralised pay-bargaining within private sector organisations accelerated from the late 1970s. Indeed, the CBI survey reports that in 1986 nearly 90 per cent of all employees in establishments with collective bargaining had their basic pay negotiated at company or establishment level. However, the situation is complicated by the fact that some employers seek an optimum balance between centralised *and* decentralised bargaining arrangements (Kinnie 1987), whilst others retain central or corporate control within which local pay bargainers operate (Marginson 1986).

Table 14: *Most important bargaining level for most recent pay increase in manufacturing, private services and public services, 1984 and 1990*

	Manual employees 1984	1990	Non-manual employees 1984	1990
				per cent
Manufacturing				
multi-employer	41	37	20	33
single employer	21	19	36	24
enterprise	38	44	44	43
Private services				
multi-employer	56	35	38	20
single employer	33	52	52	76
enterprise	11	13	10	4
Public sector				
multi-employer	81	81	86	84
single employer	18	18	13	16
enterprise	1	1	1	–

Source: WIRS 1992

Towers (1992) highlights a number of factors explaining the trend towards decentralised pay bargaining levels. These include:

- trade union weakness;
- corporate decentralisation preceding decentralised bargaining;
- the growth of performance-related pay;
- the pressures for employers to link worker productivity with appropriate pay increases.

The IPM (Palmer 1990: page 27) suggests that the shift towards pay decentralisation has been heavily influenced by the need to recruit, motivate and retain employees of the right calibre to ensure business success. Employers also seem to want the freedom not only to determine pay rates and pay increases locally but also to introduce new pay strategies, including profit-sharing, merit pay and pay bonuses, more suited to their own business strategies. 'For many organisations, pay policy has become a critical element of their strategic business planning.'

Multi-employer bargaining

Multi-employer bargaining, sometimes called industry-wide or national bargaining, is where minimum terms and conditions of employment are negotiated for all employers that are party to the 'national agreement'. Multi-employer bargaining normally requires the constituent employers to belong to the appropriate employers' association (see Chapter 2). The advantages and disadvantages to employers of multi-employer bargaining are outlined in Exhibits 29 and 30 below.

Exhibit 29: *Advantages of multi-employer bargaining*

These include the following:

- it concentrates employer and union employee relations resources;
- it leaves local management to concentrate on other business issues;
- it provides equitable treatment of employees by all employers in the sector, covered by national bargaining;
- it avoids employers playing each other off in the wage bargaining process.

Exhibit 30: *Disadvantages of multi-employer bargaining*

These include the following:

- it reduces the ability of individual employers to negotiate according to local circumstances;
- it leads employers to pay something for nothing locally;
- it forces some employers to pay more than they can afford;
- it can lead to employees expecting that national pay increases will be applied to local pay rates, irrespective of effort, whilst some employers will want to pay less than what is negotiated nationally;
- it ignores local labour markets, worker productivity and employee performance;
- it concentrates union bargaining power and negotiating skills.

Single-employer bargaining

Single-employer or company bargaining is where all terms and conditions are negotiated at employer level, in either single-site or multi-site

organisations. The advantages and disadvantages of single employer
bargaining to employers are outlined in Exhibits 31 and 32.

Exhibit 31: *Advantages of single-employer bargaining*

These include the following:

- it provides uniform terms and conditions across the company for similar jobs;
- it provides stable pay differentials amongst different bargaining groups within the company;
- it provides a common approach for handling grievances and resolving disputes in the company;
- it concentrates the bargaining power of management and the negotiating skills of management;
- it provides greater predictability of labour costs for management;
- it avoids wage 'leap-frogging' and minimises wage parity claims across the company.

Exhibit 32: *Disadvantages of single-employer bargaining*

These include the following:

- it is inflexible and makes it difficult to accommodate differences in production systems, product markets, labour markets and technologies within a centralised bargaining system;
- it raises the level of management decision-making, reducing local management and employee commitment to these decisions;
- it requires very effective in-company communications;
- it can lead to over-formalisation of employee relations, be slow to respond to change and be too inflexible;
- it can be expensive because of the need to maintain a centralised employee relations system;
- it may be difficult to integrate new businesses within the employee relations system.

Enterprise bargaining

Enterprise or plant bargaining is where terms and conditions are
negotiated between management and union representatives locally,
not at corporate level. Enterprise bargaining is either *autonomous* or

coordinated. Autonomous enterprise bargaining is where each plant has the authority to settle all terms and conditions locally. Coordinated enterprise bargaining is where negotiations are conducted at plant level within limits set by the centre. The advantages and disadvantages of enterprise bargaining to employers are outlined in Exhibits 33 and 34.

Exhibit 33: *Advantages of enterprise bargaining*

These include the following:

- it provides shorter lines of communication and speeds the resolution of disputes;
- it increases the authority of local management by providing clear responsibility for employee relations;
- it increases management ability to respond flexibly to employee relations by introducing pay, conditions and incentives, geared to local conditions;
- it increases the commitment of employees through locally determined agreements;
- it dissociates union bargaining power.

Exhibit 34: *Disadvantages of enterprise bargaining*

These include the following:

- it requires management planning and negotiating skills which may not exist at plant level;
- it increases the danger of claims for 'wages parity' by the unions;
- it requires total pay decentralisation, otherwise it is difficult to maintain differentials;
- it complicates labour cost control.

Two-tier bargaining

Two-tier bargaining is where some elements of the reward package are determined at one level, whilst others are determined at another, lower level. In some cases, multi-employer agreements settle minimum pay rates or minimum earnings nationally and company agreements supplement them by providing the means for determining actual earnings, including pay flexibility, at employer level. In this way, employers combine the stability of framework agreements at industry level with maximum flexibility for individual employers, who are party to national agreements, at corporate level. Such arrangements are claimed to stabilise wage costs at industry level, whilst remaining sensitive to variations in regional and local labour markets.

In other cases, two-tier bargaining takes place within single-employer bargaining arrangements. Here basic conditions of employment can be settled at corporate centre, with pay – especially performance pay – being determined at establishment or plant level. This enables employers to obtain the best of two worlds. Even where decentralised bargaining takes place, coordination at corporate level may be retained through 'the budgetary control mechanism, where labour cost targets are often specified in line with broader targets or rates of return on sales and capital employed' (Purcell 1987: page 55).

Factors affecting bargaining levels

Determining the appropriate bargaining level is a complex task for employers and management, especially those with multi-plant operations and complex business structures. A study by ACAS (1983) suggests that certain structural and organisational factors are key determinants of an organisation's collective bargaining structure, especially bargaining levels. These factors include: the firm's product market; its forms of work organisation; the technology used; its geographic location; its business structure; the union structure; and the payment system.

A recent analysis by the IPM (Palmer 1990), which seeks to help employers identify the type of bargaining structure best suited to their own needs, discusses the internal factors, external factors and bargaining topics likely to affect an employer's decision in determining the optimum bargaining level. The internal factors include:

- company organisation (such as decision-making levels, degrees of diversity and plans for expansion);
- management style and management strengths;
- plant characteristics (such as size, technology and degrees of interdependence);
- job categories and relationships (such as wage policy, payment systems and bargaining reference groups).

The external factors are:

- union organisation (such as representation, power and membership levels);
- the industry structure (such as market competition, national collective agreements and trading relationships).

The bargaining topics likely to affect decisions on bargaining levels include: the terms and conditions which are negotiable; the procedural agreements which exist; and whether arbitration is used for resolving disputes between the employer and the unions.

General indicators of multi-employer bargaining being preferred by employers are industries having: a large number of small companies; competitive product markets; high levels of trade union membership; high labour costs relative to other costs; and geographical concentration of the sector. Single-employer bargaining is likely in companies with: single product businesses; stable product markets; a centralised corporate structure; and strong trade union organisation. Enterprise bargaining is likely in companies with: multi-product businesses; unstable product markets; multi-divisional structures; and weak trade union organisation locally.

The Negotiating process

John Dunlop, a major theoretician of employee relations, and an outstanding mediator, argues that there have been two main approved institutional arrangements for resolving conflicts of interest amongst groups and organisations in Western societies for over 200 years. These are 'the give and take of the market place and government regulatory mechanisms established by the political process' (Dunlop 1984: page 3). He sees negotiating as a positive, alternative mode of conflict resolution between competing groups, such as employers and unions, which has made inroads into both the market and governmental distributive processes. Negotiating provides benefits to both sides, involves compromise, avoids uncertainty and is flexible in its approach. Moreover, even if collective bargaining does not entirely displace market forces, he argues, the differences between negotiators in 'pure bargaining skills and power' may 'result in somewhat different terms and conditions of employment over time than would arise through markets or under governmental dictation' (page 6).

Based on his experience and research, Dunlop provides a 10-point basic framework for analysing the negotiating process:

- It takes agreement within each negotiating group to reach a settlement between them.
- Initial proposals are typically large, compared with eventual settlements.
- Both sides need to make concessions in order to move towards an agreement.
- A deadline is an essential feature of most negotiating.
- The end stages of negotiating are particularly delicate, with private discussions often being used to close the gap between the parties.
- Negotiating is influenced by whether it involves the final, intermediate or first stages of the conflict resolution process.
- Negotiating and overt conflict may take place simultaneously, with the conflict serving as a tool for getting agreement.
- Getting agreement does not flourish in public.
- Negotiated settlements need procedures to administer or interpret the final agreement.
- Personalities and their interactions can affect negotiating outcomes.

An overview

The purpose of negotiating in employee relations is to resolve any conflicts of interest or conflicts of right between employers and trade unions, through both sides modifying their original demands to achieve mutually acceptable compromises between them. The issues may relate to terms and conditions of employment, non-wage matters or combinations of these. A number of stages are discernible in the negotiating process: objective-setting; preparing; bargaining; and implementing.

Objective-setting

To enable movement to take place between the bargaining parties in the negotiating process, each side has to establish a realistic spectrum or set of bargaining objectives. As shown in Figure 14, these consist of an 'ideal settlement point' [ISP], a 'realistic settlement point' [RSP] and a 'fall back point' [FBP]. The ISP is what the negotiators would ideally *like to achieve* through negotiation, if possible. The RSP is what they *intend to achieve*, whilst the FBP is what they *must achieve* at the very minimum, and without which no settlement can result. The bargaining range of each side lies between its ISP and its FBP, with final settlement taking place between each of the parties' FBPs. Where the FBPs of the two sides do not overlap, there is a 'bargaining gap' between them and, unless there is a modification of their bargaining objectives, no negotiated compromise is possible.

Figure 14: *Hypothetical wage-bargaining objectives for management and unions*

Management Side	ISP	RSP	FBP					
	*	*	*					per cent wage rise
	3	4	5	6	7	8	9	
		*		*		*		
Union Side		FBP		RSP		ISP		

Preparing

Identifying, collecting and deciding how to use relevant information across the bargaining table are key elements in preparing for negotiating. Information relates to a number of areas including: facts, precedents, personalities, power and issues. Decisions have to be taken by the bargaining teams about what information is to be disclosed to the other side, when it is to be disclosed and what is to be withheld. In this sense, 'knowledge' or information is power and it can provide a cutting edge in the negotiating process if it is used tactically and authoritatively by either or both sides. Information is normally provided to support and justify the propositions made by each party, as well as to challenge each other's propositions. Bargaining conventions dictate that initial negotiating propositions focus on each party's ISP, with neither side revealing its full strength initially.

Preparing also involves each team deciding who is to be the lead negotiator, who is to take records at the meetings and who is to observe. The leader's role is to conduct the negotiation for the bargaining team. The leader does most of the talking, makes proposals, trades concessions and calls adjournments. Recorders take notes, ask questions, summarise situations and generally keep negotiations on track, especially when the going gets tough. Recorders support the lead negotiator but never 'take over' the main negotiating role.

Observers 'read' negotiations. They do not normally say much but analyse the negotiations, pick up the subleties and moods of the participants and provide inputs of new information and ideas during adjournments, as appropriate.

Bargaining

Bargaining involves a number of phases which are described in more detail below. Atkinson (1980) identifies four phases: clarifying the other side's position; structuring the expectations of the other side; getting movement; and closure. Kennedy and his colleagues (1984) propose three similar phases to Atkinson, once the parties have determined their bargaining objectives. These are: 'arguing'; 'proposing'; and 'exchanging' and 'agreeing'. They also identify three sub-phases. These are: 'signalling' within the arguing phase; 'packaging' within the proposing phase; and 'closing' within the exchanging and agreeing phase. What differentiates each phase from the other is the skills and activities appropriate to them. However these phases are defined and delineated, they provide a 'negotiating landscape' within which negotiators direct their resources, skills and knowledge, structure their behaviour and act out their roles, according to the situations facing them.

Implementing

This is the process by which both parties are responsible for carrying out the decisions and outcomes determined by the parties jointly. Final decisions need to be recorded, put in writing and signed by both sides. This avoids further conflict over interpreting what has actually been agreed between the negotiators!

Arguing

In this initial phase of bargaining, each side makes its opening statements and the arguments underpinning them. Both parties normally only reveal their ISPs and are reluctant to concede anything to the other side in terms of information or clues to their real negotiating objectives. The underlying aim of the negotiators is to justify the positions of their own sides, to maximise the information obtained about the other side's RSP and to reveal the minimum information about their own. There is intense listening on both sides, questioning for clarification and challenging the other side to justify its negotiating stance. Each side remains non-committal about the other party's proposals, whilst testing its commitment to its case. There is mutual seeking of information but little exchanging takes place at this phase. This is because arguments cannot be negotiated; they only set the contexts and parameters of each side's opening positions.

The process of 'signalling', identified by Kennedy and his colleagues (1984: page 62), is where qualifications are 'placed on a statement of a position.' The initial statements of the parties are absolute ones. For example, 'We'll never agree to that'; 'Your offer is totally unacceptable to our members'; or 'Your proposal is nonsense.' Signalling provides the parties with the opportunity to move towards each other in the early stages of negotiation, after the initial stonewalling responses of both sides. Examples of signalling by one of the parties could be: 'Well, we could discuss that point' (meaning that it is negotiable) or 'We would find it very difficult to agree to that' (meaning that it is not impossible to do so). Skilled negotiators reward signalling behaviour where possible. It moves the parties away from their opening gambits and creates the possibilities for concessions later. To be productive, signalling needs to be reciprocated. It is important to reward signals, not obstinacy. This is done by responding positively to the other side with phrases such as: 'We're always prepared to consider reasonable proposals.'

Proposing

A proposition in the negotiating process is an offer, or a claim, made by one of the parties to the other, moving it away from its original position. Initial proposals tend to be tentative and are non-committal. They aim at reassuring the other party and at marking out the parameters within which exchanges can take place between them and agreement can finally be reached. Proposals become more specific as negotiations proceed, thus providing a means for moving towards real bargaining or concrete exchanges between the parties later. Propositions are conditional, never absolute. They are stated in the following way: 'If you are prepared to do "A", then we will consider doing "B".' Generally, negotiators open with realistic proposals and move only slowly towards each other. Choosing the opening position therefore is crucial.

Propositions are normally firm on generalities, such as 'We are determined to settle this issue quickly.' But they are flexible on specifics, such as 'We propose an offer of £X.' The party receiving a proposal needs to listen to it carefully and not to reject it out of hand, so that it can respond and provide a counter-proposal. Opening conditions are normally large, whilst opening concessions are normally small. However, since negotiators learn their craft through experience, and about each other through observation, these influence the ways in which they structure their proposals, respond to initiatives and act out their negotiating roles.

'Packaging' is the term used by Kennedy and his colleagues to describe the bridging that is made between the opening movements of the parties and their shifting into final agreement. 'It is, effectively, the activity which draws up the agenda for the bargaining session' (Kennedy *et al.* 1984: page 89). Packaging aims to facilitate convergence between the parties, from where they are, after the arguing and proposing phases have taken place, to where they can finally agree a settlement. This entails:

- identifying the other party's reservations about coming to an agreement, its negotiating objectives and its bargaining priorities;
- considering its possible 'signalled' concessions;
- each side reviewing its own negotiating objectives, bearing in mind its ISP, RSP and FBP, and those of the other side.

This enables each side to determine whether there is enough movement between them to produce a package and how it can modify it or adapt it to meet some of the other side's reservations.

Each side has to consider:

- the concessions it wants;
- the room it has for manoeuvre;
- the concessions it is prepared to signal in the package;
- what it wants in return.

This enables each party to tell the other what 'package' is on offer, thus providing a negotiating platform, including the readiness to trade concessions, which prepares the ground for exchanges between them. These exchanges of concessions follow the general rule of not giving anything away without getting something back in return. The pattern is: 'If you move on that issue, then we will move on this one.' In trading concessions, each party needs to value them in terms of their perceived value to the other party. This means evaluating the worth of a concession to the other party, its cost to your side and what is wanted in exchange for it.

Exchanging and agreeing

This is the most crucial phase of the bargaining process. Unless the parties are able to make final exchanges and concessions between them, bargaining reaches an impasse and a failure to agree is recorded. The key to reaching a successful agreement is for each of the parties to come up with positive propositions, which remain linked but are conditional on movement by the other side. The sorts of statements made by the parties are: 'If your side agrees to A, then we will agree to B.' By continuing to put conditions on what they are prepared to exchange, negotiators ensure that they do not concede anything without getting something back in return.

Linking all the issues ensures that every item in the package is listed by both sides. This means that when either party raises an issue, it can be dealt with in the context of the package as a whole. This provides the negotiators with some degree of flexibility and leverage. They also have the opportunity to link each concession to corresponding concessions on other items, as they move towards final agreement. All the items are negotiated conditionally upon the package as a whole being agreed. Keeping items linked makes them available for trading and exchange, as bargaining proceeds to its concluding stages. The more items that there are to exchange, the stronger the bargaining positions of the negotiators. The process of linking facilitates moves on one issue with trade-offs for something else. In this way, single items in the negotiating package are not picked off in a piecemeal way. And the negotiators are provided with more room for manoeuvre, providing that the linking amongst the items is realistic.

Closing a negotiation requires judgement. If the parties are unable to close their bargaining activity, their continued negotiating can result in further concessions that collectively may be costly to each side. One way of closing is for one side to make a 'final' concession to the other, preferably on a minor issue. A second way is by summarising what has been agreed to date, stressing the concessions which have been made and emphasising the benefits of agreeing to what is on offer. A third way is through an adjournment. This enables the other side to have time to consider what is on 'final' offer. Fourth, one side can present the other with an ultimatum. This states, in effect, that unless what is on offer is accepted, a failure to agree will result. Finally, the choice of alternatives may be given to the other side. This enables it to consider which alternative is preferable, whilst not changing what is actually on offer.

Once final agreement has been reached, it must be listed in detail and recorded in writing. Both sides must be absolutely clear what has been agreed, with all relevant points being listed, clarified and explained as necessary. Where there is any disagreement on any item, negotiations must continue until agreement is reached. In short, what has been agreed has to be clearly summarised, accurately recorded and finally signed by both the parties.

Collective agreements

Collective agreements are the outcome of collective bargaining, determined between employer and union representatives. Being bilateral employment rules, they differ from company rules and employer policy statements, which are unilateral in origin. The collective nature of these rules is also reflected in the fact that the terms and conditions of employment, and employee relations procedures, incorporated in collective agreements, apply to groups of workers covered by them. Substantive agreements cover any kind of payments and a wide range of working conditions. Procedural agreements spell out the steps by which employee relations processes are to be carried out. These include: machinery for negotiation, consultation and arbitration; negotiating, handling grievances and resolving disputes; discipline and dismissal; and facilities for trade union representatives.

The formulation of collective agreements

Good practice suggests that formal, written collective agreements are now the norm in employee relations. Although over-formality is not conducive to good employee relations, written agreements are preferred by employers and unions for a number of reasons:

- They focus attention on problem areas and lead to joint policies bringing about agreed solutions.

- Written agreements create order in employee relations and facilitate change. They overcome, for example, the problems involved where either management or union negotiators move on for one reason or another.
- They provide continuity in employee relations, enabling decisions to be determined in the light of past practice, precedent and accepted norms.

In some cases, agreements are drafted by management, with the final details being considered and agreed by the parties jointly. In other cases, unions take the initiative and management respond to what is proposed. In yet other cases, the development of agreements is best handled by a joint working party.

The legal status of collective agreements

A collective agreement is defined in law as any agreement or arrangement made by or on behalf of one or more trade unions and one or more employers or employers' associations, relating to one or more of the matters listed in the TULRCA 1992. These are (section 178):

(a) terms and conditions of employment, or the physical conditions in which any workers are required to work;
(b) engagement or non-engagement, or termination or suspension of employment or the duties of employment, of one or more workers;
(c) allocation of work or the duties of employment between workers or groups of workers;
(d) matters of discipline;
(e) a worker's membership or non-membership of a trade union;
(f) facilities for officials of trade unions; and
(g) machinery for negotiation or consultation, and other procedures, relating to any of the above matters, including the recognition by employers or employers' associations of the right of a trade union to represent workers in such negotiation or consultation or in the carrying out of such procedures.

The distinctive feature of British collective agreements is that they are not legally enforceable between the employers and unions negotiating them. As the TULRCA 1992 states (section 179): 'a collective agreement shall be conclusively presumed not to be a legally enforceable contract', unless it is in writing and contains a provision stating that it is intended to be enforceable. Unlike in many other countries, collective agreements in Britain do not have a 'contractual function' between the parties making them, they are 'binding in honour' only. But they do have a 'normative function'. This means that the terms, conditions and rules determined by them become incorporated into individual contracts of employment, expressly or sometimes by implication.

The non-enforceability of collective agreements was underlined by the *Ford Motor Company* v. *AUEF and TGWU* case in 1969. The company brought a legal action alleging breach of contract against the unions, on the grounds that they had supported their members' strike action in breach of agreed collective bargaining procedures. The High Court decided that the unions were not liable because their collective agreements with the employer were not intended to be legally enforceable contracts. The Court argued that, as experienced negotiators, management and unions had had no intention of creating legal enforceability, so there was no contract between them – only 'an unenforceable gentleman's agreement'. This judgement was not taken to appeal, and although the Industrial Relations Act 1971 presumed all collective agreements to be legally binding unless the parties declared them otherwise, almost every collective agreement between 1971 and 1974 contained a clause stating that 'this is not a legally enforceable agreement' (Weekes *et al.* 1975).

The customary way of securing the normative function of collective agreements is to incorporate their provisions into the personal contracts of employment of each worker. Whilst in some countries collective agreements have an automatic effect upon employment contracts, in Britain they do not. The best way for the employment contract to incorporate the collective terms relating to pay, conditions and benefits is to incorporate them expressly. The most useful vehicle for doing this is the written statement of particulars given to employees within two months of starting employment where the employees work eight or more hours a week. A problem with trying to incorporate the terms of a collective agreement as implied terms is that the normal rules of contract law determine that nothing can be implied into a contract affecting any matter covered by an express term. Thus personal contracts of employment cannot be overridden by collective agreements.

The incorporation of procedural clauses of collective agreements into individual contracts is less clear-cut and more problematic. Procedures dealing with individual employee rights, such as those relating to grievances and disciplinary matters, provide little problem. For example, the EPCA 1978 requires employers to set out matters relating to discipline and grievances in the note accompanying a worker's written particulars in a way that envisages these procedures being incorporated into individual contracts of employment. There is more doubt about procedures concerned with workers' collective action, such as no-strike clauses, restrictions on industrial action until the procedure to avoid disputes is exhausted or other collective procedures.

One problem with these procedures is that they sometimes involve questions of policy. In the case of *British Leyland* v. *McQuilken*, for example, the employer had made an agreement with the union that, in the closing down of a department, all employees would be interviewed for retraining or redundancy. McQuilken was not interviewed because management changed its policy but he was told he could transfer to another place or be retrained. He claimed a redundancy payment and went to an industrial tribunal. The tribunal declared the refusal to implement the agreement as constructive dismissal. On appeal, the EAT rejected this on the grounds that the terms of the agreement between the employer and the union did not alter McQuilken's individual contract of employment. 'That agreement was a long-term plan, dealing with policy rather than with the rights of individual employees.'

Types of agreement

There are a variety of types of collective agreements. Collective bargaining is an infinitely flexible process of employee relations and the format of collective agreements reflects this. So far, earlier discussions have focused primarily on what may be described as fairly standardised approaches to the content of substantive and procedural agreement (see Chapter 3). This section is more selective in its approach and focuses on some of the 'newer' types, and less common forms, of collective agreement such as 'technology agreements', 'new-style agreements', 'flexibility agreements' and 'partnership agreements'.

Technology agreements

Technological change is endemic to the work process (see Chapter 6). Since the 1980s especially, micro-electronic and related technologies have been continuously applied to a range of industries, occupations and sectors, with non-manual employment being particularly affected by these changes. Although research shows that it is common for these changes to be imposed unilaterally by management, largely without consultation with staff (Daniels 1987), in some cases attempts have been made to negotiate the introduction of 'new technology' and new working methods between management and unions. This is done to facilitate the introduction of new equipment, train people to use it and reduce the anxieties associated with change, thus providing benefits to the employer and to employees in conditions of uncertainty. Such agreements are sometimes referred to as 'technology agreements'.

A number of negotiating issues arise with the introduction of new technology, each of which has procedural and substantive implications for employee relations. The negotiating issues include: job contraction; job content; job control; and health and safety at work (Winterton and Winterton 1985). Job contraction is synonymous with new technology, and potential job losses account for many of the fears felt amongst employees when new technology is being introduced into organisations. Job content, too, can be adversely affected either by the de-skilling of the work of employees or by dehumanising it, as a result of technological change. The impact of new technology on individual job control is two-fold. First, it can result in workers having less discretion in the ways in which their jobs are performed. Second, where technology creates less-skilled work, job control shifts from workers to management, since these operations are easier for management to direct. Also, although new technology reduces some physical hazards at work, there is also evidence of its potentially damaging effects where it results in irregular shift work, social isolation or physical strain, such as repetitive strain injury.

The sorts of procedural issues arising from the introduction of new technology cover include its impact on: existing procedures and bargaining arrangements; employee training; and the monitoring and operation of new technology. Existing procedures likely to be affected by technological innovation are: union recognition; grievances and disputes; discipline; redeployment and redundancy; and the level at which bargaining takes place. Employee training is an important aspect of introducing new technology, and procedures need to be determined regarding both the job training needs of employees and the employee relations training needs of union representatives. Two main procedural mechanisms are used to monitor new technology: either joint management–union study teams or outside consultants.

The sorts of substantive issues arising from the introduction of new technology arrangements cover a number of matters. These include: how the savings generated from productivity increases are to be shared between management and workers; how any job losses are to be managed; the impact of changes on terms and conditions of employment; and their impact on health and safety. The benefits of increased productivity can be shared in a number of ways. These include: higher wages; shorter working periods; early retirement; and additional leave. Where job losses result, these can be achieved by a variety of means including: natural wastage; redeployment; voluntary redundancy; or compulsory redundancy, with the relevant terms with being negotiated and agreed between the parties.

Procedural provisions may need to be made to improve the quality of working life after the introduction of new technology. These can take the form of: additional breaks; job rotation; job enrichment; and job design. The problems associated with the health and safety hazards connected with new technology need to be addressed. These can cover such matters as eye strain, shift working, the implications of robotics and any psychological hazards arising from the work environment. Introducing new technology can also affect equality of opportunity at work in matters such as job grading, promotion, patterns of work and job retraining. Procedural adjustments need to be made here too.

New-style agreements

New-style agreements (NSAs) contain a number of procedural elements distinguishing them from standardised or more traditional procedural arrangements. As Burrows (1986) indicates, a major feature of NSAs is that their negotiating and disputes procedures are based on the mutually accepted 'rights' of the parties, expressed in the recognition agreement. The intention is to resolve any differences of interest on substantive issues between the parties by negotiation, with pendulum arbitration providing a resolution of these issues where differences persist.

The general principles underlying NSAs aim to reinforce the harmony of interests between the company, the signatory union and its employees. Employees are not required to join the union but are encouraged to do so. NSAs frequently stress the need for quality, teamwork and flexibility in the work process, for avoiding unnecessary industrial action which disrupts production and for open and direct communications between the company and its employees. Only one union is recognised for the purposes of negotiation, consultation and information-giving to staff. And all these processes are normally carried on within a 'company council' consisting of management and employee representatives. Employee representatives are elected by a secret ballot of all the workforce, with the balloting process being supervised by the local full-time union officer. Company and union often provide joint training for these representatives to enable them to carry out their duties satisfactorily and effectively.

The negotiating procedure for determining new substantive issues within NSAs normally incorporates two underlying principles. The first is that during negotiations – and during conciliation and arbitration – there is to be no recourse to industrial action. Second, management and the union often affirm their commitment to resolving issues within the company but, where there are any remaining differences between them, if they fail to agree, these are resolved through binding conciliation or arbitration. Arbitrators are required to make a decision, based on the 'final offer' of one or other of the sides. There is no 'split' decision. Pendulum arbitration of this sort, it is argued, not only encourages realistic bargaining positions by each of the parties but also provides a means of peacefully resolving persisting disputes of interest between the company and its workforce.

Individual grievances and collective issues of 'rights', in contrast, are resolved through the grievance procedure and procedure to avoid disputes respectively. The latter states that there is to be no industrial action, whilst the issue is in procedure. Where such matters are not resolved 'in house', they may be referred to ACAS or another third party who may conciliate or arbitrate, with the terms of reference being agreed by the parties, within the time limits set for determining the issue.

Procedures also frequently exist for ensuring the fullest use of human resources and labour flexibility in the single-union company. These include agreed changes in working practices likely to affect productivity and staffing levels, and can involve the use of appropriate industrial engineering and human resource planning techniques. Finally, to ensure labour flexibility and organisational change, provisions are made for training and retraining the workforce for future human resource requirements.

Flexibility agreements

Collective agreements aimed at changing entrenched working practices, and removing job demarcations, by introducing labour flexibility in firms, have been a common feature of employee relations since the 1980s. In its assessment of the scope and nature of some of these flexibility agreements, Industrial Relations Review and Report (1992) concludes that there are limits to the usefulness of such agreements in introducing flexible working practices. Whilst the companies investigated no longer faced 'who does what' disputes, they questioned the extent to which the total interchangeability of labour is desirable. Further, in technologically sophisticated environments, in particular, it appeared to be uneconomic to train the whole workforce in complex skills which are only used by small numbers of employees.

Of the four organisations examined, two – Mobil Coryton and Babcock Energy – changed working practices at times of financial difficulty. The other two – Toshiba Consumer Products and the Co-operative Wholesale Society (CWS) at Deeside – introduced new working practices on greenfield sites but also against a background of economic difficulties. These studies focused on six aspects of flexibility deals: flexibility developments; flexibility and labour force size and composition; the extent to which flexibility had progressed; training needs and their implications; the collective bargaining effects; and the impact of flexibility on corporate performance.

The flexibility agreements at Toshiba and Mobil established the principle of a total end to demarcation so that these companies did not feel any need for any substantial changes in working practices subsequently. In the CWS, broad flexibility measures were expanded to a single group of employees who combined both production and maintenance skills. At Babcock, the initial flexibility agreement listed specific changes in required working practices. This was followed by a later agreement on broad flexibility, with further changes focusing on individual issues.

The flexibility deals at Mobil and Babcock contributed to labour force reductions, with substantial hiving-off of some job activities to subcontractors. Toshiba, in contrast, being a greenfield site operation, did not use much contract labour but, in adapting to product market fluctuations, varied its use of temporary staff to maintain the stability of its permanent workforce.

At Babcock, the principle was established that multi-skilled craftworkers would not have the specialist skills required in a complex industry. Its agreement was based on the need to train workers in 'secondary' skills. At Mobil and Toshiba, the flexibility agreements were based on the principle of multi-skilling, so reducing the risks of demarcation disputes. In practice, however, some employee specialisation was essential, especially in conditions of technological sophistication. In these companies, production-maintenance flexibility was limited to production workers doing minor maintenance on the plant for which they were responsible. Flexibility seemed to have progressed furthest at the CWS but even here it was not economic to provide all employees with all the skills required within the workplace. In general, it seems that these flexibility deals increased the breadth of workforce skills, but not their depth.

In all four companies, it appeared that flexibility provisions meant that new workers required certain skills training. Both Babcock and Toshiba operated their own apprenticeship schemes, whilst Mobil had wound its scheme down. This enabled Mobil to direct some of its resources at a skills training centre in a local town. It also provided opportunity for the workforces of its subcontractors to become adequately skilled.

At both Toshiba and the CWS, the employee relations structures remained as they had been. Toshiba had one of the earliest single-union agreements and the CWS combined its consultative and collective bargaining machinery. Babcock did not consider that introducing labour flexibility had had a great effect on union influence. However, because of contracting out and union mergers, a smaller number of unions was recognised than had been the case some 10 years earlier. At Mobil, on the other hand, culture change was seen as laying the groundwork for targeting employee relations practices at individual employees and their performance. This, it was envisaged, might lead to a change in the role of trade unions in the future.

In terms of the impact of labour flexibility on corporate performance, all four case studies found it difficult to separate the effects of introducing labour flexibility from those of other company innovations. All the companies felt that labour flexibility had contributed to organisational well-being, especially in producing acceptable labour productivity levels. Mobil and the CWS added that an employee relations climate free of demarcation disputes was a direct result of changed working practices.

Partnership agreements

These are a relatively new type of collective agreement. They generally emphasise three inter-related elements:

- the development of mutually acceptable pay review formulae;
- the establishment of single status for all employees;
- cooperation between management and union(s) as an obligation within the partnership arrangements.

Pay review formulae can incorporate a number of elements. These include changes in the retail price index, the employer's position in relevant pay markets and the employer's financial and operational performance, which can provide a profit-related pay element in the pay package. The main features of pay review formulae are that they are open, rational and mutually agreed in advance by the employer and the union(s), normally for an agreed period. This enables all parties – including employees – to understand the principles upon which pay is based.

Single status for all employees in partnership agreements is commonly rooted in three main principles:

- that since all employees contribute to customer or client satisfaction, they should all have good terms and conditions of employment;
- that change is best introduced through discussion and agreement with all those involved;
- that any additional costs because of single status can be offset by improved customer provision.

Single status programmes typically incorporate the following sorts of procedural and substantive provisions: single table negotiating and consultative arrangements; standard working hours; monthly pay; an integrated pay structure; expectations about productivity improvements and job flexibility; and job security arrangements, sometimes including a 'no compulsory redundancy' agreement.

The mutuality and cooperation expected between management and union(s) in partnership agreements is normally set out in the general principles of their procedural arrangements. A good example of this is provided in the partnership agreement negotiated between Welsh

Water and the Signatory Unions (1991: page 15). This states that both the company and the recognised unions agree that it is in the best interests of employees and the company to maintain constructive and cooperative relationships at all times. The principles underpinning this agreement are:

- Promoting openness on problems and issues of mutual concern.
- Valuing good communications both to employees and Trade Unions.
- Consulting and involving employees and their representatives at an early stage of formulating proposals for change.
- Ensuring that the focal point of dealing with employee issues is as near to the workplace as possible, and that any problems are resolved wherever possible through informal discussion at the lowest possible organisational level.
- Conducting formal consultation and negotiations on a joint basis covering all employees, wherever it is practical and relevant to do so.
- Devoting formal consultative meetings to matters of concern and relevance to all employees and the business.

The institutional arrangements for facilitating the partnership approach to employee relations and partnership agreements is often a company council. This is a representative body consisting of employer and union representatives which has a number of functions. These normally include: acting as a negotiating forum; acting as a consultative forum; establishing sub-committees and working parties; facilitating the resolution of grievances and disputes; and promoting the agreed principles of employee relations between the employer and the union(s).

Assignments

(a) What are the advantages and disadvantages to employers of collective bargaining as a method of determining terms and conditions of employment and for regulating relations between employers and employees?

(b) What is the case for and against legally enforceable collective agreements? What are the main implications for employers, unions and employees where 'collective contracts' are negotiated?

(c) Read Adnett (1989: Chapter 2). What are the main features of the neo-classical model of the labour market and that of the structural model? How do these models relate to the labour markets in which your organisation operates?

(d) Read Kahn-Freund (1954) in Flanders, A. (1969: pages 59–85). Comment on his analysis of how 'intergroup' conflicts between employers and unions are regulated through collective bargaining in Britain, Europe and the USA. How does he account for the differences amongst the bargaining systems?

(e) Read Chamberlain and Kuhn (1965: pages 162–90). How do they conceptualise bargaining power? How useful is their analysis for practical bargaining purposes?

(f) Read Walton and McKersie (1965: Chapter VII, pages 222–80). Examine the nature of attitudinal structuring and why it is an important sub-process in collective bargaining. What tactics can be used by negotiators to change the attitudes of their opposite numbers in the bargaining process, applying the concepts of either 'balance theory' or 'reinforcement theory'?

(g) Use the bargaining power model to assess the relative balance of power in your organisation, when either the union presented its last wage and conditions claim to your employer or management made its last wage proposal to the union. Did the bargaining outcome fit with your analysis?

(h) Read Towers (1992: pages 7–11). What does he identify as the reasons for employers withdrawing from multi-employer bargaining, what are the experiences of decentralised bargaining for employers and what are the wider organisational effects of it?

(i) Identify the organisational conditions – such as product markets, labour markets, technology, business structure and so on – where (1) multi-employer (2) single employer and (3) enterprise bargaining is most favourable to employer interests.

(j) What are the advantages and disadvantages to *unions* of (1) multi-employer-level bargaining? (2) single-employer-level bargaining? (3) enterprise-level bargaining? Under what conditions are each of the above levels most favourable to union negotiators?

(k) The unions representing white-collar staff in your organisation have presented management with their annual pay claim. This is for a 5 per cent across-the-board wage increase, a reduction in weekly hours of 20 minutes and improved sickness benefits for their members. Identify the sort of information that management would need to collect in this situation, where it might be collected and how it might be used in the negotiating process.

(l) Read Atkinson (1980: pages 137–54). What are some of the main tactics used by negotiators to get movement by their opponents in the latter stages of negotiating? Alternatively, what are some of the tactics used to get closure (pages 155–80)?

(m) Bring in a set of procedural and/or substantive collective agreements of your organisation to the group you are studying with and make a presentation of the main content and features of these agreements.

(n) Read Burrows (1986: pages 72–92) and comment on the content and practicalities of the single-union deal signed by Nissan (UK) and the AEU.

(o) Read Industrial Relations Services Employment Trends No. 505 (Industrial Relations Review and Report, February 1992: pages 11–15). Analyse and report on the flexibility package concluded at Rolls Royce Motor Cars.

References

ADNETT, J. 1989. *Labour Market Policy*. London: Longman.

ADVISORY CONCILIATION AND ARBITRATION SERVICE 1983. *Collective Bargaining in Britain: its Extent and Scope*. London: ACAS.

ATKINSON, G. 1980. *The Effective Negotiator*. Newbury: Negotiating Systems Publications.

BRANDEIS, L. 1934. *The Curse of Bigness*. Quoted in CHAMBERLAIN, N. and KUHN, J. 1965. *Collective Bargaining*. NY: McGraw-Hill.

British Leyland UK Ltd v. *McQuilken* [1978] IRLR 245.

BURROWS, G. 1986. *No-Strike Agreements and Pendulum Arbitration*. London: IPM.

CHAMBERLAIN, N. and KUHN, J. 1965. *Collective Bargaining*. NY: McGraw-Hill.

CONFEDERATION OF BRITISH INDUSTRY 1988. *The Structure and Processes of Pay Determination in the Private Sector: 1979–1986*. London: CBI.

DANIEL, W. 1987. *Workplace Industrial Relations and Technical Change*. London: Pinter.

DOERINGER, P. 1986. 'Internal labor markets and non-competing groups'. *American Economic Review*. 76(2).

DOERINGER, P. and PIORE, M. 1971. *Internal Labor Markets and Manpower Analysis*. Massachusetts: Lexington.

DUBIN, R. 1954. 'Constructive aspects of industrial conflict'. In KORNHAUSER, A., DUBIN, R. and ROSS, A. (eds) 1954. *Industrial Conflict*. NY: McGraw-Hill.

DUNLOP, J. 1950. *Wage Determination under Collective Bargaining*. NY: Macmillan.

DUNLOP, J. 1984. *Dispute Resolution*. London: Auburn.

DUNN, S. and GENNARD, J. 1984. *The Closed Shop in British Industry*. London: Macmillan.

FARNHAM, D. and PIMLOTT, J. 1990. *Understanding Industrial Relations*. London: Cassell.

FLANDERS, A. 1968. 'Collective bargaining: a theoretical analysis'. In FLANDERS, A. 1970. *Management and Unions*. London: Faber and Faber.

FLANDERS, A. (ed.) 1969. *Collective Bargaining: Selected Readings*. London: Penguin.

Ford Motor Co. v. *AUEF and TGWU* [1969] 2 QB 303.

FOX, A. and FLANDERS, A. 1969. 'Collective bargaining: from Donovan to Durkheim'. In FLANDERS, A. 1970. *Management and Unions*. London: Faber and Faber.

HICKS, J. 1932. *Theory of Wages*. NY: Macmillan.

HOXIE, R. 1921. *Trade Unionism in the United States*. NY: Appleton.

HYMAN, R. 1975. *Industrial Relations*. London: Macmillan.

INDUSTRIAL RELATIONS REVIEW AND REPORT 1992. *Industrial Relations Services Employment Trends*. 505, February.

INDUSTRIAL RELATIONS REVIEW AND REPORT 1992. *Industrial Relations Services Employment Trends*. 512, May.

INTERNATIONAL LABOUR OFFICE 1986. *Collective Bargaining*. Geneva: ILO.

KAHN-FREUND, O. 1954. 'Intergroup conflicts and their settlement'. *British Journal of Sociology*. 5(3).

KINNIE, N. 1987. 'Bargaining within the enterprise: centralized or decentralized?' *Journal of Management Studies*. 214(5).

LEVINSON, H. 1966. *Wage Determination under Collective Bargaining*. NY: Wiley.

MARGINSON, P. 1986. 'How centralized is the management of industrial relations?' *Personnel Management*. October.

MILLWARD, N., STEVENS, M., SMART, D. and HAWES, A. 1992. *Workplace Industrial Relations in Transition*. Aldershot: Dartmouth.

PALMER, S. 1990. *Determining Pay: A Guide to the Issues*. London: IPM.

PEN, J. 1952. 'A general theory of bargaining'. *American Economic Review*. 42.

PHELPS BROWN, H. 1966. 'The influence of trade unions and collective bargaining on pay levels and real wages'. In MCCARTHY, W. 1987. *Trade Unions: Selected Readings*. London: Penguin.

PURCELL, J. 1989. 'How to manage decentralized bargaining'. *Personnel Management*. May.

SCHELLING, T. 1963. *The Strategy of Conflict*. London: University Press.

STEVENS, C. 1963. *Strategy and Collective Bargaining Negotiation*. NY: McGraw-Hill.

TOWERS, B. 1992. *Issues in People Management No. 2: Choosing Bargaining Levels – UK Experience and Implications*. London: IPM.

Trade Union and Labour Relations (Consolidation) Act 1992.

WALTON, R. and MCKERSIE, R. 1965. *A Behavioral Theory of Labor Negotiations*. NY: McGraw-Hill.

WEBB, S. and WEBB, B. 1913. *Industrial Democracy*. NY: Longman.

WEEKES, B., MELLISH, M., DICKENS, L. and LLOYD, J. 1975. *Industrial Relations and the Limits of the Law*. Oxford : Blackwell.

WINTERTON, J. and R. 1985. *New Technology: the Bargaining Issues*. Nottingham: Universities of Leeds and Nottingham in association with the IPM.

Chapter 10

Employee Involvement, Consultation and Participation

Collective bargaining, as an employee relations strategy, is based on a policy of union incorporation in employment decision-making with employers (see Chapters 2, 3, 9). It is a joint approach to employee relations and depends on employees being organised into independent trade unions, the unions being recognised by the employer for negotiating purposes and a fair balance of power existing between the two sides in the bargaining relationship. Employee involvement practices, in contrast, which have grown in importance and scope in recent years (Millward *et al*. 1992), are not generally based on trade union organisation. They tend to be employer driven and unitary in their employee relations emphases. They are normally task or job centred, aimed at individual employees and based on a management policy of employee commitment. Joint consultation, in turn, although collectively based, is also unitary, integrative and managerialist in its focus. A number of attempts and experiments in worker participation, involving employee representatives in strategic decision-taking with senior management at corporate level, were made in the public sector in Britain during the late 1970s, with varying degrees of success (Ferner 1988). Unlike in Western Europe, where employees often have legal rights to representation on company boards, such as in Denmark, Germany and the Netherlands, and in works councils or works committees (Incomes Data Services 1991), there is no statutory, or even voluntary, provision for worker participation in management in Britain. Indeed, worker participation remains a controversial and contentious issue amongst companies, employers and managers in Britain.

Employee involvement practices

Companies in Britain with over 250 employees are required to state in their annual reports, as a result of the Employment Act 1982, what action they have taken to promote 'employee involvement' practices within their organisations. They have to describe what steps they have taken to introduce, maintain or develop employee involvement arrangements in the following areas:

- information and communication between management and employees;
- economic awareness of their businesses;
- financial participation by employees in the companies employing them;
- consultative arrangements.

Information and communication systems are the means by which employers provide systematic information on matters of concern to employees. Economic awareness schemes are aimed at achieving a common understanding by employees of the economic and financial factors affecting the performance of the company employing them. Financial participation is aimed at encouraging the involvement of employees in their company's financial performance, through employee share schemes or other means. Consultation, in the sense that it is used here, normally refers to 'informal consultative arrangements'. These are the processes through which employers provide regular channels of communication, between management and individuals or with small groups of employees, so that the views of employees can be taken into account by management when it takes decisions likely to affect employee interests at work.

Employee commitment

Employee commitment is at the heart of employee involvement programmes. Although 'commitment' and 'involvement' are different concepts, they are closely linked, since both are concerned with how employers can encourage employees to identify with a company's business interests through a variety of communication processes, employee relations activities and corporate policies. Employee commitment, in outline, is the extent to which employees identify with the organisation's work ethic, cooperate with its goals and objectives and contribute to corporate performance. Employee involvement, in contrast, is the term normally used to denote the processes set up within an organisation to enable its employees to become involved in decisions largely affecting the ways in which their work is done.

The argument, from the employer's point of view, for trying to win a high level of employee commitment to work, jobs and the company, in contrast with merely seeking instrumental compliance by employees to management decisions, is based on a number of assumptions. These include the claims that employees who are committed:

- devote their energies to working for the employer rather than for their own private interests;
- favour the company in which they are employed rather than other companies;
- give additional time and effort to the company when this is needed;
- give priority to corporate values and employer interests when these seem to be in conflict with those of external bodies such as trade unions or professional associations.

The degree to which employees are committed to their work, job and employer can be inferred from their feelings, attitudes, behaviour and actions whilst at work. According to White (1987), employee commitment denotes three kinds of feelings or behaviour relating to the company in which an individual is employed. First, employees believe in and accept the goals, values and ethos of their employer. Second, employees are willing to work beyond what is normally expected under their contracts of employment: there is an extended 'psychological contract' between employer and employee. Third, there is a desire by employees to maintain membership of the organisation, rather than to leave it. Further, because commitment is voluntary and personal, it cannot be imposed by management, it cannot be initiated by others but it can be withdrawn by those offering it, if they decide to do so.

A number of factors appears to influence employee commitment. These include:

- gender and marital status;
- education and length of service;
- personality;
- individual needs;
- the dominant societal culture.

It also seems that underlying employer attempts at increasing employee commitment is the assumption that it improves organisational performance. Employee commitment is claimed to relate to corporate performance in three ways (White 1987: page 13). These are:

First, strong *commitment to work in general* is likely to result in conscientious and self-directed application to work, regular attendance, minimal disciplinary supervision, and a high level of effort.

Second, . . . *strong commitment to a specific job* will also result in a high level of effort insofar as good performance is related to self-esteem, including ambition and career plans . . .

Third, *commitment to the organisation* . . . includes the intention to stay, and is associated with turnover. As might be expected, commitment normally also becomes weaker as the event of leaving draws nearer. It is difficult to assess which is cause and which the effect but there is a definite link between a fall in expressed commitment and turnover. This, of course, adds to the costs of production when it necessitates recruitment, training and supervision.

The concept of employee commitment is clearly a complex one and is associated with several objectives, but the commitment of employees at work certainly affects a variety of organisational variables. These include: absenteeism, turnover, effort and the quality of performance within organisations. It therefore has a number of implications for personnel and corporate policies. These include:

- generating early commitment amongst new employees;
- designing strategies for improving commitment;
- maintaining the reciprocity between the rewards received and the contribution being made by employees;
- reducing turnover by increasing commitment;
- developing participative strategies for introducing new technology;
- implementing appropriate personnel policies, sometimes in association with employee representatives.

Employee involvement

The term 'employee involvement' first began to appear in management literature in the late 1970s. After its National Conference in 1978, the CBI published its first set of guidelines on employee involvement (CBI 1979). These were aimed at promoting the voluntary development of employee involvement practices within companies. What the CBI was talking about, at that time, was an open style of management, operated by managers with the necessary skills, self-confidence and 'pride in their jobs', so as to facilitate appropriate communication and consultation arrangements with employees. This approach, it was believed, would help managers achieve the consent which they needed to put their decisions into action. It would also, it was anticipated, bring about 'collaboration and involvement in the common purpose of the company and the mutual interest which all employees have in the success of the business' (CBI 1979: page 4).

The objectives of such a strategy were to achieve a more competitive and efficient British industry, through improved employer–employee relationships, by ensuring that decision-making took place with the understanding and acceptance of the employees concerned. 'In this way, companies can reduce conflict by fostering cooperation and making the most of the individual employee's contribution' (page 6). The CBI suggested that arrangements for involving employees could therefore be directed at:

- promoting understanding of their contribution to wealth creation in their companies;
- promoting employee involvement in job content and job purpose;
- ensuring employees were aware of the reasons for management decisions;
- ensuring employees were aware of the business situation of their enterprises;
- informing employees of their company's future objectives and plans.

The CBI went on to say that it was very easy 'to get hung up on words' (CBI 1979: page 3). However:

> We have decided to use the word 'involvement' in order to avoid the emotional and political overtones of other words. There has, however, been so much talk and political argument about 'industrial democracy', 'participation', 'consultation' and 'a participative style of management' that we are in danger of missing the woods for the trees.

The CBI's stance, it was claimed, was based on its long-standing policy that employee involvement was best developed voluntarily, not though legislation, and in accordance with the circumstances of the industry and the company concerned. There was no universal blueprint for employee involvement practices.

The CBI's current statement of principles on employee involvement builds on its earlier position and the recent experiences of its members.

It believes that employee involvement (CBI 1990: page 7):

- Is a range of processes designed to engage the support, understanding and optimum contribution of all employees in an organisation and their commitment to its objectives
- Assists an organisation to give the best possible service to customers and clients in the most cost effective way
- Entails providing employees with the opportunity to influence and where appropriate, take part in decision-making on matters which affect them
- Is an intrinsic part of good management practice and is therefore not confined to relationships with employee representatives
- Can only be developed voluntarily and in ways suited to the activities, structure, and history of an organisation.

The CBI goes on to argue that employee involvement promotes business success. It does this by: fostering trust and a shared commitment to an organisation's objectives; demonstrating respect for individual employees; and enabling employees to get maximum job satisfaction. There are a range of means for generating management-led employee involvement practices. These include: two-way communications between management and employees; regular consultation; devolving decision-making to the lowest possible levels; training in communication skills; financial participation; harmonising terms and conditions of employment; and seeking individual contributions aimed at 'continuous improvement' in the organisation.

Information and communication

Information provision involves any process used by management for communicating with employees on issues affecting the organisation and employee interests at work. The information provided may be passed on in writing, verbally or visually, with combinations of these methods normally being used. In ACAS's view (ACAS 1989), successful workplace communication enables organisations to function effectively and employees to be properly informed about corporate developments. Done effectively, it helps (page 4):

- employees perform better and become more committed to their company's success
- managers perform better and make better decisions

- create greater trust between managers, trade unions and employees
- reduce misunderstandings
- increase employees' job satisfaction.

Both the CBI (1977) and the IPM (1981) support the view that information provision should focus on the five 'Ps'. These are:

- progress;
- profitability;
- plans;
- policies;
- people.

Progress refers to information about the success of the organisation in achieving its corporate goals and targets. It covers three categories of information: markets; costs; and the working environment. The sort of information that can be provided by management in this area is outlined in Exhibit 35.

Exhibit 35: *Examples of information on company progress*

These include:

- Markets
  - sales
  - market share
  - trading position
  - state of the order book
  - contracts gained or lost

- Costs
  - return on capital
  - labour costs per unit of output
  - inflation
  - raw material and input prices
  - productivity
  - quality
  - waste measures
  - number of employees

- Working environment
  - accident and safety records

The importance of profitability to a company can be demonstrated by providing relevant financial information to its employees. This often incorporates the company balance sheet, statements of income and expenditure and more specific information relating to 'value added', how the company is financed and how its income is spent. This information needs, as far as possible, to be free from accounting jargon and to encourage greater awareness by employees of the sources of corporate income, investment and expenditure and their impact on business activity and the firm's future prospects.

As far as company plans are concerned, employees are normally most interested in the ones affecting them directly, particularly those relating to expansions, closures, relocations and reorganisations. The information provided here normally includes details on:

- investment;
- relocations and reorganisations;
- amalgamations and redeployments;
- expansion;
- training;
- human resources issues.

A company's policies, especially on human resourcing, employee relations and training, need to be explained to all employees, along with the reasons for them. These cover areas such as pay, conditions, holidays, sickness benefits, pensions and employee relations procedures. As these policies are updated, they can be disseminated to employees so that they are kept continuously informed on all matters affecting their job and employment interests.

Information about people covers such matters as:

- appointments;
- resignations;
- retirements;
- promotions;
- vacancies;
- awards.

Other more personal information relating to births, deaths and marriages and to sporting and social events is also sometimes communicated to employees. This is done to facilitate employee awareness of

what is happening amongst colleagues and to encourage group maintenance at the workplace.

Communicating in writing

There is a wide variety of methods by which management can provide
written information to employees. The following forms of written communication are the ones most commonly used by managements in
organisations.

Notice boards

These are a cheap and easy way of getting instant, current messages
across to employees. They can provide information clearly, accurately
and positively, although if the notice board is in a bad position, no one
may read the notices provided. Notice boards may also get cluttered,
information may get lost and it may be presented in an unattractive and
unimaginative way. On the other hand, information may be read by one
individual and passed on to others verbally.

Letters to employees

These are useful for presenting information on a single, important
topic. They can be sent to an employee's home, put in pay packets or
circulated internally. Internal memos are a variant of these but they
focus on specific issues so that they are not confused with management
directives or employer instructions.

Bulletins and briefing notes

These are used to update employees, especially middle and junior managers, on important matters. They need to be up to date and well
informed, taking account of the latest information and details available
from senior management.

Newsletters

Newsletters provide the lower tiers of formal written communications
in organisations and are useful means for enabling junior managers to
inform their staff of issues relevant to them. They are most successful

where they are used as an informal adjunct to the 'company' newspaper or house journal. Means need to be provided for retrieving such information and updating it when necessary.

House journals

Well-produced house journals, steering a neutral course between employer and employee interests, can provide a useful, regular communication medium within organisations. Unfortunately, they are expensive to produce and distribute, they need professional journalistic direction and their content can be so bland that they fail to attract the interest of their potential readership. A well-designed, well-edited and well-produced house journal, however, can be a very effective means for enabling management to provide employees with relevant organisational information and for employees to have their say about in-house matters which concern them.

Employee handbooks

These are an important and often neglected source of one-off communication from management to employees. And through continuous updating, they allow a lot of basic information to be provided to employees over time. The sorts of information covered include:

- the history and background of the organisation;
- its products or services;
- its objectives, structures and methods of operating;
- the main employment conditions and benefits to employees;
- the principal rules of the organisation.

Employee reports

It is increasingly common for larger companies to provide an annual report to all their employees. The annual report is an ideal place for bringing together all the information provided to employees over the year, in an up-to-date form. It normally includes financial information, general information about sales, investment and employment, future trends and other relevant indicators of 'corporate health and wealth'. Annual employee reports need to be attractively presented, free from jargon and readable. In this way, employees are more likely to become aware of how they contribute to organisational performance and effectiveness. They are better able to understand the company's sources of income, investment and expenditure. And, with information presented to employees in a systematic, fair and easily understood manner, greater trust can be engendered between management and its workforce.

Communicating interactively

There are a number of options available to management for communicating verbally with employees. These 'interactive' methods normally enable two-way communication to take place between management and employees. The method used depends on the size of the group being communicated with, what is being communicated and to whom it is being communicated. Used effectively, they enable genuine feedback to be generated between management and workforce and trust and openness to be reinforced between them.

Meetings

These include departmental meetings and mass meetings. The departmental meeting represents a step towards the briefing group system, which is examined below. Departmental meetings represent the bottom end of the communication chain and they are the basic means of enabling departmental managers to pass on information to staff from higher management, as well as of taking up points and issues raised by members of their own departments. Such meetings are often fairly informal, although they are likely to have pre-circulated agendas and agreed rules for conducting business. They also tend to be held fairly frequently and therefore may provide a useful forum for enabling departmental heads to meet staff regularly and for staff to put their points of view to management, and the issues of immediate concern to them, as they arise.

Mass meetings are more formal, set-piece occasions. They enable members of senior management to address all staff at a given location, on specific issues. They are not normally held very frequently and the opportunity for interaction between management and employees is more limited than for departmental meetings. However, with skilful use of 'question and answer' sessions, exchanges can take place and the usefulness of the meetings can become enhanced as a result of this. Because of their size, however, such meetings require professional planning if they are to be successful. Speakers need to be sufficiently briefed, well prepared and clearly structured in their presentations, using appropriate visual aids and learning technologies to get their messages across.

Briefing or discussion groups

These have been popularised by a number of organisations and management interest groups, especially the Industrial Society, since the 1970s (Garnett 1980). In essence, a briefing group system seeks to bring down the levels of verbal communication, between management and workforce, below those of departmental or unit meetings, into workgroups. There are a variety of types of briefing groups but a 'briefing group system' is defined by the Industrial Society (1970) as:

> A group which is called together regularly and consistently in order that the decisions, policies and the reasons for them, both at company and departmental levels, may be explained to other people. Those briefed communicate in turn to their own briefing group so that information is systematically passed down the management line, in a number of interlocking steps . . . The objective of a briefing group system is to convey understanding of a communication to every employee through face to face contact with his/her supervisor.

The benefits claimed of briefing groups are that they enable supervisors to take on the role of workgroup communicators. They also provide for face-to-face communication amongst people who know each other well. They are likely, therefore, to be informal and to allow genuine two-way communication to take place within them.

The size of briefing groups varies from about 4 to 18 members who meet for up to half an hour monthly or bi-monthly, under the leadership of their supervisor. Typically, these groups focus on the five 'Ps', outlined above. The two most important elements in creating and sustaining effective briefing group systems are the commitment of senior management and the training of group leaders. Supervisors, in particular, have to be made aware that operating the briefing group system is part of their job, and not an optional extra to be ignored during periods of pressure. Equally, every effort needs to be made to ensure that briefing group leaders receive appropriate training in running their groups, and in understanding the aims and objectives of the system, so that the groups can operate effectively.

Conferences and seminars

These are meetings of selected or specified employees who come together to study, discuss and examine a particular problem. Emphasis is placed on questioning and group discussion. For example, when major organisational changes are envisaged, full-day conferences or seminars are a useful means of creating communication channels between senior management and those likely to be affected by the changes. Conferences and seminars can be in-house or off-premises, with the latter being particularly useful where management wants to encourage an informal atmosphere. For successful results and outcomes, conferences and seminars need to be organised in accordance with a number of accepted guidelines. These include:

- the meeting should be of manageable size to ensure informality and the flow of ideas;
- it should last at least one day;
- management presentations should be short, snappy and to the point;
- delegates should be encouraged to ask questions, put their views and work collaboratively;
- all ideas provided should be followed up, analysed and acted upon.

Quality circles

A quality circle is a group of people within an organisation who meet together on a regular basis to identify, analyse and solve problems on quality, productivity or other aspects of daily working life, using problem-solving techniques. Membership of such groups, which usually have 4 to 12 members, is normally voluntary and members are commonly from the same work area or do similar job tasks and activities. The reasons for introducing quality circles into organisations are to develop employees, to facilitate communications, to improve quality, to increase competitiveness and to make cost savings. Having met together, quality circles then present solutions to management and are usually involved in implementing and monitoring them.

Where quality circles are used effectively, it has been shown that they develop individuals, provide personal progression for circle members, improve managerial leadership, promote teamwork and contribute to quality improvements (Russell and Dale 1989). Appropriate attitudes, skills and behaviour by managers are essential, if quality circles are to succeed, grow and develop. Top management commitment is crucial for the effectiveness of quality circles. This means management willingness to listen and respond positively to quality circle presentations, to implement their outcomes and to monitor implementation. Middle and supervisory managers, however, can be obstacles to the success of quality circles, where they fear loss of managerial control. One way in which this problem is addressed is by creating such things as quality circle leaders, facilitators and steering groups. But it is also sometimes necessary to establish a 'parallel' organisational structure, one concerned with production and the other with change. In other words, quality circles can exist as parallel structures in organisations, in tandem with the operating hierarchy, and be mainly concerned with facilitating change.

Apart from some misgivings about the members of quality circles being selected rather than elected, many trade unionists are not opposed to quality circles in principle. Their main concern is that quality circles may be manipulated by some managements to undermine the role of trade union representatives in the workplace and they therefore could lead to a weakening of the union function and even to union derecognition. Yet some quality circles have workplace representatives as their leaders, whilst one piece of research contends that most of the issues dealt with by quality circles have few employee relations implications (Bradley and Hill 1987). Another approach used to mitigate trade union anxieties about quality circles is the creation of a joint management–union steering group at the outset. By involving both parties from the beginning, the initiators of quality circles can be clear about the intentions, objectives and expectations of quality circles from the start. They are then better able to create the conditions conducive to trust and openness amongst management, workers and union representatives.

Health and safety committees

Joint management–worker or management–union health and safety committees provide useful, interactive channels for information and communication between employers and employees at workplace level. Improving health and safety in the workplace is an integrative activity in which both employers and employees have a common concern. Unhealthy working conditions and accidents at work cause considerable hardship to individuals, create additional expense for organisations and damage the reputations of employers. Positive health and safety measures, to which all employees can contribute, are a vital part of management's responsibility. Joint committees on health and safety are a valuable medium for management–worker dialogue and can ensure that the highest standards of health and safety are established and maintained within the enterprise. Effective joint committees can help to produce healthy and safe working environments by:

- ensuring that there are regular inspections in the workplace;
- monitoring health and safety records;
- analysing records and statistics;
- making sure that appropriate training takes place;
- keeping in touch with new developments;
- seeing that legislation is implemented;
- stimulating health and safety awareness;
- providing specialist advice within the workplace.

Where they are active and properly constituted bodies, joint health and safety committees benefit the employer, employees and, where they are recognised, the trade unions.

Attitude surveys

Structured, regular attitude surveys within organisations provide a systematic means for managements to investigate the opinions and views of employees on issues of specific relevance to both employer and workers and to get valuable feedback on them. Attitude surveys are undertaken for various reasons including:

- diagnosing organisational problems;
- assessing the effects of organisational change;
- measuring employee attitudes prior to and subsequent to a programme of change;
- providing feedback on management policies, actions and plans;
- identifying matters of collective concern to employees.

Suggestion schemes

These are used to encourage employees to put forward ideas about improving methods of working, cutting costs, increasing productivity or modifying any aspect of the work environment which might benefit the organisation and/or its workforce. Financial or other rewards are normally provided to individuals whose ideas are accepted and put into operation by the employer. Special forms or suggestion boxes are provided by the employer and publicity can be given through the house journal, posters and employee pay packets.

Training

Training is an important form of communication. It can help employees understand the information given to them and encourage them to play a fuller part in the ways an employer conducts its affairs. Training is needed because information about corporate performance or management activities sometimes involves specialist terminology and data that is difficult to interpret. Well-designed training courses are a useful way of giving employees factual information about their employment. Training events can provide explanations of what is happening in the organisation, and opportunities for questions to be put to management and answers to be given on issues raised by course members. Training in communication skills is also important for those who have to communicate. It can enable managers to:

- become more aware of the importance of effective workplace communications;
- understand their roles and responsibilities as communicators;
- improve their ability to communicate.

Such training is particularly important for supervisors who have a critical communication role but may have limited experience in doing it well.

Communicating visually

Some organisations have taken communications a step further by linking them to sophistication aids like films and videos. They have done this because:

- linking the spoken word with the visual gets messages across more effectively;
- it ensures consistency in the information that gets across;
- some employees prefer such an approach.

Films are useful for getting information over to large groups. Unfortunately, they are expensive and the medium is rather inflexible, because films soon get out of date and parts of them cannot be updated. Videos, on the other hand, are gaining in popularity. This is because of their advantages of providing 'in-house' productions, flexibility and relatively low cost. The ease of preparing videos allows them to be kept up to date, whilst the use of play-back facilities ensures that the message to be transmitted can be got across very effectively. Some organisations are using videos to enable their senior managers to give 'corporate updates' and top-level communications to staff, on periodic but regular bases.

Financial participation

Financial participation is a form of employee involvement which, like all other forms of employee involvement, is employer driven, unitary in its emphasis and normally centred on individuals. The approach is used by companies to encourage employees to identify more closely with their firm's aims and objectives and to promote the idea that their common interest lies in maximising corporate profits. It is hoped that employees will see the advantages of cooperation, flexibility and teamwork and the disutility of conflict and the pursuit of uncoordinated self-interest at work (Ridley 1992). The main types of financial participation schemes used by employers in Britain are profit-sharing, profit-related pay, employee share ownership and gainsharing, all of which, by definition, are limited to private sector businesses. This approach to seeking employee commitment has to some extent been encouraged by legislation since the early 1980s. This has arisen, in part at least, because, in the view of successive governments, financial participation breaks down the 'them and us' attitudes between management and employees in the private sector. As such, it is thought likely to bring about a greater identity of interest between the two parties at enterprise level.

Profit-sharing

It is a widespread view that there is an inexorable trend towards profit-sharing in Britain, the EC, Japan and the USA. Yet Japanese bonus payments – which are paid only in larger firms – vary very little over time and increase in line with earnings. In Germany, where almost all employees are covered by financial participation arrangements as a result of the Capital Formation Act, the legislation requires employers to make a fixed financial contribution to a form of savings for employees, chosen by them, but not necessarily in their own companies. Even in the USA, regarded by some as the home of profit-sharing, only some 16 per cent of full-time employees are covered by actual profit-sharing arrangements. The vast majority of schemes in the USA provide deferred payments which are usually invested on behalf of the employees in savings plans for their retirement (Incomes Data Services 1992).

'Pure' profit-sharing is paid to employees at management's discretion. It is the 'residue' profit allocated for payment to employees, after the company's obligations to its shareholders have been fulfilled. It is left entirely to management to decide:

- the proportion of total profit to be used for profit-sharing;
- the amount to be allocated to individual employees (and the rationale for this);
- the frequency of such bonus payments.

Profit-sharing, then, is a periodic bonus paid by an employer, out of corporate profits, which is added to the employee's basic pay. Experience suggests, however, that problems arise for management when they use periodic profit-sharing bonuses as a substitute for a competitive wage. Flanders and his colleagues (1968) found, for example, in their study of the John Lewis Partnership, that there was a much higher level of staff dissatisfaction with basic pay than with profit-sharing. In other words, profit-sharing is only likely to work where employees have reasonable pay levels, good conditions of employment and confidence in management's basic approach to employee relations. It is no remedy for bad employee relations.

A significant feature of profit-sharing is the way in which payouts average around 5 to 6 per cent of annual salary over time. According to Matthews (1989), where profit-sharing bonuses become too large or too small, they are often terminated by the company and their replacement schemes normally pitch their bonuses at around the 5 per cent level. Difficulties arise where, because of trading difficulties, bonuses fall to zero. Yet the durability of some schemes is surprising. This is normally where there is an ideological commitment to them by the management and owners, who continue to support the scheme, however poorly the company is performing financially.

To some extent, the introduction of profit-sharing is optimised when the market conditions facing companies are tight. Tying profit-sharing arrangements to the overall performance of the company or enterprise carries a strong message of collective responsibility for corporate efficiency during difficult times. There are clear advantages in introducing a scheme when initial costs are low, with the likelihood that payments will improve in the future. On the other hand, problems are created by continually rising payments, especially if the scheme is presented as an incentive. By the very nature of incentives, they fluctuate each year. But if profits are maintained at a constant level, or are on a rising curve, the expectation is that profit-sharing payments will remain as they are or will increase too.

Profit-related pay

There has been a growth in profit-related pay in recent years (Millward *et al.* 1992). The introduction of profit-related pay into the corporate sector was stimulated by the Finance Act 1987. After an initial surge, schemes tailed off, but interest in them revived after the Finance Act 1991. This Act doubled the tax relief on such schemes and model rules were published to help employers implement them. The sudden rush of schemes was also stimulated by the major accountancy firms that provided clients with formula-based schemes to avoid paying tax on elements of basic pay.

Part of government thinking about the introduction of profit-related pay is the assumption that financial participation by employees in the economic success of their firms encourages loyalty to their employer and support for the profit motive. But it is also linked with the aim of getting firms to substitute a variable profit bonus for basic pay. An implication of this is that paying flexible wages encourages firms to retain their employees in difficult economic times and to reward them when times are good.

Employee share ownership

There is also growing interest by both employers and government in employee share ownership (ESO). There are three main types of ESO:

- *Approved Deferred Share Trust (ADT) schemes.* In these, profits are put in a trust fund which acquires shares in the employing company for employees. These shares are then allotted to participating employees according to a set formula. Employees must retain the shares for a specified period to avoid tax liability.

- *Save as You Earn (SAYE) share option schemes.* These schemes are where employees can buy their employer's shares from the proceeds of a SAYE savings contract. Employees then accumulate savings over a five or seven year period and use them to purchase shares at a predetermined price. There is no liability to income tax, although capital gains is payable.

- *Discretionary or executive share option schemes.* These are, by definition, limited to company executives. They are used both to reward executive employees and to reinforce their loyalty to their company.

Other types of share ownership scheme are found in partly employee-owned firms like the National Freight Corporation (NFC). NFC, an internationally based company, was formed when the National Freight Consortium was privatised in the early 1980s. It was floated on the Stock Exchange in 1989 and more than 90 per cent of its employees are now shareholders, although they only own about 20 per cent of the company's equity. To protect the principles on which the company was established, employee shareholders have a double vote on all issues. This is provided that they collectively hold more than 10 per cent of the equity. The employee ownership philosophy of the company enables the NFC to use it as a marketing tool. Each individual employee is in contact with customers, which is a good sales pitch. In addition, employee ownership helps maintain a strong corporate identity which might otherwise be lost.

Gainsharing

The main distinguishing feature of gainsharing is that it is a group incentive payment linked to productivity, based on a formula which in turn is linked to past performance. Also, unlike some other financial participation schemes, it can involve trade unions in the way it operates. The thinking behind gainsharing is the desire of management to promote a team philosophy amongst employees by rewarding them collectively for improvements in performance. Gainsharing is most commonly found in the USA but a prominent example in Britain is at British Steel. This scheme was developed in the early 1980s and took the form of a quarterly pay bonus, based on the ratio of added value to employment costs, together with more sophisticated measures such as quality of output and delivery to time.

One of the most common gainsharing schemes is the Scanlon Plan. One version is based on the ratio of labour costs to total production value, with negotiators agreeing on a normal ratio so that any savings are distributed to employees on a monthly basis. Management's profit from the plan is derived from increased sales with no corresponding increases in costs. The plan allows for revisions to be made to the basic formula where there are changes in product prices or increases in basic pay. Schemes can also be revised where capital investment takes place which obviously raises productivity without additional employee effort.

Another approach is that of 'added value', a concept developed by A. W. Rucker, again in the USA. Added value is defined as the difference between sales revenue and the cost of goods and services bought in. It represents, in effect, the 'wealth' created by a company. Rucker showed that labour costs, expressed as a proportion of added value, remain stable over long periods. It can thus provide a measure of productivity. The weakness of the Rucker scheme – and of the Scanlon Plan – is that the ratios used may be affected by factors that have little to do with the productivity of employees. Technological changes, or changes in prices or product mix, may affect sales revenue without affecting wage costs.

Gainsharing appears to be a better motivator than profit-sharing – although they are not mutually exclusive. It is particularly attractive where labour costs are a high proportion of total costs. And gainsharing schemes can be geared to improvements in quality, delivery and the cost of waste. They are also more flexible than profit-sharing. On the other hand, gainsharing can inhibit change, its formulae can be difficult for employees to understand and such schemes require a lot of monitoring and communication on the part of management and supervisors. Gainsharing also assumes that employees actually influence performance measures, whereas in many organisations they do not.

Total quality management

Total quality management (TQM) has become a major issue for many companies in Britain in recent years. Yet the term is often used imprecisely, loosely and without defining what 'total quality' actually is. The 'management of quality' in Britain is not a new concept but, with the move away from the traditional role of quality inspection, there has been a tendency to label all approaches to quality management as total quality. This is inaccurate and fails to take account of the complex origins of TQM, the diversity of TQM practices and the links it has with employer attempts to obtain employee commitment and to structure employee involvement intiatives in organisations (Marchington *et al.* 1992).

Origins and variations

The origins of TQM can be traced back to the search by Japanese companies for quality improvements in the 1950s. By the 1960s, ideas on quality improvement combined the pioneering works of Deming (1986) and Juran (1989) with the concepts of statistical process control and teamwork. It was around this time that the first quality circles were introduced in Japan. Both Deming and Juran argued that quality control should be conducted as an integral part of management control, with 'continuous improvement' as the ultimate goal. In asserting that 'quality is free', Crosby (1978) argued that, in expressing their concerns with quality issues, managements are also dealing with people situations. His approach was closely linked with those of Deming and Juran but stated, in essence, that quality starts with sets of attitudes for which management has the major responsibility. But changing attitudes within organisations, at all levels, takes time and needs to be managed on a long-term, proactive basis. The development of quality control into total quality control (TQC) emerged from these debates, with TQC becoming known as TQM by the late 1980s.

TQM is distinguished from quality circles in a number of ways. According to Wilkinson and his colleagues (1992), quality circles have five main characteristics that contrast with TQM. They are voluntary groups, 'bolted on' to organisations, acting 'bottom-up' and operating at departmental or unit level. Their aim is to improve employee relations. TQM, on the other hand, is compulsory, an integrated quality system, 'top-down' and company-wide. Its underlying purpose is quality improvement. Nevertheless, TQM has implications for employee relations. Employees take greater responsibility for quality, are accountable for its achievement and work in teams. In addition, TQM is supposed to place greater emphasis on employee self-control, personal autonomy and individual creativity. The active cooperation of employees is expected, rather than just their compliance with management policy decisions and the employment contract. However, since TQM comprises both production and employee relations elements, it 'highlights tensions between, on the one hand, following clearly laid-down instructions whilst, on the other, encouraging employee influence over the management process' (Wilkinson *et al.* 1992: page 6).

The British Quality Association provides three definitions of TQM. The first focuses on its soft, qualitative characteristics: customer orientation, culture excellence, removal of performance barriers, training, competitive edge and employee participation. The second emphasises its hard, operations management aspects: systematically measuring and controlling work, setting performance standards and using statistical control procedures to assess quality. The third definition incorporates a mixture of hard and soft approaches to TQM and consists of three features: an obsession with quality, the need for a scientific approach to total quality and the view that all employees are part of the same team.

In Britain, TQM focuses on variants of the hard and mixed approaches. Oakland (1989), for example, views TQM as improving business effectiveness, flexibility and competitiveness and meeting customer requirements both inside and outside the organisation. He sees TQM as a triangle and a chain – indicating the interdependence of customer–supplier links throughout the organisation – with the three points of the triangle representing management commitment, statistical process control and teamworking. Dale and Plunkett (1990: page 6), whilst focusing on the statistical and operational characteristics of TQM, also link it with employee relations arguing that the 'key features of TQM are employee involvement and development and a teamwork approach to dealing with improvement activities.' Collard (1989) regards TQM as a management discipline aimed at preventing problems from occurring in organisations by creating attitudes and controls that make problem prevention possible. For him, improved quality need not lead to increased costs. Indeed, costs are likely to fall because of a decline in failure rates and reduced costs of detection.

The basic elements of TQM

A useful general definition of TQM is provided by the Institute of Management Services (1992: page 5). It emphasises that TQM is not simply a system for achieving zero defects in the products or services provided by a company but that it also involves people. In its view, TQM is:

> A strategy for improving business performance through the commitment and involvement of all employees to fully satisfying agreed customer requirements, at the optimum overall cost, through the continuous improvement of the products and services, business processes and people involved.

TQM, in short, is focused on achieving business success through satisfying customer needs. This is facilitated by involving every employee within the organisation in achieving this end and by expecting employees to see others, both internal and external to the organisation, as customers for their services.

There is no 'blue print' for developing, implementing and evaluating a TQM programme within an organisation. It is contingent upon organisational circumstances, management preferences and the resources available. However, a number of common elements can be identified by examining the literature on TQM. These are:

- the emphasis on continuous improvement;
- the need for commitment from top management;
- the issue of attitudinal change;
- the impact of TQM on the organisation as a whole.

There are also human resource implications arising from TQM, such as training, development and the creation of appropriate organisational structures. These are examined in the next section.

Since the focus of TQM is continuous improvement aimed at satisfying customer needs and providing value for money, at optimum cost to the organisation, this requires that everyone in an organisation that has introduced TQM should become involved. This includes:

- using a defined process of delivering quality;
- continuously identifying opportunities for improvement;
- delivering improvement through structured problem-solving techniques.

People also have to use error prevention mechanisms, practise corrective feedback mechanisms and apply key business processes, across the whole organisation, rather than within individual functions alone. The idea of continuous improvement means that people have to understand and identify any quality problems early on, at all levels in the organisation, and accept their responsibility for doing this. Continuous improvement is based on continuous measurement and evaluation, with this taking place both within the organisation and externally with clients or customers.

For TQM to be successful, its proponents argue that it needs effective leadership and long-term commitment by management – with managers acting as role models, leading and empowering change within their organisations. This needs to be supported by a culture of 'learning together', with guidance and support for the learning process being provided by management. TQM also incorporates clearly defined business objectives, communicated by managers and understood and owned by all employees. It is also management's task to encourage and empower every employee to adopt appropriate ownership behaviour (Hakes 1991). This includes ownership of outputs, customer problems and improvement actions. Most importantly, TQM focuses on success through people. This involves invoking solutions by consensus, providing education and training opportunities based on user needs, and facilitating teamwork and effective intra-organisational communications.

This means that top management has a major responsibility to continuously reinforce a TQM programme through its example as a group. Whether in meetings, newsletters or in-house journals, management has to demonstrate its complete commitment to total quality. In this sense, some writers assert that changing management attitudes is the key to developing successful TQM and that this must start at the very top of an organisation. To show this commitment, it is argued, top management should make sure that everybody, from top to bottom in the enterprise, is clear about its long-term goals and objectives. This affects styles of management, communication systems and the way things are done within the organisation.

The issue of attitude change is critical in introducing, maintaining and implementing TQM programmes. Because of the consequences of TQM, it requires a complete change of attitudes, expectations and the prevailing culture in an organisation. These consequences may include: reductions in staffing, for example amongst inspectors and those administering complaints procedures; lack of staff knowledge of the techniques used in TQM, such as new statistical and control techniques; and anxieties about the implications of change. TQM also involves more participative management styles, with middle management having less control over the supervisory and quality processes. Further, changes in management style, with greater devolution of management responsibilities, are often seen as a threat by middle managers. The need for attitude change is not confined to managers, however – it is required of all the workforce but it particularly applies to management.

As an organisationally based process, TQM focuses on the best use of resources for the total organisation, organisational flexibility and responsiveness to change. It is also concerned with customer/supplier relationships which embrace not only external and internal customers but also external and internal suppliers. It is concerned, in short, with all those people who are bound together in long-term business relationships inside and outside the organisation. Other aspects of the TQM process include: measuring peformance in terms of agreed customer requirements, customer satisfaction and process efficiency; anticipating customer needs; and delivering products and services which 'delight' customers. This requires identifying and adopting best working practices, as well as monitoring continuous improvement.

Some human resource implications

There are three main sets of human resource implications arising from the introduction of a TQM programme. These comprise:

- the need for management leadership to facilitate employee motivation;
- training and development implications;
- the creation of an appropriate organisational structure to facilitate TQM.

A major feature of introducing TQM into any organisation is often the need to change corporate culture into one that is more people-oriented. This entails leadership at all levels, opportunities for employee empowerment and the development of relevant skills within the workforce. Managers act as motivators, stimulating employees to accept responsibility for satisfying the agreed needs of their customers, whilst also encouraging employees to become committed to total quality. Meetings need to run effectively, team-building skills need to be facilitated and communication skills need to be developed. Another aspect of motivation is providing recognition, rewards and performance feedback to the employees concerned.

Training for TQM aims to develop self-motivated, self-reliant employees and enable them to achieve both their personal goals and those of the organisation, whilst satisfying the requirements of their customers. It commonly focuses on:

- the top–down cascading of ideas and information;
- workgroup training, with managers leading the training of their teams;
- relating the training content to the team's actual work.

The content of TQM training includes quality delivery, quality improvement and quality management. There is also the need to develop interpersonal skills amongst people within the workplace, such as team-building, motivating, leadership and communicating skills.

Collard (1989) is both descriptive and prescriptive about the training needs arising from TQM. He claims that a total quality training programme combines three elements:

- management skills training;
- training in quality management techniques, such as in the use of appropriate statistical techniques;
- corporate culture development.

He also identifies four levels of training for: top management; middle management; task group leaders; and facilitators. The development of group leadership, group working and communication and presentation skills for managers, for example, is seen as being particularly important. These include competency in: chairing meetings; developing the skills of group members; and developing appropriate leadership styles. Other behavioural skills that need to be developed include: problem-solving techniques; presentation techniques; and brainstorming. In Collard's view, organisations need to develop company-specific training programmes, not off-the-shelf packages. These should incorporate the concept of continuous development, with total quality training 'occurring regularly for all levels, not just at the beginning of the programme. The training should seek to extend and develop understanding of the basic techniques' (page 138).

Developing an appropriate organisational structure and a quality function includes a number of measures, such as:

- providing a quality support organisation to help management develop a strategy to implement the total quality process;
- coordinating the application of quality management;
- tracking the cost of quality.

It is also necessary to coordinate quality management systems and integrate health, safety and customer considerations into products, services and business processes. This is important in order to ensure effective communication structures and to facilitate employee involvement and cooperation in each case.

Joint consultation

Joint consultation is a complex process. It has a long history which can be traced back at least to the recommendations of the Whitley Committee in 1917–18. Its influence as an employee relations process has fluctuated widely however: decline in the interwar years; resurgence during the second world war; decline again during the 1950s and 1960s; further resurgence in the 1970s and early 1980s; and renewed decline in the late 1980s and early 1990s (Millward and Stevens 1986; Millward *et al.* 1992). As Hibbett (1991: page 664) comments: 'consultation based on formal committee structures appears to have reduced somewhat . . . In recent years companies appear to have concentrated on expanding employee involvement arrangements other than formal consultation', with employees being consulted individually or in small groups. Whatever its history and present importance, however, there are four different models of joint consultation (see also Chapter 3):

- the non-union model;
- the marginal model;
- the competitive model;
- the adjunct model.

These models need to be borne in mind, if the structures and content of joint consultation are to be understood and evaluated.

Factors influencing joint consultation

Marchington (1989) identifies four main factors influencing the development of joint consultative machinery within organisations. These are:

- management philosophy;
- union organisation and worker resistance;
- trust and cooperative relations;
- the external environment.

Most joint consultative arrangements are initiated by management, therefore the model of consultation that is adopted within an organisation reflects the management's dominant employee relations philosophy and its basic intentions in managing people. Management's underlying purpose in supporting the non-union, marginal and competitive models of joint consultation, for example, is to weaken trade unions and to maintain power by opposing or even confronting the unions. In contrast, in adopting the adjunct model of joint consultation, management does so with the expectation that this will result in cooperation with the unions and their incorporation in the employee relations process, rather than in conflict and discord with them.

Related to this is the strength of union organisation and the willingness of workers to resist management plans for setting up and running joint consultative arrangements on management's terms alone. Again the non-union, marginal and competitive models are more likely to be established where unionism is weak or where worker organisation is channelled into staff associations, 'house' unions or company-based 'works councils'. Where joint consultation is used to undermine trade unionism or to bypass it, unless this is resisted by the unions and their members, union representatives are in effect marginalised or excluded from the consultative process. As Cressey and MacInnes (1984) point out, with the power balance favouring managements, it is management that determines what items to take to joint consultative committees, the form of discussion within them and the outcomes arising from them.

In adjunct joint consultation, union representatives are more likely to have joint ownership of the consultative machinery and the right to refer issues to the negotiating machinery. This increases their commitment to the consultative process. Moreover, as Marchington and Armstrong (1983) indicate, where shop stewards are well organised, they value joint consultation. But where they are poorly organised, they are generally neutral or negative about it.

It is also argued that high trust between management and union representatives is an important ingredient in 'good industrial relations' (Purcell 1981). High trust is more likely to be part of adjunct joint consultation than it is in other consultative arrangements. However, high trust, where it exists, is more common in soft product market conditions than in hard ones. As Marchington (1989: page 397) concludes: 'If employers are attempting to prevent or marginalise unions, a tight economic climate makes consultation less necessary since the unions are further weakened, and the time for involvement is less available.' Conversely, where the adjunct model is adopted, economic recession might well induce both sides to continue maintaining good working relationships together, within both the consultative and the negotiating machinery. This is likely to ensure that high trust is sustained between the parties, even in difficult external circumstances.

Finally, the level of decision-making within an organisation also has an impact on the efficacy of joint consultation. Where management decision-making is largely centralised, this is unlikely to give much authority to local consultative committees. This fits the marginal or competitive models of joint consultation. In contrast, where management decision-making is devolved, or at different levels within an organisation, this is more likely to provide the consultative process with added authority. This fits the adjunct model of joint consultation, especially where the consultative machinery is linked hierarchically throughout the organisation.

Constitutional arrangements

The constitutional arrangements for setting up and operating joint consultative committees (JCCs) vary widely. Where joint consultation is entirely management driven, such as in the non-union, marginal and competitive models, the constitutional arrangements for JCCs are obviously determined by management decision alone. It is management that decides the terms of reference, membership, structures, frequency of meetings and the agenda of such committees. The underlying purpose of such committees is to keep them firmly under management control, either by excluding the union presence (the non-union model) or by weakening union influence (the competitive and marginal models). The terms of reference of these types of JCCs are normally unitary in purpose, whilst membership on the 'staff' side is usually drawn from employee representatives, rather than from union representatives. Sometimes these employee representatives are elected by their constituents, in other cases they are appointed by management. These JCCs are located largely at site level and rarely have links higher up the organisation. The frequency of meetings varies but is likely to lie within the range of monthly, quarterly or half-yearly meetings. The agenda of these sorts of JCCs is likely to be soft, with management using them largely as downward information-providing bodies, rather than as opportunities for asking employees about their views on workplace matters and listening to them before decisions.

Adjunct JCCs are formally constituted bodies, at site and/or corporate level, established through negotiations between management and union representatives. They are normally the result of formal joint consultation agreements. And it is the joint responsibility of both management and unions to ensure that the consultative arrangements, established within the procedure, comply with their terms of reference and the constitution embodied within the agreement.

Adjunct joint consultation

Joint consultation is at its most advanced when it is of the adjunct variety. The sorts of arrangements set out for adjunct JCCs are outlined below.

Aims

The underlying purpose of adjunct joint consultation is to establish arrangements that involve the signatory unions in the consultative process between management and the employees covered by the joint consultation agreement. In this sense, adjunct joint consultation is normally concerned with those matters of mutual concern to management and employees that are not covered by the negotiating procedures. Matters may be discussed within the consultative machinery, prior to negotiation, and be referred to the negotiating machinery subsequently. But adjunct joint consultation is a problem solving, two-way information exchange process between the parties rather than a bargaining or a 'top-down' process.

Adjunct joint consultation enables management, employees and the unions to consider and, as far as is practicable, to resolve the problems facing them. In this sense it may be considered as an integrative process. Joint consultation thereby increases the effectiveness of the organisation's operations to the mutual benefit of both the employer and its employees. JCC systems of this type are thus ways of improving staff morale, reducing tensions between management and employees, increasing job satisfaction and raising employee productivity.

Perkins (1986: page 44) sees the underpinning aims of effective joint consultation as being four-fold:

- Joint consultation ensures continuity of structure, enabling it to be used as a method of communication on all matters of concern to management and employees.
- Used correctly, it reinforces the trust and goodwill existing between management, employees and unions.
- It provides problem-solving procedures between management and employee representatives, although these are only meaningful if they precede final decisions.
- It allows employees to raise their own issues and grievances, to receive management's views and to instigate action where appropriate.

Effectively constituted and properly managed joint consultation, in short, enables employees, through their union representatives, to discuss and consider matters of mutual concern to them and management, thus allowing them to influence management proposals before final decisions are taken.

Functions

Exhibit 36: *The functions of JCCs*

These can include discussions on:

- productivity, efficiency and quality;
- safety at work;
- education and training;
- working conditions such as leave, holiday arrangements, working hours, absenteeism, meal breaks, transport and catering facilities;
- the health and welfare of employees;
- the welfare of retired employees;
- staffing levels;
- new equipment.

The primary function of local JCCs at plant, site or works level is to provide regular and recognised opportunities for the joint consideration, by management and employee representatives, of all issues affecting them which are not covered by joint negotiating machinery. They are also recognised channels of communication between the parties to any matter put on the JCC agenda by either management or employee representatives. Examples of the functions of JCCs are provided in Exhibit 36 but these are neither exclusive nor exhaustive, and some JCCs have narrower functions than those which are listed.

Membership, structure and rules

Adjunct JCCs are based on the principle that shop stewards or other trade union members represent employees within the consultative system. Such representatives, however, act on behalf of all their constituents, regardless of whether or not they are union members. The number of union representatives usually takes account of the number and types of employees working in the plant, site or workplace. Management representatives, in turn, are selected by senior management, again in accordance with the joint consultation agreement.

Many JCCs only operate locally, but in multi-plant or multi-site organisations arrangements are sometimes made to coordinate the consultative machinery throughout the organisation, by means of vertically linked consultative committees. JCCs at organisational level have union members drawn from locally based consultative committees. But these trade unionists are not usually elected directly by the employees within the plants. They are drawn from amongst the shop stewards on the lower-level committees. In some cases, full-time union officers take on the role of employee representatives at corporate level. Management representatives, as is normally the case, are appointed to such committees by senior management.

The rules of JCCs are found in the constitutions determined by the joint consultation agreement. Terms of reference, for example, are essential to establish what subjects are matters for consultation and what subjects are negotiable. Guidance is given on the objectives of the consultative procedure and the means by which these are to be affected. Examples of JCC rules are illustrated in Exhibit 37.

Exhibit 37: *Examples of JCC rules*

These include:

- title of the JCC;
- parties to the agreement;
- preamble;
- aims of the JCC;
- means of achieving the aims;
- functions;
- definitions;
- membership;
- retirement of members;
- casual members;
- substitutes;
- co-options;
- periods of office;
- secretariat;
- meetings;
- quorum;
- decisions and recommendations;
- agenda;
- minutes;
- variation or termination of the agreement.

The agenda is often the most important part of JCC meetings and its contents reflect whether or not the committee is really working. Agendas and other relevant papers must be circulated well in advance, except where meetings are held at short notice, if the JCC is to operate effectively. It is the nature of joint consultation meetings that agendas tend to reflect management topics, especially at local level, so every effort must be made to get employee representatives to submit their own items for discussion.

Resolving conflicts

It is normally the right of a signatory union, or of a group of signatory unions, or of management, to require a matter to be dealt with through the negotiating procedure, rather than the consultative machinery, where it thinks this is appropriate. Further, if a JCC fails to resolve any disagreement on a matter on which it is competent to take a decision, this matter is normally dealt with in the formal negotiating procedure. Finally, where a JCC exercises its advisory or consultative functions in ways likely to affect any other JCC within an organisation, it usually transmits its recommendation on that matter to the JCC concerned.

Worker participation

Throughout this book the emphasis has been on how the potential conflicts arising from the pay–work bargain are managed in an advanced capitalist economy like that of Britain. There are four policy choices available to managements in determining their employee relations strategies, including how work relations are structured, how work is organised and what emphasis they should adopt in managing people at work. These policy choices are (see also Chapter 2):

- worker subordination (effected through managerial prerogative);
- union incorporation (effected through collective bargaining and formal joint consultation);
- employee commitment (effected through employee involvement practices);
- worker participation (effected through worker directors, board level representation and enterprise committees).

These management policy thrusts are not necessarily mutually exclusive: they can operate in parallel within the same organisation, with different policies being used for different groups of employees. The traditional management policy in Britain for much of the nineteenth century was worker subordination. During the first three-quarters of the twentieth century, union incorporation became the dominant policy model, particularly when this was supported by the state during the years of the employee relations consensus (see Chapter 7). More recently, since the mid 1980s, with increasing product competition, rising unemployment and growing market deregulation, employee commitment has become a favoured policy choice for increasing numbers of employers. Worker participation, however, has not been either a management policy issue or a major political one in Britain since the late 1970s, when the report of the Bullock Committee of inquiry into industrial democracy was published (Department of Trade 1977). This is largely because of hostility to it by successive Conservative governments and the changed balance of power in the labour market and workplace favouring employers and management.

Approaches to worker participation

Worker participation is any employee relations process which enables employees to share in the making of enterprise or corporate decisions. In Britain, managements and management organisations generally argue that worker participation is best operated at the individual or small group level. This is most usefully done, it is contended, by providing opportunities for individuals and small groups to 'participate' in the ways their jobs are organised, in quality circles, in the ownership and profits of the company employing them, in TQM initiatives at departmental and corporate levels and in the communication, information and consultative channels of their employer. This type of 'worker participation', which is management defined and employer centred, can be best described as task and work-based participation, aimed at individual employees. It is low-level participation, soft on power and management driven, and is essentially a managerial definition of the term 'worker participation'.

In Britain, trade unions, in contrast, claim that the best method of advancing worker participation at work is collective bargaining. In this view, collective bargaining becomes less a method of sharing in the making of managerial decisions than a method of promoting 'industrial democracy' in the workplace and at employer level. Democracy, in essence, means providing the opportunity to influence the making of decisions by individuals and groups whose vital interests are affected by these decisions. The concept of industrial democracy, therefore, envisages employees having the right to exert influence over those decisions most affecting their daily working lives. These include the economic, social and personnel aspects of the workplace and of the enterprise employing them. Industrial democracy, it is argued, calls for real worker participation in the decision-making process, through the agency of trade unions. Conversely, it implies a sharing of the right to manage in those areas involving employee representatives. In this sense, industrial democracy is high level, power centred, and union and worker driven. It is for this reason that British employers are hostile to such a concept of 'worker participation in management' or what the unions describe as industrial democracy.

It is arguable, however, that industrial democracy goes beyond traditional collective bargaining. Collective bargaining is a power relationship and is a process of interest group representation in certain limited areas of personnel decision-making. It is an assertion of power, or of countervailing power, in a procedural framework negotiated between management and union representatives. The emphasis is on resolving conflicts of interest between the parties, with the outcomes of collective bargaining being determined by the relative balance of negotiating power between them. Collective bargaining only becomes industrial democracy where the negotiating agenda is widened beyond that of the pay–work bargain – the 'managerial concept' of collective bargaining (see Chapter 9) – and where an integrative or cooperative approach to the management–union relationship is adopted by both parties.

Marsden (1978) views industrial democracy as a contest over collective control within enterprises. It takes a variety of forms resulting from the struggle for control and from power shifts between the competing parties – employer and employees, and management and unions. The outcomes of this struggle depend on the level and scope of participation exercised and the ways in which effective worker participation is determined. In effect, worker participation can take place at enterprise or corporate level. But since participation at corporate level challenges the right to manage more than it does at enterprise or workgroup level, it is even more strongly resisted by management and management interest groups than at other levels.

There are two routes, in effect, through which industrial democracy/ worker participation can be advanced. One is by the 'bottom–up' process of local initiatives driven by workers and their trade unions. This aims to develop participative working relationships with employers and management. In Britain, the voluntary, bottom–up route, led by shop stewards, has been the preferred method for trade unions and their members. This strategy is likely to be successful in well-organised enterprises and industries, with strongly based trade unions, in conditions of full employment. It is less likely to achieve results where there are high unemployment, hostile employers and weak trade unions. Moreover, since the bottom–up model is based on adversarial employee relations, it is difficult to reconcile with the objective of creating consensus within the enterprise and integrative management–union relationships.

The other route to worker participation is the 'top–down' process of supportive public policy, with legal enactment or centrally determined 'framework' collective agreements between employer and trade union confederations. This, in contrast, has been the preferred approach in most of Western Europe since the end of the second world war. Works councils at plant level, co-determination at board level and other sets of participatory rights for workers have been the product of political struggle and political representation at government level. Unlike the bottom–up model, the top–down model is based on the idea of social partnership between employers and unions and management and workers. It is rooted in providing a set of legal rights and responsibilities for the parties to employee relations, based either on statute law or on legally enforceable collective contracts. This model of worker participation aims to create identity and harmony of interest between management and workers, in order to increase the enterprise's potential for wealth creation and to weaken the likelihood of industrial conflict. It also seeks to institutionalise cooperative and trusting working relations between employers and employees, at both the workplace and corporate level.

Participation in the workplace

Formal systems of worker participation in the workplace are at their most advanced in Western Europe. Most EC member states have some form of statutory provision or agreed systems for facilitating worker participation at workplace level. The precise mechanisms vary according to each country's legal framework for employee relations, the relative strengths of employers and unions, the coherence and unity of the trade union movement and the dominant culture of employee relations (Ferner and Hyman 1992). The Netherlands and Germany, for example, have highly legalistic systems, with extensive and detailed powers for worker representatives. In Denmark and Italy, by contrast, worker participation is built into central collective agreements. It is these which provide broadly defined obligations for employers and employees in determining their participation arrangements.

Legal systems

The most institutionalised system of worker participation at workplace level is provided in Germany. Here industrial democracy or worker participation is embodied in the concept of co-determination (see Chapter 3). This is based on the principle of co-decision-taking between management and elected worker representatives on a number of issues considered to be vital to each party. At the level of the workplace, this is done through the institution of 'works councils', although since the Works Constitution Act 1972, workers are represented not only at plant level but also at company level. The most important participation rights of German works councils are outlined in Figure 15. These cover a wide range of issues and give German workers some measure of joint control in areas affecting their conditions of employment, working practices and workplace organisation. Assessments of the effectiveness of German works councils vary. Berghahn and Karsten (1989) argue that works councils have strengthened the position of workers in the enterprise. Jacobi and his colleagues (1992: page 243), on the other hand, claim that: 'in general, works councils' participation rights are strong in relation to social policy; weaker in the case of personnel issues; and weaker still in financial and economic matters.'

Figure 15: *Main participation rights of German works councils*

Rights	Social matters	Personnel matters	Economic matters
Co-determination	working time holidays payment system piecework work organisation	staff files selection training	social plan
Veto		recruitment redeployment wage groupings dismissal	
Consultation and information	labour protection accidents	HR planning appeals	major plans new plant job content

In the Netherlands, the dominant form of worker representation at enterprise level is through the statutory system of works councils. These must be established by employers in any enterprise employing at least 100 employees or at least 35 employees working more than one-third of normal working hours. They are employee-constituted bodies, elected by all the employees within an enterprise who have at least six months' service. The size of the works councils varies according to the size of the enterprise and all employees can stand for election providing they have at least one year's service with the employer. Works councillors have protection against dismissal, time off with pay to attend works councils meetings and time off with pay for relevant training. But they are also bound by the requirements of confidentiality and must not disclose their employer's business or trading secrets, even when their periods of office as works councillors have finished (Incomes Data Services 1991).

Works councils in the Netherlands are obliged to meet with management at least six times a year. They have rights of information, consultation and veto. Employers, for example, are required to provide works councils with all the information reasonably required for them to carry out their tasks (Visser 1992). This information includes:

* the legal constitution of the employer;
* its annual accounts;
* reports on the general conduct of the business;
* at least once annually, a report on employment trends in the enterprise and its social policy.

The main issues on which employers are required to consult works councils are:

* transfers of control of the enterprise;
* acquisitions and joint ventures;
* closures or relocations;
* changes in the enterprise's activities;
* the recruitment of employees;
* the commissioning of expert advice by the employer.

The agreement of the works council is also required where the employer seeks to amend provisions relating to:

* hours and holidays;
* job evaluation schemes;
* pensions or profit-sharing;
* health and safety at work;
* grievance procedures;
* rules relating to recruitment, dismissal, promotion, training and appraisal.

Systems of statutory works councils are also established in other European states such as in Belgium, France, Greece, Portugal and Spain. They vary in their legal and constitutional details (Ferner and Hyman 1992) but they all basically provide sets of legal rights and duties for employers, works councils and elected employee representatives at enterprise level. In some cases, such as in Belgium and France, works councils are paralleled by other representative bodies at enterprise level. In Belgium and France, for example, in addition to statutory works councils there are 'trade union delegations', which are made up of elected trade union representatives and have collective bargaining functions. In Belgium, trade union delegations are not statutory bodies but are established by central collective agreements between employer and union confederations. In France, in contrast, trade union delegations are regulated by law, which provides their members with paid time off work to carry out their duties, with protections against dismissal – during their periods of office – and with consultative and negotiating rights.

In most cases, apart from those of the Netherlands, Italy and Portugal, there is also a statutory duty on employers to establish plant-based health and safety committees. These complement works councils and their main functions are to elect employee safety representatives and to ensure that issues relating to the health and safety of employees are discussed regularly with management. They are also legally required to oversee health and safety issues, improve working conditions and ensure that employers comply with relevant health and safety legislation.

Voluntary systems

In Denmark, employee representation at workplace level is based on a voluntary, corporatist approach and is largely through union-based shop stewards and 'cooperation committees', established through centralised, framework collective agreements. There is, for example, a long tradition of shop steward representation of employees in Denmark and agreed provisions for their election, status and role within the workplace. Central and industry-wide agreements define their functions, prescribe their activities and regulate their employee relations duties. In essence, shop stewards are direct links between management and employees on issues relating to workplace terms and conditions. They are also a focal point through which local grievances are articulated, channelled and resolved. In larger organisations, with many shop stewards, they establish joint union delegations and union 'clubs' incorporating several different unions. In acting within the authority of framework and national agreements, Danish shop stewards are expected to act with restraint and to help maintain good working relations and joint cooperation within the workplace between management and employees.

The principle of employee relations cooperation in Denmark is extended through the creation of cooperation committees at workplace level. Their aim is to promote industrial harmony, business competitiveness and employee job satisfaction in the workplace. The Cooperation Agreement, between the Danish Employers Confederation and the Federation of Trade Unions, stresses the importance of active participation by employees and their union representatives in the arranging and organising of their daily working lives. It also facilitates the setting-up of cooperation committees in enterprises with more than 35 employees. These consist of managers, senior personnel who are not union members, directly elected employees and shop stewards.

The rights and duties of cooperation committees, under the Cooperation Agreement, are (Incomes Data Services 1991: page 29):

- Establishing principles for the work environment and human relations, as well as the principles for the personnel policy pursued by the enterprise . . .
- Establishing the principles of training and retraining for employees who are to work with new technology.
- Establishing principles for the in-house compilation, storage and use of personnel data.
- Exchanging views and considering proposals for guide-lines on the planning of production and work, and the implementation of major changes in the enterprise.
- Assessing the technical, financial, staffing, educational and environmental consequences of the introduction of new technology and major changes to existing technology.
- Informing employees about proposals for incentive systems of payment . . . Also informing employees about the possibility of setting up funds for educational and social security purposes.

Cooperation committees are not empowered, however, to deal with matters covered by collective bargaining. But employers are required to inform employees of their firm's financial position, its prospects and any major changes likely to occur in the future.

Employee relations in Italy are in a state of considerable fluidity and instability (Ferner and Hyman 1992) but, in workplace relations, employee participation remains based on union organisation, not on works council legislation. Collective agreements remain the principal source of workers' rights to information and consultation, whilst the Workers' Statute 1970 confers a number of rights on the most representative unions at enterprise level. The principal national agreements, for example, generally include provisions outlining the information and consultation rights of trade unions. At company level, firms with over 200 employees must provide information to trade union representatives on significant changes to the production process or work organisation and on planned large-scale transfers of employees. Where there are over 350 employees, information must be provided about investment and the employment and environmental implications of new working operations or an extension of existing operations.

Under the Workers' Statute 1970, employees have the right to set up representative bodies for dealings with management within the enterprise, provided that such bodies are initiated by the employees, the employer has over 16 employees and the bodies are under the auspices of the most representative trade unions. Trade union representatives have the right to represent members in the workplace and to be involved in bargaining. They are entitled to time off work to undertake their duties, to unpaid leave of absence for other union duties and not to be dismissed by the employer, except for serious misconduct.

Board-level participation

Statutory worker participation arrangements providing for employee representation on company boards exist in Denmark, the Netherlands and Germany. This representation is normally facilitated through the device of two-tier board structures, consisting of an upper-tier 'supervisory' board and a lower-tier 'management' board. Supervisory boards determine overall company policy and must be consulted on important corporate decisions, whilst management boards are concerned with day-to-day operations and issues. Employee representatives sit on the supervisory board.

In Denmark, the law provides for employee representatives on the supervisory boards of all limited liability companies and companies limited by guarantee. They have the same rights and duties as other board members. The supervisory board must ensure that employees are given information about the company's circumstances, including finances, employment and production plans. The arrangements in the Netherlands have existed since 1971. They require all public limited companies with more than 100 workers to establish a supervisory board with employee representatives. The most advanced system of board-level co-determination is in Germany, where there are three models of board-level participation. In joint stock and limited liability companies and limited partnerships with more than 2,000 employees, the supervisory board consists of equal numbers of employee and shareholder representatives, with the size of the board varying according to company size. Enterprises with more than 1,000 employees in the coal, iron and steel industries have supervisory boards consisting of an equal number of employee and shareholder representatives. In companies with between 500 and 2,000 employees, one-third of the members of the supervisory board must be employee representatives. As in the other countries, employee board members have the same rights and duties as shareholder members (Lane 1989).

In France, there is no statutory system of employee representation at board level. However, under a decree of October 1986, companies may provide for a number of employee representatives on the board of directors, with renewable periods of office of up to six years. Additionally, the Auroux laws provide rights for employees to express their views on the content, conditions and organisation of work. These rights are essentially collective and the legislation stipulates that agreements on employees' rights should be concluded between employers and unions where companies employ 50 or more employees and have trade union delegates. Nevertheless, individuals may go straight to members of management with opinions or problems, without having to go through the normal employee representation channels (Goetschy and Rozenblatt 1992).

Assignments

(a) By what criteria would you assess whether or not your organisation operates an 'employee commitment' strategy? You might consider your analysis under headings – which are neither exclusive nor exhaustive – such as: jobs; workgroups; departments; other units of organisation; products/services; type of organisation; functional roles within the organisation; corporate values; or work in general.

(b) Identify and critically evaluate the methods of information provision used by management in your organisation.

(c) Read Millward *et al.* (1992: pages 165–72) and identify the major trends in employee communication highlighted by the WIRS survey.

(d) As head of department, provide a draft agenda for your next departmental meeting. What sort of preparation will you have to do to make the meeting a success?

(e) Prepare a position paper for your chief executive outlining the case for introducing (or revising) a briefing group system in your organisation.

(f) Present a report on the structure, operation and effectiveness of quality circles in your organisation.

(g) What would be the 'pros' and 'cons' of introducing a profit-sharing scheme in your company?

(h) Read Marchington and his colleagues (1992: pages 33–42). Report on the impact of employee involvement practices on employees, managers and trade union representatives, as outlined in this research.

(i) Read either Collard (1989), or Dale and Plunkett (1990), or Hakes (1991), or Oakland (1989) and make a presentation on the elements of TQM as examined by one of these authors.

(j) To what extent has 'total quality' been introduced in your organisation? Report on the issues, problems and human resource implications arising from this.

(k) Provide a report on the joint consultative arrangements in your organisation. How effective are they from a management point of view? What is a typical list of agenda items?

(l) Draft a constitution for a workplace JCC.

(m) Read Ferner and Hyman (1992) and provide a report on one European system of industrial relations analysed in this book. Indicate how this system differs from that of Britain.

(n) What are the cases for and against employee representation on company boards as happens in other parts of the EC? On what grounds do British employer groups oppose this type of worker participation?

(o) Read Lane (1989: pages 224–48) and provide a comparison of the patterns of industrial democracy in Germany, France and Britain.

References

ADVISORY CONCILIATION AND ARBITRATION SERVICE 1989. *Workplace Communication*. London: ACAS.

BERGHAHN, V. and KARSTEN, D. 1989. *Industrial Relations in West Germany*. London: Berg.

BRADLEY, K. and HILL, S. 1987. 'Quality circles and management interests'. *Industrial Relations Journal*. 26(1), Winter.

COLLARD, R. 1989. *Total Quality: Success through people*. London: IPM.

CONFEDERATION OF BRITISH INDUSTRY 1977. *Communication with People at Work*. London: CBI.

CONFEDERATION OF BRITISH INDUSTRY 1979. *Guidelines for Action on Employee Involvement*. London: CBI.

CONFEDERATION OF BRITISH INDUSTRY 1990. *Employee Involvement – Shaping the Future*. London: CBI.

CRESSEY, P. and MACINNES, J. 1984. *The relationship between economic recession and industrial democracy*. Glasgow: Centre for Research in Industrial Democracy and Participation, University of Glasgow.

CROSBY, P. 1978. *Quality is Free*. NY: McGraw-Hill.

DALE, B. and PLUNKETT, J. 1990. *Managing Quality*. London: Allen.

DEMING, W. 1986. *Out of Crisis*. Cambridge, Mass.: MIT.

DEPARTMENT OF TRADE 1977. *Report of the Committee of Inquiry on Industrial Democracy*. London: HMSO.

FERNER, A. 1988. *Governments, Managers and Industrial Relations*. Oxford: Blackwell.

FERNER, A. and HYMAN, R. 1992. *Industrial Relations in the New Europe*. Oxford: Blackwell.

FLANDERS, A., WOODWOOD, J. and POMERANTZ, R. (1968). *Experiment in Industrial Democracy*. London: Faber.

GARNETT, J. 1983. *The Manager's Responsibility for Communication*. London: Industrial Society.

GOETSCHY, J. and ROZENBLATT, P. 1992. 'France: the industrial relations system at a turning point?' In FERNER, A. and HYMAN, R. *Industrial Relations in the New Europe*. Oxford: Blackwell.

HAKES, C. (ed.) 1991. *Total Quality Management*. London: Chapman and Hall.

HIBBERT, A. 1991. 'Employee involvement: a recent survey'. *Employment Gazette*. December.

INCOMES DATA SERVICES 1992. *Industrial Relations*. London: IPM.

INCOMES DATA SERVICES 1992. *IDS Focus: Sharing Profits*. 64, September.

INDUSTRIAL SOCIETY 1970. *Systematic Communication by Briefing Groups*. London: Industrial Society.

INSTITUTE OF PERSONNEL MANAGEMENT 1981. *Communication in Practice*. London: IPM.

JACOBI, I., KELLER, B. and MUELLER-JENTSCH, W. 1992. 'Germany: codetermining the future?' In FERNER, A. and HYMAN, R. 1992. *Industrial Relations in the New Europe*. Oxford: Blackwell.

JURAN, J. 1989. *Juran on Leadership for Quality*. NY: Free Press.

MARCHINGTON, M. 1989. 'Joint consultation in practice'. In SISSON, K. (ed.) 1989. *Personnel Management in Britain*. Oxford: Blackwell.

MARCHINGTON, M. and ARMSTRONG, R. 1983. 'Shop steward organisation and joint consultation'. *Personnel Review*. 12(1).

MARCHINGTON, M., and GOODMAN, J., WILKINSON, A. and ACKERS, P. 1992. *New Developments in Employee Involvement*. London: Employment Department.

MARSDEN, D. 1978. *Industrial Democracy and Industrial Control in West Germany, France and Great Britain*. London: Department of Employment.

MATTHEWS, D. 1989. 'The British experience of profit sharing'. *Economic History Review*. November.

MILLWARD, N. and STEVENS, M. 1986. *British Workplace Industrial Relations 1980–1984*. Aldershot: Gower.

MILLWARD, N., STEVENS, M., SMART, D. and HAWES, W. (1992). *Workplace Industrial Relations in Transition*. Aldershot: Dartmouth.

OAKLAND, J. 1989. *Total Quality Management*. London: Heinemann.

PERKINS, G. (ed.) 1986. *Employee Communications in the Public Sector*. London: IPM.

PURCELL, J. 1981. *Good Industrial Relations*. London: Macmillan.

RIDLEY, T. 1992. *Motivating and Rewarding Employees – Some Aspects of Theory and Practice: Work Research Paper 51*. London: ACAS.

RUSSELL, S. and DALE, B. 1989. *Quality Circles – a Broader Perspective: Work Research Unit Occasional Paper 43*. London: ACAS.

VISSER, J. 1992. 'The Netherlands: the end of an era and the end of a system'. In FERNER, A. and HYMAN, R. 1992. *Industrial Relations in the New Europe*. Oxford: Blackwell.

WHITE, G. 1987. *Employee Commitment: Work Research Unit Occasional Paper 38*. London: ACAS.

WILKINSON, A., MARCHINGTON, M., GOODMAN, J. and ACKERS, P. 1992. 'Total quality management and employee involvement'. *Human Resource Management Journal*. 2(4).

Chapter 11

Industrial Action

Industrial action or a 'trade dispute' takes place whenever employers and employees, and/or the organisations representing them, are unable to resolve their differences peacefully and constitutionally in determining, regulating or terminating the pay–work bargain. In law, a trade dispute means any dispute between 'employers and workers, or between workers and workers, which is connected with one or more of the following matters' (TULRCA 1992: section 218):

(a) terms and conditions of employment, or the physical conditions in which any workers are required to work;
(b) engagement or non-engagement, or termination or suspension of employment or the duties of employment, of one or more workers;
(c) allocation of work or the duties of employment between workers or groups of workers;
(d) matters of discipline;
(e) the membership or non-membership of a trade union on the part of a worker;
(f) facilities for officials of trade unions; and
(g) machinery for negotiation or consultation, and other procedures, relating to any of the foregoing matters, including the recognition by employers or employers' associations of the right of a trade union to represent workers in any such negotiation or consultation or in the carrying out of such procedures.

Where a trade dispute takes place, this results in a temporary breakdown of the employment relationship between employer and employee, the imposition of industrial sanctions by either or both parties (or their agents) against the other and the emergence of industrial conflict between them.

Kornhauser and his colleagues summarise the nature of industrial conflict neatly and succinctly (1954: page 13). They describe it as: 'the total range of behavior and attitudes that express opposition and divergent orientations between individual owners and managers on the one hand and working people and their organisations on the other hand.' In taking any kind of industrial action against one another, the parties to employee relations are using their economic and social power to try and coerce the other party into conceding an employment decision – whether over wages, conditions, job security or working arrangements – which cannot be resolved by negotiation, compromise or third-party intervention. Industrial action and the use of industrial sanctions, therefore, involve the application of naked force by one or more of the parties to employee relations against the other. This undermines good working relations between them, imposes financial costs on them and might even threaten the social order, if matters were to get out of control.

Because of this, the state takes an active role in regulating industrial conflict. If the state cannot achieve industrial peace by persuasion, argument or third-party intervention, it provides certain legal backstops to contain and constrain what it defines to be legitimate industrial action. These are aimed at protecting those damaged by industrial action, keeping the sanctions within acceptable constitutional bounds and discouraging what the state defines as politically destabilising employee relations conflict (see Chapters 3, 4, 7 and 8).

The functions and forms of industrial sanctions

The taking of industrial sanctions, by any of the parties to employee relations, represents the breakdown of trust, cooperation and goodwill between them. Industrial sanctions, therefore, tend to be the means of last resort used by the parties in attempting to resolve their differences arising from the pay–work bargain. When employers, employees or their agents take industrial sanctions against one another, it is because they believe that it is only by imposing their unilateral power on the other side that they can achieve their employee relations goals.

The aim of industrial sanctions is to weaken the other side's resolve in opposing what is on offer at the bargaining table. If the employees are not unionised, then the employer's ability to impose its unilateral decisions on them is less likely to be resisted, because they have no countervailing collective power to use against management. If the employees are unionised, however, the employer is obliged to take account of the employees' collective power, and its potential impact on the outcome of the conflict, in taking its decision. It also has to listen to what is being proposed by the union leaders on behalf of their members.

Similarly, in deciding whether to take industrial sanctions against their employer, employees and their union leaders have to take account of the likely outcome in terms of costs to them, whether a successful outcome to the action is possible and the consequences of the action for employee relations in the future. In all trade disputes, the potential for coercive power between employer and employees, or between management and unions, is a crucial determinant of the propensity to apply industrial sanctions, the form that the sanctions might take and their likely outcomes on the conflict between the parties.

Theories of industrial conflict

There are three main competing sets of theories seeking to explain the nature of industrial conflict between employers and employees and between management and unions (Farnham and Pimlott 1990). These are:

- structural or Marxist theory;
- unitary or 'human relations; theory;
- functionalist theory.

In outline, Marxist theory sees industrial conflict between employers and employees as inevitable and deep-rooted, since it emerges out of the class and power relations within capitalist societies. Human relations theory sees industrial conflict as anti-social, dysfunctional and disruptive of enterprise harmony and effectiveness. Functionalist theory sees industrial conflict as having positive benefits for the parties to employee relations, as long as it is channelled into appropriate institutional mechanisms and resolved accordingly.

Marxist theory

Marxist theory views industrial conflict as rooted in the economic structures of capitalist societies. It is a theory of social change and, although there are a number of schools of Marxian scholarship, Marxism is essentially a method of analysing power relationships in society. It assumes:

- that the capitalist mode of production is but one stage in the development of human society;
- that class conflict is the catalytic source of change within capitalism;
- that out of the dialectical conflict between the social classes, with opposed economic interests, social change takes place, leading eventually to the socialist state.

As Allen (1976: page 21) writes:

> When reality is viewed dialectically it is seen as a process involving interdependent parts which interact on each other. When reality is also viewed materialistically it is seen as phenomena predominantly influenced by economic factors. The dialectical relationship between economic factors, therefore, provides the prime motivation for change. This briefly is what Marxism in the first instance is about.

In the bourgeois capitalist state, the competing class interests are between those of profit-seeking capitalists and the wage-earning proletariat. The struggle for economic hegemony between them is deemed to be inevitable, irrevocable and irreconcilable. Industrial conflict between employer and employee, and between management and union, is merely a reflection of the dominant class interests within capitalism and is synonymous with class conflict. As such, employee relations conflict, between those buying labour in the market place and those selling it, is seen as a permanent feature of capitalism (Hyman 1975). Industrial conflict, in its various forms, in short, arises out of economic contradictions within the capitalist mode of production and is a means for advancing and fighting the class struggle and the class war. The protagonists are those owning and representing private capital and those supplying their skills for wages in the labour market. In an eocnomic system driven by market forces, private ownership of the means of production and profit-seeking, mutual accommodation between capital and labour is impossible and continuous class conflict between them is inevitable.

Human relations theory

The unitary or human relations theory of industrial conflict is at the opposite end of the theoretical spectrum. This set of theories holds, in essence, that conflict at work between employer and employee is

dysfunctional, that trade unions cause industrial conflict and that industrial conflict in any form is a corroding and disruptive social influence
in the workplace and the wider society. The ideas and concepts associated with what is sometimes misleadingly called the 'Human Relations
School' were first gestated and publicised by American industrial sociologists such as Mayo (1946), Roethlisberger (1946) and Warner and
Low (1947). Their ideas were further refined and developed by the
more sophisticated 'neo-human relations' theorists such as McGregor
(1960) and Argyris (1964). The main implications of their analyses are
that conflict at work is unnatural, subversive and destabilising and, as it
cannot be suppressed, it should be eradicated by enlightened management policies and participative styles of management.

All of Mayo's research was carried out with the permission and collaboration of management. For Mayo, management embodies the central purposes of society and, with this initial orientation, he never
considered the possibility that organisations might contain conflicting
interest groups, such as management, workers and unions, as distinct
from different attitudes or 'logics'. For him, industrial conflict was a
social disease, whilst the promotion of organisational equilibrium, or a
state of 'social health', should be management's prime aim and objective. The issue that Roethlisberger sought to address was (1946: page
112): 'how can a comfortable working equilibrium be maintained
between the various groups in an industrial enterprise such that no
group . . . will separate itself out in opposition to the remainder?'
Warner and Low (1947) had similarly overwhelmingly negative con-
notations of industrial conflict. The subjective bias in their writing
towards stability, harmony and social integration within organisations
meant that they saw conflict exclusively as a dissociative and disinte-
grative phenomenon, although they conceded that 'frictional' conflicts
could arise from personality differences, poor management and bad
communications. Industrial conflict, by this view, is a pathological
social condition, upsetting the 'normal' state of organisational equilibrium, and must be avoided at all costs.

Functionalist theory

The functionalist theory of industrial conflict, in contrast, sees conflict
as inevitable in any human situation. Individuals group together in
society for associative purposes – such as in politics and employee
relations – and inter-group conflicts arise which, if resolved, result in

new behavioural norms, thus eliminating the sources of dissatisfaction amongst the groups involved. Moreover, as Coser (1956: page 31) writes: 'far from being necessarily dysfunctional, a certain degree of conflict is an essential element in group formation and the persistence of group life.' In employee relations, this means that conflict creates links between employers, management and unions. It modifies the norms for readjusting these relationships, leads each party to match the other's structures and organisation and makes possible a reassessment of their relative power in achieving consensus or agreement amongst themselves. In this way, industrial conflict serves as a social balancing mechanism maintaining and consolidating the instrumental relationships amongst employers, employees and unions.

For functionalists, industrial conflict is therefore generated by the divergent interests of the parties in the employment relationship. With industrial enterprises being the dominant institutions of modern society, 'where few command and many obey', Dahrendorf (1959: pages 250–53) takes issue with the scientific management and human relations views that the 'true interests' of management and workers are identical. He asserts that:

> . . . Taylor's exclusive emphasis on the community of interests among all participants of the enterprise is plainly insufficient for the explanation of certain phenomena, such as strikes, and that it is therefore necessary to assume a conflict of latent interests in the enterprise emerging from the differential distribution of authority.

The significance of the functionalist theory of industrial conflict for employee relations is the need for the parties to the pay–work bargain to accept the inevitability of potential conflict between them, to institutionalise it and to resolve it through appropriate constitutional mechanisms. Only then is it likely that either or both parties will resort to unilateral force, and the use of industrial sanctions, to achieve their employee relations goals. This will only happen after these institutional arrangements have broken down. Furthermore, the application of industrial sanctions by any of the parties to employee relations is only possible within the limits of the law.

Manifestations of industrial conflict

In practice, industrial conflict takes a variety of forms. Writers such as Kornhauser and his colleagues (1954) and Hyman (1989) distinguish

Figure 16: *Manifestations of individual and unorganised industrial conflict*

Worker behaviour	Management behaviour
absenteeism	autocratic supervision
withholding effort	tight discipline
time-wasting	harassment of workers
industrial sabotage	discrimination at work
labour turnover	demoting individuals
complaints	one-sided propaganda
rule-breaking	speeding up work
low morale	anti-union propaganda
'griping' against management	'slagging off' the workforce

between industrial conflict that is individual and unorganised and that which is collective and organised. Individual and unorganised conflict, for example, takes place at the personal and interpersonal levels. It involves certain types of worker behaviour and managerial behaviour and manifests itself in a variety of ways, as outlined in Figure 16. The essence of unorganised industrial conflict is that it is unpredictable, is not directed into conflict resolving channels and is difficult to manage.

Examples of how collective and organised industrial conflict manifest themselves are provided in Figure 17. These relate to management–union conflict and are more formalised types of industrial conflict. Although strikes are often considered to be the main manifestation of organised conflict, it is clear from Exhibit 39 that collective industrial conflict is not limited to strike activity alone. Nor does collective conflict only manifest itself in the workplace. It also takes place in the socio-political spheres through elections, lobbying, public relations activities and educational propaganda by both employers and unions.

Patterns of strike activity in the UK

Strike activity is not an easy term to define and the official statistics of the United Kingdom (UK), collected by the Employment Department (formerly the Department of Employment and earlier still the Ministry of Labour) only cover what are described as 'stoppages of work'.

Employee Relations

Figure 17: *Manifestations of collective and organised industrial conflict*

In the workplace	In society
restrictions of output	political lobbying
going slow	union political affiliations
working to contract	corporate political donations
removal of overtime	political demonstrations
strikes and lockouts	using the media
closing down plants	educational propaganda

Technically, a stoppage of work is any trade dispute between employers and workers, or workers and workers, which is connected with terms and conditions of employment. The official statistics exclude disputes not resulting in stoppages of work, such as working to rule or going slow, and stoppages involving fewer than 10 workers or those lasting one day or less, except where the total number of working days lost is greater than 100. The statistics also include lockouts by employers and unlawful strikes. But they do not distinguish between: strikes and lockouts; 'lawful' and 'unlawful' stoppages; and, since 1981, 'official' and 'unofficial' disputes.

In practice, a strike is any stoppage of work, or withdrawal of labour, initiated by workers, whilst lockouts are stoppages of work initiated by employers who prevent their employees working, by refusing entry to the workplace. A lawful strike is one undertaken in accordance with the legal requirements of the TULRCA 1992, as amended. To be lawful, strikes must be between workers and their direct employer, must relate to matters covered in section 218 of the Act and can only take place after a properly conducted strike ballot has been held, thus providing legal immunities to the strike leaders and the union(s) involved. Unlawful strikes are not protected by legal immunities and can result in injunctions and fines being awarded against the unions. An official dispute, or more properly a 'constitutional' one, is where strike action occurs which is in accordance with agreed negotiating procedures between the employer and the union(s). Unofficial or 'unconstitutional' disputes, in contrast, are in breach of agreed procedures for avoiding disputes.

Another meaning sometimes given to an 'official' dispute is one which is supported by the union(s) and is in accordance with union rules. 'Official' disputes of this sort normally involve the payment of strike benefits to the workers taking industrial action. Similarly, the term 'unofficial' disputes can also refer to industrial action which is not normally in accordance with union rules and where the unions do not pay any benefits to the striking workers.

Strike statistics

In analysing stoppages of work annually, the Employment Department uses three measures of strike activity. These are: the number of working days lost; the number of workers involved in stoppages of work; and the number of stoppages.

Working days lost

The number of working days lost is the total time lost as a result of trade disputes in the basic working week, over a given period, usually a year. Overtime and weekend working are excluded, with allowances being made for public and known annual holidays and for absences from work due to sickness and unauthorised leave. Where strikes last less than the basic working day, the hours lost are converted to full-day equivalents. Similarly, days lost by part-time workers are also converted to full-day equivalents. In disputes where employers dismiss their employees and subsequently reinstate them, the total working days lost include the days lost by the workers during the period of dismissal.

Workers involved

The number of workers involved in stoppages of work are those individuals directly and indirectly involved at the establishment where the dispute occurs. Workers indirectly involved are those who are not themselves party to the dispute but are laid off because of it. Workers at the other sites who are indirectly affected are not counted. This is because of the difficulty of deciding the extent to which a particular employer's reduction in output or services is due to the effects of a strike elsewhere or to some other cause. Workers involved in more than one stoppage during the year are counted for each stoppage in which they take part. Part-time workers are counted as whole units.

Number of stoppages

This records the total number of stoppages, lasting more than one day, over the year. Because of recording difficulties, the number of working days lost per year is normally regarded as a better indicator of the impact of trade disputes than the number of recorded stoppages.

Stoppages of work

A time series of stoppages of work in the UK for the period 1971–91 is shown in Table 15. A number of conclusions may be inferred from Table 15. First, the number of working days lost per year varied widely over this 20-year period, with relatively high figures for some years – such as 1972, 1979 and 1984 – and some low ones, especially since 1985. The unusually high number of working days lost in certain years were due, in the main, to large individual stoppages. In 1972, for example, a miners' strike over a national wage increase accounted for 10.7 million (45 per cent) of the 23.9 million working days lost for that year. Similarly, in 1979, a strike by engineering workers accounted for 16 million (54 per cent) of the 29.5 million working days lost in that year. And in 1984, the days lost in the miners' strike, in protest against pit closures, accounted for 22.4 million (83 per cent) of the 27.1 million working days lost during that year (Bird 1992a). It is important therefore to consider the size of the major stoppages in each period when making comparisons between individual years.

Second, the annual average number of working days lost per 1,000 employees declined substantially during the 1980s, compared with the 1970s. For the 10 years 1971–80, the annual average was 572 working days lost per 1,000 employees, whilst for the 10 years 1981–90, it was 288 working days. Even more starkly, if the miners' dispute is discounted in 1984, then the annual average for the period 1981–90 falls to only 160 lost working days per 1,000 employees. The 1980s were clearly one of relatively low levels of industrial conflict in the UK compared with the 1960s and 1970s (Smith *et al.* 1978).

Third, the average number of workers involved annually in stoppages of work for the five years 1971–75 was 1,375,000. This rose to 1,667,000 workers per year, on average, for the five years 1976–80, falling to 1,289,000 workers per year for the five years 1981–85. For the five years 1986–90, the annual average fell even more dramatically to 840,000 workers.

Table 15: *Stoppages of work in progress: the UK 1971–91*

Year	Working days lost ('000s)	Working days lost per 1,000 employees	Workers involved ('000s)	Stoppages
1971	13,551	612	1,178	2,263
1972	23,909	1,080	1,734	2,530
1973	7,197	317	1,528	2,902
1974	14,750	647	1,626	2,946
1975	6,012	265	809	2,332
1976	3,284	146	668	2,034
1977	10,142	448	1,666	2,737
1978	9,405	413	1,041	2,498
1979	29,474	1,273	4,608	2,125
1980	11,964	521	843	1,348
1981	4,266	195	1,513	1,344
1982	5,313	248	2,103	1,538
1983	3,754	178	574	1,364
1984	27,135	1,278	1,464	1,221
1985	6,402	229	791	903
1986	1,920	90	720	1,074
1987	3,546	164	887	1,016
1988	3,702	166	790	781
1989	4,128	182	727	701
1990	1,903	83	298	630
1991	761	34	176	369

Source: Employment Department

Fourth, the number of recorded stoppages during the 1970s averaged around 2,300 per year. During the 1980s, they fell to a little over a thousand stoppages per year on average and, for the five years 1986–90, to an average of about 840 stoppages per year.

The causes of industrial action

Ever since the nineteenth century, government has recorded information on the principal causes of industrial stoppages in the UK. Government officials review all the available information from employers, conciliation officers and newspaper reports and then identify what is stated by the parties to be the main reason for each strike. Table 16 shows that the dominant issue in the strikes occurring in the UK during the period 1925–90 was pay. Over this 65-year period, pay was cited as the main reason for over two-thirds (68 per cent) of the working days lost. Although the relative importance of pay issues declined progressively up until the immediate postwar period (1945–54), it subsequently recovered in the 20 years after 1955. During the 1980s, pay once again declined in relative importance but still remained the most important single cause of working days lost annually, at around 58 per cent of the total.

Table 16: *Number and percentage of working days lost over pay: the UK 1925–90*

Period	Number (000s)	Over pay (000s)	Over pay per cent
1925–34	200,935	175,751	87.5
1935–44	18,956	11,405	60.2
1945–54	20,694	10,293	49.7
1955–64	38,910	27,586	70.9
1965–74	90,164	74,217	82.3
1980–90	78,118	45,309	58.0

Source: Department of Employment and Employment Department

The pay issues causing disputes between employers, employees and unions are wide ranging. They include union demands for:

- increases in wage rates or bonuses;
- the restoration of pay differentials;
- special rates for particular jobs or for the conditions in which the work is performed;
- guaranteed earnings.

Pay disputes also commonly occur over reductions in earnings, changes in payment systems and the grading or regrading of jobs. Other pay issues which have been identified as likely to cause disputes between managements and workers include conflicts over cash allowances, holiday pay and fringe benefits.

Table 17 provides a detailed analysis of the percentage of working days lost by principal cause of dispute, for all industries in the UK, for the years 1980–91. Again, stoppages over pay accounted for most of the working days lost in every year, except for 1984 and 1985 when redundancy issues predominated. In 1991, whilst pay was the major issue causing disputes (41 per cent of the total), redundancy was a close second (33 per cent). It is also noticeable that in 1988 about a third of all working days lost were caused by issues relating to staffing and the allocation of work.

Table 17: *Working days lost in the UK by cause of dispute 1980–91*

| Year | Cause – percentage of total | | | | | | |
	Pay	Hours	Redun-dancy	Trade union matters	Conditions of work	Staffing	Dismissal/discipline
1980	89	1	3	2	1	2	2
1981	62	5	15	7	1	4	6
1982	66	5	16	2	1	6	3
1983	58	3	17	2	4	8	8
1984	8	0	87	1	0	2	1
1985	25	3	67	1	1	2	2
1986	59	3	15	3	3	13	4
1987	82	2	5	1	2	5	4
1988	51	0	7	4	1	33	3
1989	80	8	4	2	1	4	1
1990	58	25	2	2	3	8	3
1991	41	2	33	1	9	8	7

Source: Employment Department

International comparisons

From the analysis provided so far, it is clear that the number of working days lost, the number of workers involved and the number of recorded stoppages in the UK vary annually and over time, due to a variety of complex economic and related factors. It is also clear that the principal causes of trade disputes in the UK vary over time too. To obtain a balanced overview of the UK's 'strike rate', or its numbers of working days lost per 1,000 employees, comparisons can be made with the strike rates in 19 other advanced capitalist countries, out of the 24 that are members of the Organisation for Economic Cooperation and Development (OECD). This is done for all industries and services in Table 18, for the period 1982–91, although some care must be exercised in interpreting the data, due to differences in the methods used for selecting and compiling data on industrial disputes in the countries represented. Also, since there are considerable variations between

Table 18: *Industrial disputes in OECD countries: working days lost per 1,000 employees, all industries and services 1982–91*

Country	Averages		
	1982–86	1987–91	1982–91
UK	420	130	270
Denmark	250	40	140
France	80	50	60
Germany	50	10	30
Greece	560	7,640	3,710
Ireland	450	190	320
Italy	700	300	520
The Netherlands	20	10	20
Portugal	150	70	110
Spain	520	650	580
Japan	10	–	5
USA	120	70	90
Canada	490	360	430
Austria	–	10	5
Finland	530	180	360
Norway	170	30	100
Sweden	60	100	80
Switzerland	–	–	–
Australia	280	220	250
New Zealand	550	230	390

Note: the averages for Greece, Italy, Portugal and Japan are based on incomplete data

Source: Employment Gazette

years in the incidence of working days lost, with some years being heavily influenced by a small number of very large stoppages, international comparisons based on the average for a number of years are more useful than annual comparisons alone, as shown in Table 18.

First, it can be seen from Table 18 that there are quite wide differences in the strike rates between each of these countries within given periods and between different periods of time. For the whole period 1982–91, for example, seven countries – Greece, Spain, Italy, Canada,

Table 19: *Industrial disputes in OECD countries: working days lost per 1,000 employees in strike-prone industries 1982–91*

Country	Averages		
	1982–86	1987–91	1982–91
UK	980	240	610
Denmark	560	90	330
France	150	80	120
Germany	100	10	50
Greece	920	5,360	4,470
Ireland	510	350	430
Italy	280	440	360
The Netherlands	40	40	40
Portugal	270	110	200
Spain	520	770	650
Japan	20	10	10
USA	310	210	260
Canada	940	760	850
Austria	–	–	–
Finland	760	180	470
Norway	300	30	170
Sweden	10	170	90
Switzerland	–	–	–
Australia	610	530	570
New Zealand	2,740	520	890

Note: the averages for Greece, Italy, Portugal and Japan are based on incomplete data

Source: Employment Department

New Zealand, Finland and Ireland – had consistently higher strike rates than the UK. Similarly, in the period 1982–86, the UK ranked eighth out of the 20 countries, whilst in the period 1987–91, it ranked ninth. According to Bird (1992b), the UK's average of 130 lost working days per 1,000 employees for the period 1987–91 is approximately one-eighth of a working day lost per employee or about one working hour per week. This represents a 70 per cent decrease in the UK strike rate for the years 1987–91, compared with the previous five-year period. This decrease was greater than for all the other OECD countries, except Denmark (80 per cent), Norway (80 per cent) and Germany (90 per cent).

Second, some countries have consistently high strike rates and others relatively low ones. Greece, Spain and Italy are in the former category. Switzerland and Japan – with less than five lost days per 1,000 employees – and Austria, the Netherlands and Germany, with an average of 10 lost days per 1,000 employees for the period 1987–91, are in the latter category. Countries like the UK, Australia and Portugal lie in the middle range of strike activity.

Third, there was a general downward trend in the incidence of working days lost per 1,000 employees in OECD countries for the whole period 1982–91, with strike rates being generally higher for the period 1982–86 than for the years 1987–91. This is apart from Greece, Spain and Sweden, where strike rates rose in the late 1980s. In the case of Greece, there were general strikes in both 1987 and 1990 and these account for its relatively large numbers of working days lost per 1,000 employees for the period 1987–91.

One feature of trade disputes is the variation in strike activity amongst different industrial sectors. Some industries are particularly strike prone such as mining and quarrying, manufacturing, construction, and transport and communication (see below). This variation, and the contrasting industrial structures of different countries, in part explains why some countries have relatively high or low rates of strike activity compared with others. To help reduce this effect, Table 19 compares the working days lost per 1,000 employees in these four strike-prone sectors in 20 of the OECD's 24 member states, for the period 1982–91. Overall, for the period 1982–91, the incidence of working days lost per 1,000 employees in these strike-prone industries was between one-and-a-half times to twice as high as for all industries and services (Table 18), although it was three times as high in the USA. Nevertheless, like all industries and services, these strike-prone ones also experienced a general decrease in strike rates over this period.

Influences on industrial action

Employee relations are not conducted in a vacuum (see Chapters 1, 4 and 6). They take place in specific economic, institutional and political contexts. It is these broad categories of factors which have been identified by scholars as the main ones influencing industrial action, patterns of strike activity and the outcomes of industrial conflict between employers and unions. There is, however, no general theory of strikes or industrial action. As Jackson (1987: page 149) concludes: 'Strikes are enormously complex and are themselves a classification of a variety of different kinds of activity under one head.' Each strike is undertaken 'for different reasons at different times and has a different meaning for different participants.' Because strikes are the most obvious form and most quantified type of industrial action, this section, like the previous one, focuses, albeit selectively, on the main factors influencing strike activity rather than other manifestations of industrial conflict.

Economic factors

A number of studies use economic variables to explain strikes or stoppages of work. These include: inter-industry comparisons; unemployment; and the business cycle.

Inter-industry comparisons

An early comparative study of the major variations in strike incidence amongst different industries, in 11 countries, was undertaken by Kerr and Siegel (1954). Their focus was on why industrial conflict was prevalent in some industries and absent in others. Previous studies had concentrated on labour market and product market factors, management and union policies, procedures for adjusting disputes and the influence of dominant personalities on industrial conflict. Kerr and Siegel showed that these factors did not explain why some industries are strike prone in many parts of the world and others are not. Their central explanation of strike propensities (see Figure 18) was in the

Figure 18: *General pattern of strike propensities*

Propensity to strike	Industry
high	mining seafaring and docks
medium high	lumber textiles
medium	chemicals printing leather manufacturing construction food
medium low	clothing gas, water and electricity services
low	railways agriculture trade

Source: Kerr and Siegel (1954)

location of workers in society, with the nature of their jobs acting as a secondary influence. Isolated masses of workers, insulated from society at large, were identified as being most likely to take strike action, frequently and bitterly, especially when employed on unpleasant tasks. Individuals and groups who are integrated into the general community, on the other hand, through a multiplicity of associations, were identified to be least likely to strike.

A more recent, detailed study of variations of inter-industry strike activity in the UK was undertaken by the Department of Employment for the period from the mid-1960s to the mid-1970s (Smith *et al.* 1978). It had six main conclusions:

- There were very considerable differences between industries in terms of their propensity to strike, with five industries – coalmining, docks, car assembly, ship building, and iron and steel – accounting for at least a quarter of stoppages and a third of the days lost.

- Stoppages were overwhelmingly a manual worker phenomenon, although stoppages amongst non-manual workers were increasing.
- On average, over the period 1966–73, almost three-quarters of stoppages, accounting for over a half of the working days lost, involved members of only one union. Furthermore, six unions, accounting for about half of total union membership, were involved in about 80 per cent of stoppages.
- Strike activity was concentrated in a very small number of plants, with the incidence of strikes rising strongly with plant size.
- There were regional differences in strike proneness, over a considerable period of time.
- High average earnings, high labour intensity and large average establishment size were associated with relatively high strike frequency, and high strike incidence, whilst a high proportion of female employees was associated with low strike proneness.

Unemployment

Another key economic variable claimed to be linked with patterns of industrial action is unemployment. Hibbs (1976), for example, looked at data for 10 countries between 1950 and 1969 and argues that there is a negative relationship between unemployment and strike activity (i.e. as unemployment falls, strike activity rises). He concludes that the inverse relationship between industrial conflict and unemployment demonstrates considerable sophistication by workers and unions in their use of the strike weapon, since they seek to capitalise on the strategic advantages provided to them by tight labour markets. Furthermore, strikes are responses by workers to movements in real wages, rather than money wages. With unemployment low, workers have the opportunity to seek alternative jobs which might offer higher rates of pay. But as the cost of labour mobility is high, they will first try to increase their wages in their present jobs, by striking if necessary. It is also argued that both unions and their members are more able to withstand stoppages of work during the periods of prosperity. Their financial resources are relatively buoyant then, and the costs incurred in striking tend to be lower than in periods of recession.

Creigh and Makeham (1982), in contrast, suggest a positive relationship between unemployment and strike activity (i.e. as unemployment rises, strike activity rises). Their study examined data relating to 15 countries between 1975 and 1979 and focuses on the role of employers in trade disputes. They argue that during periods of high unemployment employers may be less willing to resist industrial action or to take countervailing steps to avoid the disruption caused by strikes. Consequently, where strikes occur during periods of high unemployment, they are likely to last longer. However, with unemployment inversely related to levels of economic activity, an employer's strike costs, in terms of lost production, are likely to increase as unemployment falls. So employers tend to avoid strike action in these conditions. Indeed, during periods of prosperity, employers are able to pass on increased costs to their customers. Low unemployment may increase worker demands for high pay rises but it also induces employers to raise their pay offers to them.

A third set of writers claim that there is no correlation, either negative or positive, between unemployment and strike activity (Knight 1972; Shorey 1976; Smith *et al.* 1978). Clearly, the relationship between the two is a complex one. But to date, a definitive general relationship between unemployment rates and measures of strike activity, either at industry level or nationally, does not appear to have been demonstrated.

The business cycle

It has long been recognised that there are cycles of strikes and that they are possibly related to the business cycle. Rees (1952) identifies a pronounced positive correlation between them, with strikes increasing in frequency during periods of prosperity and diminishing in frequency during recessions. The timing of the relationship appears to be such that strikes typically turn down before business activity reaches a peak and turn up some time after recovery has begun. Rees's explanation is based on the assumption that the strike weapon has become the strategic tool of well-organised 'business unions', rather than the spontaneous protest of aggrieved workers, and that union strategy is the driving force in the situation.

According to Rees, the strike peak represents a maximum divergence of expectations between unions and employers. As the business cycle rises, unions are influenced by the wage increases of other unions, increases in the cost of living and buoyant labour market. Employers, in contrast, seek higher sales, higher profits and new markets. They are, therefore, likely to resist wage demands for which the unions are prepared to fight and this can result in union strike action.

The issues of special interest to employers, normally preceding the peak of the business cycle, are rises in the number of business failures, falls in investment and declines in orders. The issue of special concern to the unions is future employment prospects. As the business cycle peaks, the more pessimistic expectations may be shared by some union leaders and strikes fall off. The lag in strikes at the troughs of business cycles represents a 'wait and see' policy by union leaders. They want to be sure that the revival is genuine before risking their members' jobs.

Institutional factors

These are another set of factors that are claimed to influence industrial action. Those supporting the institutional approach explain particular aspects and patterns of industrial conflict by reference to the institutions of conflict resolution, especially that of collective bargaining. The Donovan Commission (1968), for example, sought to explain the number of unofficial strikes in Britain in the 1960s in terms of the inadequacies of multi-employer collective bargaining machinery (see Chapter 7). The Commission identified the growing gap between industry-wide pay rates and actual earnings at the workplace and argued that existing procedural agreements were failing to cope adequately with the resolution of disputes between managements and workgroups within the workplace. The Commission went on to recommend the reform of company and factory-level collective bargaining machinery. This was to be based on comprehensive company-wide agreements aimed at regulating pay, grievances, discipline and redundancy and providing facilities for shop stewards within the firm.

The idea that collective bargaining helps to identify, regularise and institutionalise industrial conflict is based on a number of assumptions:

- It is argued that collective bargaining regulates conflict between employers and employees by keeping it within acceptable bounds, providing a forum for resolving it and legitimising the joint decisions made between the representatives of the two sides.
- When there is a dispute, collective bargaining enables management and unions to pause, think and reflect upon the consequences of their actions before taking industrial sanctions against each other.
- Collective bargaining absorbs energies which might otherwise be directed into more destructive channels of industrial or social conflict.

- Collective bargaining, in providing a forum for communication between management and unions, facilitates not only improved working relations between them but also peaceful change in society generally.

Collective bargaining is predicated, however, on the premises that employers recognise and accept the nature of industrial conflict, that they agree to institutionalise it and that there are appropriate agents of worker representation.

A seminal study is that of Ross and Hartman (1960) who examined the patterns of industrial conflict in 15 countries between 1900 and 1956. Although their methodology and their findings have been challenged subsequently (Eldridge 1968; Ingham 1974; Edwards 1981), Ross and Hartman's analysis is important for two main reasons. First, their research provides a useful framework for analysing industrial conflict. Second, they have been instrumental in influencing further studies on the institutionalisation of industrial conflict and its implications for the parties to employee relations (Kassolow 1969; Clegg 1976).

Ross and Hartman's central thesis is the 'withering away of the strike'. They argue that there was a general reduction in strike activity over the period they studied. The reasons given for this were: employers had developed more sophisticated policies for dealing with employees; the labour movement was forsaking strike action in favour of political action; and the state had become more prominent as an employer. In fact, strike activity did not wither away but started to grow in the 1960s and 1970s, although, as indicated above, it diminished again in the 1980s. Whilst it has been difficult to identify consistent trends across different countries since they wrote, their thesis is persuasive for the period they reviewed.

It is important to recognise the differing employee relations contexts of the 1960s, 1970s and 1980s. In Britain at least, the 20 years after the publication of Ross and Hartman's work were characterised by full employment, Keynesianism and a large public sector. The years since the late 1970s, in contrast, have featured deregulated labour markets, supply-side economic policies and a smaller public sector. These factors most certainly affected the institutions of employee relations and the willingness of the parties to become involved in industrial action. It is not surprising, in the circumstances, that industrial action was particularly centred on the public sector during the 1980s, as it was subjected to compulsory competitive tendering, privatisation and new styles of personnel management (Farnham 1993).

The second main theme of Ross and Hartman's study is the identification of distinctive patterns of industrial conflict and the linking of them to different employee relations systems. They identified five categories of employee relations, each with its own forms of strike activity. These were: two northern European patterns; a Mediterranean-Asian pattern; a North American pattern; and three special cases – Australia, Finland and South Africa. The first northern European pattern incorporated Denmark, the Netherlands, Germany and the UK. These were characterised by a nominal propensity to strike, with strikes of low or moderate duration. The second north European grouping of Norway and Sweden featured infrequent but long strikes. The Mediterranean-Asian pattern, comprising France, Italy, Japan and India, had high participation in strikes but these were of short duration. Finally, the North American pattern of the USA and Canada had a moderately high propensity to strike and the disputes were of relatively long duration.

In comparing different employee relations systems, Ross and Hartman identified five key features, which were claimed to be associated with distinctive patterns of strikes, and these are summarised in Figure 19. Denmark, the Netherlands, Germany and the UK were characterised by mature trade unions, stable union memberships and subdued union leadership conflicts. There was a wide acceptance of trade unions by employers and centralised collective bargaining. These countries had important Labour parties, and whilst governments rarely intervened to regulate terms and conditions of employment, they did intervene in the resolution of industrial disputes. Norway and Sweden shared many of the above characteristics but had less active government intervention in management–union relations.

The Mediterranean-Asian countries, in contrast, had relatively young trade union movements, low union membership and continual union leadership conflicts. Collective bargaining was weak, left-wing parties were divided and there was considerable government intervention in industry. In North America, there was an old trade union movement, with a stable membership and little factionalism. Unions were increasingly accepted by employers, collective bargaining was decentralised and terms and conditions were largely determined privately. There was not a successful Labour party.

Employee Relations

Figure 19: *Principal features of comparative employee relations systems*

1 Organisational stability of the labour movement

   1.1 age of labour movement

   1.2 stability of membership

2 Leadership conflicts in the labour movement

   2.1 factionalism and rivalry

   2.2 strength of communism in the unions

3 State of management–union relations

   3.3 degree of union acceptance by employers

   3.4 consolidation of bargaining structure

4 Labour political activity

   4.1 a Labour party as a leading political party

   4.2 Labour governments

5 Role of the state

   5.1 extent of government activity in defining terms of employment

   5.2 dispute settlement procedures

Source: Ross (1959)

Political factors

Political power is seen by some scholars as a major variable determining long-term patterns of strikes and industrial action. Korpi and Shalev (1979: page 181) argue, for example, that where labour movements are organised effectively and coordinated politically, they try to achieve their goals not only through collective bargaining but also through political rather than strike action. On the other hand, where labour movements are fragmented, are politically weak and have little nor no political influence, strikes are likely to remain high. Thus in Scandinavian countries and Austria, which have well-organised union movements and where democratic socialist political parties have been in power for many years, strikes are rarely used to pursue union goals and objectives. In countries like the USA, Canada and Ireland, on the other hand, where labour movements are less well organised and socialist parties are weak or non-existent, strikes are more common.

> In these instances, conflicts between buyers and sellers of labour
> power continue to be manifested primarily within the employ-
> ment contract, something which is no longer the case elsewhere.
> The long duration of strikes in these countries has contributed to
> give them very high *relative volumes* of strikes (man-days idle)
> in the postwar period.

In countries like Britain, Belgium and Denmark, the relationship between the political activities of their labour movements and strike activity is claimed to be more complex. Up until the late 1970s in Britain, for example, whilst the Labour party gained periods of political power, its control of and its long-term impact on the political system were relatively insecure. Labour governments were therefore unable to manage class conflict through 'political exchange' for any long period of time. Consequently, Britain's postwar strike record was similar to that of the prewar period and the strike weapon, as a union tactic, failed to wither away. In postwar Belgium, despite labour's involvement in government, strike mobilisation was as high as it had been in the prewar period. In Denmark, although organised labour had periodic influence in Danish governments in the years up till the late 1970s, its power was less stable than in the rest of Scandinavia. According to Korpi and Shalev (1979: page 182): 'this instability may well have contributed to the continuing wave-like incidence of industrial conflict in postwar Denmark, at what is nevertheless a relatively low level by international standards.'

Another political analysis of strike activity is provided by Shorter and Tilley (1974), They argue, first, that trade unions have a crucial role in channelling worker dissatisfaction into strike action and, second, that strikes have political aims which do not simply express economic interests. Where trade unions do not have political power through representation in the political system, strikes are used to put direct pressure on governments to change their existing policies or to initiate new ones. In this sense, strikes are an expression of class conflict between workers and their organisations and the political authorities, with 'strike waves' often coinciding with periodic political crises as they have done in France and Italy.

In Shorter and Tilley's analysis, strike activity prior to the second world war was of a similar intensity throughout Western Europe. After the war, however, patterns differed. In countries such as those in

Scandinavia, where labour gained political power, strike activity declined. Where labour failed to gain political power, such as in France and Italy, strikes continued at relatively high levels and expressed the political aspirations and expectations of the working class. The USA, in contrast, was seen as a special case, because strike activity did not wither away as it had done in northern Europe. This has been explained in terms of the failure of successive Federal governments to substantially protect workers' interests through interventionist political reforms. As a result, North American 'labor unions' drew a sharp dividing line between free collective bargaining, used to protect their members' job interests, including the use of strike action if necessary, and *ad hoc* 'interest-coalition' politics used to advance union political action.

Managing industrial action

Nowadays industrial action in Britain is normally initiated by trade unions. Industrial action initiated by employers, such as lockouts, is very rare, although to what extent plant closures, transfers of businesses and large-scale redundancies are regarded by trade unions and their members as covert forms of 'industrial action' by management is a matter of debate. This section, therefore, concentrates on the main issues to be considered by employers when they face organised industrial action from trade unions. These involve both legal and non-legal issues, although the suitability of any management response depends on the nature of the dispute, the estimated costs of pursuing any particular course of action and the balance of bargaining power between the two sides (Martin 1992).

Preparing for industrial action

Every trade dispute is unique. The type of action threatened by the trade unions, the extent and scope of the expected action and the nature of the issue in dispute, all affect the ways in which management is likely to respond and plan its own counter-actions to the situation. Once it seems likely that industrial action is being planned by trade unions and their members, management has to prepare and consider its possible responses. There are four key points:

- *Assess the scale of the problem.* Management needs to identify the scope of the dispute, estimate its possible support amongst the workforce and assess the potential difficulties and costs of resolving it. This includes considering the likelihood of a settlement in the short term.

- *Make contingency plans.* In doing so, management has a number of decisions to take: how any work is to be covered during the dispute; how adequate health and safety standards are to be maintained; and how any relevant property of the employer, such as keys, vehicles or other equipment, is to be returned to management before industrial action takes place.

- *Extend the communication systems.* Over and above existing communication channels, new communication systems may be necessary whilst the dispute is in progress. This is to ensure: effective management coordination of the dispute; publicity to employees and the press; and open channels of communication with the unions and their members.

- *Plan actions in response.* This should include considering what sort of warnings are to be given to employees, unions and customers about the legal and non-legal implications of the dispute.

Some of the key points needing to be considered by management, prior to industrial action being taken, are summarised in Exhibit 38.

Exhibit 38: *Key points for management in preparing for industrial action*

These include:

- make plans before industrial action takes place;
- assess the effects the action will have;
- remember that industrial action is normally in breach of the contract of employment
- ensure that strikers do not get paid during the dispute
- bear in mind that picketing must be peaceful and at the employees' place of work
- do not use the disciplinary procedure in response to industrial action
- the law on industrial action is normally invoked by the employer
- laying off employees without pay is only lawful where there is a term in the contract allowing this

- keep in touch with those coordinating management action and seek advice where necessary
- remember that management and employees have to work together after the dispute is settled

The legal issues

The main legal issues arising from industrial action which employers have to consider are: legal immunities; balloting; and picketing.

Legal immunities

Where employees take industrial action, they are normally in breach of their contracts of employment. Also, when trade unions, their officials or others organise industrial action, they are calling for breaches of, or interferences with, the performance of employment contracts. They may also be interfering with the ability of employers to fulfil commercial contracts. Since it is unlawful, under the common law, to induce individuals to break or interfere with a contract, the legal device of statutory immunities – most commonly called 'trade union' or 'legal immunities' – enables unions and individuals organising industrial action to do so without being sued in the courts (see Chapters 4, 7, 8). Legal immunities do not, however, protect individual strikers, or those taking action short of a strike, from being dismissed, or from having legal proceedings taken against them by their employer, because they have broken their employment contracts.

For unions and strike leaders to be protected by legal immunities, the following conditions are necessary. First, there must be a trade dispute and a properly conducted industrial action ballot. Second, the action must *not*: be secondary action, which does not involve the primary or direct employer; promote a closed shop; or support employees dismissed whilst taking unofficial industrial action. Further, the action must not involve unlawful picketing.

Legal immunities only apply where a union or its officials are acting 'in contemplation or furtherance of a trade dispute' (the 'golden formula'). In law, a trade dispute must be: (1) between workers and their own employer; and (2) wholly or mainly about employment related matters. This legal definition does not cover actions:

- between groups of workers or inter-union disputes;
- between workers and employers other than their own;
- between a union and an employer where none of its workforce is in dispute with it;
- not 'wholly or mainly' due to employment related matters;
- relating to matters taking place overseas.

Where legal immunities do not apply, employers (and customers and suppliers) that are damaged by the industrial action may take civil proceedings in the courts against the union or the individuals concerned. They have to show that:

- an unlawful act has been done or is threatened;
- a contract to which they are a party has been or will be broken or interfered with; and
- they are likely to suffer loss because of this.

Unless legal immunities apply, a union is held responsible for any acts which are done, authorised or endorsed by its principal executive committee, general secretary, president or any other committee of the union. To avoid legal liability, a union or its agents must repudiate the act as soon as is reasonably practicable, after it has come to their notice. They must give written notice of the repudiation to the committee or individuals concerned. And they must do their best to give written notice of the fact and date of the repudiation to every member involved in the action and to the employer.

Where legal immunities do not apply, those damaged may seek an injunction from the courts. This may be issued on an interim basis, pending a full hearing of the case. The courts also have the authority to require any union found in breach of the law to take such steps to ensure that:

- there is no further inducement to take or continue the action;
- no further action is taken after the injunction is granted.

If an injunction is not obeyed, the employer may return to court and ask that those concerned be declared in contempt of court. Any party found in contempt may be fined or have other penalties issued against it. Unions may be deprived of their assets, through the sequestration of their funds. This means that union funds are placed under the control of a person, appointed by the court, who may pay any fines or legal costs incurred as a result of the court's proceedings. It is also possible for employers (and others) to claim damages for any losses resulting from the unprotected industrial action. There are, however, upper limits on these damages in any proceedings and these are according to the size of union membership.

Balloting

Where a union calls on its members to take part in or to continue industrial action, it must hold a properly conducted secret ballot to maintain its legal immunity. And unless *all* the relevant statutory requirements are satisfied, the ballot does not preserve this immunity. The ballot must always be held before a union calls for or otherwise organises industrial action. Those entitled to vote are all the union members who the union reasonably believes are, at the time of the ballot, to be called upon to take industrial action. There must normally be a postal ballot. The ballot paper must contain a question requiring the voters to indicate that they are prepared to take part in the action. The law also requires that the following statement must appear on every voting paper: 'If you take part in a strike or other industrial action, you may be in breach of your contract of employment' (Employment Department 1990: page 11).

Unions are required to give the employer seven days' notice of the intention to hold a ballot, the date of the ballot and a description of the employees who will vote. Not later than three days before the ballot paper is sent to any union member, the employer must be provided with a sample of the voting paper or, where there is more than one, of each voting paper. Majority support must be obtained in response to the question(s) asked. Votes must be accurately and fairly recorded and an independent scrutineer must be appointed, whose name must be on the ballot paper. As soon as is reasonably practicable after the ballot, the employer must be informed of the result and the scrutineer must make a report. Written notice must be given to the employer, specifying the employees who are to be induced to take industrial action, or to continue it, before the action commences.

Picketing

To be protected in law, pickets must comply with the basic rules embodied in the law. This is to ensure that picketing is organised lawfully and in accordance with good practice. According to the Employment Department (1992: page 5), the law requires that picketing may only:

(i) be undertaken in contemplation or furtherance of a trade dispute;
(ii) be carried out by a person attending at or near his own place of work; a trade union official, in addition to attending at or near his own place of work, may also attend at or near the place of work of a member of his trade union whom he is accompanying on the picket line and whom he represents.

Furthermore, the only purpose involved must be peacefully to obtain or communicate information or peacefully to persuade individuals to work or not to work. Picketing which is not peaceful and leads to violence, intimidation, obstruction or molestation is likely to involve offences under the criminal law.

Responding to employees

An employer's response to industrial action is normally aimed at preventing the action or, if this fails, achieving a return to work on acceptable terms as early as possible, whilst at the same time avoiding an escalation of the dispute. For these purposes, employers need to develop action plans which are coherent, flexible and effective. Considered responses need to be given to employees individually and to their unions.

Responses to individual employees are normally preceded by a written warning to them, by either a personal letter or a general circular, with some means by which they can acknowledge its receipt. Ideally, this communicaiton should make clear the nature of the employer's response to the proposed action and it should provide sufficient time for the employees to change their minds. Since employees refusing to take industrial action cannot be 'unjustifiably disciplined' by their unions, employers sometimes include information to this effect in the warning letters sent to individuals before and during industrial action.

When deciding how to respond to industrial action, employers need to answer two key questions (Local Authorities Conditions Advisory Board 1991: page 13). These are:

- has the action led to a breach of the terms of the individual's contract?
- how important is any breach which may have occurred?

Where a strike is involved, this is a fundamental breach of the employment contract, since the employees are refusing to do the work required of them, even though work is available. Action short of a strike is not so straightforward. It depends on the form of action and its effects. With go-slows, work-to-rules or bans on voluntary overtime, there appear to be no breaches of contractual terms. Where overtime is customary, however, and the ban is severely disruptive to the employer, it may be possible to argue that this has breached an implied term of the employment contract.

The nature and extent of the breach of contract, therefore, are major factors in determining an employer's responses to industrial action by some or all of its workforce. A summary of the possible responses available to employers faced by industrial action is provided in Exhibit 39. In adopting any of these actions, employers have to bear in mind the legal implications of what they are doing and any likely reactions by employees to the employer's initiatives. When employers are taking strike action, for example, there is no legal obligation on the employer to pay them, since they are not ready and willing to work under the terms of their contracts. In other cases, such as when employers propose taking disciplinary action against employees for breach of contract, the situation is less clear-cut, and indeed there are disadvantages to doing this. For example, the stage at which disciplinary action is invoked depends on the relevant procedure. Furthermore, the individual employee may not take any notice of formal warnings and then the employer may be forced to take further disciplinary action, without really wanting to.

Similarly, there are important statutory provisions regarding dismissal for industrial action. These provide that employees dismissed whilst taking part in industrial action will not be able to make a complaint to an industrial tribunal unless:

- at the date of the dismissal one or more of the employees also taking industrial action was not dismissed;
- one or more of the other employees dismissed for taking part in the action was subsequently offered re-engagement within three months of their date of dismissal, and these employees were employed at

the same establishment as the employee claiming dismissal.

Where, however, the call to take industrial action has been repudiated by the trade union, no union member who is sacked, whilst continuing to take action, is able to claim unfair dismissal, even if there has been selective dismissal or re-engagement.

Exhibit 39: *Possible responses by employers to industrial action*

These include:

- deducting pay for strike action;
- deducting pay for action short of a strike;
- refusing partial performance of the contract;
- sending employees home;
- suspending with pay;
- suspending without pay;
- using the disciplinary procedure;
- locking-out;
- summary dismissal;
- taking civil action against individual employees.

An employer failing to follow these statutory provisions will not automatically have any dismissals declared unfair by an industrial tribunal, since dismissals for taking strike action are normally considered fair. But where a union has not repudiated the action and an employer dismisses selectively from amongst those taking part in the dispute, it has to be shown that it was reasonable to do so in the circumstances. Similarly, where an employer re-engages selectively, the dismissal of other employees may not necessarily be declared unfair. The question is whether it was reasonable to re-engage some but not others. In practice, however, employers normally re-engage all sacked strikers once a dispute is settled, providing that their jobs remain after the dispute has ended.

The general effect of industrial action on conditions of employment is clear-cut as far as strike action is concerned. Employees not available for work cannot expect to receive any employment benefits. For example, the employer is under no obligation to provide occupational sick pay should an employee fall sick during strike action. However, if an employee has taken annual leave and strike action starts during this period, then in the absence of evidence to the contrary, that individual should be deemed to be on leave, not on strike. Similarly, employees who are on sick leave before industrial action starts should be assumed to be on sick leave, providing that the necessary certification is produced. Also, the operation of the Health and Safety at Work Act 1974 is not suspended during a period of industrial action and employers continue to owe a duty to any employees remaining at work and to others. The employer may need to come to an arrangement with employee representatives to ensure that essential safety measures are carried out before the strike action takes effect.

Responding to trade unions

An employer's responses to the trade unions, when a trade dispute is either threatened or is taking place, tends to centre on the issue of whether or not to take legal action against the union(s) involved. What the employer does is as much a matter of management judgement as it is of legal technicalities. The central issues are:

- What will be the likely long-term effects on relations between the employer and the union(s) if legal action is initiated by the employer?
- What will be the likely outcome on the dispute of legal intervention by the courts?

The key legal issue is that successful legal action by an employer against trade unions in the courts depends on a union losing its legal immunities when it and its members take part in what is deemed to be 'unlawful' or 'unprotected' industrial action (see page 432–434 above; also, Chapter 4). Legally, employers need to determine in the first instance whether (Employment Department 1992):

- a trade dispute is taking place;
- the 'golden formula' applies (i.e., that the action is 'in contemplation or furtherance of a trade dispute');
- a proper industrial action ballot has been conducted;
- the action is authorised by the relevant trade union(s);
- the action is primary, not secondary;
- picketing is peaceful and in accordance with the Employment Department's code of practice.

The normal civil law remedies are available to employers when unlawful industrial action takes place or is threatened. Proceedings against individual employees are rare but liability for civil claims extends beyond those taking part in industrial action. Those organising the action may also be liable, including the union officials and the union, except where they are protected by legal immunities. But legal immunities only have the effect of protecting employees as union members, not as individual employees who have no immunity for the act of breaking their individual contracts of employment.

The immediate civil remedy is an injunction. This is a court order seeking to stop the industrial action and is only normally granted if the court decides that such action is unlikely to be shown to have immunity on the full hearing of the case. An injunction is a holding measure, until a full trial decides the matter properly. An injunction is usually sought as a way of immediately preventing the action from taking place, since a full trial is only possible some time after the intended action has been carried out. The courts are generally ready to grant injunctions to employers, providing that the proposed action might not have immunity. They do this by taking account of the 'balance of convenience' between the parties. This means that judges tend to favour the party which is likely to suffer the most, if the injunction is not granted. Normally, this is deemed to be the employer. However, the courts also consider the likelihood of the union establishing at full trial that legal immunity does apply and they give the union the opportunity to put its side of the case, before granting an injunction.

Many employers, in practice, are very reluctant to use the law to resolve industrial disputes, because of the detrimental long-term effects it can have on employee relations. Much depends on the damage being done by industrial action. Moreover, an injunction may be disregarded by the union or individuals concerned and then the employer has to consider whether to institute contempt of court proceedings against the union. These may lead to fines, damages or other penalties against the union. Employers, therefore, need to give very careful consideration to the consequences of invoking the law in an industrial dispute, before making a definitive decision to proceed with it.

The return to work

Once a settlement has been reached between management and unions, a full return to normal working as soon as possible is essential. Where action has been short of a strike, there is no great difficulty. With strikes, a phased return may have to be arranged. The formal terms of the return may have to be negotiated at the time of settlement and employers should try to seek reciprocal arrangements with trade unions on the terms of the return to work. But written agreements do not always reflect all aspects of the employment relationship. For example, as far as is possible, employers should ensure that there is no victimisation of union members who did not take part in the industrial action. This might mean advising employees of their rights of appeal under trade union rules and the law, such as the right not to have 'unjustifiable discipline' taken against them.

It is normally important to restore the pre-existing employee relations climate, so that the return to work can take place without any recriminations on either side. On the employer's side, this means the job or career structures of employees should not be prejudiced by the fact that they took industrial action. The employer has to decide whether disciplinary warnings arising from misconduct during the industrial action should be kept on record or deleted. It also needs to decide what effect any break in continuous service is to have on employee benefits and conditions of employment. Employees who have been dismissed and subsequently re-engaged are normally re-appointed on the same terms and conditions, providing their posts still exist. Overall, then, employers and management have a prime role in ensuring that the return to work proceeds smoothly, fairly and in accordance with what has been formally agreed with the trade unions.

Assignments

(a) Read Dahrendorf (1959: pages 241–79). What is his theory of industrial conflict and what are its implications for the managing of employee relations? Also read Jackson (1987: pages 155–84) and compare his explanations of industrial conflict with that of Dahrendorf's analysis.

(b) Report and comment on any forms of individual and unorganised conflict in your organisation.

(c) Describe and analyse a strike with which you are familiar. Get your material *either* from a situation that you have directly experienced yourself *or* from the literature of employee relations, newspaper reports, television documentaries or individuals who have actually been involved in a dispute.

(d) Read the latest annual report on industrial stoppages in the *Employment Gazette*. What were the trends for the past year? What were the principal causes? And what were the duration and size of stoppages?

(e) Read Smith *et al.* (1978: pages 84–90). What are their main conclusions about the nature of strike activity in Britain for the period of review (1966–75)? To what extent do you think that their analysis is still relevant today?

(f) Read Clegg (1976). What is his explanation of strike-proneness?

(g) What guidance does the Employment Department's (1992) code of practice on picketing provide relating to numbers of pickets on picket lines and the organisation of picketing? What is the legal status of the code?

(i) Your organisation has been informed by the unions of their intention to take strike action as a result of a properly conducted industrial action ballot. Consider the responses you will advise the employer to take in the circumstances and draft a letter to the employees concerned warning them, individually, of the employer's intended responses.

(j) An organisation has informed the unions of its intentions of closing its manufacturing plant, and of instituting compulsory redundancies, if they do not accept lay-offs and a reduction in the terms of the present lay-off agreement. The unions are now in dispute with the company, having taken a properly conducted industrial action ballot. The company has proposed rotating lay-offs for its staff for six months, with access to independent arbitration, a 10 per cent cut in employee benefits and a profit-sharing scheme. This has been rejected by the unions and the 400 staff have been dismissed by the management and replaced by a new workforce. (1) What is the legal position? (2) What advice would you give to senior management at this stage of the dispute?

References

ALLEN, V. 1976. 'Marxism and the personnel manager'. *Personnel Management.* December.

ARGYRIS, C. 1964. *Integrating the Individual and the Organization.* Chichester: Wiley.

BIRD, D. 1992a. 'Industrial stoppages in 1991'. *Employment Gazette*. May.

BIRD, D. 1992b. 'International comparisons on industrial disputes'. *Employment Gazette*. December.

CLEGG, H. 1976. *Trade Unionism under Collective Bargaining*. Oxford: Blackwell.

CREIGH, S. and MAKEHAM, D. 1982. 'Strike incidence in industrial countries: an analysis'. *Australian Bulletin of Labour*. 8(3).

DAHRENDORF, R. 1959. *Class and Class Conflict in Industrial Society*. London: Routledge and Kegan Paul.

DONOVAN, Lord 1968. *Royal Commission on Trade Unions and Employers' Associations*. London: HMSO.

EDWARDS, P. 1981. *Strikes in the USA, 1871–1974*. Oxford: Blackwell.

ELDRIDGE, J. 1968. *Industrial Disputes*. Routledge and Kegan Paul.

EMPLOYMENT DEPARTMENT 1990. *Trade Union Ballots on Industrial Action*. London: COI.

EMPLOYMENT DEPARTMENT 1992. *Code of Practice on Picketing*. London: COI.

FARNHAM, D. 1993. 'Human resources management and employee relations'. In FARNHAM, D. and HORTON, S. (eds) 1993. *Managing the New Public Services*. Basingstoke: Macmillan.

FARNHAM, D. and PIMLOTT, J. 1990. *Understanding Industrial Relations*. London: Cassell.

HIBBS, D. 1976. 'Industrial conflict in advanced industrial countries'. *Political Science Review*. 70(4).

HYMAN, R. 1975. *Industrial Relations*. London: Macmillan.

HYMAN, R. 1989. *Strikes*. Basingstoke: Macmillan.

INGHAM, G. 1974. *Strikes and Industrial Conflict*. London: Macmillan.

JACKSON, M. 1987. *Strikes*. Brighton: Wheatsheaf.

KASSOLOW, E. 1969. *Trade Unions and Industrial Relations*. NY: Random House.

KERR, C. and SIEGEL, A. 1954. 'The interindustry propensity to strike – an international comparison'. In KORNHAUSER, A., DUBIN, R. and ROSS, A. (eds) *Industrial Conflict*. NY: McGraw-Hill.

KNIGHT, K. 1972. 'Strikes and wage inflation in British manufacturing industry 1950–1968'. *Bulletin of the Oxford Institute of Economics and Statistics*. 34(3).

KORNHAUSER, A., DUBIN, R. and ROSS, A. (eds) 1954. *Industrial Conflict*. NY: McGraw-Hill.

KORPI, W. and SHALEV, M. 1979. 'Strikes, industrial relations and class conflicts in capitalist societies'. *British Journal of Sociology*. 30(2).

LOCAL AUTHORITIES CONDITIONS OF SERVICE ADVISORY BOARD 1991. *Employers' Responses to Industrial Action*. London: LACSAB.

McGREGOR, D. 1960. *The Human Side of Enterprise*. NY: McGraw-Hill.

MARTIN, R. 1992. *Bargaining Power*. Oxford: Clarendon.

MAYO, E. 1946. *The Social Problems of an Industrial Civilization*. London: Routledge.

REES, A. 1952. 'Industrial conflict and business fluctuations'. *Journal of Political Economy*. 60(5).

ROETHLISBERGER, F. 1946. *Management and Morale*. Cambridge, Mass.: Harvard University Press.

Ross, A. 1959. 'Changing patterns of industrial conflict'. In SOMERS, G. (ed.). *Proceedings of the 12th Annual Meeting of the Industrial Relations Research Association.*

Ross, A. and HARTMAN, P. 1960. *Changing Patterns of Industrial Conflict.* NY: Wiley.

SHOREY, J. 1976. 'An interindustry analysis of strike frequency'. *Economica.* 43, no. 172.

SHORTER, E. and TILLEY, C. 1974. *Strikes in France 1830–1968.* Cambridge: CUP.

SMITH, C., CLIFTON, R., MAKEHAM, P., CREIGH, S. and BURN, R. 1978. *Strikes in Britain.* London: Department of Employment.

WARNER, W. and Low, J. 1947. *The Social System of the Modern Factory.* New Haven: Yale University Press.

Author Index

Subject Index